Benefits for Migrants Handbook

....

5th edition

Pamela Fitzpatrick, Timothy Lawrence and Colin McCloskey

Child Poverty Action Group

CPAG promotes action for the prevention and relief of poverty among children and families with children. To achieve this, CPAG aims to raise awareness of the causes, extent, nature and impact of poverty, and strategies for its eradication and prevention; bring about positive policy changes for families with children in poverty; and enable those eligible for income maintenance to have access to their full entitlement. If you are not already supporting us, please consider making a donation, or ask for details of our membership schemes, training courses and publications.

Published by Child Poverty Action Group
94 White Lion Street, London N1 9PF
Tel: 020 7837 7979
staff@cpag.org.uk
www.cpag.org.uk

A CIP record for this book is available from the British Library

ISBN: 978 1 906076 34 4

Child Poverty Action Group is a charity registered in England and Wales (registration number 294841) and in Scotland (registration number SC039339), and is a company limited by guarantee, registered in England (registration number 1993854). VAT number: 690 808117

Cover design by Devious Designs
Typeset by David Lewis XML Associates Ltd
Printed in the UK by CPI William Clowes Beccles NR34 7TL
Cover photo by Peter Olive/Photofusion

The authors

Pamela Fitzpatrick is a welfare rights worker at the Child Poverty Action Group, and a founder and Chair of Harrow Law Centre. She is a co-author of CPAG's *Welfare Benefits and Tax Credits Handbook* and *At Greatest Risk*, and a welfare rights trainer.

Timothy Lawrence is a solicitor specialising in immigration and asylum work at Southwark Law Centre in London.

Colin McCloskey is a consultant solicitor. He specialised in housing and community care work for 20 years in a legal aid practice and now works freelance. He works part time for the Asylum Support Appeals Project.

Acknowledgements

The authors would like to thank everyone who has contributed to this book. In particular, thanks are due to Tim Samuel, Fiona Ripley, Graham Tegg, Martin Williams, Beth Lakhani, Sarah Clarke, Kelly Smith and Edward Graham for their invaluable comments. Thanks also go too to the previous authors for their contribution.

We would also like to thank Alison Key for editing and managing the production of the book, Katherine Dawson for the index and Kathleen Armstrong for proofreading the text.

CPAG gratefully acknowledges the financial support of the Trust for London.

Trust for London
Tackling poverty and inequality

The law covered in this book was correct on 1 October 2010 and includes regulations laid up to this date.

Contents

About this *Handbook*   ix
Abbreviations   x

Part 1   Immigration law
Chapter 1   Immigration law: overview   3
1. Immigration law in the United Kingdom   3
2. The main types of immigration status   5
3. British citizenship and nationality   6

Chapter 2   Leave to enter or remain in the United Kingdom   8
1. Leave to enter or remain   8
2. Time-limited leave   10
3. Indefinite leave   10
4. Employment   11
5. Recourse to public funds   11
6. Sponsorship   14
7. Turkish nationals   15

Chapter 3   Asylum, human rights and international
protection   17
1. Asylum seekers   17
2. Refugee status and humanitarian protection   19
3. Discretionary and exceptional leave   20
4. Fresh claims   21

Chapter 4   European Economic Area nationals   23
1. European Economic Area nationals   23
2. Family members   27
3. Public funds   32
4. A8 nationals   33
5. A2 nationals   33
6. Exclusion and removal   35

Chapter 5   Determining immigration status   38
1. British citizens and people with the right of abode   38
2. People with leave to enter or remain   39
3. People without leave   43

4. Asylum seekers   44
5. European Economic Area and Swiss nationals   44
6. Deportation and special immigration status   45
7. Other passport issues   45

Part 2   Immigration status, residence and benefits
Chapter 6   Overview   49
1. Immigration and residence rules for benefits and tax credits   49
2. Benefits and tax credits: checklist   50

Chapter 7   Immigration control and benefits   55
1. People subject to immigration control   55
2. Public funds   62
3. Family members with different immigration statuses   64
4. Refugees   67

Chapter 8   Residence rules   70
1. Introduction   70
2. The different residence tests   71
3. Residence and presence rules for individual benefits   78
4. How a family member abroad affects benefit   103
5. Habitual residence   110
6. The right to reside   116

Chapter 9   Claims and getting paid   126
1. Introduction   126
2. National insurance numbers   126
3. National insurance contributions   131
4. Proving your immigration status, age and relationships   134
5. Getting paid if you go abroad   137
6. Other sources of help   139

Part 3   European law
Chapter 10   European Union law   145
1. The European Union and its institutions   145
2. European Union law   149
3. European Union law and benefits   151
4. Using European law in the United Kingdom   152
5. Referring a case to the European Court of Justice   153
6. European Union law and the anti-test-case rule   155
7. Interim relief   156

Chapter 11   The European Union co-ordination of social
security   159
1. Introduction   159
2. Who is covered by the co-ordination rules   161
3. Which benefits are covered by the co-ordination rules   165
4. The 'competent' state   171
5. Equal treatment   176
6. Aggregation   177
7. Exporting benefits   178
8. Overlapping benefits   180

Chapter 12   The co-ordination rules for categories of benefits   184
1. Introduction   184
2. Invalidity benefits   185
3. Old age benefits   189
4. Survivors' benefits   194
5. Benefits for accidents at work and occupational diseases   195
6. Unemployment benefits   196
7. Family benefits   201
8. Special non-contributory benefits   204
9. Death grants   206
10. Sickness, maternity and paternity benefits   207

Chapter 13   Using European Union law to claim benefits   218
1. Rights under European Union law   218
2. Right of residence and access to benefits   223
3. Workers   229
4. Workseekers   233
5. Self-employed people   234
6. Students   235
7. People who are self-sufficient   235
8. Service providers and users   236
9. Retired or permanently incapacitated workers and self-employed
people   238
10. A8 and A2 nationals   239
11. Family members   241
12. Primary carers of children in education   243
13. People who are economically inactive   244

Chapter 14	International agreements	250
1. Reciprocal agreements		250
2. Council of Europe conventions and agreements		256
3. European Union co-operation and association agreements		257

Part 4	Support for asylum seekers	
Chapter 15	Support for asylum seekers	263
1. Support for asylum seekers: overview		263
2. Who is entitled to asylum support		266
3. Exclusions from asylum support		269
4. When asylum support can be suspended or discontinued		270
5. Temporary asylum support		272
6. Who is entitled to Section 4 support		272
7. When Section 4 support can be suspended or discontinued		282
8. Other forms of support		284

Chapter 16	Applications	292
1. Applying for asylum support		292
2. Deciding if you are destitute		293
3. Applying for Section 4 support		300

Chapter 17	Payment and accommodation	303
1. Asylum support		303
2. Contributions and recovery		309
3. Section 4 support		311

Chapter 18	Appeals	316
1. The right to appeal		317
2. Appeal procedures		317
3. Decisions the First-tier Tribunal can make		325

Appendices		335
Appendix 1	Glossary of terms	335
Appendix 2	Information and advice	343
Appendix 3	Useful addresses	346
Appendix 4	Useful publications	351
Appendix 5	Leave to enter endorsements	355
Appendix 6	Reciprocal agreements	376
Appendix 7	Passport stamps and other endorsements	378
Appendix 8	Abbreviations used in the notes	394

| Index | | 399 |

About this *Handbook*

This *Handbook* is intended to bridge the gap between guides on welfare rights and those on immigration. It is designed to be used by migrants and their advisers wanting advice on benefit entitlement. By 'migrants' we mean people, including British citizens, who have come or returned to Great Britain from abroad and people who have left Great Britain to live abroad or are temporarily abroad.

The *Handbook* covers the benefit rules that are most likely to affect migrant claimants and their families, and the practical problems they are likely to face. It is not a complete guide to the benefit rules and should be used together with general guides, such as CPAG's *Welfare Benefits and Tax Credits Handbook*.

How to use this book

Your benefit rights may depend on your immigration status.

In **Part 1** we provide a brief outline of the immigration system and explain the terms used in immigration law which appear in the rest of the book. Part 1 aims to provide welfare rights advisers with a general framework of immigration law. In some cases, it may contain enough information for you to use the rest of the *Handbook* to work out your benefit entitlement. However, if you are unclear about your immigration status or the effects of claiming benefit, you should obtain advice from a specialist immigration adviser.

Part 2 provides information on the general rules that apply to migrants claiming benefits.

Part 3 covers European Union law and how it applies to social security benefits.

Part 4 provides information on the support available to asylum seekers.

Abbreviations

AA	attendance allowance	IB	incapacity benefit
ASAP	Asylum Support Appeals Project	IND	Immigration and Nationality Department
ARC	application registration card		
BIA	Border and Immigration Agency	IOM	International Organization for Migration
CA	carer's allowance		
CAB	Citizens Advice Bureau	IS	income support
CRD	Case Resolution Directorate	JSA	jobseeker's allowance
CTC	child tax credit	MA	maternity allowance
CTB	council tax benefit	MP	Member of Parliament
DCI	Departmental Central Index	NASS	National Asylum Support Service
DLA	disability living allowance	NAM	New Asylum Model
DWP	Department for Work and Pensions	NI	national insurance
		PC	pension credit
EC	European Community	REA	reduced earnings allowance
ECHR	European Convention on Human Rights	SAL	standard acknowledgement letter
		SAP	statutory adoption pay
ECSMA	European Convention on Social and Medical Assistance	SDA	severe disablement allowance
		SMP	statutory maternity pay
ECtHR	European Court of Human Rights	SPP	statutory paternity pay
ECJ	European Court of Justice	SSP	statutory sick pay
EEA	European Economic Area	The Revenue	HM Revenue and Customs
ESA	employment and support allowance		
		UK	United Kingdom
EU	European Union	UKBA	UK Border Agency
HB	housing benefit	WTC	working tax credit

Part 1

Immigration law

Chapter 1

Immigration law: overview

This chapter covers:
1. Immigration law in the United Kingdom (below)
2. The main types of immigration status (p5)
3. British citizenship and nationality (p6)

The chapters in Part 1 of this *Handbook* provide sufficient information to identify immigration status in order to establish a person's entitlement to social security benefits.

Note: immigration law has serious implications for people and it is a criminal offence for anyone to give immigration advice unless they are qualified to do so.[1] Government agencies also share information and an application for benefits may prompt an investigation into an applicant's immigration status, which could have serious adverse consequences. If your immigration status is uncertain or there is a need for further immigration advice, you should contact a suitably qualified adviser (see Appendix 2).

1. Immigration law in the United Kingdom

The right to live, work and settle in the United Kingdom (UK) is regulated and controlled by a complex system of laws. The main provisions of the UK's current immigration law are in the:
- Immigration Act 1971;
- British Nationality Act 1981;
- Immigration Act 1988;
- Asylum and Immigration Appeals Act 1993;
- Asylum and Immigration Act 1996;
- Immigration and Asylum Act 1999;
- Nationality, Immigration and Asylum Act 2002;
- Asylum and Immigration (Treatment of Claimants, Etc) Act 2004;
- Immigration, Asylum and Nationality Act 2006; *and*
- UK Borders Act 2007.

The above Acts are supplemented by statutory instruments (regulations), the Immigration Rules and numerous government policies. The Government has indicated that it intends to legislate further to consolidate and simplify this structure.

There are also various international treaties and conventions to which the UK is a party. These include:

- the 1951 Convention Relating to the Status of Refugees and its 1967 Protocol, commonly referred to as 'the Refugee Convention';
- the European Convention on Human Rights and Fundamental Freedoms 1950, incorporated, in part, into UK law by the Human Rights Act 1998;
- European Council Directive 2004/83/EC on minimum standards for the qualification and status of third-country nationals or stateless people as refugees or as people who otherwise need international protection, and the content of the protection granted ('the Qualification Directive');
- European Council Directive 2003/9/EC, laying down minimum standards for the reception of asylum seekers ('the Reception Directive'); *and*
- European Council Directive 2004/38/EC on the right of citizens of the European Union and their family members to move and reside freely within the territory of the member states ('the Citizens' Directive').

The **Secretary of State for the Home Department** (Home Secretary) is responsible for the **Home Office**, within which is the agency that deals with immigration control. This is presently called the **UK Border Agency (UKBA)**.

Entry clearance officers stationed in overseas posts are responsible for immigration control prior to entry to the UK, and now mainly operate behind commercial organisations responsible for the initial processing of applications. Entry clearance officers decide whether to give entry clearance (**entry visas** or **visas**) to applicants under the Immigration Rules (see Chapter 2). This includes entry clearance for reuniting refugees and people with other types of international protection in the UK with their families (see Chapter 3). They also decide whether to issue **family permits** under European Union law (see Chapter 4).

Immigration officers are generally responsible for processing people who arrive at the various UK ports of entry and for removing people from the UK. They have the power to arrest people suspected of having committed a criminal offence under immigration law. They can also arrest and detain people who are liable to be detained in order to enforce their departure from the UK under immigration law.

Civil servants in the UKBA are mainly responsible for deciding applications for leave to remain in the UK after entry, including applications for asylum.

Detainee custody officers are responsible for immigration detention.

The **Identity and Passport Service** is an executive agency of the Home Office, responsible for issuing UK passports and identity cards.

Police officers are responsible for registering certain people who require leave to enter and remain in the UK, arresting people suspected of having committed a criminal offence under immigration law, and arresting and detaining people who are liable to be detained in order to enforce their departure from the UK under immigration law.

The **Immigration and Asylum Chambers of the First-tier Tribunal and the Upper Tribunal** are responsible for hearing and determining appeals against decisions of entry clearance officers, immigration officers and the Secretary of State.

The **Asylum Support Chamber of the First-tier Tribunal** is responsible for determining appeals against decisions refusing asylum support.

Judges of the High Court, Court of Appeal and Supreme Court hear applications for reviews of decisions by the Home Secretary and her/his officers, and of decisions by the First-tier Tribunal and Upper Tribunal. Judges also now sit in the First-tier Tribunal and the Upper Tribunal.

Cases may also be brought in the **Court of Justice of the European Union** (previously the **European Court of Justice**) that concern European Union law matters, and in the **European Court of Human Rights** in matters concerning the European Convention on Human Rights.

---

2. The main types of immigration status

There are four main types of immigration status under which people may be lawfully present in the United Kingdom (UK). You may be in the UK:
- with the right of abode (this includes British citizens – see p6);
- with leave to enter or remain (see Chapter 2);
- as an asylum seeker, refugee or with another form of international protection (see Chapter 3);
- as a national of the European Economic Area (EEA), or as a family member of an EEA national, with a right of residence under European Union (EU) law (see Chapter 4).

If you do not have the right of abode, you are usually '**subject to immigration control**'.[2] This means you may only live in the UK with permission and are subject to regulations provided by immigration laws.[3]

Citizens of the other member states of the EEA and their family members have certain rights to enter and reside in the UK on conditions agreed by the member states, primarily for economic purposes (see Chapter 4). You do not require leave to enter or remain in the UK while you remain entitled to do so by virtue of such a right, and you are not subject to immigration control during this time.[4]

Turkish nationals have special rights to establish themselves in the UK for economic purposes under agreements of 'association' between the European Community and Turkey (see p257).

---

3. **British citizenship and nationality**

British nationality may be acquired:
- by birth. This may depend on the date and location of the birth, and on the nationality/citizenship, and immigration and/or marital status of the person's parents (see p7); *or*
- by applying to the Home Secretary for naturalisation or registration; *or*
- as result of legislative changes.

There are six different forms of British nationality, only one of which ('British citizenship') gives the right of abode in the United Kingdom (UK). British nationals may be either:
- British citizens;
- British overseas territories citizens;
- British subjects;
- British protected persons;
- British nationals (overseas); *or*
- British overseas citizens.

Some of these forms of nationality are rare and some will eventually disappear.

Multiple nationalities

Unlike some systems of nationality or citizenship law, UK law permits you to be a British national and also a national of any number of other countries.

British nationals, the right of abode and immigration law

British citizens and some Commonwealth citizens have the right of abode in the UK.[5]

Nearly everyone who has the right of abode in the UK is a British citizen. All British citizens have the right of abode, but most of those who hold some other form of British nationality do not. Some Commonwealth citizens, including people who hold another British nationality, also have the right of abode, but it has not been possible to gain the right of abode since 1983 without also being a British citizen. Commonwealth citizens who had the right of abode then still have it, but since the beginning of 1983 the only way to obtain the right of abode is by becoming a British citizen.

People with the right of abode are free to live in, and to come to and go from, the UK, provided they can prove they have this right.

British nationals who do not have the right of abode generally require leave to enter or remain in the UK, but may have certain advantages over other foreign nationals under the Immigration Rules and in applications for full British citizenship.

Acquiring British citizenship on birth

Most people born in the UK before 1 January 1983 automatically acquired British citizenship on that date (the exceptions were children of diplomats and 'enemy aliens').[6]

If you were born in the UK on or after 1 January 1983, you only acquired British citizenship if your mother or father was a British citizen at the time of your birth or was 'settled' in the UK – eg, they had indefinite leave to remain or permanent residence.[7] Before 1 July 2006, if only your father was a British citizen or settled, you only acquired British citizenship if your parents were married at the time. From 1 July 2006, this restriction has no longer applied and the UK Border Agency has a policy of permitting the registration of children born before this date to British or settled fathers who were not married to the child's mother at the time.

From 1 January 1983, a child born overseas acquires British citizenship by descent if either parent is a British citizen, unless that parent is her/himself a British citizen by descent – eg, the parent was born overseas.[8]

Note: these are basic examples of how British citizenship may be acquired. There are many other routes, which are beyond the scope of this *Handbook*.

Notes

1 Part V IAA 1999

2. The main types of immigration status
  2 s1(1) IA 1971
  3 s1(2) IA 1971
  4 s7 IA 1988; reg 30 and Sch 2 I(EEA) Regs

3. British citizenship and nationality
  5 s1(1) IA 1971
  6 s11 BNA 1981
  7 s1 BNA 1981
  8 s2 BNA 1981

Chapter 2

∙∙∙

Leave to enter or remain in the United Kingdom

This chapter covers:
1. Leave to enter or remain (below)
2. Time-limited leave (p10)
3. Indefinite leave (p10)
4. Employment (p11)
5. Recourse to public funds (p11)
6. Sponsorship (p14)
7. Turkish nationals (p15)

---

1. Leave to enter or remain

People without the right of abode (see p6) must usually obtain leave to enter or remain in order to live in the United Kingdom (UK) for a specific purpose. If granted, the leave may be subject to conditions. Purposes for which leave may be given include taking employment, studying, a visit and as the dependant of a person lawfully in or entering the UK.

The Immigration Rules set out the categories of purpose for which leave to enter or remain can be granted, together with the conditions that must be met. The Rules also outline the requirements that must be met by applicants, the grounds on which leave may be refused, curtailed or revoked and the criteria for deportation of people whose presence in the UK is considered to be against the interests of the public – eg, foreign national criminals. The Rules change frequently, but a consolidated version is published on the UK Border Agency (UKBA) website (www.ukba.homeoffice.gov.uk). Leave may also be granted outside the Immigration Rules (see p20).

Published policy guidance confirms the Government's interpretation of the requirements, which must be followed by officials, and the circumstances in which discretion will be used to grant leave outside the Immigration Rules. This adds an additional layer of complexity.[1]

Applying for leave

If you wish to enter the UK, you may need to obtain entry clearance (a visa or entry visa) from an entry clearance officer overseas before travelling. Nationals of 'visa national' countries must always obtain a visa before travelling to the UK. Nationals of non-visa national countries may apply at the port of arrival for entry for certain purposes, but this is mainly restricted to short-term visits. Nationals of any country who intend to stay for longer periods must usually obtain entry clearance before travelling. The list of visa national countries is published in Appendix 1 to the Immigration Rules on the UKBA website (www.ukba.homeoffice.gov.uk).

Leave to remain after entry to the UK is obtained by applying to the UKBA.

Conditions of your leave

Leave to enter or remain in the UK may be given subject to a limited number of conditions. If you fail to observe the conditions attached to your leave, you may commit a criminal offence. It could also lead to your current leave being curtailed or revoked, future applications for leave being refused and you being arrested, detained and removed from the UK.

The main conditions attached to leave granted under the Immigration Rules are:
- a restriction on the time you may remain in the UK;
- a requirement to register your residential address with the police;
- restrictions on your ability to take employment or to access 'public funds' (see p11).

Note: people without the right of abode but with indefinite leave to remain in the UK have no conditions attached.

Special categories

Some categories of people are exempt from some of the usual conditions attached to permission to enter and remain in the UK. The main categories of people who are exempt are seamen, aircrew, diplomats and members of the UK or visiting armed forces.[2]

Nationals of the European Economic Area and Switzerland and their family members have separate rights and conditions of entry and residence in the UK (see Chapter 4).

Turkish nationals also have special rights to establish themselves or provide services in the UK for economic purposes under agreements of 'association' between the European Community and Turkey (see p257).

2. Time-limited leave

Leave may be granted for a limited period of time, which may or may not be extended, depending on the requirements for the various categories under the Immigration Rules.

Note: any limited leave is automatically extended beyond the date it was due to expire if you make a valid application to extend or vary the leave before the expiry date. Your leave is extended until the UK Border Agency (UKBA) makes a decision on your application and, if this is refused, until any rights of appeal are exhausted.[3] Certain types of application have been subject to delays in processing by the UKBA for several years (eg, applications from people who applied to extend their leave given outside the Immigration Rules for human rights reasons or by a blanket policy of not returning people to a war-torn country – see Chapter 3 for more information) and there are still many people with leave that remains extended in this manner. This does not apply if an appeal is made against a refusal of leave to remain by a person who did not have leave to enter or remain at the time s/he applied.

3. Indefinite leave

Indefinite leave to enter or remain in the United Kingdom (UK) is leave without a time restriction. Indefinite leave is sometimes referred to as 'settlement'.

There are no conditions (eg, on employment and claiming 'public funds' – see p11) attached to indefinite leave.[4] However, if you have been granted indefinite leave, you may be restricted from claiming benefits if the leave was given on the basis of an undertaking by a sponsor that s/he would be responsible for your maintenance, and your sponsor may be liable to repay any benefits claimed (see p14).

Indefinite leave may lapse or be revoked. You could also be deported on the grounds that your presence in the UK is not conducive to the public good (usually following a criminal conviction).

If you have indefinite leave, you can leave the UK and return as a returning resident if you:
- wish to return to settle in the UK; *and*
- have not been away from the UK for more than two years (unless there are special circumstances, such as a previous long residence); *and*
- did not receive assistance from 'public funds' towards the cost of leaving the UK. **Note:** 'public funds' in this context is the scheme that allows people to be reimbursed the costs of resettling in their country of origin. It does not refer to the fact that you may have been claiming benefits and other 'public funds' while in the UK (see p11).[5]

4. **Employment**

Certain types of leave prohibit employment – eg, visitors are usually prohibited from working. Other types of leave impose a condition limiting the employment you may do – eg, if you are given leave as a student or for business activity. Leave permits a person to take up any type of employment unless it is specifically restricted.[6]

The UK Border Agency (UKBA) policy on allowing students to work is subject to change but some students may be permitted to take certain types of employment and for a restricted number of hours only during term time.[7]

If you have been given leave for specific employment (eg, under Tiers 2 or 3 of the points-based system or under a work permit) or a specific activity (such as self-employment, or as a writer, composer or artist), you may only work in the employment or undertake the activity for which you were given leave. If you wish to change employment, you must apply to the UKBA for permission.

From 27 January 1997, employers have been required to check that all new employees have the right to work in the United Kingdom (UK) and can be prosecuted for employing a migrant who cannot lawfully work. The law on the employment of migrant workers has changed several times since this date and the checks an employer is required to make (or should have made) to ensure its employees are (or were) entitled to work in the UK depend on the date the worker was first employed by the employer.

These requirements raise race discrimination issues. If you are a migrant who has been refused or dismissed from employment, you should seek specialist advice.

5. **Recourse to public funds**

Most of the purposes for which leave is given under the Immigration Rules require people to show that they (and any dependants) can and will be adequately maintained and accommodated without recourse to specified 'public funds' (see p12). A restriction from having recourse to public funds is commonly imposed on time-limited leave to remain.

This means that the presence of the person wanting to be given leave to enter or remain must not cause additional public funds to be claimed by any member of her/his family who is entitled to benefits. In addition, however, the presence of the person must not mean that s/he or anyone else in her/his family has to live below a particular standard of maintenance and accommodation.

What are public funds

Public funds are:[8]
- attendance allowance (AA);
- severe disablement allowance;
- carer's allowance;
- disability living allowance (DLA);
- income support (IS);
- income-related employment and support allowance (ESA);
- health in pregnancy grants;
- council tax benefit;
- housing benefit;
- social fund payments;
- child benefit;
- income-based jobseeker's allowance (JSA);
- pension credit;
- child tax credit (CTC);
- working tax credit (WTC); *and*
- housing and homelessness assistance.[9]

This definition of public funds is exhaustive. NHS services, education services and benefits based on national insurance contributions are not counted as public funds. Therefore, even if you have a public funds condition attached to your leave, you may still claim other benefits. Specifically, these include:
- contribution-based JSA;
- contributory ESA;
- incapacity benefit;
- retirement pension;
- widows' and bereavement benefits;
- guardian's allowance;
- maternity allowance;
- statutory maternity pay.

In certain cases, the relevant benefits, tax credits or housing legislation allow a person subject to the condition that s/he has no recourse to public funds to claim a particular benefit in her/his own right without breaching the condition – eg, claims for CTC and WTC must be made jointly in the case of a couple. If only one member of a couple is subject to immigration control, for tax credits purposes neither are treated as being subject to immigration control.[10]

What is adequate maintenance

Whether or not there is adequate maintenance depends on the number of people needing maintenance and the income of the person or family unit concerned.

The required standard of adequacy is currently considered to be that the income of the family as a whole is equal to or greater than the allowances an equivalent family would receive from IS if all were entitled to have recourse to public funds. The use of this benchmark has been justified as necessary to prevent immigrant families or communities having a lower standard of living in the UK than the poorest British citizens.[11]

It is rare then that a family, in which one or more members claim the social security benefits to which they are entitled, will be able to show that it can help support another family member who is not entitled, although support by third parties may also be counted.[12]

Unlike other benefits, DLA and AA claimed by a sponsor are counted when calculating whether a family's income is the same or higher than the IS allowance for an equivalent family.[13] It is likely that the same approach could be successfully argued to apply to industrial injuries disablement benefit and severe disablement allowance. Specialist advice should be sought if this might be an issue. All other benefits are considered to be paid at a level necessary to ensure the adequate maintenance of the recipient only.

If there is no public funds or employment condition attached to a person's leave, but s/he needed to satisfy the maintenance and accommodation requirements under the Immigration Rules before the leave was granted, the leave may nevertheless be curtailed and/or a further application refused if s/he fails to continue to meet the requirements throughout the period of leave granted.[14] Because of this, therefore, it is important to realise that certain categories of leave require you to maintain yourself without working or restrict the type or duration of employment you can do (see p11).

What is adequate accommodation

The accommodation available must comply with environmental health provisions and be capable of accommodating the number of people concerned without overcrowding. It must also be adequate on a common-sense basis.[15]

The Housing Act 1985 contains statutory definitions of overcrowding in a 'dwelling house'. A **'dwelling house'** includes both a privately owned house and one owned by a local authority. A house is overcrowded if two people aged 10 years or older of the opposite sex (other than husband and wife) have to sleep in the same room, or if the number of people sleeping in the house exceeds that permitted in the Act.

The Act specifies the number of people permitted for a given number of rooms or given floor area, but the UK Border Agency uses the room number yardstick, taking into account only rooms with a floor area larger than 50 square feet and rooms used either as a living room or bedroom – ie, kitchens and bathrooms are not included.[16]

The Immigration Rules often require that the accommodation must be owned or occupied 'exclusively' by the family unit concerned. A separate bedroom for the exclusive use of the applicant and sponsor is sufficient to meet this requirement, so a family may live in shared accommodation sharing other rooms (such as a kitchen and bathroom) with other occupants.[17]

6. Sponsorship

The Immigration Rules define a 'sponsor' as the person in relation to whom an applicant is seeking leave to enter or remain as a spouse, fiancé, civil partner, proposed civil partner, unmarried partner, same-sex partner or dependent relative.[18] The role of the sponsor is to maintain and support an applicant in the United Kingdom (UK), unless s/he can do so from her/his own resources or together with the sponsor. A parent may also fulfil this role in the case of a child applicant.[19] Support by third parties is permitted.[20]

Sponsorship undertakings

A sponsor may be asked to give a written undertaking to be responsible for a person's maintenance and accommodation for the period of leave granted and any further period of leave to remain that s/he may be granted while in the UK.[21] Undertakings are often requested for:

- dependent relatives (although not for children under 16 years of age coming for settlement);
- students relying on a private individual in the UK.

Undertakings are rarely requested for applications for leave by spouses, civil partners, fiancé(e)s, or unmarried partners.

If you have been granted leave to enter or remain as a result of a maintenance undertaking, you are excluded from claiming benefits.[22] If you subsequently claim benefit while in the UK, your sponsor may be required to pay back the value of the benefit claimed.[23] The restriction applies until the sponsored person has been in the UK for five years since the date of the undertaking or the date of entry, unless the sponsor dies, in which case the restriction lapses immediately (see p60). This restriction will also lapse immediately if the sponsored person becomes a British citizen.[24]

A maintenance undertaking may be enforceable even if it is not formally drafted.[25] In one case, a formal declaration that a sponsor was able and willing to maintain and accommodate was held not to amount to an undertaking, as it did not include a promise to support.[26]

Sponsorship under the points-based system

The old routes to working and studying in the UK (which included the Highly Skilled Migrant Programme, work permits and the Sectors-based Scheme) have been replaced with a new points-based system.

Under the new system, applicants for leave must pass a points-based assessment before they are given permission to enter or remain in the UK. There are five tiers, each of which has a different points requirement. These are:

- highly skilled workers – eg, scientists and entrepreneurs;
- skilled workers with a job offer – eg, teachers and nurses;
- low-skilled workers filling specific temporary labour shortages – eg, construction workers for a particular project;
- students;
- youth mobility and temporary workers – eg, musicians coming to the UK to play in a specific concert.

Migrants applying under any tier except highly skilled workers must be sponsored by an employer or educational institution. The sponsor must hold a certificate of sponsorship, which is a unique reference number that the sponsor issues to a migrant to enable her/him to remain in the UK. Unlike a work permit, this is not an actual certificate or paper document.

Sponsors are under a duty to report to the UK Border Agency any significant changes in the sponsored person's circumstances, suspicions that s/he is breaching the conditions of her/his leave or significant changes in the sponsor's own circumstances – eg, if s/he stops trading or becomes insolvent.

7. Turkish nationals

Turkish nationals have the right to establish themselves in the United Kingdom (UK) for economic purposes under the agreement of 'association' between the European Community (EC) and Turkey. This right is separate to and more limited than the rights of nationals of the European Economic Area and Switzerland (see Chapter 4).

The EC-Turkey Association Agreement of 12 September 1963 is known as the 'Ankara Agreement'. The purpose of the Ankara Agreement was to promote a move towards the abolition of restrictions on freedom of establishment and freedom to provide services by those who wished to move between Turkey and the EC (as it was at the date of the agreement).

This was to be achieved by prohibiting the introduction of new national restrictions less favourable than those in force on the 'relevant date'. In the case of the UK, this is the date of the UK's accession to the EC on 1 January 1973. The Immigration Rules in effect on 1 January 1973 were less restrictive in certain respects than the current Immigration Rules and Turkish nationals are entitled to have any relevant applications considered under these old, less restrictive, Rules.[27]

Notes

1. **Leave to enter or remain**
   1 See the instructions and entry clearance guidance, available at www.ukvisas.gov.uk/en/ecg
   2 s8 IA 1971

2. **Time-limited leave**
   3 The extension of leave while a right of appeal could be exercised only applies within the time limit for appealing or when an out-of-time appeal has been accepted.

3. **Indefinite leave**
   4 s3(3)(a) IA 1971
   5 paras 18-19 IR

4. **Employment**
   6 For example, highly skilled migrants (Tier 1 of the points-based system), refugee, humanitarian protection and discretionary leave.
   7 The policy is presently contained in *Tier 4 of the Points Based System: policy guidance*, July 2010.

5. **Recourse to public funds**
   8 para 6 IR
   9 Under Part VI or VII Housing Act 1996 and under Part II Housing Act 1985, Part I or II Housing (Scotland) Act 1987, Part II Housing (Northern Ireland) Order 1981 or Part II Housing (Northern Ireland) Order 1988
   10 para 6B IR and see Ch1 s7 IDI
   11 *KA (Pakistan)* [2006] UKAIT 00065; approved in *AM (Ethiopia)* and *Ors and Anor v Entry Clearance Officer* [2008] EWCA Civ 1082, 16 October 2008
   12 *Mahad (previously referred to as AM) (Ethiopia) v Entry Clearance Officer* [2009] UKSC 16, 16 December 2009

13 *MK (Somalia) v Entry Clearance Officer* [2007] EWCA Civ 1521, 28 November 2007
14 paras 322(4) and 323 IR
15 *S v Entry Clearance Officer, Islamabad (Pakistan)* [2004] UKIAT 00006
16 Ch8 s1 IDI, annex F
17 Ch8 s1 IDI, annex F

6. **Sponsorship**
   18 paras 277-95 or 317-19 IR
   19 para 297 IR; *AM (Ethiopia)* and *Ors and Anor v Entry Clearance Officer* [2008] EWCA Civ 1082, 16 October 2008
   20 *Mahad (previously referred to as AM) (Ethiopia) v Entry Clearance Officer* [2009] UKSC 16, 16 December 2009
   21 para 35 IR
   22 s115(9)(c) IAA 1999
   23 para 35 IR; ss78, 105 and 106 SSAA 1992
   24 CPC/4317/2006
   25 *R (Begum)* [2003] *The Times*, 4 December 2003
   26 *Ahmed v SSWP* [2005] EWCA Civ 535

7. **Turkish nationals**
   27 Art 41.1 Additional Protocol to the Agreement; *R (on the application of Veli Tum and Mehmet Dari) v Secretary of State for the Home Department* C-16/05 [2007] (ECJ)

Chapter 3

Asylum, human rights and international protection

This chapter covers:
1. Asylum seekers (below)
2. Refugee status and humanitarian protection (p19)
3. Discretionary and exceptional leave (p20)
4. Fresh claims (p21)

1. Asylum seekers

Applying for asylum

Leave to enter or remain may be given to fulfil the United Kingdom's (UK's) obligations under international treaties and conventions relating to the protection of human rights and refugees. A **'refugee'** is a person who is outside her/his country of nationality or former habitual residence and who has a well-founded fear of persecution in that country for reasons of race, religion, nationality, political opinion or membership of a particular social group.

People who have applied for recognition as a refugee or as a person requiring international protection in the UK are commonly called **'asylum seekers'**.

Asylum applications to the UK Border Agency (UKBA) can be made on one or more of the following grounds:
- under the Refugee Convention (see p3);
- under Article 3 of the Human Rights Convention (see p3). This prescribes that no one shall be subjected to torture or to inhuman or degrading treatment or punishment;
- under the Qualification Directive (see p3).

The most common other Human Rights Convention Article raised in immigration cases is Article 8. This protects a right to enjoy private and family life without unnecessary or disproportionate interference.

'Temporary protection' is a separate and specific category of leave introduced by the Qualification Directive. It is given to people following a declaration of the

European Union Council in recognition of a mass influx of displaced people. There have been no declarations since the Directive came into force.

The definition of an asylum seeker for the purpose of support and accommodation (see p266) is limited to people who have applied under the Refugee Convention and/or Article 3 of the Human Rights Convention – ie, an application based only on Article 8, for example, does not make the applicant an asylum seeker for asylum support purposes.[1]

Future changes

The Nationality, Immigration and Asylum Act 2002 amends the definition of asylum seeker for the purpose of support and accommodation by limiting it to 'claims made in person at a particular place designated by the Secretary of State'.[2] At the time of writing, the amendment was not yet in force, but the UKBA generally requires an asylum seeker to have made her/his first claim for asylum in person before s/he will be given asylum support.

An asylum seeker may apply for asylum at a port of entry before passing through passport control, or from inside the country, having entered the UK illegally or with leave for a different purpose under the Immigration Rules.

If a person delays making an in-country asylum application, her/his entitlement to asylum support may be affected (see Chapters 15 to 18).

If an asylum application is refused or withdrawn, it may be possible to make a fresh application (see p21).

Detention

Some asylum seekers are detained while their asylum application is 'fast-tracked' or if their application is considered to be 'manifestly unfounded'. They are detained in the expectation that their application will be considered quickly. Other asylum seekers are detained for removal to a third country (ie, not the UK or the person's country of nationality), which is deemed to be responsible for considering the application. The provisions for this have been agreed by international treaties between European Union member states and other countries.

Failed asylum seekers may also be detained, sometimes for many months or even years, while the UKBA considers that they can be removed within a 'reasonable' period of time.

Temporary admission, temporary release and bail

Asylum seekers who apply at a port of entry and in-country applicants who did not have leave at the time of their application may be given temporary admission to the UK until their application is decided. An asylum seeker who has been detained may be granted temporary release or bail.

An asylum seeker given temporary admission at a port of entry is considered not to have 'entered' the UK.[3]

Temporary admission usually imposes conditions on the asylum seeker. These include a requirement to live at a specified address, report to an immigration officer at a specified time and location, and not to engage in paid or unpaid employment. There are criminal penalties if a person does not adhere to these conditions, which may also make it more likely that s/he will be detained.

An asylum seeker's temporary admission may continue beyond the determination of her/his initial application for asylum, sometimes for many years.

Temporary admission, temporary release and bail are also given to people who have remained in the UK after their limited leave to enter or remain has expired and to people who have entered the UK illegally, whether or not they have applied for asylum.

Permission to work

If you are an asylum seeker who has not received a decision on your initial claim for asylum after one year, and the delay was not your fault, you can apply to the UKBA for permission to work.[4]

2. Refugee status and humanitarian protection

Leave to enter or remain is granted if the UK Border Agency (UKBA) recognises an asylum seeker as a refugee or as otherwise in need of protection, or in order to avoid a breach of human rights law.

Since 30 August 2005, a person recognised as a refugee is normally granted an initial five years' leave to remain, with the option of applying for indefinite leave to follow. The previous policy was to grant indefinite leave immediately.

During the limited five-year period, your refugee status can be reviewed and revoked. A review may be triggered if:

- your actions bring you within the scope of the 1951 Refugee Convention cessation clauses – eg, if you travel back to your country of origin without a reasonable explanation; [5] *or*
- there is a 'significant or non-temporary' change in the conditions in your country of origin (or part of the country) that means your continuing need for protection is now placed in doubt.

If you have been recognised as a refugee, your spouse and dependent children who formed part of your family unit prior to your departure from your country (and other dependent relatives in limited circumstances) can apply to be reunited with you in the United Kingdom (UK). There are no maintenance and accommodation requirements that must be met in these applications. Your spouse and children will be given the same leave as you.

'**Humanitarian protection**' is given to someone who needs protection from harm by others, but whose case does not fit the criteria for refugee status – eg, s/he is at risk of serious harm that is not related to one of the Refugee Convention reasons. In other cases in which a potential breach of human rights is accepted, a more limited period of discretionary leave is granted – eg, in cases based on ill health (see below).

Since 30 August 2005, a person granted humanitarian protection is given limited leave of five years. After this initial five-year period s/he may be granted indefinite leave, subject to an 'active review' of whether there is still a continuing need for protection. Before 30 August 2005, humanitarian protection was granted for three years, after which time settlement was normally granted.

If you have been given humanitarian protection from 30 August 2005, similar family reunion provisions apply to you as those that apply to refugees (see p19).

3. **Discretionary and exceptional leave**

Discretionary leave

Discretionary leave may be granted if:
* a potential breach of human rights is accepted on the grounds of ill health; *or*
* a potential breach of Article 8 of the Human Rights Convention (see p3) is accepted (the right to enjoy private and family life without interference); *or*
* there are no adequate reception arrangements to enable the removal of an unaccompanied minor (a child) to her/his country of nationality; *or*
* the individual circumstances of a case are considered by the UK Border Agency (UKBA) or the Secretary of State to be unusually compelling, including those covered by UKBA policy concessions; *or*
* there is a real risk of a breach of human rights if a person were to be removed, but her/his presence in the UK is considered not to be conducive to the public good (eg, if s/he has committed a serious crime) and/or is considered a threat to security.

The current policy is that discretionary leave may be granted for up to three years. If you apply to have your discretionary leave extended, all the circumstances at the time of your application will be reviewed. You can apply for indefinite leave to remain after you have had six years' discretionary leave, unless your presence in the United Kingdom is considered not to be conducive to the public good, in which case you must complete 10 years with such leave. In the case of an unaccompanied minor, discretionary leave may be granted for up to three years or until the child is 17 and a half, whichever is the shorter period. At 17 and a half years, if not eligible for settlement, the child's case will be 'actively reviewed'. This will not automatically result in an extension of leave or settlement.

Exceptional leave

Exceptional leave to enter or remain was abolished from 1 April 2003. Before this date, exceptional leave was granted to asylum seekers who were not recognised as refugees, but who the Home Office decided not to return to their country of nationality, often under a blanket policy relating to a particular country experiencing civil or military upheaval.

From 1 April 2003, exceptional leave was replaced with humanitarian protection and discretionary leave.

Leave outside the rules

Leave granted by discretion or under a policy that does not relate to asylum, protection or human rights may be called 'leave outside the rules'.[6]

4. Fresh claims

If you have made a human rights application or an application for asylum which has been refused or withdrawn and there is no appeal pending, you can make further representations (or 'further submissions'). The UK Border Agency (UKBA) will then consider whether these amount to a 'fresh claim' – ie, an application that is significantly different to the failed application and which has a realistic prospect of resulting in your being allowed to stay in the United Kingdom (UK).[7] It may take many years before a decision is reached. These further submissions are not restricted to Refugee Convention or Article 3 of the Human Rights Convention claims, and may, for example, be based on Article 8 of the Human Rights Convention only, or on any other grounds that might realistically lead to you being given leave. See p17 for more details.

Note: the definition of an asylum seeker (and, therefore, an asylum seeker whose claim has been rejected) under the provisions for support and accommodation in the Immigration and Asylum Act 1999 is different. This includes Refugee Convention claims and claims under Article 3 of the Human Rights Convention only.[8] The Nationality, Immigration and Asylum Act 2002 amends this definition, limiting it to 'claims made in person at a particular place designated by the Secretary of State'.[9] At the time of writing, however, the amendment was not yet in force.[10]

Failed asylum seekers (as defined under the provisions for support and accommodation of asylum seekers and failed asylum seekers in the Immigration and Asylum Act 1999) and their dependants can be supported by the Secretary of

State under Section 4 of the Immigration and Asylum Act in certain circumstances – eg, if they are destitute and have made further representations and the UKBA has yet to consider whether these amount to a fresh claim.[11]

Notes

1. **Asylum seekers**
   1 s94(1) IAA 1999
   2 s44(2) NIAA 2002
   3 Unless s/he fails to adhere to the conditions of her/his temporary admission and/or is declared to be an illegal entrant: *Szoma v SSWP* [2005] UKHL 64
   4 Art 11 EU Dir 2003/9 (the 'Reception Directive'); paras 360 and 361 IR

2. **Refugee status and humanitarian protection**
   5 Art 1C(1)-(6) Refugee Convention 1951

3. **Discretionary and exceptional leave**
   6 Ch1 s14 IDI

4. **Fresh claims**
   7 para 353 IR and asylum policy instruction 'Further Submissions', available at www.ukba.homeoffice.gov.uk/ sitecontent/documents/policyandlaw/ asylumpolicyinstructions
   8 s94(1) IAA 1999
   9 s44(2) NIAA 2002

10 There do not appear to be any places formally designated for this purpose. The Asylum and Immigration Tribunal held in relation to a similar requirement under s113 NIAA 2002 that the various addresses that the Secretary of State makes available for those intending to lodge asylum or human rights claims must be considered as designated (in s92(4)(a) *ST (Turkey)* [2007] UKAIT 00085, meaning of 'has made'), but Sedley LJ more recently remarked that no such place has ever been designated: *BA (Nigeria), R (on the application of) v Secretary of State for the Home Department* [2009] EWCA Civ 119, 26 February 2009
11 s4 IAA 1999

Chapter 4

European Economic Area nationals

This chapter covers:
1. European Economic Area nationals (below)
2. Family members (p27)
3. Public funds (p32)
4. A8 nationals (p33)
5. A2 nationals (p33)
6. Exclusion and removal (p35)

This chapter explains the rights of free movement and residence of European Union citizens and nationals of the European Economic Area (EEA). There is a significant overlap between immigration and welfare rights law in this area as a consequence of the introduction of the 'right to reside test' for benefit entitlement on 1 May 2004 (see p116).

More detail is provided in this chapter on the rights enjoyed by EEA and Swiss nationals and their families than in the preceding chapters on leave to enter or remain in the United Kingdom (UK) and asylum seekers, refugees and people requiring international protection. This is because you do not need to obtain confirmation from the immigration authorities of any rights you (and your family) are exercising as an EEA national in the UK. Your rights, therefore, may not be so readily apparent from any documentation you have – eg, an endorsement in your passport (see Chapter 5).

1. European Economic Area nationals

The European Economic Area (EEA) comprises the member states of the European Union (EU) plus Norway, Liechtenstein, Iceland and Switzerland.

The present member states of the EU are: Austria, Belgium, Bulgaria, Cyprus, Czech Republic, Denmark, Estonia, Finland, France, Germany, Greece, Hungary, Ireland, Italy,

Latvia, Lithuania, Luxembourg, Malta, Netherlands, Poland, Portugal, Romania, Slovenia, Slovakia, Spain, Sweden and the United Kingdom (UK).

Citizens of the EU member states enjoy rights of free movement and residence within the EU for, broadly, economic reasons. In certain circumstances, they are also entitled to social assistance in member states other than their own.

These rights derive from the Treaty establishing the European Community (EC), the Treaty of Rome 1957 and subsequent legislation. The European Parliament's Directive 2004/38 (the 'Citizens' Directive') codified and reviewed the existing instruments in order to simplify and strengthen these rights. The UK has implemented this Directive by the Immigration (European Economic Area) Regulations 2006. The Directive is superior to UK legislation and supersedes it if there is any discrepancy in which the UK law is more restrictive of the rights of free movement and residence specified by the Directive. Most of this chapter uses the terminology of the Regulations, as these will be the starting point of for considering your EEA rights, while noting points of difference between these and the Directive.

Nationals of Norway, Liechtenstein and Iceland benefit from the rights of free movement and residence specified by the earlier instruments and it is expected that EU Directive 2004/38 will be extended to them in due course. Swiss nationals enjoy similar rights under a 1999 agreement between the Swiss Confederation and the EC and its member states. The UK has decided, for the sake of simplicity, that the 2006 Regulations apply equally to nationals of Norway, Liechtenstein, Iceland and Switzerland as to EU citizens. EU citizens, however, may enjoy stronger rights that directly derive from the (superior) Directive where differences between the Directive and the Regulations exist.

Right of admission

EEA nationals who move to or reside in the UK do not require leave to enter or remain.[1] They have the right to be admitted into the UK provided they produce an identity card, passport or can otherwise prove their status. They are not required to obtain a visa (or equivalent) in order to gain entry to the UK.[2]

Initial right to reside

EEA nationals have an initial right to reside in the UK for three months, provided they do not become an unreasonable burden on social assistance during this period (see p32).[3]

Extended right to reside

The right to reside for longer than the initial three months depends on the EEA national or her/his family member being a 'qualified person'. A **'qualified person'** is an EEA national residing in the UK who is:[4]

- a jobseeker;
- a worker;
- a self-employed person;
- a self-sufficient person (who has comprehensive sickness insurance[5]); *or*
- a student. At the start of her/his studies, s/he must provide an assurance that s/he will not become an unreasonable burden on social assistance and must have comprehensive sickness insurance throughout the extended period.

See Chapter 13 for more details.

An EEA national who is a qualified person is entitled to reside in the UK for as long as s/he remains a qualified person,[6] unless the Secretary of State decides that her/his removal is justified on the grounds of public policy, public security or public health (see p35). [7]

Nationals of eight of the states that joined the EU in 2004 ('A8 nationals') and the two states that joined in 2007 ('A2 nationals') have certain restrictions on their being workers in the UK (see p33).

Permanent right of residence

An EEA national who has resided in the UK legally for a continuous period of five years acquires the right to reside in the UK permanently ('permanent residence'). Time spent in the UK as a qualified person or as an EEA national family member (see p27) of another EEA national counts towards the five-year period. Continuous legal residence under earlier EU instruments can also be counted,[8] and time spent in possession of a valid registration certificate that was issued on the basis that you were such a person at the time might also count, even if you have ceased to be so during the period of validity.[9]

If you are an EEA national, you may also acquire permanent residence on becoming a 'worker or self-employed person who has ceased activity'.[10] This may happen in one of three ways.

- You stop being a worker or self-employed person and have either reached state pension age or, if you are a worker, you have stopped working to take early retirement and:
  - you have been a worker or self-employed person in the UK for at least 12 months prior to your giving up work; *and*
  - you have lived in the UK continuously for more than three years prior to stopping work/self-employment.[11] Periods during which you are active as a worker or a self-employed person in an EEA state but your place of residence is in the UK (returning at least once a week) count as period of residence in the UK.[12] If you are an EEA national and your spouse or civil partner is a UK national, s/he need not meet the conditions on the length of residence or activity as a worker or self-employed person at all.
- You stop being a worker or self-employed person in the UK because you have a permanent incapacity to work and:

- you have resided in the UK continuously for more than two years prior to stopping work. Periods during which you are active as a worker or a self-employed person in an EEA state but your place of residence is in the UK (returning at least once a week) count as period of residence in the UK.[13] If you are an EEA national and your spouse or civil partner is a UK national, s/he need not meet the conditions on the length of residence or activity as a worker or self-employed person at all;[14] *or*
- the incapacity is the result of an accident at work or an occupational disease that entitles you to a pension payable in full or in part by an institution in the UK.[15]

- You are now working or self-employed in another EEA state, but your place of residence is in the UK. You must normally return at least once a week. Before working or being self-employed in the other EEA state, you must have been continuously resident and continuously active as a worker or self-employed person in the UK for at least three years.[16]

Periods of inactivity count as periods of activity if they were for reasons not of your own making, because of illness or an accident, or if you were unemployed and 'signing on' at your local Jobcentre Plus office.[17]

EEA nationals acquire permanent residency automatically. You do not need to apply.

Once you have permanent residency, it can only be lost if you are absent from the UK for more than two consecutive years[18] or if the Secretary of State decides that your removal is justified on the grounds of public policy, public security or public health (see p35). [19]

Confirmation of the right to reside

You can apply to the UK Border Agency (UKBA) for a registration certificate, which confirms your status as a qualified person, or a document certifying that you have permanent residence.[20]

Note: it is not necessary for an EEA national to hold a certificate or document in order to benefit from the rights it confirms. Your rights as an EEA national do not depend on an application being made to the UKBA.

A registration certificate may be issued for five years, or less if the period of residence envisaged will be less than five years. However, the period of validity should not be regarded as a period of limited leave to enter or remain that requires extension or imposes conditions on the holder. It is not necessary to apply for a certificate to enjoy the rights it confirms. Similarly, even though an EEA national holds a valid registration certificate, s/he does not necessarily remain a qualified person.[21]

Even if you have a right of residence, you are not automatically entitled to a document confirming your rights – you must be able to produce a valid identity card or passport in addition to proof that you have these rights.[22]

2. **Family members**

Rights of free movement and residence under the Citizens' Directive and the 2006 Regulations (see p23) extend to certain family members accompanying or joining a European Economic Area (EEA) national who moves to or resides in the United Kingdom (UK). Certain members of an EEA national's family enjoy greater rights than others. There are three main categories of family member:

- family members;
- extended family members;
- family members who have retained the right of residence.

Family members

A '**family member**' is an EEA national's:[23]

- spouse or civil partner;
- child under age 21 (or over 21 if still dependent). Children of the EEA national's spouse or civil partner are also family members;
- dependent parents or grandparents and those of the EEA national's spouse or civil partner;
- extended family members (see p28) who have been issued with a family permit, a registration certificate or a residence card that remains valid for as long as they continue to satisfy the requirements for recognition as such.[24]

Family members of students

If an EEA national is residing in the UK with an extended right to reside as a student, her/his family members are restricted to her/his:[25]

- spouse or civil partner;
- dependent child, or her/his spouse's/civil partner's dependent child (**Note:** there must be dependency whatever the child's age);
- extended family members (see p28) who have been issued with a family permit, a registration certificate or a residence card that remains valid for as long as they continue to satisfy the requirements for recognition as such.[26]

Meaning of dependent

If the definition of a family member requires her/him to be dependent on the EEA national, this means financial dependence.[27]

In order to be considered dependent, the family member must need the material support of the EEA national or her/his spouse in order to meet her/his essential needs. This must be considered independently of any claim for for any minimum income benefit – eg, income support.[28]

Extended family members

An 'extended family member' includes:
- a relative of the EEA national or her/his spouse or civil partner who was living as part of the EEA national's household, or who was dependent (see above) on the EEA national before s/he came to the UK.[29] If the relative has joined the EEA national in the UK, s/he must continue to be either part of the EEA national's household or dependent on her/him; *or*
- a relative of the EEA national or of her/his spouse or civil partner who requires personal care from that person on serious health grounds; *or*
- a person who is in a durable relationship with the EEA national – eg, an unmarried partner;
- any other relative issued with a family permit, a registration certificate or a residence card.[30]

Family members who have retained the right of residence

The following people are '**family members who have retained the right of residence**' under the 2006 Regulations.
- A family member of a qualified person who has died. S/he must have been a family member when the qualified person died, and must have resided in the UK for at least the year immediately before the death.[31]
- A child of a qualified person who has died (or a child of her/his spouse or civil partner) who was attending an educational course[32] in the UK immediately before the qualified person died and continues to attend such a course.[33]
- A child of a person who has ceased to be a qualified person on ceasing to reside in the UK (or a child of her/his spouse or civil partner) who was attending an educational course in the UK immediately before the qualified person ceased to reside in the UK and continues to attend such a course.[34] Such rights of residence are also retained if the former qualified person ceased to be a qualified person before leaving.[35]
- A parent with custody of a child who has retained a right of residence in either of the two bullet-point scenarios above.[36]
- A family member of a qualified person who has died.[37]
- A person who has ceased to be a family member of a qualified person on the termination of the qualified person's marriage or civil partnership where:
  - the marriage or partnership lasted for at least three years and the couple resided in the UK for at least one year while they were married;[38]

- the person has custody of the qualified person's child;[39]
- a court has ordered that s/he has access to the qualified person's child under age 18 and that this must take place in the UK;[40]
- there are particularly difficult circumstances which mean s/he should continue to live in the UK – eg, there has been domestic violence.[41]

Note: in all the above scenarios, the family member must have been residing in the UK in accordance with the 2006 Regulations on the date of the death of the qualified person or the termination of the marriage/civil partnership. Except if there is a child in education, the Regulations only provide for rights of residence on the termination of a marriage/civil partnership or after the death of the EEA national if one of the family members is a non-EEA national who would be classed as a worker, a self-employed person or a self-sufficient person if s/he were an EEA national. The Citizens' Directive appears to provide for these rights, but also that an extended right to reside to a European Union (EU) citizen who is a family member of another EU citizen (eg, if the latter was a worker, but the former was not) is not lost on the termination of marriage/civil partnership, or on the death or departure of the EU citizen, and without any additional conditions. However, under the Directive an EU citizen family member who retains a right of residence in these situations must become a worker, a self-employed person, a student or a self-sufficient person before acquiring permanent residence.[42]

Caselaw has confirmed that a child who is attending an educational course in the UK has a right of residence, provided s/he has, at some point, been residing in the UK as a family member of an EEA national with a right to reside as a worker. In these circumstances, a parent with custody also has a right to reside.[43]

Family members of British citizens

The 2006 Regulations also provide for a right of residence for family members of a British citizen who is returning to the UK after working or being self-employed in another EEA state. In this situation, the returning British citizen is treated as if s/he were an EEA national of another member state exercising rights of free movement in the UK. Her/his family members benefit from the rights of entry and residence without having to apply for permission to enter or remain in the UK with the British citizen under the Immigration Rules.[44] There is no requirement for the non-EEA family member to be lawfully resident in the UK before the free movement rights are exercised.[45]

If a family member of a British citizen is also a national of another EEA state, s/he has the same rights under the 2006 Regulations as a family member of an EEA national who is not a British citizen, but it appears that s/he might not enjoy rights under the Directive, as this appears only to apply to EU citizens who move to or reside in member states other than the state of which they are a national.[46]

Other rights of residence

A parent or person with actual custody of a child may derive a right to reside from any such right enjoyed by the child if her/his presence in the UK is required in order for the child's effective enjoyment of those rights. This is certainly so in the case of a parent with custody of an EEA national's child who is self-sufficient. Note, however, that the source of the child's right to reside (eg, self-sufficiency) must not depend on the parent being economically active in the UK, if s/he would not be permitted to be so if the child did not enjoy such a right.[47]

Other immediate family members may also derive a right to reside in the UK in this situation if it is necessary to maintain family unity.[48]

Right of admission

Family members have a right to be admitted to the UK, provided they produce a family permit, a residence card or a permanent residence card (see p31) or prove their status as a family member within a reasonable period of time.[49]

A family permit is like entry clearance and can be applied for from an entry clearance officer stationed overseas. A valid family permit endorsed in the holder's passport allows her/him to enter the UK at a port of entry (provided there is no fraud or material change in circumstances).

Initial right to reside

A non-EEA family member of an EEA national is entitled to reside in the UK with the EEA national while the EEA national exercises her/his initial right to reside for three months (see p24). The family member must hold a valid passport and must not become an 'unreasonable burden on the social security system' (see p32).[50]

Extended right to reside

If you are the family member of a qualified person or the family member of an EEA national with permanent residence, you are entitled to reside in the UK for as long as you remain so.[51] This applies whether or not if you are an EEA national yourself.

If you are a family member who has retained the right of residence, you are entitled to reside in the UK for so long as you remain so.[52]

If you are an extended family member, you have no absolute right to a family permit, registration certificate or residence card, but you may apply for one. The decision to issue one of these is discretionary. An extensive examination of your circumstances must be carried out and, if refused, you must be given reasons (unless this is against the interests of national security).[53]

If a family permit, registration certificate or a residence card is not granted, an extended family member does not come within the definition of family member under the 2006 Regulations and does not, therefore, have a right of residence under the Regulations.[54]

Family members of students

At the start of her/his studies, an EEA national student must provide an assurance that s/he and any family members will not become an unreasonable burden on the social security system. The EEA national student and her/his family members must also have comprehensive sickness insurance throughout the extended period.[55]

Permanent right of residence

If you are an EEA national who has resided legally in the UK for a continuous period of five years, you acquire the right to reside in the UK permanently ('permanent residence').[56]

Time spent as an EEA national family member of another EEA national counts towards this five-year period, as does any time spent as a qualified person in your own right.

If you are a non-EEA national who has legally resided in the UK with an EEA national (ie, as a family member or a family member who has retained the right of residence) for a continuous period of five years, you also acquire the right to permanent residence.[57]

Residence under the earlier EU instruments can be counted for these purposes. Residence in possession of a valid registration certificate issued on the basis that you were such a person at the time might also count, even if you ceased to be so during the period of validity.[58]

Family members of a worker or self-employed person who has ceased activity (see p238) acquire the right to permanent residence immediately.[59]

A person who was the family member of a worker or self-employed person acquires the right to permanent residence if the worker or self-employed person dies. S/he must have resided with her/him immediately before her/his death and the worker or self-employed person must have either resided continuously in the UK for at least the two years immediately before her/his death or the death was the result of an accident at work or an occupational disease.[60]

Both EEA and non-EEA nationals automatically acquire permanent residence in the circumstances detailed above. You do not need to apply.

Once acquired, the right to permanent residence can only be lost if you are absent from the UK for more than two consecutive years[61] or if the Secretary of State decides that your removal is justified on the grounds of public policy, public security or public health (see p35).[62]

Confirmation of the right to reside

If you are not an EEA national and you have a right to reside as a family member, you can apply to the UKBA for a residence card or permanent residence card as confirmation of your status. If you are an EEA national yourself and have a right to reside as a family member of an EEA national, you can apply for a registration certificate or a document certifying permanent residence.

Note: a registration card (or certificate) is only a declaration. The period of validity should not be regarded as a period of limited leave to enter or remain that requires extending or imposes conditions on the holder. You do not have to apply for one to enjoy the rights it confirms. Also, even though you hold a valid residence card, this does not necessarily mean that you remain a family member of a qualified person.

Having a right of residence as a family member or a family member who has retained the right of residence does not automatically entitle you to be issued with a document confirming these rights. You must also have a valid passport, or national identity card if you are an EEA national, as well as proof that you have the right of residence.[63]

3. **Public funds**

If you are a qualified person or a family member of a qualified person, you are not subject to the public funds requirement under the Immigration Rules (see p11). There is, however, one exception. From 1 January 2005, the primary carer, parent or sibling of a self-sufficient European Economic Area (EEA) national child may be granted leave to enter/remain on the condition that s/he can be maintained and accommodated without recourse to public funds (see below).[64]

An EEA national who is in the United Kingdom (UK) as a student or self-sufficient person must also be able to support her/himself without public funds and may lose her/his right of residence if s/he claims public funds and cannot demonstrate s/he is not an unreasonable burden on the state (see p11).

UK Border Agency (UKBA) policy is that, if an EEA national student or self-sufficient person claims public funds after having been in the UK for some time, the fact that s/he has been self-sufficient is a factor in determining whether the burden is reasonable. The length of time s/he is likely to be receiving public funds is also taken into account. Although the UKBA acknowledges that an EEA national in this situation will be treated as having a right of residence even though s/he has received public funds, its policy is not to issue her/him with a registration certificate.[65]

'**Public funds**' for these purposes are:
- income support;
- income-based jobseeker's allowance;
- housing benefit;
- council tax benefit;
- working tax credit;
- social fund payments;

- child benefit;
- any disability allowance;
- housing allocated under certain housing and homelessness provisions.[66] Social housing is not included.

Note: the above applies when the UKBA considers whether someone has been an unreasonable burden for immigration purposes. See p62 for details of the public funds rules for social security benefits purposes.

4. **A8 nationals**

Nationals of the Czech Republic, Estonia, Hungary, Latvia, Lithuania, Poland, Slovakia and Slovenia have restrictions on their right to work in the United Kingdom (UK) as citizens of the European Union (EU).[67] These restrictions applied from 1 May 2004 (the date the countries joined the EU) until 1 May 2009, with an option of extension until 1 May 2011, which the UK Government has chosen to exercise. Nationals of these countries are termed 'A8 nationals'.

A8 nationals who wish to reside in the UK as workers must register under the Worker Registration Scheme until they have completed 12 continuous months as a worker under the Worker Registration Scheme.[68] They have no rights of residence as jobseekers until they are free from the requirement to register or if they have a right to reside as a family member of a Swiss or a European Economic Area (EEA) national (excluding the initial right to reside if the latter person is also an A8 national).[69]

An A8 national's rights of residence from self-employment, self-sufficiency or studying are not subject to any such restrictions.

You should register with the Worker Registration Scheme within one month of taking up work. You are then issued with a registration certificate and card (see Figure 25, Appendix 7). The certificate only relates to the specific employment for which it is applied. If you change jobs, you should apply within one month for an amended certificate.

In general, family members of A8 nationals have the same rights as family members of EEA nationals, except that family members of A8 nationals working under the Worker Registration Scheme are issued with a family member residence stamp rather than a residence card as confirmation of their right to reside.

5. **A2 nationals**

Nationals of Romania and Bulgaria (known as 'A2 nationals') have further restrictions on their right to work in the United Kingdom (UK) as European Union (EU) citizens.[70] These restrictions apply from the date Romania and Bulgaria joined the EU on 1 January 2007 until 1 January 2012, with an option of extension for a further two years until 1 January 2014.

A2 nationals who wish to reside in the UK as workers must apply for an accession worker card, unless they are exempt (see below). Their employer may also have to apply for a work permit. A2 nationals have no right of residence as jobseekers.

Not all categories of employment require a work permit.

You are exempt from the requirement to apply for an accession worker card if you:

- are in the UK under the Seasonal Agricultural Workers Scheme and hold a valid work card issued by a Scheme operator;
- were given leave to enter or remain in the UK under the Immigration Rules before 1 January 2007 and your passport has been endorsed with a condition restricting your employment to a particular employer or employment category. If this leave to enter or remain expires before you qualify as exempt from work authorisation requirements, or you want to work in a job other than that for which the leave was granted, you must obtain an accession worker card;
- have leave to enter under the Immigration Rules and this does not place any restrictions on taking employment in the UK;
- have been working with permission (including under your terms of leave to enter or remain) in the UK for a continuous period of 12 months ending on or after 31 December 2006;
- are providing services in the UK on behalf of an employer established elsewhere in the European Economic Area (EEA);
- are also a citizen of the UK or another EEA state, other than Bulgaria or Romania, or Switzerland;
- are the family member of an EEA national exercising a Treaty right in the UK (except if you are the family member of a Bulgarian or Romanian national who is subject to work authorisation requirements), or the spouse or civil partner of a British citizen or person with settlement in the UK;
- are the family member of a Bulgarian or Romanian national who is self-employed, self-sufficient or a student; *or*
- are a highly skilled migrant and apply for a registration certificate on this basis.

You can apply for a registration certificate to confirm there are no restrictions on your taking employment in the UK, but need not do so.

An A2 national family member of an A2 national who is exempt from work authorisation requirements is entitled to a registration certificate confirming s/he is also exempt from these requirements.

A non-EEA national family member of an A2 national who is exempt from work authorisation requirements is entitled to a residence card.

A family member of an A2 national who is in the UK and is not exempt from the work authorisation requirement must also obtain an accession worker card in order to take employment in the UK. Family members of A2 nationals working under the Seasonal Agricultural Workers Scheme or under an au pair or the Sectors-based Scheme will not be given permission to take employment.

A non-EEA national family member of an A2 national holding a work authorisation document can apply for a family member residence stamp.

An A2 national family member of an A8 national registered under the Worker Registration Scheme who intends to work is exempt from worker authorisation requirements and can apply for a registration certificate confirming this.

You may also apply for a registration certificate if you are an A2 national or an EEA national yourself and you are the family member of an A8 or A2 national who is not subject to work authorisation and who is working.

6. **Exclusion and removal**

European Economic Area (EEA) nationals and their family members may be removed if they do not have, or cease to have, a right to reside.[71] They must not be removed as an automatic consequence of having recourse to public funds.[72]

EEA nationals and their family members who have a right of residence may only be excluded or otherwise removed from the UK if there is a serious threat to public policy, public security or public health.[73] If someone has permanent residence, the grounds for exclusion must be serious[74] and an EEA national who is aged under 18 cannot be excluded or removed unless it is in her/his best interests or her/his removal is imperative on grounds of public security.[75] Similarly, an EEA national who has resided in the UK for 10 years cannot be excluded or removed except on imperative grounds of public security.[76]

4

Notes

1. European Economic Area nationals

1 s7(1) IA 1988
2 Reg 11 I(EEA) Regs
3 Reg 13 I(EEA) Regs
4 Reg 6 I(EEA) Regs
5 European Commission guidance is that this means insurance under the EU co-ordination rules 1409/71 and 833/04. See also LJ in *W (China) and Anor v Secretary of State for the Home Department* [2006] EWCA Civ 1494, 9 November 2006
6 Reg 14(1) I(EEA) Regs
7 Reg 19(3)(b) I(EEA) Regs
8 *Taous Lassal* C-162/09 (ECJ)
9 See pending references to the ECJ, *Shirley McCarthy* C-434/09 and *Maria Dias* C-325/09
10 Reg 15(1)(c) I(EEA) Regs
11 Reg 5(2) I(EEA) Regs
12 Reg 5(5) I(EEA) Regs
13 Reg 5(5) I(EEA) Regs
14 Reg 5(6) I(EEA) Regs
15 Reg 5(3) I(EEA) Regs
16 Reg 5(4) I(EEA) Regs
17 Reg 5(7) I(EEA) Regs
18 Reg 15(2) I(EEA) Regs
19 Reg 19(3)(b) I(EEA) Regs
20 Reg 16 I(EEA) Regs
21 But see pending references to the ECJ, *Shirley McCarthy* C-434/09 and *Maria Dias* C-325/09
22 Reg 16(1) I(EEA) Regs

2. Family members

23 Reg 7 I(EEA) Regs
24 Reg 7 I(EAA) Regs
25 Reg 7(2) I EEA Regs
26 Reg 7 I(EEA) Regs
27 *Yunying Jia* C-1/05 (ECJ)
28 *Marie-Christine Lebon* C-316/85 (ECJ)
29 *Blaise Baheten Metock and Ors* C-127/08 [2008] (ECJ) and see *Bigia and Ors v Entry Clearance Officer* [2009] EWCA Civ 79, 19 February 2009. The person may have to have been dependent on the EEA national and/or living as part of the EEA national's household outside the UK recently.
30 Regs 8, 12(3), 16(6) and 17(5) I(EEA) Regs

31 Reg 10(2) and (6) I(EEA) Regs
32 Within the scope of Art 12 EU Reg 1612/68
33 Reg 10(3)(a)(i) and (iii) I(EEA) Regs
34 Reg 10(3)(a)(ii) and (iii) I(EEA) Regs
35 *London Borough of Harrow v Nimco Hassan Ibrahim and Secretary of State for the Home Department* C-310/08 (ECJ)
36 Reg 10(4) I(EEA) Regs
37 Reg 10(2) and (6) I(EEA) Regs
38 Reg 10(5)(d)(i) I(EEA) Regs
39 Reg 10(5)(d)(ii) I(EEA) Regs
40 Reg 10(5)(d)(iii) I(EEA) Regs
41 Reg 10(5)(d)(iv) I(EEA) Regs
42 Arts 12 and 13 EU Dir 2004/38
43 *Nimco Hassan Ibrahim* C-310/08 and *Maria Teixeira* C-480/08 (ECJ). This might also apply if the child was a family member of a self-employed or self-sufficient EEA national.
44 Reg 9 I(EEA) Regs
45 *Blaise Baheten Metock and Ors* C-127/08 (ECJ)
46 Art 3(1) EU Dir 2004/38
47 *Kungian Catherine Zhu and Man Lavette* C-200/02 (ECJ); *Baumbast and R* C-413/99. See also *M (Chen – parent: source of rights) Ivory Coast* [2010] UKUT 277 (IAC)
48 Recital 6 to EU Dir 2004/38; see also *Mary Carpenter* C-60/00
49 Reg 11 I(EEA) Regs
50 Reg 13(2) I(EEA) Regs
51 Reg 14(2) I(EEA) Regs
52 Reg 14(3) I(EEA) Regs. It is interesting that a right to reside by a family member of an EU citizen with permanent residence is not explicitly provided for in the Directive.
53 Regs 12(2) and (3), 16(5) and (6) and 17(4) and (5) I(EEA) Regs
54 *YB (EEA reg 17(4) – proper approach) Ivory Coast* [2008] UKAIT 00062
55 Reg 4(3) I(EEA) Regs
56 Reg 15(1)(a) I(EEA) Regs
57 Reg 15(1)(b) I(EEA) Regs
58 *Taous Lassal* C-162/09
59 Reg 15(1)(d) I(EEA) Regs
60 Reg 15(1)(e) I(EEA) Regs

61 Reg 15(2) I(EEA) Regs
62 Reg 19(3)(b) I(EEA) Regs
63 Regs 16(4) and 17(1) and (2) I(EEA) Regs

3. Public funds
64 para 257C IR. This might not be a lawful
    condition. See *M (Chen – parents: source
    of rights) Ivory Coast* [2010] UKUT 277
    (IAC)
65 Ch 12 European Casework Instructions,
    available at
    www.ind.homeoffice.gov.uk/
    sitecontent/documents/policyandlaw/
    ecis
66 Under Part VI or VII Housing Act 1996
    and under Part II Housing Act 1985, Part
    I or II Housing (Scotland) Act 1987, Part
    II Housing (Northern Ireland) Order
    1981 or Part II Housing (Northern
    Ireland) Order 1988

4. A8 nationals
67 A(IWR) Regs
68 Reg 2(4) A(IWR) Regs
69 Reg 1(6) A(IWR) Regs

5. A2 nationals
70 A(IWA) Regs

6. Exclusion and removal
71 Reg 19(3)(b) I(EEA) Regs
72 Reg 19(4) I(EEA) Regs
73 Reg 19(5) I(EEA) Regs
74 Reg 21(3) I(EEA) Regs
75 Reg 21(4)(b) I(EEA) Regs
76 Reg 21(4)(a) I(EEA) Regs

Chapter 5

Determining immigration status

This chapter covers:
1. British citizens and people with the right of abode (below)
2. People with leave to enter or remain (p39)
3. People without leave (p43)
4. Asylum seekers (p44)
5. European Economic Area and Swiss nationals (p44)
6. Deportation and special immigration status (p45)
7. Other passport issues (p45)

This chapter gives guidance on determining immigration (and citizenship) status for the purpose of establishing entitlement to social security benefits.

A person's immigration status in the United Kingdom (UK) can be identified by examining her/his passport and any endorsements in it by the UK immigration authorities (eg, stamps, stickers or vignettes) or, increasingly, her/his identity card. Note, however, that the holder's status may have changed since the passport, endorsement or card was issued. In addition, some people do not hold any of these.

If your immigration status is uncertain, you should contact a regulated adviser. A list of advisers and organisations is included in Appendix 2.

1. British citizens and people with the right of abode

If you have the right of abode in the United Kingdom (UK), you can prove this by presenting:
- a UK passport or an identity card issued under the Identity Cards Act 2006, describing you as a British citizen; or
- a UK passport or an identity card issued under the Identity Cards Act 2006, describing you as a British subject with the right of abode in the UK; or
- a certificate of entitlement to the right of abode.

These are now the only acceptable forms of evidence of the right of abode.[1]

If you have been granted British citizenship after applying to register or naturalise, you will receive a certificate confirming this, which may then be presented to the Home Office Identity and Passport Service when you apply for a UK passport.

Note: not all holders of UK passports have the right of abode in the UK (see p6), and some Commonwealth citizens with the right of abode do not hold UK passports.

UK passports can be issued in the UK to those whose right of abode is awaiting verification. The passport will contain the endorsement: 'The holder's status under the Immigration Act 1971 has not yet been determined.'

People with the right of abode who are also foreign nationals may have a certificate of entitlement endorsed in their foreign passport (see Figure 1, Appendix 7).

A certificate of patriality issued under the Immigration Act 1971 and which was valid immediately before 1 January 1983 is regarded as a certificate of entitlement unless the holder no longer has the right of abode – eg, if s/he has renounced this, or if there has been independence legislation.[2]

Some people with the right of abode may hold a 'confirmation of "right of abode" document'. This was a non-statutory document issued for a brief period before the commencement of the Immigration Act 1988 to dual nationals with the right of abode who had opted to travel on non-British passports.

2. People with leave to enter or remain

Entry clearance confirming leave to enter

Entry clearance is endorsed by a sticker (known as a 'vignette') placed in a person's passport or travel document, and by data stored digitally in an identity card and government database (see p41).

The vignette endorsement may be designated as a visa (for visa nationals, stateless persons and refugees), entry clearance (for non-visa nationals and British nationals other than British citizens) or a family permit (for dependants of European Economic Area nationals).

Two types of vignette are now issued. Which is used depends on the type of entry clearance given. Both types include a photograph of the holder (see Figures 2 and 3, Appendix 7). Older versions look similar, but without a photograph (see Figures 4 and 5, Appendix 7), and even older ones are a smaller sticker signed and date-stamped by an official (similar to the leave to remain endorsement vignette shown in Figure 6, Appendix 7).

Accompanying dependants whose details are included in the main applicant's passport receive their own vignettes, fixed in the main applicant's passport.

Entry clearance granting leave to enter allows you to enter the United Kingdom (UK) at a port without having to demonstrate that you satisfy the requirements of the Immigration Rules (unless the entry clearance was obtained by fraud or there has been a material change in circumstances since it was issued). The vignette endorsement is usually date-stamped on entry (see Figure 7, Appendix 7), and confirms that you have been granted leave to enter the UK, often for the remaining period of validity (see p10).

An immigration officer can vary or extend a person's leave (where permitted) on her/his arrival in the UK.

The date the entry clearance first becomes valid is usually the same as the date of authorisation and the holder may present her/himself for initial entry under the entry clearance at any time during its validity. However, entry clearance officers have the discretion to defer the date on which the entry clearance first becomes valid for up to three months after it is issued if, for example, the person wishes to delay travelling to the UK.

If you are granted entry clearance, you may travel to and remain in the UK for the purpose for which it was granted. You can travel in and out of the UK as many times as you wish, provided your entry clearance remains valid. However, if entry clearance has been authorised for multiple journeys to the UK of a fixed duration (eg, under the visitor category of the Immigration Rules), the duration of each visit is limited to a maximum of six months. This limitation is stated on the vignette under the heading 'duration of stay'.

An endorsement of entry clearance for *indefinite* leave to enter will specify a 'valid until' date. This is the date by which the holder must present the entry clearance at a port of entry to the UK or the date on which the holder's passport is due to expire; it is not a date of expiry of the leave. If the holder has presented the entry clearance at port, there should be an ink stamp showing where and on which date that occurred. The date on which the entry clearance was presented is the date on which the entry clearance took effect as indefinite leave.

If you are granted entry clearance with a vignette for leave to enter on certain conditions (eg, as a student on condition that you do not engage in employment except as authorised or that you do not have recourse to public funds), these should be stated on the endorsement (see Figure 2, Appendix 7).

See Appendix 5 for a table of the current codes used on an entry clearance vignette to show the purpose for which the entry clearance has been issued.

Leave to enter without entry clearance

Nationals of some countries cannot enter the UK for any purpose without first obtaining entry clearance (visa nationals). Others can apply at the port of entry for leave to enter for some of the purposes provided for under the Immigration Rules.

It may be difficult to identify the purpose for which an endorsement of leave to enter has been given if the application has been made at the port of entry. If limited leave has been granted, the endorsement may be an ink stamp, stating the duration of the leave period for which leave is granted and the conditions (if any) attached to the leave (see Figure 8, Appendix 7). Each stamped endorsement by an immigration officer granting leave to a person without entry clearance should be accompanied by a rectangular date stamp, showing when the leave was granted.

The example shown in Figure 9, Appendix 7 is the endorsement usually made in the passport of a person given leave to enter at a port of entry as a visitor or student on a short course (of six months or less). The endorsement shows that leave has been granted on condition that the holder does not engage in any employment or have recourse to public funds.

People returning to the UK who already have indefinite leave to enter or remain are simply given a date stamp if readmitted with indefinite leave.

If you leave the UK and return during a period of leave given for more than six months, an immigration officer may endorse a grant of leave to enter with the same conditions using an ink stamp stating this.[3]

Some people, usually Commonwealth citizens, who entered the UK before the Immigration Act 1971 came into force may have retained an expired passport with an ink entry stamp with no conditions attached. These people are referred to as 'freely landed'. They may have been treated as having been given indefinite leave to enter or remain when the 1971 Act came into force and have retained this status by remaining resident in the UK.

Leave to remain granted inside the United Kingdom

The UK residence permit replaced all former stamp and ink endorsements for permission to stay in this country for longer than six months. The permit is a vignette, similar in appearance to that used to endorse entry clearance (see p39), and includes a photograph of the holder (see Figure 10, Appendix 7).

Previously, leave may have been endorsed using a smaller vignette sticker or by a rectangular stamp accompanied by a pentagonal date stamp (see Figures 7 and 11, Appendix 7).

Identity cards

Identity cards (see Figure 12, Appendix 7) have now begun to replace the vignette (sticker) endorsements and other UK immigration status documents. The first identity cards were issued to foreign nationals from November 2008 and the intention is that all foreign nationals applying for leave to enter or remain in the UK will be required to have a card. **Note:** if you are issued with a card confirming you have been given leave to enter or remain, your passport will not be endorsed at all.

The new credit card-sized document shows the holder's photograph, name, date of birth, nationality and immigration status. A secure electronic chip attached to the card holds digitised biometric details, including fingerprints, a facial image and biographical information (including name, and date and place of birth).

The card also shows details of the holder's immigration status and entitlements in the UK, including what kind of leave s/he has and whether s/he can work. A database holds a record of the biometrics of each person to whom a card has been issued, so these can be cross-checked.

Holders of the new identity card must inform the UK Border Agency (UKBA) of specified changes in their circumstances or face prosecution or other sanctions.

Applications for further leave and appeals

Note: limited leave is automatically extended beyond the date it was due to expire if you make a valid application to extend or vary the leave before that date. It is extended until a decision is made by the UKBA and, if your application is refused, still further until any appeal rights are exhausted. The same conditions attached to the leave continue to apply during the extension.

People who have applied for their leave to be extended and are waiting for the UKBA to make a decision are unlikely to have retained their passports. In addition, certain types of application have been subject to delays (of several years) in processing by the UKBA. This can make it difficult for some people to prove that their leave is ongoing. The UKBA usually acknowledges a valid application for leave by letter, and may specifically confirm that a person has permission to work on request – eg, while s/he waits for a decision on her/his application.

A person who has been refused leave or whose leave has been revoked or cancelled but who has appealed the decision may have her/his passport if it was returned to her/him with the decision notice. If you appeal, you are not required to surrender your passport.

Travel and status documents issued to non-United Kingdom nationals

Where necessary, leave to enter, leave to remain or indefinite leave to remain may be granted by letter or by a form, rather than endorsing a passport. For example, indefinite leave to remain may be endorsed on an immigration status document if a person's passport is not available at the time indefinite leave is granted.

Leave given to refugees, humanitarian protection and discretionary leave may also be endorsed on an immigration status document (see Figures 13, 14, 15 and 16, Appendix 7).

A dependant of a refugee or person with humanitarian protection may be granted entry clearance on the basis of a refugee family reunion on a standard European Union form if s/he has no passport or cannot obtain one. The example in Figure 17, Appendix 7 shows the previous equivalent, a GV3 document, with an endorsement reading 'visa family reunion – sponsor'. The sponsor referred to is the relative with refugee status whom the dependant is joining in the UK (the endorsement does not indicate that a sponsorship undertaking has been given).

Refugees are entitled to a Refugee Convention travel document (coloured blue).

People recognised as stateless under the terms of the 1954 United Nations Convention relating to the status of stateless people are entitled to a stateless persons' document (coloured red).

Someone granted indefinite leave but not recognised as a refugee, and someone granted exceptional leave, discretionary leave or humanitarian protection for a limited period following a failed asylum application can apply for a certificate of travel (coloured black). However, to qualify for such a document, you must usually have applied to your own national authorities for a passport or travel document and been formally and unreasonably refused this.

3. **People without leave**

A person who has remained in the United Kingdom (UK) after her/his limited leave to enter or remain has expired may have committed a criminal offence and may be arrested, detained and removed from the UK. This also applies if you have remained in the UK after you have been refused further leave or had your leave revoked or curtailed and any appeal rights have been exhausted. Any conditions attached to the limited leave cease on the expiry, revokation or curtailment of the leave.

If further leave has been refused, a line may be drawn through the previous endorsement of leave. A decision refusing leave to enter at a port may be endorsed by a crossed-through ink date stamp (see Figure 18, Appendix 7).

You must be notified of any immigration decision in writing. Sending a notice to your last known address, or the address of a representative (solicitor or other regulated person) might be sufficient, so you may not necessarily be aware of a decision concerning you. Specialist advice should be sought if there is any doubt.

Other people may have entered the UK illegally and have never been granted leave.

If a person is in the UK without leave and comes to the attention of the authorities, s/he is likely to be served with a notice stating s/he is liable to be removed (see Figure 9, 20 and 21, Appendix 7). S/he may be detained for the purpose of enforcing removal, or given temporary admission, temporary release or bail.

Temporary admission, temporary release or bail usually imposes conditions on the person concerned. These can include that s/he must live at a specified address, report to an immigration officer at a specified time and location and must not engage in either paid or unpaid work. There are criminal penalties if you fail to adhere to these conditions, and doing so might make it more likely that you will be detained. You must be informed of any such condition in writing; this is usually done using a form called an IS96 (see Figure 22, Appendix 7).

4. Asylum seekers

People who have applied for recognition as a refugee or certain other forms of international protection are commonly called 'asylum seekers' (see Chapter 3).

Until early 2002, asylum seekers were issued with a standard acknowledgement letter (SAL). A 'SAL1' was issued to those claiming asylum at the port and a 'SAL2' was issued to those who claimed asylum once they were already in the United Kingdom (UK). Since 2002, the UK Border Agency has issued asylum seekers with an application registration card (ARC) (see Figure 23, Appendix 7). The ARC may state whether the applicant has any dependants or permission to work.

Asylum seekers who apply at a port of entry, and in-country applicants who did not have leave at the time of their application, are usually given temporary admission to the UK until their application is decided. If they had been detained, they might have been granted temporary release or bail. See Chapter 3 for further information.

Rarely, an asylum seeker has leave when s/he applies for asylum. In this case, the leave is automatically cancelled.

5. European Economic Area and Swiss nationals

A European Economic Area (EEA) or Swiss national may apply to the UK Border Agency (UKBA) for a registration certificate, confirming her/his status as a qualified person (see p26), or a document certifying s/he has permanent residency. This takes the form of a vignette (sticker) fixed on a card booklet, separate to your passport.

A family member of a qualified person (ie, an EEA national with a right of residence) may apply to the UKBA for a residence card, confirming her/his status, or a permanent residence card certifying s/he has permanent residency. Alternatively, s/he may have been issued with a family permit entry visa before travelling to the United Kingdom. Each of these is usually a vignette (sticker) fixed in your passport.

Note: the above documents are considered to be declaratory only. It is not necessary to obtain such a document in order to enjoy the rights recognised by it, and the period of validity should not be regarded as a period of limited leave to enter or remain that requires extending or imposes conditions on the holder.

Also, the fact that a person holds a valid residence card or registration certificate does not mean s/he necessarily retains a right of residence or remains a family member of a qualified person.[4]

See Chapter 4 for more details of the rights of EEA and Swiss nationals and their families.

6. Deportation and special immigration status

Deportation

'**Deportation**' is a procedure under which a person without the right of abode is removed from the United Kingdom (UK) and excluded from re-entering for as long as the order for deportation remains in force. Deportation is most commonly used when someone has been convicted of a serious criminal offence. Deportation is not the same as '**administrative removal**', which is the procedure for removing someone who has entered the UK illegally or breached her/his conditions of leave.

If you are being considered for deportation, you may be detained, released or bailed with conditions.

7. Other passport issues

Embarkation from the United Kingdom

Embarkation from (leaving) the United Kingdom (UK) used to be endorsed by a triangular ink stamp in the embarking person's passport (see Figure 24, Appendix 7). However, the practice has been suspended since March 1998.

New passports and endorsements

People with indefinite or limited leave may have this confirmed by an endorsement in a passport or other document that it has expired. In this situation, you can apply for the new document to be endorsed in a new or replacement passport, but the fact that the new passport or document is unendorsed does not affect your status. Holders of the new identity card (see p41) must inform the UK Border Agency of specified changes in their circumstances or face prosecution or other sanctions.

Illegible passport stamps

A person whose passport has been endorsed illegibly may be deemed to have been granted leave to enter for six months with a condition prohibiting employment,[5] or, if s/he arrived in the UK before 10 July 1998, to have been given indefinite leave to enter the UK.[6] A person who requires leave to enter the UK, but whose passport was not endorsed on entry may be considered an 'illegal entrant'.[7] Specialist advice should be sought.

Notes

1. **British citizens and people with the right of abode**
   1 s3(9) IA 1971, as amended
   2 s39(8) BNA 1981

2. **People with leave to enter or remain**
   3 s3(3)(b) IA 1971

5. **European Economic Area and Swiss nationals**
   4 But see pending references to the ECJ, *Shirley McCarthy* C-434/09 and *Maria Dias* C-325/09

7. **Other passport issues**
   5 Sch 2 para 6(1) IA 1971, as amended
   6 Sch 2 para 6(1) IA 1971 prior to amendment and as interpreted by the courts
   7 *Rehal v SSHD* [1989] Imm AR 576

Part 2

Immigration status, residence and benefits

Chapter 6

Overview

This chapter covers:
1. Immigration and residence rules for benefits and tax credits (below)
2. Benefits and tax credits: checklist (p50)

---

1. Immigration and residence rules for benefits and tax credits

Before you make a claim for benefit, it is important to establish your immigration status because this determines your entitlement to social security benefits and tax credits. It is also important because a claim for benefit might affect your right to remain in the UK. There are close links between the benefit authorities and the Home Office. Consequently, if you make a claim for benefits, the immigration authorities may be alerted to the fact that you are here unlawfully, or that you have broken your conditions of entry by claiming benefits (see p55).

The inter-relationship between immigration law and social security/tax credits law is complex and it may not be clear what immigration status you have. It is important, therefore, to get specialist independent advice before claiming a benefit or tax credit if you are unsure about your position.

It is a criminal offence for anyone to give immigration advice unless they are registered as an immigration adviser or exempt from the requirement to register.[1] It is important, therefore, that you contact a regulated adviser. See Appendix 2 for details of how to find a solicitor or adviser.

There really only two types of tests or conditions that can exclude you from social security benefits and tax credits. The first relates to whether you are a 'person subject to immigration control' (see p55). If you are defined as being a 'person subject to immigration control', you are largely excluded from accessing most social security benefits and tax credits. The second way of excluding you or restricting your access to benefits is by various residence tests (see p71). You therefore need to work through the following steps to see whether or not you will be eligible for any benefits.

Step one
Does the benefit you want to claim have any immigration or residence conditions attached to it? See below.

Step two
Are you a 'person subject to immigration control'? See p55.

Step three
Do the 'public funds' restrictions apply to you? See p62.

Step four
Do you satisfy the relevant residence and or presence tests for the benefit you want to claim? See p71.

Step five
Have you paid sufficient national insurance contributions to claim a contribution-based benefit? See p131.

Step six
Do you have any rights under European Union law? European law can help you to meet residence and presence conditions and, if you are a family member of a European Economic Area national, you should not be treated as a 'person subject to immigration control'. See Chapters 10 to 13.

2. **Benefits and tax credits: checklist**

There are now many rules which prevent a person who is newly arrived in the United Kingdom (UK) from accessing benefits. The rules can affect you even if you are a British citizen, if you have been abroad.

- If you are a 'person subject to immigration control', you are excluded from accessing most social security benefits and tax credits unless you fall within one of the limited exceptions which are set out in regulations (see p56).
- Even if you are not a 'person subject to immigration control', if you fail the 'habitual residence test' (see p110) you will be a 'person from abroad' (even if you are a British citizen) and therefore not eligible for income support (IS), income-based jobseeker's allowance (JSA), income-related employment and support allowance (ESA), pension credit (PC), housing benefit (HB) and council tax benefit (CTB).

- If you are a European Economic Area or Swiss national, you can only satisfy the habitual residence test if you have a right to reside (see p223).
- Most A8 (see p33) and A2 nationals (see p33) who come to take up employment in the UK can only have a right to reside if they are in registered or authorised work (see p33).

The chart below outlines the presence, residence, immigration and national insurance contribution conditions for all social security benefits and tax credits. Chapter 8 sets out the detailed rules on residence and presence, including the habitual residence and right to reside tests. See Chapter 9 for the national insurance contribution conditions for benefits.

Benefit	Immigration conditions	Residence conditions	Contribution conditions
Attendance allowance	Must not be a 'person subject to immigration control'	– Presence – Past presence – Ordinary residence	No
Bereavement benefits	No[2]	No	Yes
Carer's allowance	Must not be a 'person subject to immigration control'	– Presence – Past presence – Ordinary residence	No
Child benefit	Parent/carer must not be a 'person subject to immigration control'	Parent/carer: – Presence – Past presence – Ordinary residence – Right to reside Child/young person: – Presence – Ordinary residence	No
Child tax credit	Must not be a 'person subject to immigration control'	– Presence – Ordinary residence – Right to reside	No
Council tax benefit	Must not be a 'person subject to immigration control'	– Presence – Right to reside – Habitual residence	No
Disability living allowance	Must not be a 'person subject to immigration control'	– Presence – Past presence – Ordinary residence	No

Benefit	Immigration conditions	Residence conditions	Contribution conditions
Employment and support allowance (contributory)	No	No	Yes
Employment and support allowance (income-related)[3]	Must not be a 'person subject to immigration control'	– Presence – Right to reside – Habitual residence	No
Employment and support allowance in youth[4]	Must not be a 'person subject to immigration control'	– Presence – Past presence – Ordinary residence	No
Guardian's allowance	No	– Must be entitled to child benefit – Parent must be born in the UK or have resided in UK for 52 weeks	No
Health in pregnancy grant[5]	Must not be a 'person subject to immigration control'	– Presence – Ordinary residence – Right to reside	No
Housing benefit	Must not be a 'person subject to immigration control'	– Presence – Right to reside – Habitual residence	No
Incapacity benefit	No	Presence at time of claim	Yes
Incapacity benefit for incapacity in youth[6]	Must not be a 'person subject to immigration control'	– Presence – Past presence – Ordinary residence	No
Income support	Must not be a 'person subject to immigration control'	– Presence – Right to reside – Habitual residence	No
Industrial injuries disablement benefit	No	Presence at time of accident	No
Jobseeker's allowance (contribution-based)	No	No	Yes

Benefit	Immigration conditions	Residence conditions	Contribution conditions
Jobseeker's allowance (income-based)	Must not be a 'person subject to immigration control'	– Presence – Right to reside – Habitual residence	No
Maternity allowance	No	– Presence – Ordinary residence	No
Pension credit	Must not be a 'person subject to immigration control'	– Presence – Right to reside – Habitual residence	No
Reduced earnings allowance	No	No	No
Retirement pension (Category A and B)	No	No	Yes
Retirement pension (Category D)	No	– Resident for 10 years – Ordinary residence	No
Severe disablement allowance	Must not be a 'person subject to immigration control'	– Presence – Past presence – Ordinary residence	No
Social fund	Must not be a 'person subject to immigration control'	Regulated social fund: – Presence – Ordinary residence Discretionary social fund: – Presence	No
Statutory sick, maternity, paternity and adoption pay	No	No	No
Working tax credit	Must not be a 'person subject to immigration control'	– Presence – Ordinarily residence	No

Notes

1. Immigration and residence rules for benefits and tax credits

1 Part V IAA 1999. Exceptional leave has been replaced by discretionary leave and humanitarian protection for asylum seekers, but it remains for other people who may not fit within the Immigration Rules.

2. Benefits and tax credits: checklist

2 Although there are no general residence conditions, if you go abroad and are no longer ordinarily resident, you can continue to receive your benefit, but the rate of benefit is frozen at the rate in payment when you became no longer ordinarily resident in the UK.

3 Sch 3 para 19 WRA 2007

4 Sch 1 para 4(1)(c) WRA 2007; reg 11 ESA Regs

5 Reg 9 HPG(EA) Regs

6 Reg 16 SS(IB) Regs

Chapter 7

Immigration control and benefits

This chapter covers:
1. People subject to immigration control (below)
3. Public funds (p62)
4. Family members with different immigration statuses (p64)
5. Refugees (p67)

Chapter 8 provides information on the various residence tests and Chapter 14 covers the various international agreements that exist between the United Kingdom and other countries. Chapters 10 to 13 contain detailed information on European Union law and how it affects social security.

1. People subject to immigration control

The term **'person subject to immigration control'** is used both in immigration and social security law. This section deals with the definition of a 'person subject to immigration control' for benefits purposes. However there is considerable overlap between the two areas of law and, in order to work out whether you are a 'person subject to immigration control for benefit purposes, you need to know your immigration status. For full details on who is subject to immigration control for immigration purposes, see Chapter 2.

A 'person subject to immigration control' for benefit purposes is excluded from entitlement to most benefits. However, there are limited exceptions to this general rule which allow some 'persons subject to immigration control' for benefit purposes to claim certain benefits. Note, however, that if you can claim benefits which are classed as public funds (see p62) under these or other rules, but you have leave to enter or remain with a condition that you do not have recourse to public funds, this could affect your immigration position.

There are special rules for families in which one (or more) person is subject to immigration control and others are not (see p64).

In order to work out whether or not you are a 'person subject to immigration control' for benefit purposes and, if so, whether or not you can obtain the benefit you want to claim, you need to do the following.

- Check whether you are a 'person subject to immigration control' for benefit purposes (see below). If you are not, you can claim the benefits you want, provided you meet the other conditions of entitlement.
- If you are a 'person subject to immigration control', you should check whether the benefit you want to claim is covered by the rules that exclude you from entitlement (see p59).
- Even if you are a 'person subject to immigration control' and the benefit you want to claim is one from which people subject to immigration control are generally excluded, you should check whether you fall within any of the limited exceptions to this rule (see p60).
- If you cannot claim the benefit you want, but you have a partner who is not a 'person subject to immigration control', or if you can but other members of your family are subject to immigration control, check the special rules on p64.
- If you, or a member of your family, have leave to enter or remain in the United Kingdom (UK) subject to the condition that you do not have recourse to public funds, but you (or another member of your family) can claim benefits, check whether this could affect your/their immigration status (see p62).

In addition, there are some special rules that only apply to refugees (see p67).

Note: even if you are not excluded from entitlement to a benefit because you are a 'person subject to immigration control' you may still not be entitled if you do not satisfy the relevant residence or presence rules (see Chapter 8).

Who is a 'person subject to immigration control'

If you are defined as a **'person subject to immigration control'** under the benefit rules, you are not eligible for most UK benefits.

Only a non-European Economic Area (EEA) national can be a 'person subject to immigration control' for benefit purposes. So a British citizen or a citizen of another EEA state is never a 'person subject to immigration control' for benefit purposes.

If you are not an EEA national, you count as a 'person subject to immigration control' if you:

- require leave to enter or remain in the UK, but do not have it (see p57);
- have leave to enter or remain with a public funds restriction (see p62);
- have leave to enter or remain given as a result of a maintenance undertaking (see p58).

Only people falling within one of the above categories can be refused benefit as a 'person subject to immigration control'. Therefore, if you do not fall within the above definition, you cannot be refused benefit on this basis, although you may still be refused for other reasons – eg, if you fail certain residence tests (see p71).

However, even if you come within the above definition, benefit regulations specifically exempt certain groups of people from the restrictions to benefit (see p60). The exemptions vary according to the type of benefit concerned. There are also some transitional regulations that give benefit entitlement to some people.

You require leave to enter or remain, but do not have it

If you are not an EEA national and require leave to enter or remain in the UK and do not have it, you are a 'person subject to immigration control' for benefit purposes.[1]

The following non-EEA nationals do not require leave to enter or remain:

- a family member of an EEA national who has a right to reside on that basis in the UK (see p27);
- a person with the right of abode/certificate of patriality (see p6);
- a British national with a right of readmission to the UK.

All other non-EEA nationals require leave to enter or remain in the UK. If you are not an EEA national and not in any of the above three groups, you will be a 'person subject to immigration control' if you do not have leave to enter or remain. See p8 for more information on when leave to enter or remain is granted.

In practice, you are a 'person subject to immigration control' for benefit purposes if you:

- are an asylum seeker with temporary admission;
- have overstayed your limited leave to remain;
- have entered the UK illegally;
- are subject to a deportation order.

Note: if you are an overstayer or an illegal entrant and, therefore, a 'person subject to immigration control', a claim for benefit made by you or a family member may mean that the Home Office is alerted to your presence and status in the UK.

You have leave to enter or remain with a public funds restriction

If you are not an EEA national and you have leave to remain, but it was granted on condition that you do not have recourse to public funds, you are a 'person subject to immigration control' for benefit purposes.[2]

Most forms of time-limited leave are granted subject to such a condition, except people granted asylum for a time-limited period, people with humanitarian protection and people with leave granted outside the Immigration Rules (see p10). People with some form of indefinite leave (see p10) never have that leave on the basis that they have no recourse to public funds, although they may be subject to a sponsorship agreement (see p14). If you have leave to enter or remain with a condition that you do not have recourse to public funds and you receive them, this can affect your immigration status (see pp11 and 62).

You have leave to enter or remain given as a result of a maintenance undertaking

A 'maintenance undertaking' is sometimes referred to as a 'sponsorship agreement'. Generally, such undertakings are only requested for elderly relatives, children aged 16 to 18, or other more distant relatives of people with settled status, who are themselves seeking indefinite leave to remain. An undertaking is not usually required for a spouse or for younger children.

See p14 for more information about sponsors and sponsorship arrangements.

You count as having leave to enter or remain given as a result of a maintenance undertaking if:

- there is a written document, signed by your sponsor and given to the Home Office, which contains a promise by that sponsor that s/he will maintain and accommodate you in the future.[3] It does not matter if this written promise is not on an official form[4] (such as Form RON 112 or Form SET(F)), provided it is clear that a promise about the future conduct of the sponsor has been given. An example of a document that does *not* amount to a promise would be if the sponsor has said 'I am able and willing to support X'. This is not a promise to support you, but a statement saying s/he is able to;[5] *and*
- the maintenance undertaking played some role in the decision to grant you leave to enter or remain.[6] This will generally be the case if you were required to show that you would not be a burden on public funds to get your leave.

Confusion sometimes arises when a person has been granted indefinite leave to remain under the family reunion rules for refugees. In these cases, the refugee whose family member(s) is joining her/him in the UK is often described on the family member's travel document as a 'sponsor'. However, immigration law does not require that a refugee's family member should not be a burden on public funds and so, in these cases, generally there will not be a written undertaking. Even if there is, this will not have played a role in the decision to grant the family member leave.

If it is unclear whether or not your leave was granted because of a maintenance undertaking, the onus is on the Department for Work and Pensions (DWP), or other benefit authority, to prove that it was.[7] If you are in this situation, you should get immigration advice (see Appendix 2). If you have leave to remain because of a maintenance undertaking, you may still be able to claim benefits – in particular, if more than five years have elapsed since you came to the UK or since the maintenance undertaking was given, whichever is later (see p60).

Liabilities of sponsors

If you are the sponsor of a person who claims benefit, it is possible that you will be asked to repay any income support (IS), income-based jobseeker's allowance (JSA) or employment and support allowance (ESA) paid to the person you have sponsored.[8] However, this provision is rarely used because benefit rules usually exclude sponsored migrants from claiming these benefits during the period of sponsorship.

The DWP can recover any IS, income-based JSA or income-related ESA paid to a sponsored immigrant from the person who gave the undertaking.[9] Recovery is through the magistrates' court (in Scotland, the sheriff's court). It also has a power to prosecute for failure to maintain the claimant.[10] In the past, the DWP has used the threat of court action to persuade sponsors to provide some financial support to claimants. In practice, if the sponsor could not support the claimant, the DWP usually took no further steps. Court action has been rare in the past and is not likely to be considered if the sponsor is in receipt of benefits her/himself.

Note: the definition of 'sponsored immigrant' for the purpose of the rules on liability to maintain is different from the definition used to define a 'person subject to immigration control'. Under the liability-to-maintain rules, a sponsored immigrant is a person for whom a sponsorship undertaking has been given after 22 May 1980.[11] There is no five-year rule, so there is no cut-off point, and a sponsor would, in theory at least, remain liable indefinitely.

As the DWP has the power to recover benefit or to take court action, if the DWP approaches you about an undertaking you have made, you should seek independent advice. Any liability to maintain should not delay an award of benefit to which the claimant is entitled.

People subject to immigration control and benefits

If you are a 'person subject to immigration control', in general, you cannot get the following benefits:[12]

- IS;
- income-based JSA;
- income-related ESA;
- pension credit (PC);
- housing benefit (HB);
- council tax benefit (CTB);
- child benefit;
- attendance allowance (AA);
- disability living allowance (DLA);
- severe disablement allowance;
- social fund payments;
- child tax credit (CTC);
- working tax credit (WTC).

You can get any benefit not listed above, provided you meet the normal rules of entitlement. Most of the benefits not listed are those which are paid on the basis of past employment or payment of contributions.

You may be able to get the above benefits even if you are a 'person subject to immigration control', provided you meet certain conditions (see below). Even if cannot claim benefits yourself, a family member might be able to claim a benefit, which includes an amount for you (see p64).

Who is not excluded from claiming benefits

Means-tested benefits

You are not excluded from getting any of the means-tested benefits listed below, even if you are a 'person subject to immigration control, if:[13]

- you are a national of a country that has ratified the European Convention on Social and Medical Assistance or the Council of Europe Social Charter (1961) (this includes all EEA countries, Croatia, Macedonia and Turkey) and you are lawfully present in the UK. An asylum seeker with temporary admission is lawfully present and consequently is not excluded from the benefits listed below. However, you will still need to satisfy the residence tests for benefits;[14]
- you have leave to remain given as a result of an undertaking (see p58) and you have been resident in the UK for at least five years since either since the date the undertaking was given or the date when you came to the UK, whichever is later.[15] If there are gaps in your residence (eg, because you go to live in another country for a period), you can add together periods of residency to meet the five-year rule.[16] You can still count as resident in the UK during short periods of absence abroad if you your circumstances show that you have remained resident in the UK during your absence;[17]
- you have leave to remain given as a result of an undertaking (see p58), but the person (or all the people) who gave the undertaking has died;
- you have time-limited leave on condition that you do not have recourse to public funds (see p62) and your income from abroad has been temporarily disrupted.[18] In this situation, you can get the benefits listed below for up to 42 days in that period of leave;[19]
- you are an asylum seeker who has transitional protection. In some cases, this can include a separated partner or adult children of an asylum seeker. See CPAG's *Welfare Benefits and Tax Credits Handbook* 2005/06 for details. It is unlikely, however, that anyone still falls within this category.

The relevant means-tested benefits are:
- CTB;
- health in pregnancy grants;[20]
- HB;
- income-based JSA;
- income-related ESA;[21]
- IS;

- PC;
- social fund payments.

Note: if you are a family member of an EEA national who has the right to reside on that basis in the UK, you do not require leave to enter or remain in the UK. You are not a 'person subject to immigration control' and cannot be excluded from benefits.

In addition, you are not excluded from claiming a payment from the social fund if you are lawfully working in Great Britain and are a national of Algeria, Israel, Morocco, San Marino, Tunisia or Turkey.

A 'person subject to immigration control' (see p56) who is not excluded from claiming a crisis loan may still not be entitled if s/he fails the habitual residence test for IS, income-based JSA, income-related ESA or PC (see p110).[22] It will be necessary to show the social fund officer that you are able to repay the loan.[23]

Non-contributory benefits

You are not excluded from getting any of the non-contributory benefits listed below, even if you are a 'person subject to immigration control', if:[24]

- you are a person with leave to remain, given as a result of a maintenance undertaking (see p58) **Note:** there is no five-year rule;
- you are a family member of an EEA national.[25] The EEA national does not need leave to remain in the UK, but a social security commissioner has held that s/he must have a right of residence in European Union (EU) law (see p241);[26]
- you, or (if you are living with her/him) a member of your family, are lawfully working in Great Britain and are a citizen of a state with which the EU has an agreement concerning equal treatment in social security. This applies to citizens of Algeria, Morocco, San Marino, Tunisia and Turkey (see Chapter 14). A social security commissioner has held that an asylum seeker who had worked in the UK was able to fulfil the condition of 'lawfully working' and was therefore eligible for benefit;[27]
- for AA, DLA and child benefit, you are covered by a reciprocal arrangement;
- you are protected by the transitional rules on asylum seekers and others with limited leave.

The relevant non-contributory benefits are:

- AA;
- carer's allowance;
- child benefit;
- DLA;
- ESA in youth;[28]
- incapacity benefit for incapacity in youth;[29]
- severe disablement allowance.

Tax credits

You are not excluded from WTC and CTC, even if you are a 'person subject to immigration control', if either:[30]

- you have leave because of a maintenance undertaking, but the person who sponsored you has died or you have been resident in the UK for a period of at least five years from the date of the undertaking or the date you arrived, whichever is later; *or*
- you have limited leave with a public funds restriction (see p11) and you are temporarily without funds because money from abroad has been disrupted and there is a reasonable expectation that your funds will resume. In this case, you can get tax credits for 42 days.

For CTC only, there is a further exemption if you are lawfully working in Great Britain and are a citizen of a state with which the EU has an agreement on equal treatment in social security. This applies to Algeria, Israel, Morocco, San Marino, Tunisia and Turkey.

For WTC only, there is a further exemption if you are lawfully present in the UK and are a national of a state which has ratified the European Convention on Social and Medical Assistance or a state which has ratified the Council of Europe Social Charter 1961. This includes all EEA countries, Croatia, Macedonia and Turkey.

2. **Public funds**

If you have leave to enter or remain in the United Kingdom (UK) subject to a requirement that you do not have recourse to public funds, you are a 'person subject to immigration control' for benefit purposes. Similarly, if this applies to a member of your family, s/he is a 'person subject to immigration control' for benefit purposes.

It is the fact that you (or s/he) are a 'person subject to immigration control' that generally prevents you from getting benefits under benefit law. However, you (or your family member) may still be able to claim benefits under the exceptions to these rules discussed on p60, or someone may be able to claim an increase in benefits in respect of you under the rules about family members with different immigration statuses. If you (or a family member) claim under these rules, however, you may break the conditions under which you (or s/he) were given leave to enter or remain in the UK – eg, by having recourse to public funds. It is therefore important to check the rules in this section to see whether this is the case.

'**Public funds**' are:
- attendance allowance (AA);
- carer's allowance (CA);

- child benefit;
- child tax credit (CTC);
- council tax benefit (CTB);
- disability living allowance (DLA);
- health in pregnancy grants (but see note below);
- housing benefit (HB);
- income-related employment and support allowance (ESA);
- income-based jobseekers's allowance (JSA);
- income support (IS);
- pension credit (PC);
- severe disablement allowance;
- social fund payments;
- working tax credit (WTC).

Housing and homelessness assistance are also public funds (see p32 for more information).

Note: although not yet included in the Immigration Rules, the Immigration Directorate Instructions include health in pregnancy grants in the definition of public funds.[31] It is, therefore, probably best to treat this benefit as though it were public funds.

The Immigration Rules do now make clear that a person is not to be treated as having (or potentially having) recourse to public funds merely because s/he is (or will be) reliant on any public funds provided to her/his sponsor, unless, as a result, the sponsor is (or would be) entitled to increased or additional public funds. The exception is if a couple would be entitled to increased or additional public funds as a result of a their joint entitlement to benefits.

Note, however, that while such 'indirect recourse' does not breach a public funds restriction, future entitlement to, for example, IS or income-based JSA cannot be used to satisfy the maintenance and accommodation requirements that often apply when relatives apply to come to the UK (see p32).

The Immigration Rules also make clear that you will not be regarded as having recourse to public funds if you are entitled to any of the above benefits under the rules described on pp60–62.[32] Problems can arise for HB and CTB. Even if a family member of the claimant is a 'person subject to immigration control' for benefit purposes, the claimant's applicable amount still includes amounts for her/him. Similarly, the maximum amount of HB payable may be greater under the size rules than it would otherwise have been because of the inclusion of such a family member(s). If the HB/CTB payable as a result is more than it would have been had the family member(s) not been included in the claim, it may count as additional recourse to public funds and could be a breach of the immigration conditions attached to the leave of the person with the public funds restriction.

From 31 March 2009, the Immigration Rules were changed to confirm that people applying for entry clearance (see p8) cannot rely on additional benefits that they or their sponsor would become entitled to after their arrival. A person making an application from outside the UK will be regarded as having recourse to public funds if s/he relies on any future entitlement to any public funds that would be payable. This is an immigration control measure rather than a benefits restriction. See p11 for more information.

If you have a public funds restriction and you try to claim any benefits listed as public funds, it may come to the attention of the Home Office. Therefore, a claim may affect your right to remain in the UK or get an extension of your stay. In practice, however, under social security law a person with limited leave is unlikely to be eligible for any of the above benefits.

Contributory benefits are *not* public funds. Therefore, it is theoretically possible for a person who is defined as a 'person subject to immigration control' (see p55) to claim a contribution-based benefit. However, in order to be entitled, most contributory benefits require you to have paid sufficient national insurance contributions (see p131).

It is clear from the definition of public funds that receipt of publicly provided services, such as National Health Service treatment, does not constitute having recourse to public funds, although access to health treatment by those without a benefit entitlement is becoming more restrictive.

If the stamp giving you leave to enter or remain states that you must not have recourse to public funds, you will break the terms of your leave and commit a criminal offence if you claim one of the benefits that count as public funds (see p62) even if that condition should not have been attached to your category of permission.[33] If this condition has been attached in error, you may want to ask the Home Office to remove it, but you should seek expert advice before making such a request.

3. Family members with different immigration statuses

Sometimes, members of the same family may have different immigration statuses. For example, a husband may be a British citizen or have indefinite leave to remain, while his wife may have limited leave to remain as a spouse with a public funds restriction and so be a 'person subject to immigration control' for benefit purposes.

Couples with different statuses often have difficulties with benefit claims. One of the couple may be eligible for benefit, but s/he may have difficulty convincing the benefit authorities that s/he is eligible and, in particular, that s/he satisfies the national insurance number requirement (see p126).

A major consideration is often whether or not a claim will jeopardise the immigration position of the partner who wishes to settle in the United Kingdom

(UK) (see p62). If a couple are refugees, one of the couple may have been granted leave to remain or full refugee status while her/his partner waits for a decision on her/his asylum claim and, therefore, remains an asylum seeker. Some benefits have rules that deal with this type of situation. For example, the income support (IS), income-related employment and support allowance (ESA) and income-based jobseeker's allowance (JSA) rules all allow a couple with 'mixed' immigration statuses to claim benefit at the single person's rate (see below). However, the couple is still treated as a couple and any income or capital available to the 'person subject to immigration control' (see p55) will impact on the benefit entitlement of the other member of the couple. Pension credit (PC) has a similar rule, but treats the 'person subject to immigration control' as not being a member of the same household (see p66). The effect of this is that her/his income and capital are not taken into account in the benefit assessment.[34]

Income support, income-based jobseeker's allowance and income-related employment and support allowance

If your partner is not a 'person subject to immigration control' (see p56) but you are, s/he can claim IS, income-related ESA and income-based JSA under the normal rules, but s/he will not receive any benefit for you or any other family member who is a 'person subject to immigration control'. Full housing costs are payable.[35] You are still treated as a couple, so your joint resources are taken into account. Full entitlement to benefit arises once indefinite leave has been granted, except if you are subject to a formal undertaking and it is five years or less since either this was given or you entered the UK, and your sponsor is not dead.

Both partners in a couple who are not 'persons subject to immigration control' and lone parents who are not 'persons subject to immigration control' can claim IS for children who are.[36] If you are a 'person subject to immigration control', however, you cannot claim benefit for your children even if they are not subject to immigration control.

The additional amounts paid for children in these benefits have now been largely abolished and replaced with tax credits. However, the child may mean that the claimant is entitled to claim IS as a lone parent, and there may be some people who remain entitled to additional amounts for children under transitional provisions. See CPAG's *Welfare Benefits and Tax Credits Handbook* for further details.

A person can qualify for JSA without having to satisfy the joint-claim rules if her/his partner is a 'person subject to immigration control'. For more information about joint-claim JSA, see CPAG's *Welfare Benefits and Tax Credits Handbook*.

Pension credit

The rules for PC are similar to those for IS, JSA and ESA, with one important difference. Although a single-person rate is paid to couples with different immigration statuses, you are not treated as a couple for calculating your resources.[37] Therefore, any income the 'person subject to immigration control' has and/or any work s/he does do not affect the other person's entitlement.

Housing benefit and council tax benefit

If one partner in a couple is not a 'person subject to immigration control', that person can claim full benefit. However, there is no provision to pay benefit at a single person's rate. Housing benefit and council tax benefit are both paid at the couple rate. This may be a potential problem for the partner who is a 'person subject to immigration control' as it is possible there could be recourse to public funds (see p11) if a claim is made (see p63).

Health in pregnancy grants

A 'person subject to immigration control' is not entitled to a health in pregnancy grant and only the person who has given birth can be the claimant. If a couple have different immigration statuses and the woman who has given birth is the 'person subject to immigration control', the couple are not entitled.

Tax credits

If members of a couple have different immigration statuses, one of which allows that person to claim tax credits, the claim is determined as follows.

If the couple have responsibility for a child, the claim is treated as though both members of the couple were *not* subject to immigration control.[38] This means that a claim can be made. From March 2005, a person who is entitled to tax credits is not regarded as having recourse to public funds (see p62).[39] Therefore, a couple with children who have different immigration statuses do not put their immigration position at risk by making a claim for tax credits.

If the couple do not have responsibility for a child, the second adult element in working tax credit is not paid unless the 'person subject to immigration control' is a national of Croatia, Macedonia or Turkey and is lawfully working in the UK.[40]

Children

For most benefits, the immigration status of a child is irrelevant. The only differences are as follows.

Income support, income-based jobseeker's allowance and income-related employment and support allowance

A child's immigration status only affects entitlement to these benefits if the claimant is not a 'person subject to immigration control', but her/his partner is.

Disability living allowance

If a child is born in the UK to parents who are both 'persons subject to immigration control', the child is not a 'person subject to immigration control' until such a time as an application to regularise her/his status is made to the UK Border Agency. S/he may qualify for disability living allowance if s/he meets the usual disability conditions for the benefit.

4. Refugees

A refugee cannot be a 'person subject to immigration control', nor can her/his family members who have joined her/him under the family reunion rules.

Refugees

If you have been granted refugee status (see p19), you are not a 'person subject to immigration control' and you are not affected by the public funds rules. You can generally claim all benefits subject to meeting the general rules of entitlement. Benefit rules often give equal treatment to refugees. This is in line with the 1951 United Nations Convention on refugees, which obliges the United Kingdom (UK) authorities to provide refugees who are here lawfully with 'the same treatment with respect to public relief and assistance as is accorded to their nationals'.[41]

Backdated tax credits and child benefit

You can make a backdated claim for the child benefit and child tax credit that you were not entitled to while waiting for a decision on your asylum application to the date on which you claimed asylum. This backdating provision only applies to refugees. Therefore, if you claimed asylum but were granted humanitarian protection or discretionary leave, you cannot ask for this backdating.[42]

Note: it is not possible to backdate payments of means-tested benefits in this way.

The claim for backdated tax credits or child benefit must be made within three months of your being notified that refugee status has been granted.[43] There is no extension of this period, even if you have good reasons for a delay or you are given the wrong advice by your solicitor or other adviser.

If you have a solicitor acting for you in this matter and s/he receives notification of your grant of refugee status, the three-month time limit starts from the date your solicitor is notified.

If you claim within the three-month time limit, your claim for tax credits or child benefit can be treated as though it was made on the day you applied for asylum, even if this is several years ago. Generally with tax credits you are required to reclaim each year. However, under the special backdating rules for refugees, the claim is treated as having been renewed each April.[44]

When calculating your entitlement to backdated tax credits, HM Revenue and Customs will take into account any income to which you were entitled and you must provide information about your income and work during the relevant period. The amount of any asylum support you received is deducted from the arrears of tax credits you are paid.[45] No amounts are deducted from child benefit.

Claiming income support while studying

One of the categories of people who are entitled to income support are refugees who are studying English. If you have been granted refugee status, you can claim income support while you are studying if:

- you are attending an English course for more than 15 hours a week; *and*
- on the date the course began, you had not been in the UK for more than 12 months.

This rule only applies to those with refugee status, not to people who claimed asylum but have been granted humanitarian protection or discretionary leave.[46]

Notes

1. **People subject to immigration control**
   1 s115(9)(a) IAA 1999
   2 s115(9)(b) IAA 1999
   3 s115(10) IAA 1999
   4 *R (Begum) v Social Security Commissioner* [2003] EWHC 3380 (Admin); CIS/2474/1999; CIS/2816/2001 and CIS/47/2002
   5 *Ahmed v SSWP* [2005] EWCA Civ 535
   6 CIS/3508/2001
   7 R(PC) 1/09
   8 ss78 and 104 SSCBA 1992
   9 s106 SSAA 1992
   10 s105 SSAA 1992
   11 ss78(6)(c) and 105(3) SSAA 1992
   12 s115(1) IAA 1999; TCA 2002
   13 s115(9) IAA 1999; regs 2 and 12 and Sch Part I SS(IA)CA Regs
   14 *Szoma v SSWP*, reported as R(IS) 2/06 and see *Yesiloz v London Borough of Camden* [2009] EWCA Civ 415
   15 Reg 2(1) and Part 1, para 1 Sch SS(IA)(CA) Regs
   16 R(IS) 2/02
   17 CPC/1035/2005
   18 Reg 2(1) and Part 1, para 1 Sch SS(IA)(CA) Regs
   19 Reg 2(8) SS(IA)(CA) Regs
   20 Reg 9 HPG(EA) Regs
   21 Sch 3 para 19 WRA 2007
   22 SF Dir 16(b)
   23 SF Dir 22
   24 s115(9) IAA 1999; regs 2, 12 and Sch Part II SS(IA)CA Regs; reg 16(1)(b) Social Security (Incapacity Benefit) Miscellaneous Amendments Regulations 2000, No.3120; reg 11(3) ESA Regs
   25 s7(1) IA 1988
   26 CDLA/708/2007
   27 CFC/2613/1997(*25/00). In order for this to apply, the asylum seeker is likely to need permission from the Home Office to work.
   28 Sch 1 para 4(1)(c) WRA 2007; reg 11 ESA Regs
   29 Reg 16 SS(IB) Regs
   30 Reg 3(1) TC(Imm) Regs

2. Public funds

31 Ch 1 s7 IDI
32 The Immigration Rules make specific
    reference to entitlement to benefits
    under s115 IAA 1999 by virtue of
    regulations made under sub-sections (3)
    and (4) of that section or s42 TCA 2002.
33 s24(1)(b)(ii) IA 1971

3. Family members with different immigration statuses

34 Reg 5(1)(h) SPC Regs
35 **IS** Sch 7 para 16A IS Regs
    JSA Sch 5 para 13A JSA Regs
    ESA Sch 5 para 10 ESA Regs
36 **IS** Regs 21(3), 70, 71 and Sch 7 para
    16A IS Regs
    JSA Reg 85 and Sch 5 JSA Regs
    ESA Reg 70 and Sch 5 ESA Regs
37 Reg 5(1)(h) SPC Regs
38 Reg 3(2) TC(Imm) Regs
39 para 6B IR, HC 395
40 Reg 11(4)(b) WTC(EMR) Regs

4. Refugees

41 Art 23 United Nations Convention
    Relating to the Status of Refugees 1951
42 Such claims must be made within three
    months of notification of refugee status;
    reg 3(5) TC(Imm) Regs; reg 6(d)
    CB&GA(AA) Regs. Similar rules for IS, HB
    and CTB were abolished in June 2007.
43 Reg 3 TC(Imm) Regs
44 Reg 3(6)(b) TC(Imm) Regs
45 Reg 3(9) TC(Imm) Regs
46 Sch 1B para 18 IS Regs

Chapter 8

···

Residence rules

This chapter covers:
1. Introduction (below)
2. The different residence tests (p71)
3. Residence and presence rules for individual benefits (p78)
4. How a family member abroad affects benefit (p103)
5. Habitual residence (p110)
6. The right to reside (p116)

This chapter describes the different residence and presence conditions for benefits and outlines the effect of going abroad on your entitlement to benefits and tax credits. It does not help you determine if you are entitled to benefit in the first place. For details of the general conditions of entitlement to these benefits, see CPAG's *Welfare Benefits and Tax Credits Handbook*. To determine your immigration status, see Part 1 of this *Handbook*. For the effect of your immigration status on your entitlement to benefits and tax credits, see Chapter 7. If you are moving to or from a European Economic Area state, the rules may be different and you should see Chapter 13. For details on getting paid abroad, see Chapter 9.

Note: even if you meet the residence tests, you can still be excluded from benefit if you are a 'person subject to immigration control' (see p55).

------

1. Introduction

There are residence and presence conditions for the following benefits:
- attendance allowance;
- carer's allowance;
- child benefit;
- council tax benefit;
- disability living allowance;
- employment and support allowance (ESA) in youth;
- guardian's allowance;
- health in pregnancy grants;
- income support;
- income-based jobseeker's allowance (JSA);

- income-related ESA;
- housing benefit;
- incapacity benefit (IB) for incapacity in youth;
- pension credit;
- Category D retirement pension.

There are also some presence conditions for the following contribution-based benefits:
- state retirement pensions;
- contributory ESA;
- contribution-based JSA;
- IB.

Your entitlement to benefits and tax credits depends on the following.
- **The benefit rules for Great Britain and Northern Ireland.** These determine your presence and residence and the effect of your absence on your entitlement to various benefits and tax credits. These distinguish between temporary and permanent absences (see p78).
- **Reciprocal agreements.** These exist between the United Kingdom (UK) and some other countries and may qualify you for benefits if you have recently come to the UK or while you are abroad (see Chapter 14).
- **The European Union (EU) rules on social security**. These allow you to 'export' certain benefits to other European Economic Area (EEA) member states and to rely on contributions paid in, and periods of employment and residence in, other member states in order to qualify for benefits in another member state (see Chapters 11 and 12). The EU rules assist people who have recently arrived in the UK as well as EEA nationals who go abroad to another EEA state.

2. **The different residence tests**

The benefit rules contain a number of different types of presence and residence tests. These include tests for:
- presence (see below);
- past presence (see p72);
- ordinary residence (see p72);
- habitual residence (see p77);
- the right to reside (see p77).

Presence

All social security benefits and tax credits have rules about presence and absence. You must usually be present at the time you make your benefit claim and continue to be present apart from some temporary absences. See p78 for details of the presence conditions for each benefit. If you are going abroad to another European Economic Area (EEA) state, you are likely to have enhanced rights under European Union (EU) law (see Chapter 13).

In order to show that you are **present** in Great Britain, you must show that you are in Great Britain. This means that you are physically present.[1] If a benefits authority wants to disqualify you from benefit because you were absent from Great Britain, it must show you were absent throughout that day. This means that, on the day you leave Great Britain and the day you arrive in Great Britain, you count as present.

Past presence

The past presence test simply means that you must have been present for a fixed period of time. The following benefits have a past presence test:

- attendance allowance (AA);[2]
- carer's allowance (CA);[3]
- child benefit;[4]
- disability living allowance (DLA).[5]

The rules for past presence vary according to the benefit involved. For detailed information, see p78.

Ordinary residence

The following benefits and tax credits have an ordinary residence test:

- AA;[6]
- CA;[7]
- child benefit;[8]
- child tax credit (CTC);[9]
- DLA;[10]
- incapacity benefit for incapacity in youth;[11]
- employment and support allowance (ESA) in youth;[12]
- health in pregnancy grants;[13]
- Category D retirement pension;[14]
- working tax credit.[15]

The House of Lords has said that **ordinary residence** means:[16]

> a person's abode in a particular place or country which he has adopted voluntarily and for settled purposes as part of the regular order of his life for the time being, whether of short or long duration.

It should usually be clear whether residence is voluntary or for a settled purpose.[17] The caselaw on ordinary residence shows that:

- the term should be given its ordinary everyday meaning.[18] Ordinary residence can start on arrival in Great Britain, or it can start before (see below);
- a person in Great Britain for a temporary purpose can be ordinarily resident in Great Britain (see below);
- a person who lives in Great Britain but has no fixed abode can be ordinarily resident;[19]
- ordinary residence can continue during absences from Great Britain, but leaving to settle abroad will normally end ordinary residence (see p74);
- a person who spends most of the time (or even almost all of the time) outside Great Britain can still be ordinarily resident;[20]
- a person can be ordinarily resident in more than one place or country;[21]
- ordinary residence is different from the concept of 'domicile'.[22]

Special rules apply to children (see p74) and to people whose place of residence is beyond their control (see p74).

Ordinary residence on arrival

Ordinary residence can begin immediately on arrival in Great Britain.[23] In a family law case, a man who separated from his wife in one country (where he had lived and worked for three years) and went to live at his parent's house in another, was found to become immediately ordinarily resident there.[24] The Court of Appeal said that, where there is evidence that the person intends to make a place her/his home for an indefinite period, s/he is ordinarily resident when s/he arrives there. In another case, a court decided that a woman returning from Australia after some months there had never lost her ordinary residence in England. However, if she had, she became ordinarily resident again when the boat embarked from Australia.[25] In a case involving students (*Shah*), the students had to show that they were ordinarily resident within a few weeks of first arriving in the United Kingdom (UK), but it was not argued that they could not be ordinarily resident because they had only just come to Great Britain.[26]

Temporary purpose

To be ordinarily resident in Great Britain, you do not have to intend or be able to live here permanently. The purpose can be for a limited period and Lord Scarman said that, 'education, business or profession, employment, health, family, or merely love of the place spring to mind as common reasons for a choice of regular abode.'[27] You may have several different reasons for a single stay – eg, to visit relatives, get medical advice, attend religious ceremonies and sort out personal affairs.[28]

The reason must be a settled one. This does not mean that the reason has to be long-standing,[29] but there must be evidence of it. In most of the cases on ordinary residence, the courts have looked back to see whether a person had been ordinarily resident months or years beforehand.[30] This is much easier than deciding whether a person has recently become ordinarily resident.

There is no minimum period of residence before you are ordinarily resident. If, for example, you have arrived in the UK and started work, the benefit authorities should consider how long you are likely to reside in the UK. If you intend to live here for the time being, they should accept your intention as sufficient, unless it is clearly unlikely that you are going to be able to stay. The benefit authorities should not make a deep examination of your long-term intentions.[31] The type of accommodation you occupy may be relevant.[32]

Involuntary residence

A person who is held in a place against her/his will not become ordinarily resident. These cases, however, are very rare. Examples given by the courts are kidnap victims and people stranded on a desert island.[33] The courts have recognised that circumstances that limit or remove a person's choice may not stop her/him from being ordinarily resident where s/he resides.[34] A woman who became mentally ill on a visit to England and remained in an asylum until she died over 50 years later was ordinarily resident in the UK by the time she died, even though she never decided to stay here.[35]

Deportation to the UK does not prevent you becoming ordinarily resident here.[36] The issue is whether your residence is part of your settled purpose. If you have decided to live in the UK, it does not matter if the reason you have made that decision is because you were deported here.

Children

If you are a child or young person, ordinary residence is decided using the same rules as for adults.[37]

The only benefit for children under 16 with an ordinary residence test is DLA. The residence of a child aged under 16 is usually decided by her/his parent(s) or person(s) with parental responsibility (or, in Scotland, parental rights and responsibilities). Therefore, if the child lives with that person, the child will usually have the same ordinary residence as her/him.[38] So, a child joining a parent or other person with parental responsibility may become ordinarily resident almost immediately.[39] If there is only one person with parental responsibility, the child has the same ordinary residence as that person.[40]

If there are two such people who live apart, one of them should get the consent of the other to a change of residence of the child, otherwise the child may be treated as abducted. A child who is abducted is considered still to have the same ordinary residence as the person(s) with parental responsibility.[41] Agreement to a change of residence may be assumed if the other person takes no action.[42]

Absence from the United Kingdom

If you are ordinarily resident, you may lose this status if you go abroad, depending on:

- why you go abroad;
- how long you stay abroad;
- what connections you keep with the UK – eg, accommodation, furniture and other possessions.[43]

If you decide to move abroad for the foreseeable future, you will normally stop being ordinarily resident in the UK on the day you leave.[44] A possible exception to this is where your plans are clearly impractical and you return to the UK very quickly.

If your absence abroad is part of your normal pattern of life, your ordinary residence will not be affected.[45] This applies even if you are out of the UK for most of the year.[46] For example, if you spend each summer in the UK but all winter abroad, you may be ordinarily resident in the UK.

You remain entitled to some UK benefits if your absence abroad is only temporary. For other benefits, there are additional requirements that relate to the purpose of your absence and the length of time you are away. For some benefits, absences from Great Britain, temporary or otherwise, are of little importance. For the rules for each benefits, see the appropriate section in this chapter.

Temporary absence

If your absence abroad is extraordinary or temporary, and you intend to return to the UK, your ordinary residence will not be affected.[47]

In one case, a British woman who spent 15 months in Germany with her husband over a period of three years kept her ordinary residence in the UK. She had always intended to return here.[48]

However, if you are away from the UK for a long time and do not keep strong connections with Great Britain, you may lose your ordinary residence, even if you intend to return. In one case, a citizen of the UK and colonies lived in the UK for over four years and then returned to Kenya for two years and five months because her business here failed and there was a business opportunity in Kenya. She intended to make enough money to support herself on her return to the UK. Her parents and parents-in-law remained in the UK. She was found to have lost her ordinary residence during her absence.[49]

'**Temporary absence**' is not defined in the legislation and there are no clear rules determining whether your absence will be treated as being temporary. The only guidance available is the caselaw of the courts and the social security commissioners and Upper Tribunal, which sets out the factors the Department for Work and Pensions (DWP) must consider in determining whether the absence is temporary. It also provides examples of situations that will lead to a decision that your absence is not temporary. Every absence is unique and distinct, and so your case will be given individual consideration. It is important, therefore, that you provide full details of:

- why you wish to go abroad;

- how long you intend to be abroad; *and*
- what you intend to do while you are abroad.

Each of these considerations needs to be taken into account, and it is your responsibility to demonstrate that your absence is to be a temporary one.[50]

Intention will always be an important factor but will never, on its own, be conclusive.[51] For example, a person may wish to return but find there are obstacles, such as an unexpected change in family responsibilities, which prevent her/him from returning for the foreseeable future. This may mean that her/his absence ceases to be temporary, despite her/his initial intentions.

Example

Momin returns to visit his family in Bangladesh for a three-month period. While he is there, his father has an accident and dies, leaving his disabled mother alone. As the only child of the family without other immediate dependants, it falls on Momin to care for his mother until suitable long-term arrangements can be made. There are no nursing homes or similar institutions to care for his mother and, by the time he returns to the UK, it is more than two years since he left.

There is no set period for a temporary or non-temporary absence, although commissioners have tended to treat a period of 12 months or more as demonstrating a non-temporary absence.[52] There is no reason in principle why an absence of several years cannot still be considered temporary, but the circumstances would need to be exceptional.[53] The number and lengths of other absences (past and intended) may also be taken into account in determining whether the immediate absence is temporary.[54]

If the purpose of the trip abroad is obviously temporary (eg, for a holiday, to visit friends or relatives or for a particular course of medical treatment) and you buy a return ticket, your absence will be viewed as temporary.

The nature of an absence can change over time. If an absence, after the factors mentioned above have been considered, is found to be temporary at the beginning of the period, it does not mean that it will always remain temporary.[55] If circumstances change while you are abroad (eg, you go abroad for one reason and decide to stay abroad for a different purpose), your absence may in time come to be regarded as no longer temporary.

Example

Zeinab receives DLA, housing benefit (HB) and council tax benefit (CTB). When she travels to visit family she leaves her council flat, and the absence is accepted as temporary by both the DWP and the local authority. Two months later, she writes to say she intends to stay four months longer, as she is receiving medical treatment which is helping her. This is accepted as still temporary, and benefit continues to be paid. After six months her DLA stops, as she has received the maximum payment of 26 weeks' benefit (see p96). A further two months later she writes again to say her new partner has work locally and she intends to remain there with him for a year or more before returning to the UK. Both the DWP and the local authority decide that her absence is no longer temporary, and payments of HB and CTB are stopped (see p84).

Note: if the rules for an individual benefit refer to 'temporary absence' and 'temporarily absent', the absence is often qualified by other specific conditions which vary from benefit to benefit. For some benefits, you must 'intend' to return to Great Britain within a specific period and for others you must 'intend' the absence to be temporary as well as its actually being temporary. In many cases, these differences should not affect the outcome.

Note also: when calculating the period over which you are temporarily absent from the UK, the day you leave and the day you return are counted as days in the UK.[56] This is a general rule which will apply unless the regulations dealing with a particular benefit specify otherwise.

Habitual residence

The habitual residence test affects the following benefits:

- income support (IS);
- income-based jobseeker's allowance (JSA);
- income-related ESA;
- pension credit (PC);
- HB;
- CTB.

In addition, if you do not count as habitually resident or you would not be treated as passing the test were you to claim IS, income-based JSA, income-related ESA or PC, you are not entitled to a social fund crisis loan, unless it is to alleviate the consequences of a disaster.

For further details, see p110.

The right to reside

The right to reside test is the most complex residence test. It mainly affects EEA nationals. The benefits affected by the right to reside test are:

- IS;
- income-based JSA;
- income-related ESA;
- HB;
- CTB;
- PC;

- health in pregnancy grants.
- child benefit;
- CTC

For further details, see p116.

---

3. Residence and presence rules for individual benefits

Note: for more information about the general rules of entitlement, see CPAG's *Welfare Benefits and Tax Credits Handbook*.

Means-tested benefits

To be entitled to income support (IS), income-based jobseeker's allowance (JSA), income-related employment and support allowance (ESA), pension credit (PC), housing benefit (HB) and council tax benefit (CTB), you must:

- be present in Great Britain; *and*
- be habitually resident in the 'common travel area' – ie, the United Kingdom (UK), Republic of Ireland, Channel Islands and the Isle of Man.

Note: to count as habitually resident, you must have a right to reside (see p116).

There is no clear past presence test and, therefore, in theory you may claim any of these benefits on the first day that you are present in the UK. However, if you satisfy the presence test, you must then also satisfy the habitual residence test (see p110) and, in some cases, the right to reside test (see p116).

Once you have established your right to any of these benefits, it is possible to continue to be paid during certain temporary absences abroad.

Premiums

Premiums are paid as part of your weekly entitlement to IS, income-based JSA, income-related ESA, PC, HB and CTB. Many premiums are dependent on your receiving another benefit – eg, disability living allowance (DLA), attendance allowance (AA) or carer's allowance (CA). If your absence abroad means that you lose entitlement to the qualifying benefit, you also lose the relevant premium, although the carer premium continues to be paid for a further eight weeks. You may not be entitled to the premium as soon as you return, since you may need to satisfy again the presence test for the qualifying benefit.

If you are receiving premiums, it is important to consider the full implications of any absence abroad on your benefit entitlement. It may be possible for you to time your absences in such a way that your premiums are not affected.

Income support

To be entitled to IS, you must:
- be present in Great Britain (see p71).[57] **Note:** the legislation refers to Great Britain, but there are reciprocal agreements with Northern Ireland so that, in effect, you can be present anywhere in the UK;
- have a right to reside and be habitually resident (see p77).

Temporary absence abroad

Once entitled to IS, you remain entitled during a temporary absence abroad of either four or eight weeks (see below) and, in some circumstances, indefinitely. It is not necessary for any IS payments to be *received* before your temporary absence, but you must have claimed and satisfied the conditions of entitlement. Regardless of the reasons for your absence, you only remain entitled to IS if:[58]
- when you leave, you intend your absence to be temporary; *and*
- the period of your absence is unlikely to exceed 52 weeks; *and*
- you continue to satisfy all the other conditions of entitlement to IS.

You can get IS for **up to four weeks** if:
- you were entitled to IS immediately before going abroad; *and*
- your absence is temporary; and unlikely to exceed 52 weeks; *and*
- you continue to satisfy the other rules of entitlement for IS while abroad; *and*
- you are going to Northern Ireland; *or*
- you and your partner are both abroad and your partner qualifies for a disability, severe disability, pensioner, enhanced pensioner or higher pensioner premium; *or*
- you are incapable of work; *and*
  - you have been continuously incapable for the previous 28 weeks and you are terminally ill or receiving the highest rate DLA care component; *or*
  - you have been continuously incapable for 364 days; *or*
  - you are going abroad specifically for the treatment of your incapacity from an appropriately qualified person; *or*
- you fit into one of the groups of people who can claim IS.[59] However, this does not apply if you are getting IS on the basis of being:
  - a person in relevant education; *or*
  - involved in a trade dispute, or in the first 15 days after you have returned to work following the dispute; *or*
  - incapable of work other than in the situations above, or appealing a decision not to treat you as incapable of work.

You can get IS **for up to eight weeks** if:[60]
- you were entitled to IS immediately before going abroad;
- your absence is temporary and unlikely to exceed 52 weeks;
- you continue to satisfy the general conditions of entitlement to IS while you are abroad; *and*

● you are taking a child abroad specifically for medical, physiotherapy or similar treatment from an appropriately qualified person. The child must count as part of your family (see p103).

You can get IS **indefinitely** if:
● you were entitled to IS immediately before going abroad; *and*
● your absence is temporary and for the purpose of receiving NHS treatment at a hospital or other institution outside Great Britain.

HB and CTB may continue to be paid in addition to any IS you are paid during your absence (see p84).

Housing costs

During your four- or eight-week temporary absence from Great Britain, you remain entitled to any housing costs paid as part of IS, provided:[61]
● your home is not let or sub-let to anyone else;
● you intend to return to live in it;
● the period of your absence is unlikely to exceed 13 weeks.

In certain circumstances, you may remain entitled to your housing costs for a period of 52 weeks.[62] See CPAG's *Welfare Benefits and Tax Credits Handbook* for details of these circumstances.

Income-based jobseeker's allowance

To be entitled to income-based JSA, you must:
● be present in Great Britain (see p71).[63] **Note:** the legislation refers to Great Britain, but there are reciprocal agreements with Northern Ireland so that, in effect, you can be present anywhere in the UK;
● have a right to reside (see p77); *and*
● be habitually resident (see p77).

Temporary absence abroad

Once entitled to income-based JSA, you remain entitled during a temporary absence abroad of either four or eight weeks and, in some circumstances, indefinitely. It is not necessary for any JSA payments to be *received* prior to your temporary absence, but you must have claimed and satisfied the conditions of entitlement.

If you are entitled to income-based JSA while in Great Britain, you can be treated as still in Great Britain and therefore remain entitled during a temporary absence for a period of up to one, four or eight weeks, provided your absence is unlikely to exceed 52 weeks.[64] You must satisfy all the other conditions of entitlement for income-based JSA,[65] including that you are available for and actively seeking employment (see p81). Unless you go to Northern Ireland (in which case, you may remain entitled for up to four weeks), you must satisfy certain other conditions in order to be treated as present in Great Britain.[66] These overlap with the circumstances in which you can be treated as available for and actively seeking work despite your absence (see below).

HB and CTB may continue to be paid in addition to any income-based JSA you are paid during such an absence (see p84).

Available for and actively seeking employment

To get income-based JSA, you must be available for and actively seeking employment.[67] You could cease to satisfy these jobseeking conditions if you go abroad. However, when you go abroad you will still be treated as available for and actively seeking employment for:[68]

- **a maximum of one week** if you are temporarily absent from Great Britain for three days or more in that week to attend a job interview. You must notify an employment officer of your absence;[69] *or*
- **a maximum of four weeks** if you are part of a couple and you are getting the pensioner, enhanced pensioner, higher pensioner, disability or severe disability premium for your partner and both you *and* your partner are absent from Great Britain for three days or more in each of the four weeks; *or*
- **a maximum of eight weeks** if you take your child abroad for medical treatment by an appropriately qualified person and you are absent for three days or more in each of the eight weeks;[70] *or*
- **a maximum of three months** if you go to another European Economic Area (EEA) state (see p23).

In all cases, in order to remain entitled to benefit, the temporary absence must be unlikely to exceed 52 weeks.[71]

Even if you satisfy the above requirement, you are only treated as still present in Great Britain:

- if you are going abroad in order to attend an interview, you are:[72]
  - not actually absent from Great Britain for more than seven continuous days; *and*
  - able to demonstrate to your employment officer on your return that you attended the interview;
- if you are taking your child abroad for medical treatment, the treatment is:[73]
  - for a disease or physical or mental disablement;
  - performed outside Great Britain;
  - performed while you are temporarily absent from Great Britain by or under the supervision of a suitably qualified person.

You are also treated as available for and actively seeking employment if you are:[74]

- part of a couple and you are looking after your child while your partner is temporarily absent from the UK;

• temporarily looking after a child on a full-time basis because the person who normally looks after her/him is ill, temporarily absent from the home or is looking after another family member who is ill.

Entitlement is for a maximum of eight weeks in both cases. In addition, you must look after the child for at least three days in every week you wish to be treated as actively seeking employment.[75]

People in receipt of a training allowance

People in receipt of certain training allowances but not receiving training can get income-based JSA without being available for or actively seeking employment and do not require a jobseeker's agreement.[76] In these circumstances, you can still get JSA for four weeks if you are temporarily absent from Great Britain and entitled to a training allowance without having to show that your absence is unlikely to exceed 52 weeks.[77]

Holidays from jobseeking

You can take a 'holiday' from jobseeking and still remain entitled to JSA. You may spend a maximum of two weeks in any one 12-month period (not calendar year) not actively seeking work and living away from home.[78] You must:
• tell your employment officer about your holiday – in writing, if requested; *and*
• fill out a holiday form so you can be contacted if employment becomes available.

Although you are exempt from *looking* for work during this period, you still have to be *available* and willing to return to start work during the holiday. In practice, therefore, absences abroad during this period are unlikely to be allowed.

Housing costs

During your one-, four- or eight-week temporary absence from Great Britain, you remain entitled to any housing costs paid as part of income-based JSA, provided:[79]
• your home is not let or sub-let to anyone else;
• you intend to return to live in it;
• the period of your absence is unlikely to exceed 13 weeks.

Income-related employment and support allowance

To be entitled to income-related ESA, you must:
• be present in Great Britain (see p71).[80] **Note:** the legislation refers to Great Britain, but there are reciprocal agreements with Northern Ireland so that, in effect, you can be present anywhere in the UK;
• have a right to reside (see p77); *and*
• be habitually resident (see p77).

Temporary absence abroad

Once entitled to income-related ESA, you remain entitled during certain temporary absences abroad. The length of time you can continue to receive benefit depends on what you are doing abroad. It is not necessary for any ESA payments to be *received* prior to your temporary absence, but you must have claimed and satisfied the conditions of entitlement.

You can continue to be entitled to income-related ESA:

- **for up to four weeks** if the period is unlikely to be more than 52 weeks and you continue to satisfy the other conditions of entitlement;[81]
- **for up to 26 weeks** if the absence is:
  - in connection with arrangements made for treating a condition directly related to your capability for work; *or*
  - because you are accompanying a dependent child in connection with arrangements made for treating her/his condition;
- **indefinitely** if it is to receive NHS treatment outside Great Britain or because you are living with a family member who is in the armed forces. Before leaving Great Britain, you must have received permission from the Department for Work and Pensions (DWP).

In all cases, the period of absence must be unlikely to exceed 52 weeks and you must continue to satisfy the other conditions of entitlement. Any treatment must take place outside Great Britain and must be by, or under the supervision of, a person appropriately qualified to carry out that treatment. Before leaving Great Britain, you must contact Jobcentre Plus and obtain permission to do so.[82]

Housing costs

During your temporary absence from Great Britain, you remain entitled to any housing costs paid as part of income-related ESA, provided:[83]

- your home is not let or sub-let to anyone else;
- you intend to return to live in it;
- the period of your absence is unlikely to exceed 13 weeks.

In certain circumstances, you may remain entitled to your housing costs for a period of 52 weeks. See CPAG's *Welfare Benefits and Tax Credits Handbook* for details of these circumstances.

Pension credit

To be entitled to PC, you must be you must:

- be present in Great Britain (see p71).[84] **Note:** the legislation refers to Great Britain, but there are reciprocal agreements with Northern Ireland so that, in effect, you can be present anywhere in the UK;
- have a right to reside (see p77); *and*
- be habitually resident (see p77).

Temporary absence abroad

In certain situations, you can be treated as still present in Great Britain and thus can continue to be entitled to PC during periods of temporary absence. You are treated as not present if you do not satisfy the habitual residence test and/or you do not have a right to reside (see p77).

Once you have satisfied the presence test, you can continue to receive PC during certain temporary absences.[85] These are:

- **for a period of 13 weeks** if the absence is unlikely to exceed 52 weeks and while absent from Great Britain you continue to satisfy the other conditions of entitlement to PC;
- **for an indefinite period** if you or your partner are receiving treatment in a hospital or other institution outside Great Britain and the treatment is being provided under certain NHS provisions. You can be treated as being present in Great Britain for as long as the treatment continues.[86] However, this only applies if you satisfied the conditions for entitlement to PC immediately before you or your partner left Great Britain.[87]

During a temporary absence abroad, you can remain entitled to HB and CTB for a period of either 13 or 52 weeks (see below).

Housing benefit

In order to qualify for HB, you must meet the general conditions of entitlement including that you are liable to pay rent. In addition, you must:

- be present in Great Britain (see p71).[88] **Note:** the legislation refers to Great Britain, but there are reciprocal agreements with Northern Ireland so that, in effect, you can be present anywhere in the UK;
- have a right to reside (see p77); *and*
- be habitually resident (see p77).

Temporary absence abroad

You remain entitled to HB for the first 13 weeks of any period of temporary absence for your home provided:[89]

- you intend to return to occupy the dwelling as your home; *and*
- the property is not let or sub-let while you are away; *and*
- you are unlikely to be away for more than 13 weeks; *and*
- you meet the other conditions of entitlement to benefit.

You remain entitled to HB for the first 52 weeks of any period of temporary absence from your home provided:[90]

- you intend to return to occupy the dwelling as your home; *and*
- the property is not let or sub-let while you are away; *and*
- you are unlikely to be absent from the property for longer than 52 weeks (although, under exceptional circumstances, you may be permitted to extend

the period you remain away by a short amount, which DWP guidance interprets as meaning a maximum of a further three months); *and*

- you fall into one of the following categories:[91]
    - you are sick and in hospital; *or*
    - you or your partner or child are undergoing medically approved treatment or convalescence abroad; *or*
    - you are on a training course abroad approved by or on behalf of a government department, a local authority, any Secretary of State, Scottish Enterprise or Highlands and Islands Enterprise or one operated on their behalf by a local authority; *or*
    - you are caring for someone who is sick abroad and the care you are providing is medically approved; *or*
    - you are caring for a child whose parent or guardian is temporarily absent from her/his home because s/he is receiving medical treatment; *or*
    - you are receiving medically approved care not in residential accommodation abroad; *or*
    - you are a student eligible for HB. For more information, see CPAG's *Welfare Benefits and Tax Credits Handbook*; *or*
    - you left your home as a result of fear of violence and you are not entitled to HB for the accommodation you now occupy.[92]

In determining whether you intend to return home, account will be taken of whether you have left your personal belongings in the dwelling.[93]

The period of temporary absence begins on the first day that you are absent from home.[94] It begins again each time you leave, even if you only return for a very brief period.[95] However, you will not necessarily remain entitled by returning to your home for short periods and leaving again. You are only entitled to HB (and CTB) to help you pay for accommodation which you and your family (if any) *normally* occupy as your home.[96] If you have another home abroad which you or members of your family also occupy,[97] your absences from the UK could affect your entitlement to benefit if they are long enough or regular enough to mean that your 'main' home ceases to be in the UK. However, you will not lose benefit on these grounds if members or your family normally occupy a home abroad, but are not part of your household.[98]

Council tax benefit

In order to qualify for council tax benefit you must:

- be present in Great Britain (see p71).[99] **Note:** the legislation refers to Great Britain, but there are reciprocal agreements with Northern Ireland so that, in effect, you can be present anywhere in the UK;
- have a right to reside (see p77); *and*
- be habitually resident (see p77).

You must also be liable to pay council tax for the accommodation in which you live.[100] If your main home is abroad, you may avoid liability for council tax altogether.[101] However, this carries a risk, because demonstrating that your main home is abroad would adversely affect your HB entitlement (see p84) and could have a negative effect on other benefits you may wish to claim.

For more information about council tax, see CPAG's *Council Tax Handbook*.

Temporary absence abroad

If you are temporarily absent from Great Britain, you can continue to get CTB for a period of either 13 weeks or 52 weeks. The rules are almost the same as for HB (see p84).[102] You may also avoid liability for council tax itself by showing that your dwelling is exempt.[103] Absences abroad may mean this is the case if the property is left unoccupied.

Tax credits

To claim tax credits you must:
- be present in the UK at the time of your claim (see p71);
- be ordinarily resident in the UK (see p72); *and*
- for child tax credit (CTC), have a right to reside (see p77).

Temporary absence abroad

In certain situations, it is possible to be treated as present and ordinarily resident during some temporary absences.

If you remain ordinarily resident and your absence is unlikely to exceed 52 weeks, tax credits continue to be paid during:[104]
- **the first eight weeks** of any temporary absence;
- **the first 12 weeks** of any period when you are temporarily absent from the UK if that absence (or any extension to that period of absence) is in connection with:
  - the treatment of an illness or disability of you, your partner, a child for whom you are responsible or another relative of either you or your partner; *or*
  - the death of your partner, a child for whom you are responsible or another relative of you or your partner.

This means that you not only continue to satisfy the residence conditions for entitlement to tax credits during the period of an award, but you could also make a fresh or renewal claim while abroad (but see p107 if you are a member of a couple). If you spend longer abroad than the permitted periods, you may no longer satisfy the residence conditions for your tax credits.

Crown servants are exempt from the presence test if, immediately prior to their posting, they were ordinarily resident in the UK or were in the UK in connection with the posting, or if they are the partner of a Crown servant and were accompanying her/him on the posting.[105]

European Union (EU) law allows you to receive CTC for children who are living in other EEA states. See p201 for further details.

Child benefit

To claim child benefit, you and the child for whom you are claiming must be present in the UK (see p71), be ordinarily resident (see p72) and have a right of residence (see p77).[106]

You are treated as not present if:

- you are not ordinarily resident in Great Britain;[107]
- you do not have a right to reside in the UK;[108]
- you are out of the country for longer than the permitted periods.[109]

Temporary absence abroad

If you remain ordinarily resident in the UK and your absence is unlikely, from the start of the absence, to exceed 52 weeks, child benefit continues to be paid:[110]

- **during the first eight weeks** of any temporary absence; *or*
- **during the first 12 weeks** of any period when you are temporarily absent from the UK if that absence, or any extension to that period of absence, is in connection with:
  - the treatment of an illness or disability of you, your partner, a child for whom you are responsible, or another relative of either you or your partner; *or*
  - the death of your partner, a child for whom you are responsible, or another relative of you or your partner.

The child for whom you are claiming must, in general, also be present in the UK. However, a child will be treated as present if her/his absence abroad is temporary for:[111]

- **the first 12 weeks** of any period of absence; *or*
- **any period** during which the child is absent for the specific purpose of being treated for an illness or physical or mental disability which began before her/his absence began; *or*
- **any period** during which the child is absent only because:[112]
  - s/he is receiving full-time education at a recognised educational establishment in another EEA member state (including A2 and A8 states – see Chapter 4) or in Switzerland; *or*
  - s/he is engaged in an educational exchange or visit made with the written approval of the recognised educational establishment which s/he normally attends.

Note: if a child is born outside the UK during a period in which her/his mother is treated as present in the UK, the child is also treated as present.

EU law allows you to receive child benefit for children living elsewhere in the EEA while you are living and working in the UK. If you are receiving a pension and you are living in another EEA state with your children, you are also entitled to receive child benefit under EU law.[113] See Chapter 12 for further details.

Guardian's allowance

To be entitled to guardian's allowance, you must be entitled to child benefit and the above rules apply.

Temporary absence abroad

Guardian's allowance can continue to be paid while you are absent abroad, but it will not be uprated during your absence unless you are moving to another EEA state (see p201).[114]

A further condition of entitlement to guardian's allowance is that at least one of the child's parents must have been born in the UK or have, at some time after reaching the age of 16, spent a total of 52 weeks in any two-year period in the UK.[115]

EU law allows you to receive guardian's allowance for children living elsewhere in the EEA. See Chapter 12 for further details.

Contribution-based jobseeker's allowance, contributory employment and support allowance and incapacity benefit

Contribution-based benefits tend not to have many residence conditions attached to them. However, with all contributory benefits, you need to satisfy the national insurance (NI) contribution conditions,[116] which means that you are unlikely to qualify for any contributory benefit unless you have lived and worked in the UK for several years. This means there is an inbuilt residence requirement to the general rules of entitlement. For the contribution conditions, see CPAG's *Welfare Benefits and Tax Credits Handbook*.

If you are an EEA national and moving from another EEA state, you may be able to rely on EU social security rules which allow you to use contributions or work from another EEA state to qualify for a contributory benefit in the UK (see p177). If you are a national of, or come from, a country with which the UK has a reciprocal agreement on social security, you may be able to rely on a reciprocal agreement to qualify for contributory benefits in the UK (see Chapter 14).

Temporary absence abroad

Contribution-based jobseeker's allowance

The rules on absences for contribution-based JSA are the same as for income-based JSA (see p80).[117]

In addition, for contribution-based JSA, you are still treated as present in Great Britain if you are outside Great Britain because you are an offshore worker[118] *or* because you are a mariner and you are left outside Great Britain, provided you report to a consular officer or chief officer of customs within 14 days or as soon as reasonably practicable. If you fall into one of these categories, you remain entitled to benefit despite your absence from Great Britain, provided you fulfil all the other entitlement conditions.

In order to allow you to look for work elsewhere in the EEA, you can receive contribution-based JSA for a period of up to three months in another EEA state (see p198).[119] It will be paid to you in that country.

Contributory employment and support allowance

In order to qualify for contributory ESA, you must be present in Great Britain.[120] The rules on absences for contributory ESA are the same as for income-related ESA (see p82).

Incapacity benefit

Incapacity benefit (IB) was replaced by ESA for new claims from 28 October 2008. However, existing claimants continue to receive IB until a future date, when the DWP will move them onto ESA.

If you are temporarily absent from Great Britain, you can remain entitled to IB.

Unless you are receiving either AA or DLA, or you are a member of the family of a serving member of the armed forces and are temporarily absent because you are living with that person,[121] you can only remain entitled to IB for the first 26 weeks of any such absence.[122] The Secretary of State must certify that it would be consistent with the proper administration of the benefits scheme for you to qualify for benefit despite your absence.[123]

Irrespective of whether you are in receipt of AA or DLA or come within the armed services exception, you also need to satisfy one of the following conditions.[124]

- You are going abroad for treatment of an incapacity which began before you go abroad. This must be the reason why you are going abroad; you cannot simply decide to receive treatment while you are away.[125] The treatment itself must be carried out by some other person[126] and must usually be of a medical nature: convalescence or a trip abroad for a change in environment will not qualify.[127]
- Your incapacity is the result of an industrial injury (see CPAG's *Welfare Benefits and Tax Credits Handbook* for what this means) and you go abroad in order to receive treatment which is appropriate to that injury.[128]

- At the time you go abroad, you have been continuously incapable of work for six months and you remain continuously incapable of work for the time that you are abroad and claiming benefit. In this case, it is not necessary for your absence to be for the purpose of receiving treatment.

You can also get IB for the whole of the period of the temporary absence if one of the above three conditions applies to you and you have been continuously absent from Great Britain since 8 March 1994.[129]

You are treated as present in Great Britain and therefore entitled to IB if you are outside Great Britain because you are an offshore worker[130] or because you are a mariner. If you fall into this category, you remain entitled to IB despite your absence from Great Britain, provided you fulfil all the other entitlement conditions.

Under EU law, IB can also be 'exported' to another EEA member state (see p189).

Retirement pensions

Category A and B pensions

Both Category A and B retirement pensions are contributory benefits. Category A pension depends on either your own or your spouse's or civil partner's contribution record. For details of the contribution conditions, see CPAG's *Welfare Benefits and Tax Credits Handbook*. There are no residence or presence rules for either category, but you are unlikely to qualify unless you or your late spouse/civil partner lived and worked in Great Britain for several years. Special rules apply if you have worked for all or part of your working life in other EEA states, allowing you to add together periods of insurance under the schemes of the different countries in which you have worked (see p177).

It is possible to qualify for a reduced-rate Category A or B pension if you have paid insufficient NI contributions to satisfy the contribution conditions in full. Reduced-rate pensions are frequently paid to people who have arrived in Great Britain part way through their working lives, and to people who have spent periods of their working lives abroad and not paid sufficient contributions to maintain their pension entitlement. In certain cases, where people have worked abroad, contribution records from the two countries can either be aggregated to build up an entitlement to a pension based on the combined totals, or part pensions from both countries can be paid. For details, see p189.

If you are relying on your spouse's/civil partner's contribution record, you may be entitled to a pension, even if you have never worked in or been to the UK and you still remain abroad. You can also claim a retirement pension based on your own or your spouse's/civil partner's contributions even if you are not living in Great Britain when you reach pension age.

Example

When Muhith came to work in the UK he always intended only to stay a few years to earn enough to support his family. His wife Sumena never travelled here. Over the years the family came to depend on Muhith's UK earnings. Some years before he reached pension age he became ill and returned home, where he later had a heart attack and died. Sumena can claim a retirement pension based on her husband's contribution record as soon as the age conditions are met.

If your entitlement to part or all of a Category A or B pension depends on your NI contributions, your pension will be updated annually in the usual way if your spouse/civil partner or former spouse/civil partner whose contributions are used is ordinarily resident (see p72) in Great Britain on the day before the date of that uprating.[131]

You are still entitled to annual uprating of your Category B pension even if you are not ordinarily resident in Great Britain if:[132]

- the spouse/civil partner on whose contributions the Category B pension is based has died or you are divorced from her/him; *and*
- you have married or entered into a civil partnership again; *and*
- your new spouse/civil partner was not entitled to a Category A pension before the uprating date; *and*
  - *either* you were still married or in a civil partnership on the day before the uprating date; *or*
  - you married or entered into a civil partnership with her/him on or after that date.

Category D pension

There are residence requirements for Category D retirement pensions.

Category D pensions are for people aged over 80 years. You must:[133]

- have been resident in Great Britain for at least 10 years in any continuous period of 20 years ending on or after your 80th birthday; *and*
- have been ordinarily resident in Great Britain on:
  - your 80th birthday; *or*
  - a later date on which you claimed Category D pension.

A Category D pension is generally worth less than a Category A or B pension. The pensions 'overlap', which means that if you are entitled to a Category A or B pension, the above residence and presence conditions are not important. Absences from Great Britain during the 20-year period prior to your 80th birthday could affect your entitlement to benefit, as could absences around the time of your 80th birthday or the date of your claim. If you wish to spend time abroad or live abroad after you are 80, it is important to plan your absences carefully because you will be unlikely to qualify for any other benefit while abroad. Dependants' additions are not paid with a Category D pension.

Uprating

After establishing entitlement to any retirement pension, you continue to be entitled to it regardless of any absences from Great Britain.[134] However, absences abroad can still affect the *amount* of benefit you receive. If you spend a sufficient amount of time abroad so that you cease to be ordinarily resident (see p72) in Great Britain, the amount of benefit you receive is frozen for any day on which you are absent. This means that benefit for those days is paid at the rate when you stopped being ordinarily resident or the rate at which it was first paid if that was later.[135] Your benefit is not uprated in line with the usual annual upratings. These rules do not apply in countries with which the UK has a reciprocal agreement that allows for continued uprating of pension payments (see p255). The difference between these two groups of countries is not a breach of the Human Rights Act 1998.[136] Your benefit is uprated if you go to live in an EEA state.

However, you are still entitled to an uprated benefit, even if you are not ordinarily resident, if your entitlement is based on the contributions of your spouse/civil partner and s/he is ordinarily resident in Great Britain on the day before the benefit is uprated.[137]

In all of these cases, you are entitled to the uprated amount of benefit again after your return to Great Britain, provided you are once again ordinarily resident. You should, therefore, try to time any permanent retirement abroad so that you can take the maximum benefit with you.

You are only entitled to the age addition of 25p payable with your pension when you are 80 for any day you are absent from Great Britain if you:[138]

- are ordinarily resident in Great Britain; *or*
- were entitled to the age addition before you stopped being ordinarily resident in Great Britain; *or*
- are entitled to an increased rate of any category of retirement pension under a reciprocal agreement (see Chapter 14).

Bereavement benefits

Bereavement benefits comprise bereavement payment, widowed parent's allowance and bereavement allowance.

The only presence and residence conditions that apply to these benefits are those that relate to bereavement payment (see p93).[139]

Payment of bereavement benefits depends on whether your late spouse/civil partner satisfied the NI contribution conditions (see CPAG's *Welfare Benefits and Tax Credits Handbook* for details), although you may qualify if s/he died as the result of an industrial disease or an accident at work, even if the contribution conditions are not met. Bereavement benefits can be paid whether or not you are working, and any savings you have are not taken into account. See CPAG's *Welfare Benefits and Tax Credits Handbook* for details.

Widows and widowers who are living abroad, but whose late spouse/civil partner has worked and paid NI contributions in Great Britain, should check their benefit entitlement. The time limit for claiming bereavement benefits is three months[140] (12 months for bereavement payment[141]), although this can be extended if the bereaved person was unaware of her/his spouse/civil partner's death.[142] Once entitlement to bereavement benefits has been established, the rules on entitlement while abroad are the same as for retirement pension (see p90).

Bereavement payment

You are only entitled to this lump-sum payment if either:

- you were in Great Britain at the time of your spouse/civil partner's death; *or*
- your spouse/civil partner was in Great Britain at the time of her/his death; *or*
- you returned to Great Britain within four weeks of your spouse/civil partner's death; *and*
- you meet the contribution conditions for widowed parent's allowance or bereavement allowance.

The payment is made at a single, once-only rate, with no additions for any dependants. If you have a family member who is a 'person subject to immigration control' (see p56), this does not affect your entitlement.

Absences from Great Britain are only significant for someone who wished to claim the lump-sum bereavement payment and who (if s/he or her/his spouse/ civil partner was not in Great Britain at the time of her/his death) has to come to Great Britain within four weeks of the death in order to claim the payment.

Bereavement allowance

This can be paid for up to 52 weeks. You must have been aged at least 45 but still under pension age by the date of death of your spouse/civil partner. Your entitlement will end if you remarry or enter into a civil partnership during the year. No additions are paid for dependants.

Widowed parent's allowance

This benefit is paid to people who have the care of children, or to women who are pregnant at the time of their spouse's/civil partner's death. It is paid instead of bereavement allowance, and the two allowances cannot be paid together. Payment is not limited to a 52-week period. In order to qualify you must be responsible for a 'qualifying child', who must be:[143]

- living with you; *or*
- maintained by you, at least to the value of the child addition to widowed parent's allowance plus the amount of child benefit; *and either*
- the child of you and your late spouse/civil partner; *or*

- a child for whom you or your late spouse/civil partner were receiving child benefit at the time of death; *or*
- a child for whom you were receiving child benefit at the time of death and you were residing with your late spouse/civil partner at that time.

This means that the only dependants taken into account for the purposes of widowed parent's allowance are qualifying children, and the conditions of qualification are the same as for child benefit (see p87).

Industrial injuries benefits

Industrial injuries benefits are:
- disablement benefit;
- reduced earnings allowance (REA);
- retirement allowance;
- constant attendance allowance;
- exceptionally severe disablement allowance.

You are only entitled to any of these benefits if you:
- have an accident which 'arises out of and in the course of' employed earner's employment or a disease which is 'prescribed in relation to' employed earner's employment;[144] *and*
- were in Great Britain when the accident happened[145] or engaged in Great Britain in the employment which caused the accident or disease.

Apart from the above requirement for the injury to have a connection with the UK, to get **disablement benefit** or **retirement allowance** you do not have to satisfy any other presence or residence conditions.[146] As a result, your absences from Great Britain do not affect your entitlement to these benefits provided you satisfy the requirements relating to your work and your accident or disease. Both are uprated annually regardless of where you live.

To qualify for **REA, constant attendance allowance or exceptionally severe disablement allowance** as the result of an accident at work, you must have been in Great Britain (which includes adjacent UK territorial waters[147]) when the accident happened.[148] To qualify as a result of a disease, you must have been engaged in Great Britain in the employment that caused that disease (even if you have also been engaged outside Great Britain in that employment).[149] You must also be present at the time of your claim.

There are exceptions to these rules for various categories of worker, as follows.[150] You can qualify for benefit in respect of an accident which happens or a disease which is contracted outside Great Britain while you are:
- employed as a mariner or airman or airwoman;[151]
- employed as an apprentice pilot on board a ship or vessel;[152]

- on board an aircraft on a test flight starting in Great Britain in the course of your employment.[153]

In these cases, there are also more generous rules for defining when accidents arise out of and in the course of your employment, and for complying with time limits under benefit rules.[154]

You can qualify for benefit if, since 1986, an accident happens or you contract a disease outside Great Britain while you are paying British NI contributions, either at Class 1 rate or at Class 2 rate as a volunteer development worker.[155]

Benefit is not payable until you return to Great Britain after the accident or contracting the disease.

There are special rules to stop you losing benefit if you move between Great Britain and Northern Ireland.[156] You may also be able to use special rules if you have lived in another EEA state (see Chapter 12) or a country with which the UK has a reciprocal agreement (see Chapter 14), even if you are not a national of that country. There are also rules enabling you to retain benefits while working as an offshore worker.[157]

Temporary absence abroad

Disablement benefit and retirement allowance are not affected by absence abroad.

You remain entitled to **constant attendance allowance and exceptionally severe disablement allowance** for a period of six months (beginning with the first date on which you are absent) during which you are temporarily absent (see below for what constitutes a temporary absence) from Great Britain.[158] If your period of temporary absence is longer than six months, the Secretary of State has the discretion to allow you to continue to receive benefit.[159]

You remain entitled to **REA** for a period of three months (beginning with the first date on which you are absent) during which you are temporarily absent from Great Britain.[160] If your period of temporary absence is longer than three months, the Secretary of State has the discretion to allow you to continue to receive benefit.[161] For constant attendance allowance or exceptionally severe disablement allowance, as well as for REA, the Secretary of State will consider the reasons for your absence and any other relevant matters.

To be entitled to REA:[162]

- your absence from Great Britain must *not* be in order to work or engage in any other economic activity; *and*
- your claim must have been made before you leave Great Britain; *and*
- you must have been entitled to REA before going abroad.

You count as present in Great Britain for the purposes of REA while you are employed as a mariner or airman or woman.[163]

It has not been possible to make new claims for REA since 1990 unless the accident or illness to which the claim refers occurred before then. This means that if you lose your entitlement to your current claim by a longer period of absence abroad, you will lose this benefit and not be able to reclaim it on your return.

Disability living allowance and attendance allowance

In order to receive DLA and AA you must:[164]
- be present at the time of your claim (see p71);
- be ordinarily resident (see p72);
- satisfy the past presence test – ie, you have been present in Great Britain for a total of 26 weeks in the last 52 weeks, or 13 weeks for children under six months of age (see below).

Past presence test

You must have been present for 26 weeks out of the last 52 weeks to satisfy the past presence test.[165] You do not have to satisfy this requirement if:
- you are terminally ill.[166] However, you must still be present and ordinarily resident in Great Britain in order to be entitled;[167] or
- you are an EEA national (including a British citizen) who has worked at some point in any EEA state or a family member of an EEA national who has come to the UK from another EEA state.

If you have been abroad, it may be difficult for you to show that you satisfy the criteria for the mobility and/or the care component of DLA for the necessary three months prior to the claim. If you experience difficulties with this, you should seek advice.

You are treated as present in Great Britain for these rules, including the 26-week rule, if you were abroad only because you are:[168]
- a serving member of the armed forces; or
- living with a serving member of the armed forces and are the spouse, civil partner, son, daughter, stepson, stepdaughter, father, father-in-law, stepfather, mother, mother-in-law or stepmother of that person; or
- a mariner or airman or airwoman;[169] or
- an offshore worker.[170]

You may also be treated as present in Great Britain during a temporary absence (see p97). This may help you meet the 26-week presence rule.

Note: if you are terminally ill, the 26-week presence rule is waived.[171]

For children aged less than six months, the 26-week period is reduced to 13 weeks.[172] Because presence does not start until birth,[173] a child born in Great Britain must be 13 weeks old before being entitled to DLA, unless s/he is terminally ill, in which case the 13-week period is waived. If DLA entitlement begins before a child is six months old, the period of 26 weeks continues to be reduced to 13 weeks until the child's first birthday.[174]

Temporary absence abroad

If you go abroad, you are still treated as present in Great Britain and therefore entitled to benefit if you are:

- temporarily absent from Great Britain and you have not been absent for a period of more than 26 weeks, provided the absence was intended to be temporary at the outset;[175] *or*
- temporarily absent from Great Britain for the purpose of being treated for an incapacity or a disabling condition which began before you left Great Britain, provided the Secretary of State certifies that it is consistent with the proper administration of the system that you should continue to receive benefit;[176] *or*
- abroad as a serving member of the armed forces, an airman or woman or mariner, or a continental shelf worker, or if you are living with a close relative (see p103) who is a serving member of the forces.[177]

If you satisfy any of the above requirements for any particular day, you are also treated as present in Great Britain for the purpose of the past presence test (see p96).[178]

If, by the time you wish to go abroad, you have reached age 65 and are receiving the lowest rate care component or the lower rate mobility component of DLA, you should be aware that, if you break your claim, you may not requalify for benefit when you return.[179] This is because claims must normally be made by age 65, and an absence longer than the period for which benefit can continue to be paid will mean you will be too old to meet the qualifying conditions for DLA, and may be unable to satisfy the stricter tests which apply to AA. See CPAG's *Welfare Benefits and Tax Credits Handbook* for more details.

Carer's allowance

The residence and presence conditions for CA are the same as for DLA and AA except that there is no waiver of the 26-week rule for people who are terminally ill.[180]

Temporary absence abroad

If you go abroad, you remain entitled to CA (and you are still treated as present in Great Britain for the purposes of the 26-week rule) if your absence is temporary and it is for:[181]

- a continuous period that does not exceed four weeks and was always intended to be temporary (in practice, the disabled person would need to travel with you or you would fail to satisfy the ordinary conditions of entitlement, but see below); *or*

- the specific purpose of caring for the disabled person who is also absent from Great Britain and who remains entitled while absent to AA, DLA care component at the highest or middle rate, or constant attendance allowance. 'Specific' here does not have to mean the sole purpose, but the major purpose of the absence.[182]

You also remain entitled to CA if you go abroad without the person for whom you care provided:[183]

- the absence is for a continuous period that does not exceed four weeks and was always intended to be temporary; *and*
- you have only temporarily stopped providing care of at least 35 hours a week; *and*
- you have provided the necessary amount of care for at least 14 weeks in the period of 26 weeks before you go abroad *and* you would have provided that care for at least 22 weeks in that period but were unable to because either yourself or the person for whom you care had to go into a hospital or a similar institution for medical treatment. However, you lose your benefit if the person for whom you care loses her/his entitlement to AA or DLA after s/he has been in hospital or care home for four weeks (or 12 weeks if s/he is under 16 years of age and in receipt of DLA).

You are therefore able to take a four-week temporary holiday from caring every six months in which either you or the person for whom you care is abroad and you are still able to receive benefit for this period.

Statutory sick, maternity, paternity and adoption pay

The rules on entitlement to these benefits concentrate more on whether you count as an employee and have a continuous period of employment in the UK, rather than whether you are physically present here.

You only count as an employee if you are:

- an employed earner for Great Britain NI purposes (even if you work outside Great Britain);[184] *or*
- you are employed in an EEA member state (including A8 or A2 states – see Chapter 4);[185] *or*
- an offshore worker;[186]
- a mariner (but see below);[187] *or*
- an airman or airwoman.[188] Only mariners or airmen and airwomen who meet certain rules count as employees.[189] These are not dealt with here.

Temporary absence abroad

There are no requirements of presence or residence for statutory sick pay (SSP), statutory maternity pay (SMP), statutory paternity pay (SPP) or statutory adoption pay (SAP). You remain entitled to these benefits wherever you are based, provided you meet the normal rules of entitlement.[190] Your entitlement to SSP, SMP, SPP and SAP is not affected by any absence from Great Britain, but you can only receive SSP while you remain an employee.[191]

Your employer is not required to pay you SSP, SMP, SPP or SAP if:[192]

- your employer is not required by law to pay employer's Class 1 NI contributions (even if those contributions are in fact made) because at the time they become payable your employer:[193]
  – is not resident or present in Great Britain; *or*
  – has a place of business in Great Britain; *or*
- because of an international treaty or convention your employer is exempt from the Social Security Acts or those Acts are not enforceable against your employer.

In some cases, the rules require notice to be given about SSP or SMP, either by you to your employer, or by your employer to you. If you are in one of the circumstances where notice is required but it cannot be given because you are outside the UK, you (or your employer) are treated as having complied with the rules if the notice is given as soon as is reasonably practicable.[194] For details of when notice must be given, see CPAG's *Welfare Benefits and Tax Credits Handbook*.

Maternity allowance

There are no residence or presence rules for maternity allowance (MA). To be entitled, however, you must have been in employment either as an employed or a self-employed person for at least 26 weeks in the 66 weeks before the week in which your baby is due. MA is payable for a period of 39 weeks, starting at any time from the beginning of the 11th week before the week in which your baby is due to the week following the week in which you give birth to your baby.[195] So, in order to satisfy the 'recent work' test, you must have been employed or self-employed in Great Britain.[196] As a result, a lengthy recent absence abroad may mean that you fail to establish your entitlement to MA. You may, however, still be able to claim MA if you:[197]

- have been working abroad and you return to Great Britain; *and*
- remained ordinarily resident in Great Britain during your period of absence (see p72); *and*
- have received earnings at least equal to the threshold figure of £30 per week.

If you are an EEA national, you can rely on work carried out in any EEA state (including the A8 and A2 states – see Chapter 4) to satisfy the conditions for MA.

The social fund

The social fund is divided into two parts:
- **the regulated social fund**, comprising:
  - Sure Start maternity grants;
  - cold weather payments;
  - funeral expenses; *and*
  - winter fuel payments;
- **the discretionary social fund**, comprising:
  - budgeting loans;
  - community care grants; *and*
  - crisis loans.

Regulated social fund

You must be ordinarily resident in Great Britain, but otherwise the presence and residence tests for the regulated social fund are dictated by the presence and residence conditions attached to the various means-tested benefits on pp78–85. You should refer to the section in this chapter dealing with the relevant benefit to identify the effect of absences from Great Britain on your entitlement to benefits from the regulated social fund.

Maternity grants and funeral expenses

You are entitled to a **Sure Start maternity grant** if:
- you or your partner have been awarded one of the following qualifying benefits:[198]
  - IS;
  - income-based JSA;
  - income-related ESA;
  - PC;
  - working tax credit (WTC) which includes the disability or severe disability element;
  - CTC paid at a rate which exceeds the family element;
- one of the following applies:[199]
  - you or a member of your family are pregnant or have given birth in the last three months (including stillbirth after 24 weeks of pregnancy[200]);
  - you or your partner have adopted a child who is less than 12 months old;
  - you and your spouse/civil partner have a parental order allowing you to have a child by a surrogate mother; *and*
- you have received health and welfare advice from a health professional relating to your baby or your maternal health (except in the case of a stillborn child[201]).[202]

You qualify for **funeral expenses payments** if:
- you or your partner have been awarded one of the following qualifying benefits:[203]

- IS;
- income-based JSA;
- income-related ESA;
- PC;
- HB;
- CTB;
- WTC which includes the disability or severe disability element;
- CTC paid at a rate which exceeds the family element;
- you or your partner are treated as responsible for the funeral expenses. See CPAG's *Welfare Benefits and Tax Credits Handbook* for more information about this;[204]
- the funeral takes place in the UK (but see below);[205]
- the deceased was ordinarily resident in the UK when s/he died.[206]

If you are treated as a worker for the purposes of EU law (see p229), the rules concerning ordinary residence and the place of funeral are both extended to the EEA and Switzerland.[207]

You can get a funeral payment for a funeral that takes place in any member state of the EEA if you are a worker or a family member of a worker who has died. This also applies to people who are economically active other than being in employment – eg, who are self-employed or self-supporting. See Chapters 10 to 13 for full details of the rights of EEA nationals.

There are no special rules concerning temporary absences, but since you or your partner must be in receipt of one of the qualifying benefits on the date of claim, payment is governed by the same rules as the qualifying benefit.

Cold weather payments

Cold weather payments are payable if, on at least one of the days during the qualifying week of cold weather, you have been awarded PC or, in some cases, IS, ESA, CTC or JSA.[208] See CPAG's *Welfare Benefits and Tax Credits Handbook* for more details.

There are no special rules concerning temporary absence.

Winter fuel payments

Winter fuel payments are available to anyone aged 60 or over to help towards the cost of fuel bills. The only condition, apart from age, is that you must be ordinarily resident in Great Britain in the qualifying week – ie, a week set by the DWP and announced in advance of winter.[209] Eligibility does not depend on receiving any other benefits. You do not usually need to make a claim if you have received a winter fuel payment in the past, but if this is the first year in which you become entitled to a payment, or if you have been away from Great Britain for long enough to have lost your entitlement in the meantime, you should contact your local DWP office to make a claim. You are entitled to claim a backdated payment if, at the time of the qualifying week, you were a 'person subject to immigration control' (see p56) but have since been granted leave (usually recognition as a refugee), which covers the relevant week.[210]

Temporary absence does not affect your entitlement as long as you remain ordinarily resident (see p72).

Discretionary social fund

Payments from the discretionary social fund can only be paid to meet needs which occur in the UK.[211] It is only necessary, therefore, to show that you are in the UK for a sufficient period to allow your particular need to be established here.

Budgeting loan

In order to get a budgeting loan, you need to be receiving IS, income-based JSA, income-related ESA or PC when the decision is made on your application, and you or your partner must have been receiving that qualifying benefit for 26 weeks before that date.

There are no special rules concerning temporary absence, but since you or your partner must be in receipt of one of the qualifying benefits for a budgeting loan, payment is governed by the same rules as the qualifying benefit.

Community care grant

You can get a community care grant if, when you make your application, you are receiving IS, income-based JSA, income-related ESA or PC.[212]

If you have been staying in institutional or residential care and it is likely that you will receive IS, income-based JSA or PC when discharged, you should also be able to receive a grant.[213] A claim should be made within six weeks of the date you expect to be discharged. The High Court has decided that, in these cases, the 'community' refers only to Great Britain, so you can only claim successfully on this basis if you lived in Great Britain before the time you made your application.[214] If your claim is made in any other circumstances, and providing you are in receipt of a qualifying benefit, there is no other presence or residence test to satisfy.

There are no special rules concerning temporary absence, but since you or your partner must be in receipt of one of the qualifying benefits for a community care grant, payment is governed by the same rules as the qualifying benefit.

Crisis loan

You do not need to be entitled to, or receiving, any other benefit in order to get a crisis loan.[215]

If you would be classed as a 'person from abroad' were you to claim IS, income-based JSA or income-related ESA, or you would be treated as not in Great Britain were you to claim PC (ie, because either you are not habitually resident or you do not have a sufficient right of residence to obtain one of these benefits), you are not entitled to a crisis loan, unless it is to alleviate the consequences of a disaster.[216]

4. How a family member abroad affects benefit

Your entitlement to social security benefits and tax credits can be affected by other family members. This section sets out the impact of having a family member abroad. **Note:** different rules apply if your family member is living in another European Economic Area (EEA) state (see Chapter 11).

Member of the family
Member of the family means the spouse, civil partner, son, daughter, stepson, stepdaughter, father, father-in-law, stepfather mother, mother-in-law and stepmother. References to 'step-parent and stepchildren and in-laws' includes such relationships arising through civil partnerships.

One partner in a couple is abroad

If you have a partner who is abroad, your benefit entitlement may be affected. If the absence is temporary, you will still be treated as a couple.

However, you are no longer treated as a couple if:[217]
- your partner and/or you do not intend to resume living with each other.[218] (You may intend to resume living with each other, but your intentions may depend on something beyond your control, such as getting a visa or a job. If this applies, you may be able to argue that your intention does not count because it depends on these things and therefore you are not a couple for social security purposes);[219] *or*
- your absence from each other is likely to exceed 52 weeks, unless there are exceptional circumstances and the absence is unlikely to be substantially more than 52 weeks; *or*
- your partner is detained in custody pending trial or sentence upon conviction or under a sentence imposed by a court; *or*
- your partner is on temporary release.

If your partner is the claimant, see p78.

Your partner's absence is from *you*, not from the family home, so these rules can apply even if your partner has never lived in your current home.[220] The length of the absence is worked out from when it started to when it is likely to finish. If circumstances change so that the likely total absence gets longer (or shorter) (eg, because of illness), the absence may become too long (or sufficiently short) to count as temporary under these rules.

Example

Rifat joins Amjad in Pakistan for three months. She then returns home to the United Kingdom (UK) but, because of sickness, claims income support (IS). Amjad applies for a visa to come to the UK. Because Amjad's absence from Rifat is likely to substantially exceed 52 weeks, Rifat is treated as a single person and is entitled to IS. Three months later, Amjad is refused a visa on maintenance and accommodation grounds and he appeals. One year later he wins his appeal and a visa is issued. Before he can travel to the UK, his mother falls ill and he stays in Pakistan to care for her. Her illness is only expected to last a short time so Amjad expects to travel to the UK within a month. However, because his total absence from Rifat is now substantially more than 52 weeks, he is not treated as her partner even though the absence is expected to end soon.

If a couple is likely to be separated for more than 52 weeks, they can argue that they are not temporarily absent from one another and that the absence should be treated as permanent. This means that any benefit claim by the person in the UK should be treated as though s/he were single. An absence of more than 52 weeks might occur, for example, because:

- before applying for a visa to meet the Immigration Rules, the partner in the UK must get a job (or a job offer) in order to meet the maintenance and accommodation rules;
- the partner in the UK is waiting for recognition as a refugee, or for indefinite leave to remain;
- the partner in the UK is waiting for a decision on a visa application. This often takes months;
- one partner is waiting for the outcome of an appeal against a visa refusal. The likely length of your separation depends on how likely you are to be refused a visa. Refusal rates are high in African and Asian countries.

When a person counts as your partner

Household

Under the rules for IS, income-based jobseeker's allowance (JSA) income-related employment and support allowance (ESA), pension credit (PC), housing benefit (HB) and council tax benefit (CTB), a person can only count as your partner if you share the same household.[221]

A '**household**' is something abstract, not something physical like a home. It is made up of either a single person or a group of people held together by social ties.[222] A person cannot be a member of two households at the same time.[223] A person can be temporarily absent from the home, but still be a member of the household.[224] If it is not obvious whether people share a household, the important factors are:

- whether they share the same physical space – eg, a house, flat or room(s) in a hostel;
- whether they carry out chores for the benefit of them all – eg, cooking, shopping, cleaning.

Each benefit has special rules allowing certain temporary absences of one partner from other members of the family to be ignored when considering whether there is a common household. These special rules do not override the above normal rules about what is a household.[225] This means that, even if the temporary absence is ignored, your general situation may have sufficiently changed for your partner no longer to be in your household. This is most likely to apply if your partner is now a member of a different household abroad.

A person can count as your partner even though you are not married or in a civil partnership. In practice, if your partner is abroad and you are not married or in a civil partnership, the Department for Work and Pensions will not usually treat you as a couple for benefit purposes.

If you have never actually shared a household with your partner, you cannot be treated as being temporarily absent from one another.[226]

Example
Rifat marries Amjad in Pakistan. They have a week-long honeymoon. Rifat then returns to her home in the UK. Amjad intends to apply for a visa to join her in the UK. He works full time but earns the equivalent of £10 a week. Rifat loses her job and has to claim income-based JSA. The honeymoon was too short to count as sharing a household. Because they have never shared a household, the rules about ignoring temporary absences do not apply and Amjad does not count as Rifat's partner.

Income support, income-based jobseeker's allowance and income-related employment and support allowance

If your partner is working full time while abroad, you may be refused IS, income-based JSA or income-related ESA because of the means test attached to these benefits. In addition, f or most means-tested benefits, if you have a partner abroad you will continue to be treated as a couple and your partner will be considered temporarily absent.[227]

If your partner is temporarily absent from Great Britain, but you are in Great Britain, for the first four weeks of your IS/JSA/ESA claim (or eight weeks if your partner is taking a child or young person abroad for treatment under the rules described on p79):

- your applicable amount continues to include an amount for your partner;[228] *and*

- your partner counts as a member of your household, so her/his income and capital is taken into account in the usual way.[229]

Note: this does not apply if your partner is a 'person subject to immigration control' (see p56).

If your partner stops meeting the temporary absence rules, or is absent for more than four/eight weeks, your applicable amount is reduced to that for a single person, even though your partner's income or capital still counts as yours.[230] You may then want to argue that s/he no longer counts as your partner (see p104).

Pension credit

The rules for PC largely mirror those for IS, income-based JSA and income-related ESA (see above). The major difference is that, if your partner is a 'person subject to immigration control' (see p56), s/he is treated as not being a member of your household. Consequently, her/his income or work does not affect your claim for benefit.

Housing benefit and council tax benefit

If you are **getting IS, income-based JSA or income-related ESA,** your partner's absence does not affect the amount of your HB and only affects CTB in exceptional circumstances (see below). This is because you are treated as having no income or capital, so you are entitled to maximum HB/CTB regardless of whether your applicable amount is for a single person or a couple.[231] The local authority dealing with your HB/CTB claim should not make enquiries about your partner's absence.

If you are **not being paid IS, income-based JSA, or income-related ESA,** the HB/CTB rules about who counts as your partner and temporary absences are the same as for IS, income-based JSA and income-related ESA (see p105), except:[232]

- there are no special rules for partners;
- for CTB, there are no exceptions to the general rule that a temporary absence is ignored. However, absences that are likely to be more than 52 weeks may not count as temporary anyway. In practice, local authorities deal with CTB in the same way as HB.

If a person abroad counts as your partner under these rules:

- your partner's income and capital are taken into account as if they were your income and capital.[233] There are special rules on calculating capital abroad (see CPAG's *Welfare Benefits and Tax Credits Handbook*);
- your applicable amount includes an amount for your partner;[234]
- you lose any entitlement to family premium at the lone parent rate (which applies to some pre-6 April 1998 claimants – see CPAG's *Welfare Benefits and Tax Credits Handbook*);[235] *and*

- for HB, your partner's absence does not affect the fact that you normally occupy your accommodation as your home.[236]

These rules mean that your HB/CTB is usually the same as if your partner were living with you. This is different from the IS/income-based JSA/income-related ESA/PC rules, under which you may often be worse off.

If a person abroad does *not* count as your partner, your applicable amount is for a single person, not a couple, so your HB/CTB may be paid at a lower rate.

In very unusual cases, the person abroad may still be liable for current council tax, even though s/he no longer counts as your partner under CTB rules.[237] This is because the rules on council tax liability are different from those on CTB entitlement. If this happens, your CTB is calculated on the basis of your 'share' (ie, half the council tax) even though you are legally liable to pay all the council tax.[238] If this applies, the local authority can top up your CTB to the amount of your liability. You should ask it to do this and also try to get your partner's name removed from the list of liable people. For more details, see CPAG's *Council Tax Handbook*.

For more information about HB/CTB and temporary absences, see pp84 and 86.

Tax credits

For child tax credit (CTC) and working tax credit, if your partner goes abroad, other than for a temporary absence for an 'allowed period', you must make a fresh claim as a single person. The '**allowed periods**' are:[239]
- the first eight weeks of any temporary absence;
- the first 12 weeks of any temporary absence if that absence is in connection with certain illnesses or a death in the family.

Increases in non-means-tested benefits

You may be entitled to an increase in the following benefits for your spouse or civil partner or for a dependent adult:
- incapacity benefit (IB). **Note:** this was abolished for new claims from 27 October 2008, but if you are already in receipt of IB it remains possible to make a first claim for an adult dependant increase;
- carer's allowance (if you claimed and were entitled before 6 April 2010);
- maternity allowance (if you claimed and were entitled before 6 April 2010);
- Category A retirement pension (if you claimed and were entitled before 6 April 2010).

These increases in benefit are still payable while your spouse/civil partner or dependent adult is abroad, but only if you are residing together outside Great Britain and you are not disqualified from receiving the benefit because of any absence from Great Britain.[240] You are treated as residing together during any temporary absence (see pp90, 97 and 99) from each other.[241] Even if you both intend to be permanently absent from Great Britain, as long as your absence from each other is only temporary, the increase is not affected.[242]

There are special rules if your spouse or civil partner is in another EEA member state (see Chapters 11 and 12) or if you are a national of Algeria, Israel, Morocco, San Marino, Tunisia or Turkey (see p257).[243]

A child is abroad

If you are responsible for a child and that child goes abroad, your benefit entitlement may be affected.

Income support and income-based jobseeker's allowance

In general, you no longer can get additional amounts for children in IS or income-based JSA. Instead, CTC is paid. However, if you made your claim before 6 April 2004, your IS or income-based JSA applicable amount may still include an amount for each child for whom you are responsible.[244] In these circumstances, this amount only continues to be paid while the child is a member of your household (see p104).[245] Therefore, you may lose this additional amount of benefit if your child goes abroad as s/he may no longer be treated as part of your household.

If the child is abroad for longer than the allowed periods (see p79), your IS/income-based JSA is calculated without an additional amount for the child.

If you claimed either IS or income-based JSA after the child went abroad and you were not entitled to the other benefit immediately before claiming, these periods run from the date of claim.[246]

Employment and support allowance and pension credit

The status of the child is irrelevant for ESA and PC claims. Therefore, if you have a child who is abroad, your benefit entitlement will not be affected.

Housing benefit and council tax benefit

There are two ways in which a child for whom you are responsible and who is abroad can affect your HB and/or CTB.

- Unless you are in receipt of IS, income-related ESA, income-based JSA or PC, your HB/CTB applicable amount includes an amount for each child for whom you are responsible.[247] This only applies to a child who is in your household (see p104).[248] If the child ceases to count as a member of your household, your applicable amount will decrease and if your assessable income is more than your new applicable amount, you will be entitled to less HB/CTB.
- You may receive amounts of HB for a property which is of a larger size because of the inclusion of children in your household than you would do if they were not living with you. Therefore, if the children stop counting as members of your household, the maximum amount of HB to which you are entitled might reduce.

For either of the above to happen, the child must cease to count as part of your household. For HB/CTB, a child's temporary absence from your household is ignored when considering whether s/he remains a member of the household. For HB, the exceptions to this rule are if:[249]
- the child and/or you do not intend to resume living together; *or*
- your absence from each other is likely to exceed 52 weeks, unless:
  - there are exceptional circumstances – eg, if you have no control over the length of the absence; *and*
  - the absence is unlikely to be substantially more than 52 weeks.

For CTB, there are no rules setting out exceptions to the general rule that a temporary absence is ignored. However, absences that are likely to be more than 52 weeks may not count as temporary anyway. In practice, local authorities are likely to deal with CTB in the same way as HB.

Child benefit and guardian's allowance

Generally, in order to claim child benefit, the child for whom you are claiming must be present in the UK. However, a child will be treated as present if her/his absence abroad is temporary, during:
- the first 12 weeks of any period of absence; *or*
- any period during which the child is absent for the specific purpose of being treated for an illness, or physical or mental disability which commenced before her/his absence began; *or*
- any period during which the child is absent only because:
  - s/he is receiving full-time education at a school or college in another EEA member state (including the A8 and A2 states – see Chapter 4) or in Switzerland; *or*
  - s/he is engaged in an educational exchange or visit made with the written approval of the school or college which s/he normally attends.

A child is treated as present in the UK if s/he is living in another EEA state while you are working in the UK, provided no equivalent of child benefit is paid in that EEA state. If a child is born outside the UK during a period in which the mother could be treated as present in the UK, the child will also be treated as present.

Child tax credit

You are only entitled to CTC if you or your partner are responsible for a child or young person.[250] The child does not have to be present or ordinarily resident in the UK, only the claimant.[251] You are responsible for a child under the CTC rules if the child is normally living with you. A child is treated as normally living with you if s/he is living in another EEA state while you are working in the UK, provided no equivalent benefit is paid in that EEA state.

5. **Habitual residence**

The 'habitual residence test' was introduced on 1 August 1994 and applies to:
- income support (IS);
- income-based jobseeker's allowance (JSA);
- income-related employment and support allowance (ESA);
- pension credit (PC);
- housing benefit (HB);
- council tax benefit (CTB).

In order to qualify for one of these benefits, you must be habitually resident in the 'common travel area' – ie, the United Kingdom (UK), Ireland, the Channel Islands and the Isle of Man.

Note: as Ireland forms part of the common travel area, Irish citizens are treated more favourably than other nationals of the European Economic Area (EEA).[252]

The way in which the habitual residence test operates for each benefit is slightly different, but the outcome is the same. If you are not habitually resident in the common travel area, you are not entitled to IS, income-based JSA, income-related ESA, PC, HB or CTB.[253]

If you fail the test, you are classed as a '**person from abroad**' for IS,[254] income-based JSA,[255] income-related ESA, HB[256] and CTB.[257] For PC, if you fail the test, you are treated as not in Great Britain.[258] The effect of this is that you are not entitled to these benefits. You have an applicable amount of £nil for IS, JSA and ESA, you are treated as not liable for rent or council tax for HB and CTB, and you are treated as not meeting the presence test for PC.[259]

The habitual residence test is both complex and subjective. There has been a significant amount of caselaw on the test and this has helped to clarify and to reduce its impact. However, from 1 May 2004, the test is linked to the right to reside test (see p77). If you do not have a right to reside, you cannot be habitually resident for the above benefits.

The way the test works is as follows.
- Are you deemed to be habitually resident? If so, you should not be subjected to any further examination in respect of habitual residence or right to reside (see p116). If you meet the other general conditions of entitlement, you should be eligible for benefit.
- If you are not deemed to be habitually resident, do you have a right to reside sufficient to claim the benefit you want? If the answer is no, you will be deemed not to be habitually resident and cannot qualify for benefit (see p118).
- If you do have a right to reside but you are not deemed to be habitually resident, have you established your habitual residence in the common travel area (see p111)?

- If you were already habitually resident (either because you were deemed to be habitually resident or because you had established your habitual residence in the common travel area) and you have been abroad, was your absence temporary (see p115) or are you a returning resident (see p114)?

People deemed to be habitually resident

You are deemed to be habitually resident (including meeting the right to reside test) if you:
- are an EEA national who is a 'worker' or a 'self-employed person' (see p229);
- are an EEA national who retains the status of 'worker' or 'self-employed' person (see p231);
- are the family member (see p103) of an EEA national in either of the above two groups;
- are someone with a permanent right of residence as a former worker or self-employed person who has retired or is permanently incapacitated, or you are the family member of such a person;
- are a refugee;
- have leave outside the rules (this includes exceptional leave to enter or remain and humanitarian protection);
- have been deported, expelled or otherwise legally removed from another country to the UK (but this does not apply to anyone who is a 'person subject to immigration control' – see p56);
- left Montserrat after 1 November 1995 because of the volcanic eruption;
- left Zimbabwe to come to the UK after 28 February 2009 but before 18 March 2011 and you have received assistance from the UK government to settle in the UK;
- for HB and CTB only, receive IS, income-based JSA, PC or income-related ESA.[260]

If you are not deemed to be habitually resident, you must show that you have established habitual residence in the common travel area and that you have a right to reside sufficient to claim the benefit you want.

Establishing habitual residence

There is no definition of habitual residence in the regulations. However, there is now a considerable amount of caselaw on the meaning of habitual residence and from this caselaw certain principles have emerged.

A person must be habitually resident in the common travel area (see p110), must have a right to reside, and must be 'resident for an appreciable period of time'.[261] The length of the appreciable period depends on your case, but may be short – eg, a month.[262] However, as there is no fixed minimum period,[263] it might be a matter of days. It can include visits to prepare for settled residence made before that residence is actually taken up.[264]

The factors that are relevant when deciding whether you are habitually resident include whether:[265]
- you have a right to reside;
- you have brought your possessions to the UK;
- you did everything necessary to establish residence before coming to the UK;
- you have a right of abode (see Chapter 1);
- you have brought, or are seeking to bring, your family;
- you have ties with the UK.

No 'appreciable period' is necessary if:
- you have been habitually resident in the UK in the past, even though the length of your absence means that the previous habitual residence has come to an end. This exception comes from a comment made in a House of Lords case that 'there may indeed be special cases where a person concerned is not coming here for the first time but is resuming an habitual residence previously had.'[266] The Department for Work and Pensions (DWP) often uses this exception in favour of UK citizens returning after a long period living in one of the former colonies;
- you can take advantage of European Union (EU) law (see p115).

To be habitually resident, you must be seen to be making a home here, but it does not have to be your only home or a permanent one.[267] So a long-standing intention to move abroad (eg, when debts are paid) does not prevent a person from being habitually resident.[268]

You can be seen to be making a home here even though you have very few or no resources. For example, approaching housing associations and trying to find work could help show that you are making a home here.

The practicality or 'viability' of your arrangements for residence might be relevant when deciding whether or not you are resident and the length of the appreciable period.[269] A person who has no money to support her/himself in Great Britain, but who intends to stay, is likely to be resident here for the foreseeable future because s/he cannot afford to go anywhere else. So a person with no income will have a short appreciable period. Lack of viability can only make it more difficult to show habitual residence if it means that you are likely to leave the UK soon.

Events after the benefit claim or decision may show that your intention was always to reside in the UK.[270] For example, if you are refused income-based JSA because the DWP does not accept that you have a settled intention to stay in the UK, the fact that you are still here by the time of the appeal hearing may help show that you always intended to stay. The decision about whether or not you are habitually resident has to be made on the 'balance of probabilities'. If the probabilities in favour of each answer are exactly equal, the decision should be that you *are* habitually resident. This is because the benefits authority has to show that you are *not* habitually resident.[271]

In one case, the House of Lords confirmed that: [272]

> It seems to me plain that as a matter of ordinary language a person is not habitually resident in any country unless he has taken up residence and lived there for a period … it is a question of fact to be decided on the date where the determination has to be made on the circumstances of each case whether and when that habitual residence has been established… the requisite period is not a fixed period. It may be longer where there are doubts. It may be short.

A social security commissioner in one case made the following points.[273]
- The burden of proof in habitual residence cases lies with the decision maker not the claimant.
- A person must be resident for an appreciable period of time before s/he can be treated as habitually resident.
- What counts as an appreciable period depends on the facts of each case. There is no minimum period before a person acquires habitual residence.
- The current home need not be the only home nor need it be intended to be a permanent one, but it must be a genuine home for the time being.
- Once you have acquired habitual residence, it is not lost if you go abroad for a temporary purpose.

In another case, a commissioner confirmed the following.[274]
- What constitutes an appreciable period depends on the circumstances of the particular case.
- In general, the period lies between one and three months and cogent reasons would need to be given by the First-tier Tribunal supporting a decision in which a significantly longer period had been required.
- Whether the residence is viable is a factor that is relevant to the test but must be given appropriate weight and not overemphasised.
- The danger of overemphasising viability is that the only claimants who can establish habitual residence will be those who have sufficient access to funds not to need the benefit, and that cannot be right as the habitual residence test is a test of entitlement, not a bar to it.

Showing that you are habitually resident

Showing that you are habitually resident can be very difficult. It is best to collect as much evidence as you can of your connection to the UK. You will normally be interviewed. You should explain the steps you have taken to make the UK your home. You should provide any documents that will help your case – eg, registration with a local doctor, enrolment in a school or college, evidence of looking for work, and letters from relatives and friends settled in the UK.

The DWP and local authorities often do not apply the habitual residence test properly or even consistently. In practice, the test usually means that you are denied benefits at first, but not indefinitely. Local offices may have a rule of thumb, such as three or six months, after which a person will pass the test. Applying such a blanket policy is unlawful and therefore should be challenged either by judicial review or by bringing a complaint. Practice varies between and within offices, so even if you fail the test at one office, you could pass it at another. However, once you are accepted as habitually resident, you are very unlikely to fail the test at a later date, even if your benefit claim stops or you change benefit offices.

Because establishing an appreciable period of residence is only a matter of time, if you fail the test, you should make further claims at regular intervals. You should appeal against every refusal, but the First-tier Tribunal that hears your appeal can only consider whether you were habitually resident on or before the DWP decision. Some DWP offices tell claimants the appreciable period required for them to be accepted as habitually resident. If this applies, you should reclaim when you have been resident for that period, but still appeal the earlier refusal.

Returning residents

If you have lived in the UK in the past and you are resuming your residence, you may be treated as habitually resident immediately. In a decision issued after the *Nessa* and *Swaddling* cases, a commissioner held that, in order to establish whether a person is resuming a previous residence, it is necessary to conduct a three-stage inquiry.[275] This involves looking at:

- the circumstances in which the claimant's earlier habitual residence was lost;
- the links between the claimant and the UK while abroad;
- the circumstances of the claimant's return to the UK.

The fact that your absence is only temporary, albeit for a long time, may be a point in favour of your resuming habitual residence immediately on your return to the UK. On the other hand, if you left the UK with no intention of returning, this may be a point against resuming habitual residence on return. If you remained abroad for longer than anticipated because of circumstances outside your control, this also might be a feature in favour of resuming habitual residence. The ties and contacts you have retained or established while abroad must also be considered. You must also show that you intend resettling in the UK for the time being. If the intention to settle is very strong, the period of actual residence becomes shorter.

In contrast, a commissioner in a later case held that it is necessary for a returning resident to be resident for an appreciable period even if the claimant is resuming residence.[276] The commissioner found that, although the claimant had once been habitually resident, he had ceased to be so in the five-year period in which he was absent from the UK. A claim for benefit had been made within days of his return to the UK. On that basis, the commissioner held that he had not become habitually resident at the time of his claim for benefit, but went on to find that he was habitually resident some five weeks after his return to the UK.

Returning after a temporary absence

If you have been abroad for a temporary period and prior to your absence you were habitually resident, you do not lose your habitual residence.[277] There is some overlap between a person who is a returning resident (see p114) and a person returning after a temporary absence. Temporary absence is more likely to apply to short periods of absence – eg, for a holiday or to visit relatives.

People coming to the United Kingdom for the first time

If you have come to the UK for the first time, you must show that you are habitually resident unless you are unable to rely on EU law (see below) or you fall within one of the groups deemed to be habitually resident (p111). This means showing that you have a settled intention to remain and that you have durable ties with the country of intended residence. The period, however, can be very short.

European Economic Area nationals

Some EEA nationals are exempt from the test (see p111). Those not specifically exempt may be able to rely on the co-ordination rules to claim IS, income-based JSA, income-related ESA or PC (see Chapter 11).

Habitual residence in European Union law

'Habitual residence' is also a term that is used in EU law under the EU co-ordination rules (see p204). For example, you are entitled to receive any 'special non-contributory benefits' in the EEA member state in which you reside, provided you qualify for it under that country's social security scheme.[278] For this purpose, 'residence' means 'habitual residence'.[279] However, the term habitual residence has a slightly different meaning in EU law than it does in UK law.

In order to be covered by the co-ordination rules, you must have worked in an EEA state, but not necessarily in the UK. If you are covered by the co-ordination rules (see p161), you are entitled to have the question of your habitual residence for IS, income-based JSA, income-related ESA or PC purposes dealt with under EU law rather than UK law. The co-ordination rules do not apply to HB or CTB, so the same arguments cannot be made for those benefits.

As with UK law, 'habitual residence' in EU law is not defined, but caselaw of the European Court of Justice (ECJ) explains what habitual residence means.[280] In one case, the ECJ held that habitual residence corresponds with where a person's habitual centre of interests is situated.[281] Account should be taken of the:

- length and continuity of residence before the person moved;
- length and purpose of absence;

- nature of the occupation found in the other member state; *and*
- the intention of the person concerned as it appears from all the circumstances.

This should apply to British citizens who have returned to the UK from another EEA state, but could also apply to other EEA nationals who are not British but who have strong links with the UK.

In another case, the ECJ considered whether EU law allowed some EEA nationals to override the habitual residence test.[282] The claimant had returned to the UK after working in France, but was denied benefit under the habitual residence test because he did not have an appreciable period of residence, in addition to a settled intention. The ECJ held that, in the case of a person covered by EU Regulation 1408/71, 'completion of an appreciable period of residence' could not be imposed as a requirement for benefit in addition to an intention to reside. Therefore, unlike UK law, EU law does *not* require an 'appreciable period' for habitual residence.[283] This only applies to you if you can rely on the EU co-ordination rule (see p161). It is most likely to apply if you are returning to the UK, but it might apply in other cases.

In the case of *Swaddling*, the ECJ said: 'the length of residence cannot be regarded as an intrinsic element of the concept of [habitual] residence.'[284] This has been explained in a commissioner's decision as meaning that it is not essential under EU law for the residence to have lasted for any particular length of time, but the length of residence remains a factor to be considered.[285] So, in some cases where other factors point in favour of you being considered habitually resident, this can be so from the date of your arrival in the UK.

EU law may also allow your residence in another EEA country to count towards any period of residence under UK law.[286] However, it does not allow you to use past presence in another member state to acquire habitual residence in the place where you now live. The ECJ has always taken the view that it is acceptable for a member state to require a sufficient link with that state in order to qualify for benefits. For benefits such as IS, the link is that you must establish that you are habitually resident.[287]

6. **The right to reside**

The right to reside test is a United Kingdom (UK) test that applies to certain benefits (see below), but it impacts almost solely on European Economic Area (EEA) nationals and it overlaps significantly with the rights of European Union (EU) nationals under EU law. It is therefore important that you use this section together with Chapter 13 of this *Handbook*.

The right to reside test was introduced on 1 May 2004 and applies to the following benefits:

- income support (IS);

- income-based jobseeker's allowance (JSA);
- income-related employment and support allowance (ESA);
- pension credit (PC);
- housing benefit (HB);
- council tax benefit (CTB);
- child benefit;
- child tax credit (CTC);
- health in pregnancy grants.

In addition, you cannot get a social fund crisis loan if you would not pass the habitual residence or right to reside tests for IS, income-based JSA, income-related ESA or PC were you to claim one of these benefits, unless it is to alleviate the consequences of a disaster.

For child benefit (see p87), CTC (see p86) and health in pregnancy grants, the test is part of the existing presence test for those benefits. For the other benefits listed above, the requirement to have a right to reside forms part of the habitual residence test (see p110).

Transitional protection

If you have been in receipt of either IS, income-based JSA, PC, HB or CTB from 30 April 2004 (the day before the test was introduced) and you claim one of these five benefits, you do not have to show that you have a right to reside for this later claim.[288]

Example

Jean-Pierre is French. He came to the UK in 2003 and claimed IS and HB/CTB. In 2005 he started work and so his IS stopped, but he continued to get HB/CTB as he had a low income. In 2006, he claimed IS. He did not need to pass the right to reside test to be entitled to this because he had been in receipt of HB/CTB since 30 April 2004. In 2007, he was evicted and so his HB/CTB stopped. He continue to receive IS. When he was rehoused in 2008, he did not need to pass the right to reside test because he had been receiving one of the five benefits for each day from 30 April 2004.

These rules do not assist you if it was your partner or former partner, or one of your parents, who was in receipt of the benefit.[289]

The rules do not apply to income-related ESA. However, if you have been in receipt of one of the above five benefits since 30 April 2004 and your award of IS on grounds of disability is converted into an award of income-related ESA, you will be deemed to be habitually resident and to have a right of residence.[290]

How the test operates

Means-tested benefits

In order to qualify for **IS, income-based JSA, income-related ESA, PC, HB and CTB**, you must be habitually resident in the 'common travel area' (see p110). You are not habitually resident if you do not have a right to reside in the common travel area that is sufficient to claim the benefit you want. The habitual residence test has, therefore, two stages: the original test of habitual residence (see p110) and a further right to reside test.

For **IS, income-related ESA, PC, HB and CTB**, you will not satisfy the right to reside test if your *only* right of residence is as:[291]

- an EEA national with the right of residence during your first three months in the UK;
- a workseeker;
- a family member of an EEA workseeker.

The rules are slightly different for **JSA**, in that a right of residence as a workseeker is a sufficient right to reside to claim JSA. The effect of this is that, although having a right of residence as a workseeker is not sufficient to get HB and CTB, if you are a workseeker and you claim income-based JSA, you can be passported onto HB and CTB.

Child benefit, child tax credit and health in pregnancy grants

For child benefit and CTC, your right to reside is linked to the presence test (see pp86 and 87). You need to be present in order to be entitled to benefit.

If you make a claim on or after 1 May 2004 and you do not have a right to reside, you are treated as not being present in Great Britain and therefore cannot get child benefit and CTC.[292] There are no exempt groups. Therefore, unless you become economically active, you will never qualify for benefit no matter how long you live in the UK.

If you are an EEA national and you go to another member state, you have a right of residence during the first three months of your stay, whether or not you are economically active. There are no specific restrictions in the UK benefit rules that exclude EEA nationals from entitlement to child benefit, CTC and health in pregnancy grants. They must simply have a right to reside, which they do. After this initial three-month period, however, you lose the right of residence unless you take up some economic activity. You also, therefore, lose entitlement to child benefit, CTC and health in pregnancy grants. If you do not notify HM Revenue and Customs that the three-month period has ended, you may have an overpayment of benefit, which you will have to repay.

Who has a right to reside

Whether or not you have a right to reside is a matter of law and fact, and depends on your immigration status and nationality.

This makes the right to reside test a very complex area of law because a person's immigration status is not always apparent and, in order to make accurate decisions, it is essential to have at least a basic understanding of both UK immigration law and of EU law. Some people automatically have a right to reside – eg, British citizens. Others have a right of residence under UK law and some people have a right that stems directly from EU law. For full details of who has a right to reside, see the relevant immigration chapter and Chapter 13.

British and Irish nationals, and Commonwealth citizens with the right of abode

British citizens have an automatic right of residence in the UK. Irish nationals and nationals of other countries in the common travel area have a right of residence under the UK Immigration Rules and, therefore, should not be affected by the right to reside test. Commonwealth citizens with the right of abode also have a right of residence in the UK.

People with indefinite leave, discretionary leave or humanitarian protection

A person with indefinite leave or a form of discretionary leave has a right of residence under the UK Immigration Rules and therefore has a right to reside.

People with limited leave or no leave

A person who has limited leave under the UK Immigration Rules (eg, as a spouse or a visitor) has a right of residence during that period. However, s/he is unlikely to be able to qualify for benefits, as s/he will probably be defined as a 'person subject to immigration control' (see p56).

People with deemed residence

For all the benefits affected by the right to reside test, apart from child benefit, CTC and health in pregnancy grants, UK legislation treats you as having the right to reside if you:
- are an EEA national who is a 'worker' or a 'self-employed person' (see p229);
- are an EEA national who retains the status of 'worker' or 'self-employed' person (see p231);
- are the family member (see p103) of an EEA national in either of the above two groups;
- are someone with a permanent right of residence as a former worker or self-employed person who has retired or is permanently incapacitated, or you are the family member of such a person;
- are a refugee;
- have leave outside the rules (this includes exceptional leave to enter or remain and humanitarian protection);

- have been deported, expelled or otherwise legally removed from another country to the UK (but this does not apply to anyone who is a 'person subject to immigration control' – see p56);
- left Montserrat after 1 November 1995 because of the volcanic eruption;
- left Zimbabwe to come to the UK after 28 February 2009 but before 18 March 2011 and you have received assistance from the UK government to settle in the UK;
- for HB and CTB only, receive IS, income-based JSA, PC or income-related ESA.

European Economic Area nationals

There are different types of residence for EEA nationals depending on how long a person has been in the UK and what s/he is doing here. An EEA national can have an initial right of residence as soon as s/he enters the UK, an extended right of residence generally only if s/he becomes economically active, and a permanent right of residence usually after s/he (or a family member) has been economically active for five years after entering the UK. It is also possible to retain residence if you or a family member stop being economically active.

For more details of the right of residence of EEA nationals, see Chapter 13.

Notes

2. The different residence tests

1 R(S) 1/66
2 Reg 2(1)(a)(i) SS(AA) Regs
3 Reg 9(1)(a) SS(ICA) Regs
4 Reg 23 CB Regs
5 Reg 2(1)(a)(i) SS(DLA) Regs
6 Reg 2(1)(a)(i) SS(AA) Regs
7 Reg 9(1)(a) SS(ICA) Regs
8 Reg 23 CB Regs
9 Reg 3(1) TC(R) Regs
10 Reg 2(1)(a)(i) SS(DLA) Regs
11 Reg 16 SS(IB) Regs
12 Reg 11(1)(a) ESA Regs
13 Reg 4 HPG(EA) Regs
14 Reg 10(b) SS(WB&RP) Regs
15 Reg 3(1) TC(R) Regs
16 *R v Barnet LBC ex parte Shah aka Akbarali v Brent LBC* [1983] 2 AC 309, HL, Lord Scarman at p343H
17 *R v Barnet LBC ex parte Shah aka Akbarali v Brent LBC* [1983] 2 AC 309, HL, Lord Scarman at p344G

18 R(M) 1/85
19 *Levene v Inland Revenue Commissioners* [1928] AC 217, HL
20 *Levene v Inland Revenue Commissioners* [1928] AC 217, HL; *Inland Revenue Commissioners v Lysaght* [1928] AC 234, HL
21 For example, Mr Lysaght was found to be ordinarily resident in England even though he was clearly also ordinarily resident in the Irish Free State.
22 *R v Barnet LBC ex parte Shah aka Akbarali v Brent LBC* [1983] 2 AC 309, HL, Lord Scarman at p345E-H
23 R(F) 1/62

24 *Macrae v Macrae* [1949] 2 All ER 34 (CA).
The countries were Scotland and
England which are separate for family
law purposes. In R(IS) 6/96 para 27 the
commissioner doubts the correctness of
Macrae because he considers it used a
test very close to the 'real home' test
rejected in *Shah*. He does not seem to
have heard any argument about this:
Macrae was cited in *Shah* and was not
one of the cases mentioned there as
wrong: pp342-43.

25 *Lewis v Lewis* [1956] 1 All ER 375

26 The facts are in the Court of Appeal's
judgment: *R v Barnet LBC ex parte Shah*
[1982] QB 688 at p717E

27 *R v Barnet LBC ex parte Shah aka Akbarali
v Brent LBC* [1983] 2 AC 309, HL, Lord
Scarman at p344C-D. In R(F) 1/62
education was the purpose.

28 *Levene v Inland Revenue Commissioners*
[1928] AC 217, HL

29 For example, Mr Macrae's decision to
move to Scotland was made shortly
before he went.

30 *R v Barnet LBC ex parte Shah aka Akbarali
v Brent LBC* [1983] 2 AC 309, HL

31 *R v Barnet LBC ex parte Shah aka Akbarali
v Brent LBC* [1983] 2 AC 309, HL, Lord
Scarman at p344G

32 R(F) 1/82; R(F) 1/62; R(P) 1/62; R(P) 4/
54

33 *R v Barnet LBC ex parte Shah aka Akbarali
v Brent LBC* [1983] 2 AC 309, HL

34 *Inland Revenue Commissioners v Lysaght*
[1928] AC 234, HL

35 In *Re Mackenzie* [1941] 1 Chancery
Reports 69

36 *Gout v Cimitian* [1922] 1 AC 105, PC:
deportation of an Ottoman subject from
Egypt did not stop him becoming
ordinarily resident in Cyprus

37 *Re A (A Minor) (Abduction: Child's
Objections)* [1994] 2 FLR 126, CA: on
habitual residence, but also applies to
ordinary residence

38 *Re M (Minors) (Residence Order:
Jurisdiction)* [1993] 1 FLR 495, CA: on
habitual residence, but also applies to
ordinary residence

39 *Re M (Minors) (Residence Order:
Jurisdiction)* [1993] 1 FLR 495, CA: on
habitual residence, but also applies to
ordinary residence

40 *Re J (A Minor) (Abduction: Custody Rights)*
[1990] 2 AC 562 at 578

41 *Re M (Minors: Residence Order:
Jurisdiction)* [1993] 1 FLR 495, CA

42 *Re A (A Minor) (Abduction: Acquiescence)*
[1992] 2 FLR 14, CA: on habitual
residence, but also applies to ordinary
residence

43 R(F) 1/62; R(M) 1/85

44 *Hopkins v Hopkins* [1951] P 116; *R v
Hussain* [1971] 56 Crim App R 165, CA;
R v IAT ex parte Ng [1986] Imm AR 23,
QBD

45 *R v Barnet LBC ex parte Shah aka Akbarali
v Brent LBC* [1983] 2 AC 309, HL

46 *Levene v Inland Revenue Commissioners*
[1928] AC 217, HL; *Inland Revenue
Commissioners v Lysaght* [1928] AC 234,
HL

47 *R v Barnet LBC ex parte Shah aka Akbarali
v Brent LBC* [1983] 2 AC 309, HL, Lord
Scarman at p342D

48 *Stransky v Stransky* [1954] 3 WLR 123,
[1954] 2 All ER 536

49 *Haria* [1986] Imm AR 165, UKIAT

50 *Chief Adjudication Officer v Ahmed and
others*, 16 March 1994, CA, *The
Guardian*, 15 April 1994

51 *Chief Adjudication Officer v Ahmed and
others*, 16 March 1994, CA, *The
Guardian*, 15 April 1994

52 R(U) 16/62

53 *Chief Adjudication Officer v Ahmed and
others*, 16 March 1994, CA, *The
Guardian*, 15 April 1994

54 R(I) 73/54

55 R(S) 1/85

56 R(S) 1/66

3. **Residence and presence rules for
individual benefits**

57 s124(1) SSCBA 1992

58 Reg 4(1), (2)(a) and (b) and (3)(a) and
(b) IS Regs

59 Reg 4(2)(c) and Sch 1B IS Regs

60 Reg 4(3) IS Regs

61 Sch 3 para 3(10) IS Regs

62 **IS** Sch 3 para 3(11) IS Regs
JSA Sch 2 para 3(10) and (11) JSA Regs

63 s124(1) SSCBA 1992

64 Reg 50 JSA Regs

65 Reg 50(2)(a), (3)(c) and (5)(c) JSA Regs

66 Reg 50(2)-(6) JSA Regs

67 s1(2)(a) and (c) JSA 1995

68 Regs 14, 19 and 50 JSA Regs

69 Regs 14(1)(m), 19(1)(m) and 50(6)(c)
JSA Regs

70 Reg 14(1)(c) JSA Regs

71 Reg 50(2)(c), (3)(b) and (5)(b) JSA Regs

72 Reg 50(6)(b) and (d) JSA Regs

73 Reg 50(5)(d) and (e) JSA Regs

74 Regs 14(1)(e) and (g) and 19(1)(e) and (g) JSA Regs
75 Reg 19(1)(e) and (g) JSA Regs
76 Reg 170 JSA Regs
77 Reg 50(1) and (4) JSA Regs
78 Reg 19(1)(p)(ii) JSA Regs
79 Sch 2 para 3(10) JSA Regs
80 s124(1) SSCBA 1992
81 Reg 152 ESA Regs
82 Reg 154 ESA Regs
83 Sch 6 para 5(10) ESA Regs
84 s124(1) SSCBA 1992
85 Reg 3 SPC Regs
86 Reg 4 SPC Regs
87 Reg 4 SPC Regs
88 s124(1) SSCBA 1992
89 Reg 7(13) and (17) HB Regs; reg 7(13) and (17) HB(SPC) Regs
90 Reg 7 HB Regs; reg 7(13) and (17) HB(SPC) Regs
91 Reg 7(17) HB Regs; reg 7(17) HB(SPC) Regs
92 For further details of who is treated as occupying a dwelling, see CPAG's *Welfare Benefits and Tax Credits Handbook.*
93 *R v HBRB ex parte Robertson* [1988] *The Independent,* 5 March 1988
94 Reg 7 HB Regs; reg 7 HB(SPC) Regs
95 *R v Penwith DC ex parte Burt* [1990] 22 HLR 292 at 296, QB
96 s130(1) SSCBA 1992; reg 7 HB Regs; reg 7 HB(SPC) Regs
97 Reg 7 HB Regs; reg 7 HB(SPC) Regs
98 para A3.15 GM
99 s124(1) SSCBA 1992
100 s131(3)(a) SSCBA 1992
101 s6(5) Local Government Finance Act 1992; s99(1) Local Government Finance (Scotland) Act 1992
102 Reg 8(3) CTB Regs; reg 8(3) CTB(SPC) Regs
103 Art 3 Council Tax (Exempt Dwellings) Order 1992, No.558
104 Reg 4 TC(R) Regs
105 s3 TCA 2002
106 s146 SSCBA 1992
107 Reg 23(1) CB Regs
108 Reg 23(4) CB Regs
109 Reg 24 CB Regs
110 Reg 24 CB Regs
111 Reg 21 CB Regs
112 Reg 21(1)(b)(i) CB Regs
113 Art 77 EU Reg 1408/71
114 Reg 3 Guardian's Allowance Up-rating Order 2009, No.797
115 Reg 9 GA(Gen) Regs
116 ss1(2)(d)(i) and 2 JSA 1995
117 s21 and Sch 1 para 11 JSA 1995; regs 14, 19 and 50 JSA Regs
118 Reg 11(1A) SSB(PA) Regs, as amended
119 EU Reg 1408/71
120 SI (2) WRA 2007
121 In order to qualify as a member of the family you must be the spouse, civil partner, son, daughter, stepson, stepdaughter, father, father-in-law, stepfather, mother, mother-in-law or stepmother of the person serving in the forces – see reg 2(5)(b) SSB(PA) Regs
122 Reg 2(1), (1A) and (1B) SSB(PA) Regs
123 Reg 2(1)(a) SSB(PA) Regs
124 Reg 2(1) SSB(PA) Regs
125 R(S) 2/86 and R(S) 1/90
126 R(S) 10/51
127 R(S) 1/69; R(S) 2/69; R(S) 4/80; R(S) 6/81
128 s94(1) SSCBA 1992
129 Reg 3 Social Security Benefit (Persons Abroad) Amendment Regulations 1994, No.268, which preserve the form of SSB(PA) Regs in force before 8 March 1994 for such people.
130 Reg 11(2) SSB(PA) Regs
131 Reg 5(3)(a) and (aa), (5) and (6) SSB(PA) Regs. These only disqualify where the husband/former partner is not ordinarily resident in Great Britain.
132 Reg 5(7) SSB(PA) Regs
133 Reg 10 SS(WB&RP) Regs
134 Reg 4(1) SSB(PA) Regs
135 Reg 4(3), (4), (5)(c) and (6) SSB(PA) Regs
136 *Carson, R (on the application of) v SSWP* [2005] UKHL 37; *Casewell v Secretary of State for the Home Department* [2008] EWCA Civ 210
137 Reg 5(3)(a), (aa) and (6) SSB(PA) Regs
138 Reg 8(1) SSB(PA) Regs
139 Reg 4(a) SSB(PA) Regs
140 Reg 4 SSB(PA) Regs; s1(2)(a) SSAA 1992; reg 19(2) and (3) SS(C&P) Regs
141 Reg 19(3A) SS(C&P) Regs
142 ss3 and 4 SSAA 1992
143 ss39A(3), 81(2) and (3) SSCBA 1992
144 ss94(1), 108 and 109 SSCBA 1992
145 s94(5) SSCBA 1992
146 Reg 9(3) and (7) SSB(PA) Regs
147 s172(a) SSCBA 1992
148 s94(5) SSCBA 1992
149 s109(1) SSCBA 1992; reg 14 SS(IIPD) Regs
150 ss109(2)(a), 117, 119 and 120 SSCBA 1992

151 Reg 2(1) SS(IIMB) Regs; reg 2(1) SS(IIAB) Regs. For the meaning of 'mariner' and 'airman' see regs 4-7 and Sch 2 SS(EEEIIP) Regs

152 Reg 2(2) SS(IIMB) Regs

153 Reg 2(2) SS(IIAB) Regs

154 Regs 3, 4, 6 and 8 SS(IIMB) Regs; regs 3 and 6 SS(IIAB) Regs

155 Reg 10C(5) and (6) SSB(PA) Regs

156 Reg 2 and Sch 1 SS(NIRA) Regs

157 Reg 11(2) and (2A) SSB(PA) Regs

158 Reg 9(4) SSB(PA) Regs

159 Reg 9(4) SSB(PA) Regs

160 Reg 9(5) SSB(PA) Regs

161 Reg 9(5) SSB(PA) Regs

162 Reg 9(5)(a)-(c) SSB(PA) Regs

163 Reg 5(b) SS(IIMB) Regs; for the meaning of 'mariner' and 'airman' see regs 4-7 and Sch II SS(EEEIIP) Regs

164 **DLA** Reg 2(1) SS(DLA) Regs
    AA Reg 2(1) SS(AA) Regs

165 **DLA** Reg 2(1) SS(DLA) Regs
    AA Reg 2(1) SS(AA) Regs

166 **DLA** Reg 2(4) SS(DLA) Regs
    AA Reg 2(3) SS(AA) Regs

167 **DLA** Reg 2(1) SS(DLA) Regs
    AA Reg 2(1) SS(AA) Regs

168 **DLA** Reg 2(2) SS(DLA) Regs
    AA Reg 2(2) SS(AA) Regs

169 Regs 112 and 118 SS(Con) Regs

170 s120 SSCBA 1992; reg 114 SS(Con) Regs

171 **DLA** Reg 2(4) SS(DLA) Regs
    AA Reg 2(3) SS(AA) Regs

172 Reg 2(5) SS(DLA) Regs

173 R(A) 1/94

174 Reg 2(6) SS(DLA) Regs

175 **DLA** Reg 2(2)(d) SS(DLA) Regs
    AA Reg 2(2)(d) SS(AA) Regs
    Reg 10 SSB(PA) Regs

176 **DLA** Reg 2(2)(e) SS(DLA) Regs
    AA Reg 2(2)(e) SS(AA) Regs
    Reg 10 SSB(PA) Regs

177 **DLA** Reg 2(2)(a)-(c) SS(DLA) Regs
    AA Reg 2(2)(a)-(c) SS(AA) Regs

178 **DLA** Reg 2(1)(a)(iii) and (2) SS(DLA) Regs
    AA Regs 1(a) and 2(1)(a)(iii) and (2) SS(AA) Regs

179 Reg 3 SS(DLA) Regs

180 Reg 9 SS(ICA) Regs

181 Reg 9(2) SS(ICA) Regs; reg 10B SSB(PA) Regs

182 CG/15/1993

183 Regs 4(2) and 9(2) SS(ICA) Regs

184 **SSP** ss151(1) and 163(1) SSCBA 1992
    SMP ss164(1) and 171(1) SSCBA 1992
    SPP ss171ZA(1) and 171ZJ(2) SSCBA 1992
    SAP ss171ZL(1) and 171ZS(2) SSCBA 1992
    All definition of 'employee'

185 **SSP** Reg 5 SSP(MAPA) Regs
    SMP Reg 2 SMP(PAM) Regs
    SPP/SAP Reg 3 SPPSAP(PAM) Regs

186 **SSP** Regs 4 and 8 SSP(MAPA) Regs
    SMP Reg 8 SMP(PAM) Regs
    SPP/SAP Reg 9 SPPSAP(PAM) Regs
    All s120 SSCBA 1992; reg 76 SS(Con) Regs

187 **SSP** Reg 6 SSP(MAPA) Regs
    SMP Reg 7 SMP(PAM) Regs
    SPP/SAP Reg 8 SPPSAP(PAM) Regs
    All Reg 81 SS(Con) Regs

188 Reg 7 SSP(MAPA) Regs

189 **SSP** Regs 6 and 7 SSP(MAPA) Regs
    SMP Reg 7 SMP(PAM) Regs
    SPP/SAP Reg 8 SPPSAP(PAM) Regs

190 **SSP** Reg 10 SSP(MAPA) Regs
    SMP Reg 2A SMP(PAM) Regs
    SPP/SAP Reg 4 SPPSAP(PAM) Regs

191 These rules changed on 6 April 1996 (SSP) and 18 August 1996 (SMP). Before then, entitlement normally ended when you were absent from the EU: reg 10(1) SSP(MAPA) Regs, reg 9(1) SMP(PAM) Regs before amendment.

192 **SSP** Reg 16(2) SSP Regs
    SMP Reg 17(3) SMP Regs
    SPP/SAP Reg 32 SPPSAP(G) Regs

193 Reg 145(1)(b) SS(Con) Regs

194 **SSP** Reg 14 SSP(MAPA) Regs
    SMP Reg 6 SMP(PAM) Regs
    SPP/SAP Reg 7 SPPSAP(PAM) Regs

195 ss35(2) and 165 SSCBA 1992

196 s2(1)(a) and (b) SSCBA 1992

197 Reg 2 Social Security (Maternity Allowance)(Work Abroad) Regulations 1987

198 Reg 5(1)(a) SFM&FE Regs

199 Reg 5(1)(b) SFM&FE Regs

200 Regs 3 and 5(1)(b) SFM&FE Regs

201 Reg 5(3) SFM&FE Regs

202 Reg 5(1)(c) SFM&FE Regs

203 Reg 7(3) and (4) SFM&FE Regs

204 Reg 7(7) and (8) SFM&FE Regs

205 Reg 7(9)(b) SFM&FE Regs

206 Reg 7(5) SFM&FE Regs

207 Reg 7(1A) SFM&FE Regs

208 Reg 1A SFCWP Regs

209 Reg 2(a) SFCWP Regs

210 Reg 4(2) SFCWP Regs

211 SF Dirs 23(1)(a) and 29

212 SF Dir 25
213 SF Dir 4(a)(I)
214 *R v SFI ex parte Amina Mohammed* [1992] *The Times,* 25 November 1992
215 SF Dirs 14-17
216 SF Dir 16(b)

4. **How a family member abroad affects benefit**

217 Reg 16(1)-(3) IS Regs; reg 78(1)-(3) JSA Regs. Only the rules relevant to partners abroad are dealt with here.
218 Reg 16(2)(a) IS Regs; reg 78(2)(a) JSA Regs. Either person's lack of intention counts because the rules refer to the 'person who is living away from the other members of his family' and each partner is living away from the other.
219 See CIS/508/1992 and CIS/484/1993 on a similarly worded IS housing costs rule: now Sch 3 para 3(10) IS Regs
220 **IS** Reg 16(1) IS Regs
JSA Reg 78(1) JSA Regs
ESA Reg 156 ESA Regs
Compare with the pre-4 October 1993 version of reg 16(1) IS Regs which refers to absence from the home.
221 **IS** Reg 1 IS Regs
JSA Reg 1 JSA Regs
ESA Reg 156 ESA Regs
PC Reg 1 SPC Regs
HB Reg 2 HB Regs; reg 2 HB(SPC) Regs
CTB Reg 2 CTB Regs; reg 2 CTB (SPC) Regs
222 *Santos v Santos* [1972] 2 All ER 246, CA
223 R(SB) 8/85
224 R(SB) 4/83
225 CIS/671/1992
226 **IS** Reg 16(2) IS Regs
JSA Reg 78(1) JSA Regs
ESA Reg 156 ESA Regs
All The rules say 'resume living with'
227 **IS** Reg 16 IS Regs
JSA Reg 78 JSA Regs
ESA Reg 156 ESA Regs
228 **IS** Reg 21(1) and Sch 7 paras 11 and 11A IS Regs
JSA Reg 85(1) and Sch 5 paras 10 and 11 JSA Regs
ESA Reg 69 and Sch 5 ESA Regs
229 **IS** Reg 16(1) IS Regs
JSA Reg 78(1) JSA Regs
ESA Reg 156 ESA Regs
230 **IS** Reg 21(1) and Sch 7 paras 11 and 11A IS Regs
JSA Reg 85(1) and Sch 5 paras 10 and 11 JSA Regs

231 **HB** Schs 5 para 4 and 6 para 5 HB Regs
CTB Schs 4 para 4 and 5 para 5 CTB Regs
232 **HB** Reg 21(1) and (2) HB Regs; reg 21(1) and (2) HB(SPC) Regs
CTB Reg 11(1) and (2) CTB Regs; reg 11(1) and (2) CTB(SPC) Regs
233 s136(1) SSCBA 1992
234 **HB** Reg 22(a) and Sch 3 para 1 HB Regs; reg 21(1)(a) and Sch 3 HB(SPC) Regs
CTB Reg 12(a) and Sch 1 para 1 CTB Regs; reg 12(1)(a) CTB(SPC) regs
These apply because you still count as a couple.
235 **HB** Sch 3 para 3 HB Regs; Sch 3 para 3 HB(SPC) Regs
CTB Sch 1 para 3 CTB Regs; Sch 1 para 3 CTB(SPC) regs
236 para A3.16 GM
237 These comments do not apply to arrears.
238 Reg 51(3) CTB Regs: reg 51(4) will no longer apply. Every liable resident of a dwelling is jointly and severally (ie, collectively and individually) liable to pay all the council tax. If there are two or more people liable for council tax on your accommodation, your CTB is worked out on the basis that the total liability is divided equally between them.
239 Reg 4 TC(R) Regs
240 Regs 10(2)(c) and (3) and 12 and Sch 2 para 7(b)(iv) SSB(Dep) Regs; reg 14 SS(IB-ID) Regs. The general disqualification in s113 SSCBA 1992 does not apply to adult dependant increases.
241 Reg 2(4) SSB(PRT) Regs
242 CSS/18/1988
243 CS/15000/1996
244 **IS** Reg 17(b) IS Regs
JSA Reg 83(b) JSA Regs
245 s137(1)(b) and (c) SSCBA 1992, definition of 'family'; s35(1)(b) and (c) JSA 1995, definition of 'family'
246 **IS** Reg 16(5)(a)(i) and (aa)(i) and (5A) IS Regs
JSA Reg 78(5)(a)(i) and (b)(i) and (6) JSA Regs
247 **HB** Reg 22(b) HB Regs; reg 22(1)(b) HB(SPC) Regs
CTB Reg 12(b) CTB Regs; reg 12(1)(b) CTB(SPC) Regs
248 s137(1)(b) and (c) SSCBA 1992, definition of 'family'

249 Reg 21(1)-(3) HB Regs; reg 21 HB(SPC) Regs. Only the rules relevant to partners abroad are dealt with here.
250 Reg 3 CTC Regs
251 s3(3) TCA 2002; reg 3 TC(R) Regs

5. Habitual residence
252 *Couronne amd Ors v SSWP* [2007] EWCA Civ 1086 recently considered whether the test unlawfully discriminated against British citizens from the Chagos Islands compared with British citizens of Irish ethnic or national origin either under the Race Relations Act or the Human Rights Act. The Court held that it was not unlawful for the habitual residence test to be applied to them.
253 **IS** Reg 21(3) IS Regs, 'person from abroad'
JSA Reg 85(4) JSA Regs, 'person from abroad'
PC Reg 2 SPC Regs
HB Reg 10 HB Regs; reg 10 HB(SPC) Regs
CTB Reg 7 CTB Regs; reg 7 CTB(SPC) Regs
254 Reg 21AA IS Regs
255 Reg 85A JSA Regs
256 Reg 10 HB Regs; reg 10 HB(SPC) Regs
257 Reg 7 CTB Regs; reg 7 CTB(SPC) Regs
258 Reg 2 SPC Regs
259 Reg 2 SPC Regs
260 **HB** Reg 10 HB Regs; reg 10 HB(SPC) regs
CTB Reg 7(4)(k) CTB Regs; reg 7 CTB(SPC) Regs
261 *Nessa v Chief Adjudication Officer* [1999] UKHL 41 (R(IS) 2/00)
262 *Re F (A Minor) (Child Abduction)* [1994]; R(IS) 2/00
263 R(IS) 2/00, para 24; *Cameron v Cameron* [1996] SLT 306
264 R(IS) 2/00, para 26
265 R(IS) 2/00
266 R(IS) 2/00
267 R(IS) 6/96, para 19
268 *M v M (Abduction: England and Scotland)* [1997] 2 FLR 263, CA
269 R(IS) 6/96, paras 28-30; R(IS) 2/00, para 28
270 R(IS) 2/00, para 30
271 R(IS) 6/96, para 15
272 *Nessa v Chief Adjudication Officer* [1999] UKHL 41
273 R(IS) 6/96
274 CIS/4474/2003
275 CIS/1304/97 and CJSA/5394/98
276 CIS/376/2002

277 R(IS) 6/96
278 Art 10A(1) EU Reg 1408/71
279 Art 1(h) EU Reg 1408/71
280 R(U) 7/85; R(U) 8/88 and the cases listed in that case
281 *Di Paolo* C-76/76, 17 February 1977, unreported (ECJ)
282 *Swaddling v Chief Adjudication Officer* C-90/97 [1999] 2 CMLR 679 (ECJ)
283 *Swaddling v Chief Adjudication Officer* C-90/97 [1999] 2 CMLR 679 (ECJ)
284 para 30
285 R(IS) 3/00, para 16
286 Under Art 10a(2) EU Reg 1408/71. This argument was mentioned but not resolved in R(IS) 3/00.
287 See, for example, *Collins v SSWP* C-138/02 [2006] ECR 1-02703 (ECJ)

6. The right to reside
288 Reg 6(1) SS(HR)A Regs preserved by Reg 11(2) SS(PA)A Regs
289 CIS/1096/2007
290 Reg 10A ESA(TP)(EA) Regs
291 **IS** Reg 21AA(3) IS Regs
ESA Reg 70(3) ESA Regs
PC Reg 2(3) SPC Regs
HB Reg 10(3A) HB Regs; reg 10(4) HB(SPC) Regs
CTB Reg 7(4) CTB Regs; reg 7(4) CTB(SPC) Regs
292 Reg 21 CB Regs; reg 3 TC(R) Regs

Chapter 9

. . . .

Claims and getting paid

This chapter covers:
1. Introduction (below)
2. National insurance numbers (below)
3. National insurance contributions (p131)
4. Proving your immigration status, age and relationships (p134)
5. Getting paid if you go abroad (p137)
6. Other sources of help (p139)

1. **Introduction**

All benefits have rules about claims and payments that affect all claimants. However, these rules can cause particular problems if you are a migrant, and you may have more difficulty than other claimants in making a claim for benefit.

In order to claim most social security benefits and tax credits:
- you must be able to satisfy the national insurance (NI) number requirement. This means that you have to provide your NI number or evidence for one to be allocated for yourself and your partner (see below);
- for contribution-based benefits, you must satisfy the NI contribution conditions for the particular benefit concerned (see p131);
- you must provide evidence of your identity and circumstances. This could include evidence of your immigration or residence status (see p134).

For more information about claiming benefits and tax credits and getting paid, see CPAG's *Welfare Benefits and Tax Credits Handbook*.

2. **National insurance numbers**

In general, in order to be entitled to any social security benefit or tax credit, you must satisfy the national insurance (NI) number requirement.[1]

This means you must:
- provide an NI number, together with evidence to show that the number is the one allocated to you; *or*

- provide evidence or information to enable your NI number to be traced; *or*
- apply for an NI number and provide sufficient information or evidence for one to be allocated.

The requirement applies when you make a claim for benefit. It also applies if someone, who will be included in an existing award of benefit, joins your family – eg, if your spouse joins you from abroad.[2]

The requirement must be satisfied for you and also for your partner if you are claiming benefits as a couple.[3] This is the case, even if you are not going to receive any extra benefit for her/him because s/he is a 'person subject to immigration control' for benefit purposes.[4] See below for when your partner does not have to satisfy the NI number requirement.

If you have an NI number, the requirement is met if you provide that NI number and sufficient evidence of your identity to show that this is the number allocated to you. If you are claiming a means-tested benefit or tax credits as a couple, you must show this is the case for both you and your partner.

Difficulties often arise for migrants who may not yet have been allocated a number. In these situations, the requirement is satisfied if anyone who must have an NI number has made an application for one and provided sufficient evidence to enable one to be allocated. See below for how to apply.

Sometimes there can be delays because of the NI number requirement (see p129). If you are refused benefit because you do not to satisfy the NI number requirement, see p130.

Who is exempt

You do not need to satisfy the NI number requirement:

- if you are under 16 and you are claiming disability living allowance or a health in pregnancy grant;[5]
- for stautory adoption pay, statutory maternity pay, statutory paternity pay, statutory sick pay or a social fund payment;[6]
- for housing benefit if you live in a hostel;[7]
- for tax credits if you have a 'reasonable excuse' for failing to satisfy the requirement.[8]

In addition, you do not need to satisfy the NI number requirement for your partner if:[9]

- s/he is a 'person subject to immigration control' because s/he needs leave to enter or remain in the United Kingdom (UK) and does not have it (see p55); *and*
- s/he has not previously been given an NI number.

How to apply for a national insurance number

The Departmental Central Index (DCI), which is part of the Department for Work and Pensions (DWP), allocates all NI numbers.

NI numbers are allocated automatically to children shortly before their 16th birthday, but only if child benefit is being claimed for them. If child benefit was being claimed for you when you were that age, you should have an NI number.

If you have been allocated an NI number but do not know what it is, or if you want written confirmation of your NI number, you should complete Form CA5403 and send it to HM Revenue and Customs (the Revenue).

If you have not been allocated an NI number, you can apply for one by contacting your local Jobcentre Plus office. However, you will probably not be allocated an NI number unless it is decided that you need one for either employment or benefit purposes.

A claim for benefit, or an application for a supersession of an award of benefit (eg, when a person joins your family who does not have an NI number) should be treated as an application for an NI number. The local authority, DWP office or Revenue should complete Form DCI1 and send it to the DCI.[10] However, if you, or a family member for whom you are claiming benefit, does not have an NI number and you make a claim for benefits or notify a change of circumstances, it is advisable to state clearly on the form or letter that you wish to apply for an NI number.

When the DCI receives Form DCI1 it will carry out a number of checks to ensure that you do not already have an NI number. It should then contact you to arrange an interview at the local DWP office. This is called an 'evidence of identity interview'.

You should be told what documents you will need to take to this interview. It is important to take as many as possible that establish your identity. Documents could include:[11]

- valid passport (although an expired passport may also help);
- standard acknowledgement letter issued by the UK Border Agency (UKBA);
- application registration card issued by the UKBA to asylum seekers;
- identity card issued by a European Economic Area state;
- UK residence permit;
- full driving licence;
- local authority rent book/card;
- council tax documents;
- life assurance/insurance policies;
- mortgage repayment documents;
- recently paid fuel/telephone bills in your name;
- original marriage certificate;
- original birth/adoption certificate;
- divorce/annulment papers;
- wage slip from a recent employer;
- trade union membership card;
- travel pass with photograph affixed;

- vehicle registration/motor insurance documents;
- work permit.

These are only some of the documents that you can use to prove your identity. If you have other documents, not in the above list, these may also help. Photocopies of documents can be relied on to establish your identity, but you should bring originals if you have them. If not, you should explain why you do not have the original documents.

If you do not have any documents, you should explain why this is. If some of your documents are with the UKBA, you should explain this and, if possible, provide proof of this in the form of a solicitor's letter or by providing some other evidence. The DWP should not ask you to provide documents which you obviously do not possess.

At the interview, you will be asked to complete Form CA5400. The DWP may also ask you to complete a form allowing it to contact third parties to establish your identity.

Interpreters are not normally provided at these interviews.

Guidance states that you should be issued an NI number after your interview in a benefit-inspired application, unless you:[12]

- have produced identity documents that are not genuine;
- have been unable to prove your identity;
- failed to agree to the DWP contacting third parties to establish your identity; *or*
- do not, in the DWP's view, require an NI number.

Delays

Payment of benefit can often be delayed because you (or your partner) need to apply for an NI number.

If it is a new claim for benefit, you may be able to obtain interim payments (or payments on account in housing benefit (HB) cases). There is no right of appeal against a refusal to make interim payments, but you may be able to seek judicial review against such a decision. Specialist advice is needed for this.

If there is a supersession of your benefit when a new family member joins your household and s/he does not have an NI number, your benefit may be suspended. You can argue that payment of your benefit should not be suspended in these circumstances, particularly if it is obvious that the NI number requirement is likely to be met and the only factor is a question of time. Again, the only remedy against a suspension is judicial review.

You may be able to get a crisis loan from the social fund if you are waiting for an NI number issue to be resolved.

If a national insurance number is refused

You cannot appeal directly against a decision not to allocate you an NI number.[13] However, you can appeal against any decision refusing benefit because the NI number requirement is not met. In the appeal you can argue that the NI number requirement was met.

Usually, if benefit is refused because the benefit authority says the NI number requirement is not met, the issue in dispute will be whether you applied for an NI number and provided sufficient information or evidence to enable a number to be allocated, even if the benefit authority has not considered this point.[14] Even if you have been refused an NI number, it is possible to argue successfully that you did provide sufficient information to enable one to be allocated.[15]

When you appeal against a decision that raises the issue of whether or not you have applied for an NI number and whether your application was accompanied by sufficient information or evidence to enable one to be allocated, an important issue is whether your application counts as having been legally made. The law about this is not clear. One decision suggests it is *not* made until you attend the interview,[16] but another says that the application is made when the application for benefit is made and that documents provided at the interview are not counted as part of the application.[17] The DWP takes the view that the application is made when the claim for benefit is made, but is completed at the interview.[18]

Which of these different views is correct is important because:
- if the application is made when the benefit claim is made, then if you did not attend the interview (or were not invited to one), you may still have met the NI number requirement; *but*
- if the application is not completed until the interview and you have not provided evidence of your identity until the interview, you may still meet the requirement.

Depending on your situation, you might want to argue that any of these views is correct.

Note: if the evidence and/or information you provide in support of your application indicates that documents showing your identity are with the UKBA, this may be sufficient to meet the NI number requirement.[19]

Other remedies

If you are refused an NI number, you can write to your MP and ask her/him to help. Your MP can also make a complaint to the Parliamentary and Health Service Ombudsman on your behalf. See CPAG's *Welfare Benefits and Tax Credits Handbook* for more information.

Problems with NI numbers also raise issues about race discrimination since, in practice, the NI number requirement often prejudices black and minority ethnic communities. You may therefore want to make reference to the DWP's equal opportunities policy when you contact it.[20] The Equality and Human Rights Commission may also be able to take up the issue.

Couples with different immigration statuses

A problem can arise in the case of a couple, where the two partners have different immigration statuses. The partner who is not a 'person subject to immigration control' (see p56) may find that s/he is refused benefit because her/his partner does not have, and is unable to obtain, an NI number. This may be incompatible with Article 8 of the European Convention on Human Rights (the right to respect for family life) because the only way in which the settled person can obtain benefit is to separate from her/his partner. A number of legal challenges have been started on this point, but before any case has reached the courts, the DWP has resolved the matter favourably towards the claimant. If you are in this situation, get specialist advice.

3. **National insurance contributions**

Many benefits are paid from the national insurance (NI) contributions of employees, employers, the self-employed and other people who choose to make them.

There are six types or classes of contribution payable:[21]

- Class 1, paid by employed earners and their employers;
- Class 1A and 1B, paid by employers of employed earners;
- Class 2, paid by self-employed earners;
- Class 3, paid by voluntary contributors;
- Class 4, paid by self-employed earners.

You will only have to pay NI contributions in the United Kingdom (UK) if you are treated as present and resident in the UK (see p71) and if your earnings are high enough for you and your employer to pay contributions. The type of NI contributions you pay depends on what you are doing in the UK. If contributions are not compulsory, you can choose to pay voluntary Class 2 or 3 contributions to help you meet the contribution conditions for benefits.

Contributions are collected and recorded by HM Revenue and Customs (the Revenue).

Contributions paid in Northern Ireland or the Isle of Man count towards British benefits. You may also be able to use special rules if you have lived in another European Economic Area (EEA) member state (see p177) or a country with which the UK has a reciprocal agreement (see Chapter 14) even if you are not a national of that country.

An EEA national may be able to rely on contributions made in other EEA states in order to qualify for contributory benefits in the UK. This is because European

Union social security rules allow EEA nationals to aggregate contributions paid in any member state in order to qualify for benefits in another member state (see p177 for full details).

If you wish to pay UK NI contributions while abroad, the application form is in the Department for Work and Pensions leaflet NI38.

Class 1 contributions

You are liable for Class 1 contributions in any week in which you are:
- employed in Great Britain;[22] *and either*
  - resident or present in Great Britain; *or*
  - ordinarily resident in Great Britain.[23]

There is an exception to this rule if you are not ordinary resident in the UK, are employed by an overseas employer and normally work abroad.[24] You are only liable once you have been resident in the UK for one year. This also applies to some overseas students and apprentices;[25] *or*
- employed abroad, but only for the first year of that employment (after that you can voluntarily pay Class 3 contributions) if:[26]
  - your employer has a place of business in Great Britain; *and*
  - you were resident in Great Britain before your employment started; *and*
  - you are ordinarily resident in Great Britain.

Class 1A and 1B contributions

Class 1A contributions are paid by employers for certain benefits in kind – eg, company cars. Class 1B contributions are paid by an employer who enters into a Pay As You Earn Settlement Agreement with the Revenue.

Class 2 contributions

You are liable for Class 2 contributions in any week in which you are self-employed in Great Britain and either:[27]
- you are ordinarily resident in Great Britain; *or*
- you have been resident in Great Britain for at least 26 weeks in the last year.

You can pay Class 2 contributions on a voluntary basis for any other week in which you are either employed or self-employed and present in Great Britain.[28]

If you are self-employed abroad, you can voluntarily pay Class 2 contributions if you were employed or self-employed immediately before you left Great Britain and:[29]
- you have been resident in Great Britain for a continuous period of at least three years at some time before that; *and*
- you have paid sufficient British contributions to give you a full contribution record for three previous contribution years. For details, see CPAG's *Welfare Benefits and Tax Credits Handbook*.

If you are a volunteer development worker employed abroad but ordinarily resident in Great Britain, you can voluntarily pay Class 2 contributions.[30] These are paid at a special rate and (unlike normal Class 2 contributions) count for contribution-based jobseeker's allowance. They are only payable if the Revenue certifies that it would be consistent with the proper administration of the law to allow you to do so.

Class 3 contributions

Class 3 contributions are always voluntary. You can pay them:

- for any year during all of which you were resident in Great Britain. Other conditions apply if you have recently arrived in Great Britain;[31] or
- for any year, during part of which you were outside the UK, if you meet the conditions for voluntary payment of Class 2 contributions (see p132), except that you do not need to have been employed or self-employed before you left Great Britain;[32] or
- if you have previously been paying Class 1 contributions from abroad.

Class 4 contributions

You are liable for Class 4 contributions in any week in which you are resident in Great Britain for income tax purposes.[33]

Credits and home responsibilities protection

You may be credited for Class 1 or 2 contributions in certain weeks, normally if you would satisfy the qualifying conditions for a benefit (including that you are incapable of work, or unemployed and actively seeking and available for work). Credits help meet the contribution conditions for benefits. The various types of credit each have their own residence conditions, usually linked to those for the equivalent benefit. For more details of credits, see CPAG's *Welfare Benefits and Tax Credits Handbook*.

Making the most of your contribution record

Your benefit entitlement may depend on your contribution record. For example, your right to a state retirement pension and the amount of that pension is set by the number of contributions you have made. A small shortfall in your record may make a big difference to the amount of benefit you receive. A shortfall may, in some cases, be made up by voluntary contributions.

If you have returned to the UK from abroad you should ask the Revenue Contributions Office for a copy of your contribution record. You can then check that contributions have been made while you were away. You may also be able to make up any shortfall in your record by voluntary contributions.

4. **Proving your immigration status, age and relationships**

For most people, proving immigration status, identity, age and their relationships to others (eg, marriage or parentage) is straightforward. However, some people may have problems, and migrants are most likely to be affected.

Immigration status

It is often difficult for people who have come from abroad to prove their immigration status. Often documents have been sent to the Home Office and you may not have documentation to show to the benefit authority. The Department for Work and Pensions (DWP) can contact the Home Office, but this process can take some time. Even if your documents, such as your passport, are available, these may not clearly indicate your immigration status.

If you have limited discretionary leave as a failed asylum seeker, the Home Office will have written to you stating that the Secretary of State has decided to grant you leave outside the Immigration Rules. This letter will usually refer to a grant of discretionary leave and should be sufficient to satisfy the benefit authorities.

If you have discretionary leave as the dependant of a failed asylum seeker, you may not have such a letter. Problems can arise when you have applied to renew or vary your immigration leave, and then need to make or renew a claim for benefits. While your papers are under consideration by the Home Office, you will not have proof of your current status. However, you are protected by the arrangements for 'statutory leave'. This means that the conditions of your permission to stay continue until the Home Office makes a new decision. You should be able to satisfy the benefit authorities of this by producing evidence of your most recent grant of leave and of the date you applied for further leave.

The benefit authorities are often unclear about leave outside the Immigration Rules and may confuse it with 'indefinite leave to remain'. Also, the rules for means-tested benefits do not refer specifically to discretionary leave (to which your Home Office letter will refer), but to 'exceptional leave to enter or remain in the UK granted outside of the rules made under s3(2) of the Immigration Act 1971'. For further information about proving your immigration status, see Chapter 5.

Age

Your age, or the age of members of your family, may affect your right to benefit, or the amount of benefit. This most commonly arises in claims for retirement pension, but the amount of other benefits can also be affected. For example, income support and income-based jobseeker's allowance are both paid at a lower rate to claimants under 25.

The most common situation in which the benefit authorities are likely to dispute your age is if you were born in a place where dates of birth were not accurately recorded at that time.

Benefits authority officials are generally more willing than the Home Office to accept foreign records as accurate. If you have a birth certificate, it is usually accepted as proof of your date of birth. Other evidence that can show your date of birth includes:

- passport or identity card;
- school or health records;
- army records;
- statements from people who know you and/or your family;
- astrological charts made for a baby at the time of the birth.

You may be able to show your date of birth by referring to the accepted birth dates of other relatives. For example, if you are recorded as the eldest child and your sister has been accepted as born on a date in 1937, you must have been born before that date.

Medical assessments are sometimes used as evidence of age. This involves a doctor examining you and guessing how old you are. Some doctors use X-rays as part of this assessment. In adults, this method is only accurate to within a few years at best.

A common problem is conflicting evidence. Your date of birth may have been wrongly recorded in your passport when it was issued – eg, because you gave the wrong date or because of an administrative error. Passports are commonly recorded as '1 January' when the exact date is unclear. The date in the passport may then have been used in many other official documents. It may be difficult to persuade the benefit authorities that all these dates are wrong. You should explain that all these dates come from one document, so the only real evidence for the date is the passport. If there is other evidence showing that date is not correct, the passport is not conclusive evidence.

While each piece of evidence has to be considered, the oldest documents may be more reliable, since they were made nearer to the time of the events to which they refer.

If there is no documentary evidence, the benefit authorities should accept your own statements, unless they are contradictory or improbable.

Your date of birth may be given in the document(s) as a year or a month rather than an actual date. If this applies, the DWP assumes your date of birth is the date least favourable to you. If you claim retirement pension, this is the last day of the year/month. However, this date should then be used for all other benefit decisions, even if that is more favourable to you.

If a benefits authority refuses to accept your evidence about your age and so refuses benefit or pays it at a lower rate, you should appeal and obtain independent advice.

Marriage, divorce and civil partnerships

You may need to show that you are/were married or in a civil partnership. This is most likely to apply to claims for bereavement benefits. It may also apply if there is a question of the validity of the marriage or civil partnership.

A marriage or civil partnership certificate is the best evidence. However, if one is not available, other evidence can count. Your own statement that you were married or had a civil partnership should be enough. This is because, unlike your date of birth, you can be expected to remember that you were married or had a civil partner and who your spouse/civil partner was. If there is contradictory evidence, or if you are claiming benefit as an appointee for a person whose mental state prevents her/him from making such a statement or for a person who has died, you may need to show in some other way that there was a marriage or civil partnership.

The most important of these is the cohabitation presumption. If a couple live together as if they were husband and wife or civil partners, it is presumed that they are married to each other or in a civil partnership, unless there is clear contradictory evidence to which the benefits authority can point.[34] This presumption is even stronger if the couple has children.

Parentage

You might be required to prove that you are the parent of a child – eg, if child benefit is claimed for a child by you, but you are not living with the child.[35] It may also arise if you are refused widowed parent's allowance (or awarded it at a reduced rate) because it is disputed that your child(ren) is/are of your late spouse.[36]

A birth certificate that shows that you are the parent of a child or young person should be sufficient to prove that you are (or your late spouse or civil partner was) the parent of a child. If this is not possible, you may be able to use the presumption of legitimacy. If a child was conceived by or born to a married woman, there is a legal presumption that her husband is the father.[37] If you were married to the mother, you are presumed to be the father. In the case of widowed parent's allowance, your late husband is therefore presumed to be the father of any child conceived or born during the marriage. The presumption applies even if the child was born after the wedding but obviously conceived before.[38] The presumption can be overridden by evidence that the husband is not the father.[39] For the benefit authorities to do this, there must be evidence that shows the child was probably not legitimate.[40] If you are the claimed father but the mother was married to another man, he, rather than you, is presumed to be the father.

If the mother was not married at the time of conception or birth, there is no presumption. In such cases, DNA testing may be able to establish whether the person is/was the parent of the child concerned.

5. **Getting paid if you go abroad**

Income support, income-based jobseeker's allowance and income-related employment and support allowance

If you are getting income support (IS), income-based jobseeker's allowance (JSA) or income-related employment and support allowance (ESA) and are going abroad, you should inform your local benefits office before you leave. Your payment should then continue in the same way for the allowed period while you are away. If you are claiming income-based JSA and you are going abroad in order to attend a job interview, you should notify Jobcentre Plus, who may also ask you to explain your absence in writing. If you are taking a two-week holiday from jobseeking and you are going abroad, see p82.

Housing benefit and council tax benefit

If you are going abroad, you should tell your local authority about your absence and notify it of any reduction in income that may occur – eg, if your part-time earnings are going to cease. This is because such a reduction may affect the amount of benefit to which you are entitled. Housing benefit (HB) and council tax benefit (CTB) can continue to be paid while you are out of the country for a period of 13 weeks, and in some circumstances for 52 weeks (see pp84 and 85). A new period of absence starts if you return home for even a short stay; a period of 24 hours may be sufficient.[41] On your return home, if there is a gap in your claim you should ask for backdating, but will need to show that you have good cause for a late claim.[42] If you have any difficulties getting such a claim accepted, you should contact your local advice centre.

If you are a private or housing association tenant and your HB is paid directly to you, while you are away you may need to make arrangements with your local authority to request that the benefit is paid directly to your landlord.

Contribution-based jobseeker's allowance, contributory employment and support allowance, maternity allowance and incapacity benefit

Contribution-based JSA, contributory ESA, incapacity benefit (IB) and maternity allowance can all be paid to you while you are abroad. Before going abroad, you should inform your local office of your trip and the reasons for it. You will be asked to fill out a form giving the reasons for your absence and when you intend to return to the United Kingdom (UK). You should tell your office well in advance of your trip abroad, otherwise it may not be possible to reach a decision on your claim before you leave.

If you are a European Economic Area (EEA) national or a family member of an EEA national and you are going to another EEA state, you can have your contributory JSA paid in that state for up to three months, provided you give one month's notice to Jobcentre Plus that you are going to another state to look for work. You must then 'sign on' in the second member state within one week of your arrival.

If you are receiving IB or ESA and you are due a medical examination when you go abroad, you could ask if this can be arranged abroad. If this is not agreed and you go abroad and miss your medical, you risk that the Secretary of State will refuse to pay these benefits during your absence and you may find that your benefit stops completely because you have failed to attend a medical. Depending on your reason for going abroad and missing your medical, it may be possible to argue that you had good cause for missing your appointment and therefore should not have your benefit stopped.

Retirement pensions and bereavement benefits

Both retirement pensions and bereavement benefits can be paid to you while you are abroad. If the Department for Work and Pensions (DWP) thinks you are entitled to retirement pension and it has an address at which to contact you, it will write to you a few months before you reach state pension age to determine whether or not you wish to claim. If you do not receive a letter but you think that you may be entitled, you should contact the DWP yourself (for the address see Appendix 3).

If you are happy for your benefit to be paid in the UK, you do not need to tell your local office that you are going abroad if you will not be away for more than three months. If, however, you are going abroad for more than three months, and you need your benefit transferred into an account outside the UK, you should tell your local office so that arrangements can be made to pay your benefit to you abroad. If you need to get your benefit paid into a bank account while you are abroad, you should give the DWP as much notice as possible as it is often very slow in making these arrangements. If you have not resolved this before you leave, you should authorise a friend, relative or advice agency in the UK to complete the arrangements. Your pension will be frozen at the rate it was paid when you left the UK unless you go to live in another EEA state (see p194) or a country with whom the UK has a reciprocal agreement (see Chapter 14).

Attendance allowance and disability living allowance

If you are going abroad and you are in receipt of attendance allowance (AA) or disability living allowance (DLA), you should contact your local benefits office or the overseas section of the DWP (see Appendix 3). If you are in receipt of severe disablement allowance or extra premiums paid with your HB or CTB, remember that you may lose these allowances if your absence means that you will lose entitlement to DLA or AA. It may be possible for you to time your absence to avoid this situation and to ensure that you can continue to claim on your return.

Special rules apply if you are able to rely on European Union (EU) law and you are going to another EEA member state (see Chapter 12).

Carer's allowance

If you are going abroad and are in receipt of carer's allowance (CA), you should contact your local DWP office.

If you lose your entitlement to CA, you should still be eligible for a carer premium paid with your IS, income-based JSA, HB or CTB for a further period of eight weeks, provided you are entitled to these benefits while you are away.[43] If you lose your entitlement to CA while you are abroad and the disabled person for whom you care is staying in the UK, s/he may be able to claim a severe disability premium during your absence instead. For further information, see CPAG's *Welfare Benefits and Tax Credits Handbook*.

Special rules apply if you are able to rely on EU law and you are going to another EEA member state (see Chapter 12).

---

6. **Other sources of help**

This *Handbook* is primarily concerned with information about your immigration status and your entitlement to social security benefits, tax credits and asylum support. However, there is other financial help available, to which you may be entitled, especially if you are on a low income, have children, have an illness, disability or other special needs, or if you are an older person. See CPAG's *Paying for Care Handbook* and the *Disability Rights Handbook* published by Disability Alliance for help for those with care needs.

Education benefits

Free school lunches

Children are entitled to free school lunches if their family receives:
- income support, income-based jobseeker's allowance or income-related employment and support allowance;
- child tax credit (CTC) and has an annual taxable income of £16,190 (in 2010/11) or less. However, this does not usually apply if the family is receiving working tax credit (WTC);
- guarantee credit of pension credit (PC) in England and Wales only. PC claimants in Scotland may qualify if they received CTC, as above.

Also entitled are:
- 16–18-year-olds receiving the above benefits or tax credits in their own right;
- asylum seekers in receipt of asylum support.

Education maintenance allowance

Education maintenance allowance is a means-tested payment for young people aged 16–19 who stay on in further education. Payments are made directly to the young person and are conditional on regular course attendance. They are payable for two to three years (up to four years in Scotland if there are additional support needs). The young person may receive a weekly allowance of either £10, £20 or £30 during term time, depending on the household income. S/he may also receive bonuses if s/he remains on her/his course and does well against learning objectives set out in her/his education maintenance allowance contract. A further bonus may be payable if s/he returns to study for a second year.

Education maintenance allowance does not count as income for any benefits or tax credits the young person's parent may receive, so the young person can get an allowance and her/his parent's child benefit and CTC are unaffected. Education maintenance allowance is also unaffected by any income the young person has from part-time work.

For further details, see www.direct.gov.uk/ema. See also CPAG's *Student Support and Benefits Handbook: England, Wales and Northern Ireland* and *Benefits for Students in Scotland Handbook*.

Clothing grants

Local authorities can give grants for school uniforms and other school clothes. Each authority determines its own eligibility rules. Some school governing bodies or parents' associations also provide help with school clothing.

School transport

Local authorities must provide free transport to school for pupils under 16 if it is considered necessary to enable that pupil to get to the nearest suitable school.

School charges

There is an increasing trend for schools to charge parents for equipment and trips that should be provided free of charge. Schools are allowed to ask for a voluntary contribution from parents but, if you choose not to pay, your child cannot be excluded from a lesson or school trips if the trip is part of the school curriculum. You should not be pursued for payment because any money requested from the school must be a voluntary donation only. For further advice, contact the Advisory Centre for Education at www.ace-ed.org.uk.

Social services

Local authority social services departments have statutory duties to provide a range of practical and financial help to families, children, young people, older people, people with disabilities and asylum seekers.

Some, but not all, social services support can be refused to a 'person who is subject to immigration control' or a European Economic Area national who is not economically active, but not if there would be a breach of either European Union law or your rights under the European Convention on Human Rights.

Charities

There are some charities that provide help to people in need. Your local authority social services department or local advice centre may know if appropriate charities could assist you, or you could consult publications such as *A Guide to Grants for Individuals in Need* and the *Charities Digest*, in your local library. The organisation Turn2us has a website (www.turn2us.org.uk), with an A–Z of all the charities that can provide financial help. In many cases, application for support can be made directly from the website.

The British Red Cross can provide food parcels if you are without any money or support. www.redcross.org.uk.

Notes

2. **National insurance numbers**
 1 s1(1A) and (1B) SSAA 1992; reg 5(4) Tax Credits (Claims and Notifications) Regulations 2002, No.2014
 2 *Leicester City Council v OA* [2009] UKUT 74 (AAC), paras 27 and 28
 3 s1(1A) SSAA 1992; reg 5(4) TC(CN) Regs
 4 *SSWP v Wilson* [2006] EWCA Civ 882, reported as R(H) 7/06
 5 Reg 1(A) SS(DLA) Regs; reg 5 HPG(A) Regs
 6 s1(4) SSAA 1992 and s122 SSCBA 1992
 7 Reg 4(a) HB Regs; reg 4(a) HB(SPC) Regs
 8 Reg 5(6) TC(CN) Regs

 9 **IS** Reg 2A(c) IS Regs
 JSA Reg 2A(c) JSA Regs
 ESA Reg 2A ESA Regs
 PC Reg 1A SPC Regs
 HB Reg 4(c) HB Regs; reg 4(c) HB(SPC) Regs
 CTB Reg 4 CTB Regs; reg 4 CTB(SPC) Regs
 IB Reg 2A(c) SS(IB) Regs
 CA Reg 2A(d) SS(CA) Regs
 Bereavement benefits and retirement pensions Reg 1A(c) SS(WBRP) Regs
 10 For HB/CTB this is set out in HB/CTB Circular A13/2010
 11 SNAP Guidance, 'Interview Site, Day of Appointment', para 19
 12 SNAP Guidance, 'Processing a National Insurance Number Application', para 48

13 CH/1231/2004
14 CH/1231/2004
15 Although there is some confusion about whether an NI number must be allocated if the conditions are met – compare CH/4085/2007 and para 45 of *Leicester City Council v OA* [2009] UKUT 74 (AAC)
16 *Leicester City Council v OA* [2009] UKUT 74 (AAC)
17 CH/4085/2007
18 HB/CTB Circular A13/2010
19 CH/1231/2004, para 11
20 The DWP's publication *Work and Welfare Strategy Directorate and Fraud, Planning and Presentation Directorate: race equality scheme*, which can be downloaded from the DWP's website (www.dwp.gov.uk), may be helpful in raising issues with the DWP.

3. National insurance contributions
21 s1(2) SSCBA 1992
22 s2(1)(a) SSCBA 1992
23 Reg 119(1)(a) SS(Con) Regs
24 Reg 145(2) SS(Con) Regs
25 Reg 145(3) SS(Con) Regs
26 Reg 146(2)(b) SS(Con) Regs
27 s2(1)(b) SSCBA 1992; reg 145(1)(d) SS(Con) Regs
28 Reg 145(1)(c) SS(Con) Regs
29 Reg 147 SS(Con) Regs
30 Regs 149-54 SS(Con) Regs
31 Reg 145(1)(e) SS(Con) Regs
32 Reg 147 SS(Con) Regs
33 Reg 91 SS(Con) Regs

4. Proving your immigration status, age and relationships
34 *Re Taylor* [1961] WLR 9, CA. For more cases, see Keane, *The Modern Law of Evidence*, Oxford University Press, March 2010
35 Sch 10 SSCBA 1992
36 s39A(3) SSCBA 1992
37 See Keane, *The Modern Law of Evidence*, Oxford University Press, March 2010
38 *The Poulet Peerage Case* [1903] AC 395. In Scotland, s5(1)(a) Law Reform (Parent and Child)(Scotland) Act 1986
39 For possible sources of evidence, see Keane, *The Modern Law of Evidence*, Oxford University Press, March 2010
40 s26 FLRA 1969; *S v S* [1972] AC 24 at 41. In Scotland, s5(4) Law Reform (Parent and Child)(Scotland) Act 1986

5. Getting paid if you go abroad
41 *R v Penwith DC ex parte Burt* [1988] 22 HLR 292, QBD; para A3/3.460 GM
42 **HB** Reg 83(12) HB Regs
   CTB Reg 69(14) CTB Regs
43 **IS** Sch 2 para 14ZA IS Regs
   JSA Sch 1 para 17 JSA Regs
   HB Sch 3 para 17 HB Regs
   CTB Sch 1 para 17 CTB Regs

Part 3

European law

Chapter 10

European Union law

This chapter covers:
1. The European Union and its institutions (below)
2. European Union law (p149)
3. European Union law and benefits (p151)
4. Using European Union law in the United Kingdom (p152)
5. Referring a case to the European Court of Justice (p153)
6. European Union law and the anti-test-case rule (p155)
7. Interim relief (p156)

This chapter provides a basic overview of European Union (EU) law, and the various institutions within the EU. Chapters 11 to 14 describe your rights and the benefits to which you may be entitled if you are travelling to, from or around the European Economic Area (EEA). They describe the rights you may have as a citizen of a country within the EEA (including the EU) or as a dependant of an EEA citizen.

Because this *Handbook* is about benefit entitlement for migrants, we only cover EU law that applies to migrants. For information about EU law on the equal treatment between men and women, see CPAG's *Welfare Benefits and Tax Credits Handbook*.

1. The European Union and its institutions

The European Union (EU) was established in 1957. It began as an economic body and this is reflected in its original name, the European Economic Community. It has now developed into a social, as well as an economic, union. The EU now has 27 members.

Member states of the European Union

Austria	Germany	The Netherlands
Belgium	Greece	Poland
Bulgaria	Hungary	Portugal
Cyprus	Ireland	Romania
Czech Republic	Italy	Slovakia
Denmark	Latvia	Slovenia
Estonia	Lithuania	Spain
Finland	Luxembourg	Sweden
France	Malta	United Kingdom

EU law has been extended to countries outside the EU which are covered by the European Economic Area (EEA) Agreement (see below). The EEA Agreement came into force in January 1994, when the EU joined another trading group, the European Free Trade Area. EEA nationals are covered by EU law to much the same extent as nationals of EU states. There are slight differences, however, in that EEA nationals are not able to rely on the EU Treaty. The Agreement covers the same areas as the EU Treaty, but does not have provisions equivalent to Articles 18 or 21 of the EU Treaty (see p151).

Member states of the European Economic Area

The EEA consists of the EU countries plus Iceland, Liechtenstein and Norway.

From 1 June 2002, the right to freedom of movement also applies to Switzerland. Any references to EEA nationals should therefore be interpreted as including Switzerland.

EU law applies in all the above countries, but it extends beyond the actual territory of the member states. It also applies to countries 'for whose external relations a member state is responsible'. Therefore, Spain not only includes the mainland, but also the Balearic and the Canary Islands. Portugal includes Madeira and the Azores.[1] However, there are certain exceptions to this general rule. In particular, in the United Kingdom (UK), Gibraltar is covered, whereas the Isle of Man and the Channel Islands are not.

The rights of nationals of some of the newer member states to the EU vary in just one important respect. Member states have a right to exclude nationals of the eight states which joined the EU in 2004 (the 'A8 states') and the two states which joined the EU in 2007 (the 'A2 states') from access to their labour markets. The UK has taken advantage of this power by introducing the Worker Registration Scheme for A8 nationals and authorised work for A2 nationals (see p33 for more details).

The rights of A8 and A2 nationals are exactly the same as other EU nationals in all other respects.

The governments of the EU countries allowed these restrictions for a maximum of seven years, after which A8 and A2 nationals must have the same rights as other EU nationals. The restrictions can continue:

- until 30 April 2011 for A8 nationals;
- until 31 December 2013 for A2 nationals

A8 and A2 states

The A8 states are: Czech Republic, Estonia, Hungary, Latvia, Lithuania, Poland, Slovakia and Slovenia.

The A2 states are: Bulgaria and Romania.

The institutions of the European Union

The European Parliament

The European Parliament, based in Strasbourg, participates in the adoption of EU legislation but, unlike the British Parliament, it cannot initiate or pass laws itself. Instead, it works together with the Council of the EU (see p148) to bring forth new legislation. Members of the European Parliament are directly elected by people of the member states every five years and sit in political groups reflecting their political opinions rather than their nationalities. For some types of EU law, the European Parliament is only entitled to be consulted, but in many areas it has the right to a co-decision with the Council. This gives it considerable influence over the final legislation. The European Commission (see below), which is the executive body or civil service of the EU, is accountable to Parliament.

The European Parliament has three main roles:

- **passing European laws** – jointly with the Council in many policy areas;
- **democratic supervision** over the other EU institutions and, in particular, the Commission. It has the power to approve or reject the nomination of commissioners, and it has the right to censure the Commission as a whole;
- **the EU budget.** Parliament shares authority with the Council over the EU budget and can therefore influence EU spending. At the end of the procedure, it adopts or rejects the budget in its entirety.

The Commission

The Commission, which is based in Brussels, is effectively the EU's civil service.[2] It makes proposals for European legislation. It therefore has a different role from the UK civil service, which is meant to have a non-political role.

There are 27 commissioners, one nominated by each of the member states. They are meant to be European officials rather than representatives of their states of origin.

The Commission is divided into directorates general, each responsible for a particular aspect of EU policy, and headed by a director general. The commissioners have responsibility for particular directorates ('a portfolio').

The Commission is a powerful institution of the EU and can investigate complaints from individuals about failures of member states to implement EU law. If the Commission considers that a member state is breaching EU rules, it can bring infringement proceedings against it.

The Council of the European Union

The Council is the EU's main decision-making body. It represents the member states and its meetings are attended by one minister from each EU member's national government.

The role of the Council has been strengthened since the ratification of the Lisbon Treaty in December 2009 (see p149). The Council is now officially one of the EU institutions and the Treaty of Lisbon created the post of President of the European Council.

The President is elected for a once-renewable term of two and a half years. Prior to the Lisbon Treaty, the Presidency was rotated on a six-monthly basis.

Among other responsibilities, the Council decides whether to pass legislation.[3] It is based in Brussels and is made up of the representative minister from each member state with domestic responsibility for a particular policy area. In the field of social security, the Council consists of the minister for social affairs from each member state. In the UK this is the Secretary of State for Work and Pensions.

The European Court of Justice

Note: since 1 December 2009, the European Court of Justice (ECJ) is now known as the Court of Justice of the European Union. However, in this *Handbook*, we continue to use the term ECJ.

This is the main institution you need to know about for the purposes of this *Handbook*. The ECJ is based in Luxembourg. It is responsible for ensuring EU law is observed and applied in the same way throughout the EU. Its decisions are binding on all member states. It should not be confused with the European Court of Human Rights, which operates from Strasburg and hears cases based on the European Convention on Human Rights. The ECJ consists of one judge from each state, plus a president. Judges are appointed by the member states for a period of six years. They do not all sit on each case. The Court is assisted by an Advocate General who prepares a resumé of and an opinion on the arguments before the court. Often this is adopted by the court, but not always.

The ECJ is not a court of appeal, so you cannot appeal from a national court to the ECJ. Instead, the national court can adjourn its proceedings in order to seek the opinion of the ECJ on any point of European law which arises. The national court decides the questions which need addressing and then makes the final decisions taking account of the ECJ view. This procedure arises under Article 267 of the Treaty and is called a 'reference'. Judgments of the ECJ are brief and do not offer the type of reasoning found in UK judgments. This can present difficulties for those seeking to interpret a case. However, the Advocate General's opinion is usually more detailed and will often shed more light on the reasons for a decision.[4]

The national court is not bound to refer a question of European law to the ECJ if the matter of EU law is already clear.

2. **European Union law**

The European Union (EU) is the product of a number of international treaties. The Treaty of Rome 1957 was the founding treaty and it remains in force today. However, it has been amended by a number of subsequent treaties.

The most recent change is the Treaty of Lisbon which came into force on 1 December 2009. This amended both the Treaty on the European Union and the European Community Treaty. The Treaty on the European Union was renamed the Treaty on European Union and the European Community Treaty was renamed the **Treaty on the Functioning of the European Union**, referred to in this *Handbook* as the **European Union (EU) Treaty**. What was previously termed Community law is now replaced by the term 'EU law'. The introduction of the new Treaties has resulted in a wholesale renumbering of the Treaty Articles.

The objectives of the EU Treaty, as amended, are to:

- promote economic and social cohesion through the creation of an area without frontiers;
- prohibit discrimination on the grounds of nationality;
- introduce a concept of European citizenship.

Since the United Kingdom (UK) joined the EU in 1973, the EU's legal system has had an important effect on English law. There are two important principles:

- the supremacy of EU law over domestic law. EU law has higher standing than the law of the member state. If domestic law is not consistent with EU law, a court or tribunal should not apply it;
- 'direct effect' (see below).

'Direct effect' means that EU law forms a part of our national legal system, as if it had been adopted by the UK Parliament. As a result, individuals can claim rights under that law in national courts or tribunals. Not all EU measures have direct effect. In order to have 'direct effect', an EU law must be:

- clear;
- precise; *and*
- unconditional.

The European Court of Justice (ECJ) applies this test generously, with the consequence that many provisions of EU law are directly effective. Most EU law relevant to this *Handbook* is directly effective.

Interpretation of European Union law

The European legal system and its terminology differ from domestic law. The relationship between EU law and the domestic law of member states is complex. This is inevitable, as EU law has to deal with many different legal systems. There are different principles of interpretation for EU law and UK law.

Interpretation of European law takes a 'purposive' approach.[5] This means a legal instrument is interpreted by establishing its objective. It is therefore important to interpret any EU provisions in the light of the objectives of EU law as a whole.

By contrast, UK law has traditionally been interpreted by taking the literal meaning of the words and phrases used. Only if this is ambiguous is the purpose of the legislation examined.

If there is a conflict between EU law and UK law, EU law takes precedence.[6]

European legislative instruments

Most EU law relevant to social security is in the form of Treaty Articles, Regulations or Directives (see below).

Treaties

Treaties are the constitutional framework of the EU and they have a higher status than other EU legislation. The ECJ (see p148) regularly returns to the fundamental principles of the Treaties when considering cases. Individual parts of a Treaty are divided into Articles.

Regulations

'Regulation' has a different meaning in EU law to that in UK law. In UK law, a regulation is secondary legislation made by a minister using powers given by statute. Courts and some tribunals can consider the validity of a set of regulations and, in some circumstances, declare them unlawful and strike them down.

In EU law, a Regulation is not secondary legislation. It is more akin to UK primary legislation. It is directly applicable and it overrides conflicting domestic legislation. This will be the case even if an EU Regulation is in conflict with a UK statute.

Where a Regulation is the legal instrument used, it lays down the content of the law itself and it is unnecessary for a member state to legislate in the same field. Therefore, unlike a Directive, there is no need for a member state to transpose Regulations in domestic law.

Directives

A Directive is an instrument of EU law which is addressed to the governments of member states. It is akin to an instruction to member states to change the law in a particular area. For example, the Race Directive requires member states to remove race discrimination in areas such as access to social security. The Directive is binding on the member state as to the result to be achieved, but it leaves the individual member states with discretion on how to achieve it.[7] Directives are transposed into domestic law via a statute or statutory instrument (regulations in the UK). Member states are usually given a period of two years to incorporate the Directive into domestic legislation.

The relationship between Directives and national law is complex. In particular, member states do not always interpret Directives accurately. Therefore, although a Directive has been adopted, you may still find some areas that appear to be incompatible with EU law. If there is any doubt, it is important to compare the Directive with the domestic law to see whether the Directive has been properly implemented.

Decisions

Decisions are, in some ways, similar to Directives. It is an individual act designed to be addressed to a specified person(s) or state. A decision does not require any further measures to be taken to implement it. It is a binding act with the force of law. However, it is only binding on the parties to whom it is addressed.[8]

Recommendations

Recommendations and opinions form part of what is known as 'soft law'. They are not binding on anyone, but courts and tribunals should take them into account in reaching their decisions.[9]

3. **European Union law and benefits**

There are three main areas of European Union (EU) law that are significant for benefit and tax credit purposes:
- rights of residence;
- equal treatment;
- co-ordination of social security.

These are all linked to the fundamental freedoms laid out in the EU Treaty – ie:
- freedom of movement for workers;
- freedom of movement for self-employment;
- freedom of movement for service providers;
- the general right of freedom of movement for EU citizens.

These fundamental freedoms have developed and been extended by the European Court of Justice and by amending legislation to include freedom of movement for citizens of the EU subject to conditions and limitations.

Workers, self-employed people and service providers/receivers enjoy the full range of rights including:

* the right of free movement and residence;
* protection against discrimination on grounds of nationality;
* the right to equal treatment in respect of benefits and services;
* the right to social security protection if you move to another state;
* the right of family members to reside, claim benefits and work.

The EU Treaty sets out these principles as follows.

* **Article 18** prohibits discrimination on nationality grounds.
* **Article 20** states that any national of a member state is a citizen of the EU.
* **Article 21** provides that all citizens of the EU have the right to move and reside freely within the EU subject to certain limitations and conditions laid down in the Treaty.
* **Article 45** gives workers a right to enter and reside in other member states in order to work or to look for work.
* **Article 48** provides the foundation for the co-ordination of social security schemes. It states that, in order to ensure freedom of movement for workers, migrants must be able to aggregate periods of work in other member states in order to be able to claim benefits in another and to be able to export benefits to other member states.
* **Article 49** gives self-employed people a right to 'freedom of establishment'. This means that a self-employed person may freely enter and reside in any other member state.
* **Article 55** gives the right to enter freely and reside in another member state in order to provide services. It also includes the right to receive services.

The detailed rules on these rights are in Regulations and Directives (see pp150 and 151). The variety of EU rules all have the same objectives: to make it easier for workers to move freely from member state to member state. However, whether you can rely on a particular area of EU law depends on whether you fit within the scope of that particular piece of legislation (see pp161 and 218).

4. Using European Union law in the United Kingdom

The aim of the European Union (EU) Treaty is to achieve social, as well as economic, integration. EU law is founded on the principle of non-discrimination on grounds of nationality. Article 18 provides:

Within the scope of application of this Treaty, and without prejudice to any social provision contained therein, any discrimination on grounds of nationality shall be prohibited.

EU law recognises that there is more to removing barriers to free movement than the abolition of immigration controls. The objective of free movement would, in practice, be frustrated if a migrant were to lose out on social security benefits guaranteed under the law of a member state.

Examples

A British woman may be deterred from taking up a job in France if she cannot rely on national insurance contributions paid in both countries when she comes to receive her pension, whether she returns to England or retires in France.

An Italian man may decide not to seek work in the United Kingdom (UK) if he cannot get child benefit for his children living in Italy.

If a person believes that s/he has rights under EU law, s/he can assert those rights in the appropriate UK tribunal or court.

EU legislation and EU caselaw from the European Court of Justice (ECJ) is binding on UK courts and tribunals, as well as on the Department for Work and Pensions and other benefit authorities. This means that you can rely on EU law when applying for a revision or supersession of your benefit and in appeals to the First-tier Tribunal, Upper Tribunal or court in the same way as you would use UK law. See CPAG's *Welfare Benefits and Tax Credits Handbook* for details of how to challenge social security decisions.

It is an error of law for any tribunal or court to fail to address a point of European law raised in the course of an appeal.[10] If a case involves a European Economic Area (EEA) national, the First-tier/Upper Tribunal or court should make enquiries to determine whether that person can be assisted by EU law.[11]

You can ask a tribunal or court to refer the matter to the ECJ (see below), but should seek specialist help before doing so. Legal help (formerly legal aid) is available for references to the ECJ if legal assistance would have been available before the domestic court or tribunal. Although it is possible to refer cases to the ECJ from any level of tribunal, it is probably more sensible to refer matters from the Upper Tribunal or higher courts.[12]

5. **Referring a case to the European Court of Justice**

Any United Kingdom (UK) court or tribunal can refer a case to the European Court of Justice (ECJ). However, a case should only be referred to the ECJ where the matter of European Union (EU) law is not clear. Before asking for a reference, you should always get specialist advice on this matter.

The ECJ has the power to make preliminary rulings concerning:

- interpretation; *and*
- validity.

Actions in the ECJ refer to questions on the interpretation or validity of EU law only. The ECJ has no power to interpret national legislation. Some cases are direct actions – eg, an action brought by the Commission against a member state for failure to fulfil a Treaty obligation[13] or an action brought by one member state against another.[14]

The other way in which cases reach the ECJ is when a national court refers a case under Article 267 of the EU Treaty. Where a question of interpretation of EU law arises in any court or tribunal of a member state, that court or tribunal may request a ruling on that question if it considers that a decision on the question is necessary to enable it to give judgment.

A reference under Article 267 is not an appeal. It merely provides a means for national courts to obtain a ruling on the interpretation of an EU provision. The national court then applies the ruling to national law and decides the case itself.

A reference can be made by any 'court or tribunal', which clearly includes both the First-tier and Upper Tribunals, and the domestic proceedings are then adjourned pending the outcome of the referral.

There is no absolute right to have your case referred to the ECJ unless you have no further judicial remedy. A final court of appeal must make a reference in relation to a question of EU law. In the UK, this is generally taken to mean the Supreme Court (formerly the House of Lords). However, if is not possible for you to appeal to a higher court, the lower level court or tribunal should make a reference to the ECJ if the matter is not clear.[15] Once judgment has been given by the ECJ, the member state must act to give effect to it.[16]

There is, however, no right to refer a case to the ECJ if the matter is *'acte clair'*.[17] This means that if a provision is clear (eg, because the ECJ has already ruled on the question), there is no need for the court to refer.

The ECJ has held that it is *not* necessary for a national court to make a reference if:[18]

- the question of EU law is irrelevant; *or*
- the provision has already been interpreted by the ECJ; *or*
- the correct application is so obvious as to leave no room for doubt.

The Court of Appeal has also ruled on this issue.[19] It held that a reference would not be necessary if the ECJ had already ruled on the question, or the matter was reasonably clear and free from doubt.

Individuals cannot apply to the ECJ directly. You can ask any tribunal or court to refer a question to the ECJ, but you should seek specialist advice before doing so. In view of the complexity of the law, it may be more sensible to seek a referral from the Upper Tribunal rather than the First-tier Tribunal.

The procedure

The UK court or tribunal drafts the question and submits it to the ECJ. It is then served on the parties who have two months to make written submissions. There is usually an oral hearing.

The UK proceedings are adjourned pending the outcome of the reference. The ECJ often takes a very long time to give its judgments, so a reference is likely to cause a considerable delay. It may be appropriate to ask the Department for Work and Pensions to make interim payments while waiting for a decision.[20]

The Advocate General's opinion

The judges of the ECJ are assisted by eight Advocates General. These are not judges, but they do have a judicial function. Once all the parties to a case have made their submissions and before the judges consider the case, the Advocate General gives an opinion. This offers an analysis of the legal position, much more akin to a UK judgment. Thus, reading the Advocate General's opinion often illuminates the reasoning of the ECJ. However, the opinion is not binding and it may or may not be followed by the ECJ. Where the ECJ chooses not to follow the opinion, it may be difficult to understand how the ECJ arrived at its decision.[21] The Advocate General's opinion is given to all parties to the proceedings and is published in the *Official Journal*.

The judgment and after

Once the judgment has been given, the member state must act to give effect to it, if necessary. The UK proceedings will be re-listed for hearing in the light of the judgment.

6. European Union law and the anti-test-case rule

United Kingdom (UK) social security law has an 'anti-test-case' rule.[22] If the Upper Tribunal or a court decides that a decision maker in a totally different case (the test case) has made an error of law and you make a claim or seek a revision or a supersession before or after the test-case decision, the decision maker must decide any part of your claim or revision or supersession which relates to the period before the test-case decision as if that decision had been found by the Upper Tribunal or court in question not to have been wrong.[23]

This only applies if the test case is the first authoritative decision on the issue, and not merely a later decision confirming an earlier decision.[24]

The effect of this anti-test-case rule is to limit the arrears of benefit that can be paid. The rule only applies where there is an appeal to the Upper Tribunal or a court.

The legitimacy of the UK anti-test-case rules has been challenged, but was held to be lawful.[25]

If you find that the anti-test-case rule is applied following a judgment of the European Court of Justice (ECJ), it may be worth getting further advice about a possible challenge. This is because the UK anti-test-case rules apply to a decision on an appeal. The ECJ is not an appeal court, but it is defined as such by the UK rules.

Anti-test-case rules relating to exporting benefits

The ECJ has held that attendance allowance (AA), disability living allowance (DLA) care component and carer's allowance (CA) are exportable benefits in EU law (see p178).[26] This judgment has impacted on many thousands of claimants. The Secretary of State has applied the anti-test-case rules in order to limit backdating. However, there was no appeal in that case.[27] Instead, the European Commission initiated an action at the ECJ that annulled EU legislation. Therefore, in cases concerning AA, CA and DLA care component, it is possible to argue that a person who claimed one of these benefits even before the decision of the ECJ could have been wrongly refused benefit. This has been confirmed by the Upper Tribunal, which has held that:[28]

> the decision of the ECJ on the exportability of UK disability benefits cannot be a 'relevant determination' for the purposes of section 27 of the Social Security Act 1998 and its restrictions on the effect of 'test cases' in relation to past periods.

This is a very complex issue; you should seek specialist advice if you are affected.

7. Interim relief

If a member state breaches European Union (EU) law by denying an individual the rights to which s/he is entitled under EU rules, it may be liable to pay damages. In order to claim damages (interim relief), you must show that:[29]

- the EU law at issue intended to confer rights on individuals; *and*
- there is a direct causal link between the damage you experienced and the breach of EU law by the member state; *and*
- the breach was 'sufficiently serious'.

In other words, not every breach of EU law by a member state gives individuals the right to claim damages. If a member state was diligent about attempting to apply EU law correctly, it will not be liable.[30]

Whether a breach is actionable, therefore, depends on the amount of discretion given to the member state by the EU. If the member state is given little or no discretion, the mere infringement of EU law may be sufficient for there to be a breach.[31]

Member states have discretion in the way in which a Directive is implemented, but must ensure compliance with it. There is no discretion to ignore the content of the Directive. Whether a breach is 'sufficiently serious' depends on whether the member state manifestly or gravely disregards the limits on its discretion.[32] For example, if a member state fails completely to introduce legislation to implement a Directive, the breach should clearly be actionable, whereas if a member state introduces national legislation to implement a Directive but misconstrues some aspect of the Directive, a claim for damages may be less successful.

The principle of entitlement to interim relief was established by the European Court of Justice (ECJ).[33] The ECJ said that EU law will automatically render inapplicable any conflicting provision of national law. The Court went on to state that national courts confronted with a claim based on putative rights under EU law should award interim relief, while the case is pending.

This means that it is not possible to ask for interim relief in all cases where EU rights are asserted, but only to those where the party has a case of sufficient cogency. If the First-tier Tribunal or Upper Tribunal has already held a person to be entitled to benefit under EU law, there is a much stronger argument that s/he will be entitled to benefit and, consequently, to interim relief.

The ECJ decision most favourable to such an argument is *Emmott v Minister of Social Welfare*.[34] However, the Court of Appeal in the case of *Walker-Fox* restricted the decision in *Emmott* to 'very exceptional circumstances' involving 'unconscionable behaviour' by the relevant member state.[35] For further advice on this issue, contact CPAG's advice line.

Notes

1. The European Union and its institutions

1 Art 227(1) EU Treaty. For a full list of countries covered, see para 070040 DMG

2 Arts 211-19 (ex-155-63) EU Treaty

3 Arts 202-10 (ex-145-54) EU Treaty

4 Prior to a judgment of the ECJ, the Advocate General will give an opinion on the legal position relevant to the case. The ECJ will have regard to the opinion, but is not obliged to follow it.

2. European Union law

5 *Lister and Forth Dry Dock* C-106/89 [1990] 1 AC 546
6 s2 European Communities Act 1971
7 Art 249 (ex-189) EU Treaty
8 Art 249 (ex-189) EU Treaty
9 *Grimaldi v Fonds des Maladies Professionelles* [1989] ECR 4407; see *Wadman v Carpenter Farrer Partnership* [1993] IRLR 374

4. Using European Union law in the United Kingdom

10 R(SB) 6/91; R(S) 2/93
11 CIS/771/1997
12 Traditionally, legal aid has been excluded from representation before the commissioners and tribunals. However, it was successfully argued in CF/3662/1999 that the Lord Chancellor did have the power to award legal aid under s6(8)(b) Access to Justice Act. This has now happened several times. In theory it should also be possible to secure legal aid for a hearing before a tribunal.

5. Referring a case to the European Court of Justice

13 Art 226 (ex-169) EU Treaty
14 Art 227 (ex-170) EU Treaty
15 *Hagen v Fratelli* [1980] 3 CMLR 253
16 Arts 10 (ex-5) and 227 (ex-170) EU Treaty
17 *Acte clair* is a doctrine originating in French administrative law, whereby if the meaning of a provision is clear, no 'question' of interpretation arises. It was first introduced into EU law by the Advocate General in *Van Gend en Loos* C-28/30/62. It was later applied in *Srl CILFIT v Ministry of Health* C-283/81 [1982] ECR I-03415 (ECJ).
18 *Srl CILFIT v Ministry of Health* C-283/81 [1982] ECR I-03415 (ECJ)
19 Lord Denning in *Bulmer Ltd v Bollinger SA* [1974] CA; see also *R v ILEA (ex parte Hinde)* [1985] 1 CMLR 716
20 There is a general view that interim payments should be available pending EU cases, but the DWP is rarely asked to do so. A refusal may be challengeable by judicial review, but you should seek specialist advice before proceeding.
21 See, for example, *Graham* C-92/94, involving discrimination in invalidity benefit.

6. European Union law and the anti-test-case rule

22 s27 SSA 1998
23 *CEO and Another v Bate* [1996] 2 All ER 790, HL; s27 SSA 1998; Sch 7 para 18 CSPSSA 2000
24 R(FC) 3/98; R(I) 1/03
25 *Johnson* C-410/92 (ECJ); *Steenhorst-Neerings* C-338/91 (ECJ)
26 *Commission v European Parliament and European Council* C-299/05 (ECJ)
27 *Commission v European Parliament and European Council* C-299/05 (ECJ)
28 CDLA/2078/2005; *JS v SSWP* [2009] UKUT 81 (AAC), interim decision

7. Interim relief

29 *Factortame and Others* C-221/89 [1991] ECR I-3905 (ECJ)
30 *Francovich v Italian State* [1993] 2 CMLR 66, [1991] ECR I-5357, [1992] IRLR 84
31 *Bergaderm* C-352/98 [2000] ECR I-5291 (ECJ)
32 *Brasserie du Pécheur and Factortame,* para 55 and joined cases *Dillenkofer and Others v Germany* C-178/94, C-179/94, C-188/94, C-189/94, C-190/94 [1996] ECR I-4845, para 25 (ECJ)
33 *Factortame and Others* C-221/89 [1991] ECR I-3905 (ECJ)
34 *Emmott* C-208/90 [1991] (ECJ); *ENKA* C-38/77 [1977] (ECJ)
35 *SSWP v Walker-Fox* [2005] EWCA Civ 1441; R(IS) 3/06

Chapter 11

The European Union co-ordination of social security

This chapter covers:
1. Introduction (below)
2. Who is covered by the co-ordination rules (p161)
3. Which benefits are covered by the co-ordination rules (p165)
4. The 'competent' state (p171)
5. Equal treatment (p176)
6. Aggregation (p177)
7. Exporting benefits (p178)
8. Overlapping benefits (p180)

This chapter gives an overview of the European Union (EU) social security co-ordination rules. Chapter 12 describes the detailed rules for each category of benefit.

European Economic Area nationals may also have rights arising from other areas of EU law, in particular those relating to their rights under the EU Treaty to free movement and residence. These rules are covered in Chapter 13.

1. Introduction

In order to secure and promote freedom of movement, European Union (EU) law co-ordinates all the social security systems within the European Economic Area (EEA). The intention is that people should not lose out on social security protection simply because they move to another member state.

The legal basis for the co-ordination of social security stems from the principles in Article 45 of the EU Treaty which provides that:
- freedom of movement for workers shall be secured within the EU; *and*
- such freedom of movement shall entail the abolition of any discrimination based on nationality between workers of the member states in employment, remuneration and other conditions of work and employment.

Freedom of movement would not be possible unless there was some security provided in social security benefits. This is provided for in Article 48 of the Treaty which allows for:

- the aggregation of all qualifying periods taken into account under the laws of different states for the purpose of acquiring, retaining and calculating benefit entitlement; *and*
- the payment of benefits to people resident in member states other than their state of origin.

The current co-ordination rules (Regulation 883/04) were introduced on 1 May 2010. These are intended eventually to replace the co-ordination rules found in EU Regulation 1408/71. The new rules do not completely repeal the old co-ordination rules and, for the foreseeable future, both sets of co-ordination rules will be in force. A benefit claim will be determined under the rules applicable at the time it is made. In general, this will now be Regulation 883/04.

The general rules of co-ordination allow the following.

- **The single state principle.** You can generally only claim benefit from one member state.
- **Equal treatment.** The Regulations prohibit discrimination on nationality grounds, in terms of access to or the rate of payment of benefits covered (see p176).
- **Aggregation** of periods of residence, insurance and employment paid in any EEA state towards entitlement to benefit in another (see p177).
- **Exportability of certain benefits.** The co-ordination rules allow you to take certain benefits abroad with you if you go to another member state (see p178).
- **Co-operation.** Member states undertake to co-operate in the administration of the co-ordination rules.

Where to start

In order to establish whether you are able to rely on the co-ordination rules, you need to do the following.

- Check whether you fall under the new rules under Regulation 883/04. This is largely determined by whether you are an EU national or a national of a state which is only a member of the EEA (see p161).
- Check whether you meet the general conditions for the particular co-ordination rules you fall within. This is referred to as being with the 'personal scope' of the co-ordination rules (see p161).
- Check whether the particular benefit you want to claim is covered by the co-ordination rules and which category it falls within (see p165).
- Check the detailed rules for that category of benefit (see Chapter 12).

2. **Who is covered by the co-ordination rules**

In order to be covered by the co-ordination rules, you must fall within their **'personal scope'**. There are different rules depending on whether you fall under the new or old co-ordination rules.

Who is covered by Regulation 883/04 and Regulation 1408/71

Regulation 883/04

. From 1 May 2010, you fall within the 'personal scope' of Regulation 883/04 (the new co-ordination rules) if you are, or have been in the past, subject to the legislation of one or more member state (see p162) and:[1]

- you are a national of one of the European Union (EU) member states (**Note:** this does not include Norway, Iceland, Liechtenstein or Switzerland); *or*
- you are a refugee (see p164); *or*
- you are a stateless person (see p164); *or*
- you are a family member (see p164) or a survivor (see p164) of one of the above.

Note: the new co-ordination rules have expanded from 1 May 2010 to include people who are not and never have been economically active. In the past, people who had never worked, perhaps because of a long-term disability or illness, could not rely on the co-ordination rules other than through a family member.

Regulation 1408/71

Regulation 1408/71 continues to apply to you if:

- you are a national of Norway, Iceland, Liechtenstein or Switzerland (see p163); *or*
- you are a third-country national (see p164).

You fall within the 'personal scope' of Regulation 1408/71 if you are employed, self-employed or a student (see Chapter 13) and you are, or have been in the past, subject to the legislation of one or more member state (see p162).[2]

Transitional arrangements

There is a transitional period of a maximum of 10 years during which a person remains subject to the legislation of a member state determined in accordance with the rules in Regulation 1408/71 rather than Regulation 883/04. This applies, provided your circumstances do not change.[3]

This transitional period is intended to protect a person who is already in receipt of a benefit under Regulation 1408/71 and who might otherwise have lost benefit under the new Regulation. However, you can ask to be transferred and considered under the new rules if you think you will be better off.

Subject to the legislation of a member state

EU nationals who are, or have been, subject to the legislation of one or more member states are covered by the co-ordination rules.

In the case of *Mouthaan*, the European Court of Justice (ECJ) held that a person becomes subject to the legislation of a member state when s/he complies with the substantive conditions laid down objectively by the social security scheme applicable to her/him, even if the steps for affiliation to that scheme have not been completed.[4]

Under the old rules, you could not be subject to the legislation of the United Kingdom (UK) unless you had worked in the UK and paid national insurance (NI) contributions. The only exception was if you could rely on a family member who was covered by the co-ordination rules.

The new rules have been expanded to include people who have never worked. Under Regulation 883/04, if you are potentially eligible for any social security benefit or tax credit in the UK, you should be subject to the legislation of the UK and covered by the new co-ordination rules if you are, or have been, insured under legislation of a member state (see p161).

Regulation 883/004 states that:[5]

Legislation means, in respect of each Member State, laws regulations and other statutory provisions and all other implementing measures relating to the social security branches covered by Article 3(1) of the Regulation.

The social security branches referred to in this definition include UK benefits, such as attendance allowance, carer's allowance and disability living allowance, as well as child benefit and child tax credit. None of these are dependent on being an employee or self-employed at any time. Potentially, therefore, even if you have never worked you can now be covered by the new co-ordination rules. See p169 for a full list of benefits considered to be social security benefits under Regulation 883/04.

An employed or self-employed person

The concept of an 'employed or self-employed person' for Regulation 1408/71 has a meaning in EU law that overrides any definition in the national legislation.[6] An employed or self-employed person is defined as:[7]

> any person who is insured compulsorily or on an optional continued basis, for one or more of the contingencies covered by the branches of a social security scheme for employed or self-employed persons or by a special scheme for civil servants.

The term 'worker' is not used in this Regulation and the ECJ has ruled that the two terms are not the same.[8]

You are treated as employed or as a self-employed person under the scope of Regulation 1408/71 if:

- you currently pay NI contributions; *or*
- you ought to pay NI contributions (because you fulfil the statutory criteria) even if your contributions have not, in fact, been paid;[9] *or*
- you have, in the past, been insured under the relevant scheme of insurance;[10] *or*
- you have worked, but are no longer economically active;[11] *or*
- you are a student[12] who has previously been subject to the legislation of at least one member state.[13]

If you are a part-time worker, you are still covered by the Regulation, no matter how much or how little time you devote to your activities.[14] However, you must still satisfy the NI rules (see above). If you earn less than the lower earnings limit, you are probably not covered, even though this may be discriminatory to women.[15]

Students

A student for the purposes of Regulation 1408/71 means a person who is not employed or self-employed, who studies or receives vocational training leading to a qualification recognised by the authorities of the member state and is insured under a general social security scheme or a special social security scheme applicable for students.[16] There is no definition of student in the new Regulation 883/04 because the Regulation applies to all people, whether economically active or not. However, for determining where a student is resident for the purposes of Regulation 883/04, consideration should be given to the source of the student's income.[17]

Nationals from Norway, Iceland, Liechtenstein and Switzerland

Regulation 1408/71 continues to apply to the co-ordination of Norway, Iceland, Liechtenstein and Switzerland, as agreements on Regulation 883/04 with these countries have still to be concluded.

Third-country nationals

A third-country national (ie, a person with indefinite leave in the UK who is not an EEA national her/himself) who is resident in a member state will continue to be covered by the co-ordination rules in Regulation 1408/71 rather than 883/04. This is because the UK has obtained an opt-out, allowing it to restrict third-country nationals' access to the co-ordination rules.

Refugees

A refugee is defined as being a person who is a refugee under Article 1 of the Convention on the Status of Refugees, signed at Geneva on 28 July 1951.[18] See Chapter 3 for further details of who is a refugee.

Stateless people

A stateless person is someone who does not have any nationality.[19]

Survivors

You are defined as a 'survivor' if you are a survivor in national law – eg, in the UK, a widow, widower or surviving civil partner.

Family members

Family members of a person covered by Regulation 833/04 (and also Regulation 1408/71) can rely on the co-ordination rules that cover that person. **Note:** as economically inactive people are now covered under the new rules, a person may not need to rely on being a family member to be covered.

The definition of 'family member' is slightly different under the co-ordination rules than under the definition in EU Directive 2004/38 (see p241).[20] Under the co-ordination rules, a family member is defined as being any person defined or recognised as a member of the family or designated as a member of the family or the household by the legislation under which benefits are provided. In general, this means the definition in the UK social security regulations applies – ie, a partner who is a member of your household and a child aged up to 20 for whom you are responsible.[21]

However, under the co-ordination rules, other family members can be included, provided they are mainly dependent on you.[22]

The rights you gain as a family member are often referred to, particularly by the DWP, as 'derived rights'.[23] Until recently, EU law drew a clear distinction between those rights that you could obtain yourself as an insured person under the co-ordination rule and the more limited rights that were derived. However, a decision of the ECJ suggests that the scope of derived rights may be interpreted broadly and in favour of claimants. The reasoning for this is that an insured

Chapter 11: The European Union co-ordination of social security
3. Which benefits are covered by the co-ordination rules

11

person is also likely to have rights arising from other areas of EU law – eg, as a worker (see p229). Social security entitlement of a 'worker's' family under the co-ordination rule would therefore also be deemed to be a 'social advantage' under the free movement rules and, consequently, it would not be possible to deny benefit to the family member. It seems that earlier decisions, which distinguished between the rights of the insured person and the rights of family members and survivors, are now limited to the aggregation and co-ordination rules relating to unemployment benefits (see p196)[24] and that, for all other social security benefits, family members and survivors of workers can benefit from the co-ordination rule on the same terms as workers themselves.

A family member retains her/his derived rights even when s/he is not living permanently with the insured person.[25] They are only lost if s/he divorces and, even then, in some cases if there are children, rights can be retained after divorce.

3. **Which benefits are covered by the co-ordination rules**

The benefits covered by the co-ordination rules are referred to as being within their '**material scope**'.

Regulation 883/04 covers the same benefits as those covered by Regulation 1408/71, as well as 'paternity benefits' and 'pre-retirement benefits'. The United Kingdom (UK) currently has no pre-retirement benefits.

Individual social security benefits are not directly referred to. Instead, the Regulations have broad categories of benefits such as 'old age' or 'maternity'. The EU Regulations refers to these broad categories as 'risks' and any social security benefit in a member state designed to protect against certain risks will fall into that particular category of risk. Each member state must then list the benefits it considers fall within each risk.

The risks are categorised into one of three groups. These are:
- social security benefits (see p166);
- special non-contributory benefits (see p166);
- social and medical assistance (see p168).

Those benefits deemed to be social security benefits have the most rights, special non-contributory benefits provide fewer rights, and social and medical assistance are not covered at all.

It is important, therefore, to establish the category into which a particular benefit falls, because your rights vary according to this.

11

Chapter 11: The European Union co-ordination of social security
3. Which benefits are covered by the co-ordination rules

How to establish the category of benefit

Whether a particular benefit is a social security benefit, a special non-contributory benefit or social assistance depends on factors relating to each benefit. In particular, its purpose and the conditions for eligibility,[26] rather than how it is described by the national legal system.[27]

Under EU law, a '**social security benefit**' is one which gives an individual a legally defined position entitling her/him to that benefit in particular circumstances without any individual or discretionary assessment.[28] By contrast, '**social assistance**' is a benefit or measure which makes the claimant's need one of the essential criteria for eligibility. It is usually a means-tested benefit, rather than one where entitlement is linked to a particular risk.

The European Court of Justice (ECJ) used to struggle with what it called 'hybrid' benefits – ie, those with the characteristics both of social security (giving a legally defined right in the event of a defined risk occurring) and social assistance (being generally available to the population as a whole, provided they satisfy the 'need' criterion). However, it often tended to offer a generous interpretation to the term 'social security' and held such hybrid benefits to be social security benefits. In order to deal with this problem, a new form of hybrid benefit, 'special non-contributory benefits', was introduced in 1992.

Social security benefits

Social security benefits are those benefits each member state provides for the risks listed on p169. It does not matter whether these benefits are created under a general or a special social security scheme, nor whether the scheme under which they arise is contributory or non-contributory.[29] Schemes in which employers are liable to pay benefit, such as statutory sick pay and statutory maternity pay, are covered.[30] Also covered are child tax credit and child benefit, which are administered by HM Revenue and Customs, but remain essentially social security within the scope of the Regulations. Working tax credit (WTC) does *not* fall within the scope of the Regulations.

Special non-contributory benefits

Special non-contributory benefits have been included in the co-ordination rules since 1992. These are benefits provided under legislation or schemes intended:

- to provide supplementary, substitute or ancillary cover against the risks above and which guarantee the person concerned a minimum subsistence income, having regard to the economic and social situation in the member state concerned; *or*
- solely as specific protection for people with disabilities; *and*
- to be financed exclusively from general taxation, with entitlement not dependent on national insurance contributions.

Chapter 11: The European Union co-ordination of social security
3. Which benefits are covered by the co-ordination rules

11

The benefit must also be listed in Annex X of Regulation 883/04 (Annex II of Regulation 1408/71).[31] However, the ECJ has held that the fact a benefit is or is not listed in the Annex is not conclusive. The characteristics of the benefit must be considered to determine its status.[32]

The inclusion of this new category was largely a response to the problems encountered by the ECJ in making the distinction between 'social security benefits' that were within the scope of the Regulation and 'social assistance benefits' that were not.

Article 70 Regulation 883/04 (Article 4(2)(a) Regulation 1408/71) states that, for a benefit to be a special non-contributory benefit, it must be:

- special (see p167);
- non-contributory; *and*
- intended to provide supplementary, substitute or ancillary cover against one of the social security risks covered by the Regulation (see p168) or specific protection for disabled people 'closely linked to the person's social environment'.

The main distinctions between special non-contributory benefits and social security are that special non-contributory benefits:

- are only payable in the member state in which you reside and therefore cannot be exported;
- are payable in accordance with the legislation of that member state.

This is true for both the old and the new co-ordination rules.

'Special'

Guidance on the meaning of this term is available from the European Commission.[33] It states that the following cumulative criteria are particularly relevant in determining whether a benefit is 'special'.

- The benefit has the characteristics of a social security benefit of a 'mixed type', in that it gives the beneficiary a legally defined right to benefit which is a characteristic of a social security benefit but also contains features of social assistance, in that the particular financial and/or other needs of the individual are taken into account.
- The characteristics of the category of benefit are closely linked to a particular social and economic context in the member state where the beneficiary resides.
- In the case of insufficient economic resources, the benefit is designed to provide assistance.
- The award could be subject to means-testing, although due to its general nature it is not always necessary to examine the specific circumstances of each individual case. Means-testing is an important, though not an essential, criterion, which may, in particular, take into account income from gainful activity or other social security benefits.

11

Chapter 11: The European Union co-ordination of social security
3. Which benefits are covered by the co-ordination rules

Intended to provide cover against one of the social security risks

There is very little guidance as to the meaning of this. It is possible to see that a benefit such as income-based jobseeker's allowance (JSA) is intended as a replacement for people with insufficient contributions for unemployment benefits, or that pension credit (PC) steps in to replace retirement pensions. It is not so clear that this is the case with attendance allowance (AA), carer's allowance (CA) or disability living allowance (DLA). They appear to be unique benefits that stand alone.

Social and medical assistance

The categories of risks listed as being covered by social security benefits and special non-contributory benefits are exhaustive.[34] Any branch of social security not mentioned in the list is not covered by the co-ordination rules.[35] In addition, any benefit is excluded from the co-ordination rules if it is considered to be:

- social and medical assistance; *or*
- benefit schemes for victims of war or its consequences.

It is not entirely clear which of the UK benefits would fall within this category, but it may refer to benefits such as housing benefit (HB) or WTC. It may also mean more discretionary assistance such as payments made under the Children Act 1989 or other social services support.

Declarations by member states

Each member state is required to list the benefits it considers to be social security benefits and those that are treated as special non-contributory benefits.[36] They do this in special declarations (found in an annex to Regulation 1408/71 and 883/04).[37] The ECJ has held that if a member state has listed a benefit as social security, you are entitled to rely on this declaration and thus the benefit is covered by the co-ordination rule.[38]

The UK government considers income-based JSA to be a special non-contributory benefit rather than a social security benefit. However, applying EU criteria, this may not be accurate. A commissioner and the Court of Appeal have held that, for EU purposes, income-based JSA is an unemployment benefit, although this was in respect of a different area of EU law.[39]

The Department for Work and Pensions (DWP) also treats income-related employment and support allowance (ESA) as a special non-contributory benefit, but arguably it is a sickness benefit under the Regulations, and it might even be possible to argue that it is an unemployment benefit.

If a benefit is not listed in the declaration as a social security benefit, it does not necessarily mean that it is not covered. The ECJ may treat it as such if, in fact, it has the characteristics of a social security benefit.[40]

Chapter 11: The European Union co-ordination of social security
3. Which benefits are covered by the co-ordination rules

11

How a benefit is characterised is a matter of law. If there is a dispute, the matter can only finally be resolved by the ECJ.[41] In practice, the DWP is not likely to treat a benefit as a social security benefit unless it is in the UK declaration.

The categories of benefits

Social security benefits

The risks listed for social security benefits are for:[42]

- sickness benefits;
- maternity benefits;
- paternity benefits (under the new rules only); [43]
- invalidity benefits;
- old age benefits;
- pre-retirement benefits (under the new rules only); [44]
- survivors' benefits;
- benefits for accidents at work and occupational diseases;
- death grants;
- unemployment benefits;
- family benefits.

Sickness benefits

- AA (but see below);
- CA (but see below);
- DLA care component (but see below);
- statutory sick pay;
- contributory ESA in the assessment phase.

Note: AA, CA and DLA care component have been categorised as different risks at different times – see Chapter 12 for further details.

Maternity

- maternity allowance;
- statutory maternity pay.

Paternity benefits

- statutory paternity pay.[45]

Invalidity benefits

- contributory ESA after the assessment phase;
- AA, DLA care and mobility component and CA if you were in receipt of benefit prior to 1 June 1992. If you claimed after this date, see p211;[46]
- long-term incapacity benefit (IB);
- severe disablement IB;
- income-related ESA.

11

Chapter 11: The European Union co-ordination of social security
3. Which benefits are covered by the co-ordination rules

Old age benefits
- additional pension;
- graduated retirement benefit;
- winter fuel payments;
- increments – eg, to pensions;
- adult dependants' increases of retirement pension;
- age addition in pensions;
- Christmas bonus.

Pre-retirement benefits
There are currently no pre-retirement benefits in the UK.

Survivors' benefits
- Bereavement benefits.

Benefits for accidents at work and occupational diseases
- industrial injuries disablement benefit;
- constant attendance allowance;
- exceptionally severe disablement allowance;
- reduced earnings allowance.

Unemployment benefits
Contribution-based JSA is the only benefit the UK accepts as being an unemployment benefit. However, it is arguable that both income-based JSA and ESA may also be unemployment benefits. This is not accepted by the DWP and needs to be tested by the courts.

Family benefits
- child benefit;
- child tax credit;
- dependants' additions of other benefits, such as retirement pension;
- guardian's allowance.

Family allowances (under the old rules only)
- child benefit;
- dependants' additions.

Special non-contributory benefits
- DLA mobility component;
- income support (IS);
- income-based JSA;
- PC;
- income-related ESA.

Social and medical assistance

The UK does not specify which benefits it considers to be social assistance and consequently excluded from the co-ordination rules. In the past, UK benefits, such as IS and other means-tested benefits, were considered to be social assistance. This is no longer accurate as most of the means-tested benefits are now listed as special non-contributory benefits.

There is caselaw from the ECJ on the distinction between social security and social assistance. In the case of *Fossi*, the ECJ held that social security was legislation which confers on the beneficiary a legally defined position which involves no individual and discretionary assessment of needs of personal circumstances.[47] Whereas in *Piscitello*, the ECJ described social assistance as legislation designed to provide benefits for those in need, where eligibility is not dependent on periods of employment, affiliation or insurance but there is some element of individual assessment.[48] It is not clear which UK benefits might fall within the definition of social assistance.

HB and council tax benefit are clearly not covered by the co-ordination rules, but this is due to there being no risk to which these benefits equate. Consequently, a person who owns a property and benefits from mortgage interest payments within IS, income-based JSA or income-related ESA is covered by the co-ordination rules, while a person who rents her/his home is not covered.

4. **The 'competent' state**

Under the co-ordination rules, a person is generally only able to claim benefit from one member state and is only liable to pay national insurance (NI) contributions in one member state. The Regulations refer to a person being subject to the legislation of a single member state only.[49] This is what is known as the single state principle or the '*lex laboris*' rule.

The state responsible for you is called the '**competent state**'. The competent state's social security institution is the '**competent institution**'. The Department for Work and Pensions (DWP) is the United Kingdom's (UK's) primary competent institution.

If you have been subject to the legislation of any member state, you are covered by the co-ordination rules. However, you can only qualify for UK benefits and tax credits under the co-ordination rules if the UK is the competent state. The general rule is that the state responsible for you is the state in which you last worked, but there are exceptions to this (see p173).[50]

Example

Jay was working in Germany for several years, but has just arrived in the UK to look for work. He is getting his German unemployment benefit paid while he is in the UK, but must sign on in the UK to continue to receive it. Germany is the competent state and the

German social security department is the competent institution responsible for paying benefit. This is the case even though Jay is required to sign on in the UK. However, if Jay subsequently finds work in the UK, the competent state becomes the UK and the competent institution the DWP.

You are normally subject to the legislation of the state in which you work even if you live in another member state. However, the rules differ depending on whether you are covered by the new or the old co-ordination rules.

In some circumstances, under Regulation 1408/71 you may be subject to the legislation of more than one member state. This only arises if you are simultaneously employed in one European Economic Area (EEA) state and self-employed in another.[51] This will be rare, however, and, in general, in order to avoid duplication of benefits, only one state can be the competent state.

The new co-ordination rules: Regulation 883/04

If you are economically active, the competent state is the state in which you are working. If you are not economically active, the competent state is the state in which you are resident.

Regulation 883/04 defines who is economically active. It includes:

- people who are working as employed or self-employed;
- people receiving a cash benefit as a consequence of their employment (but this does not apply to pensions or to invalidity, survivors' or industrial injury benefits);
- members of the armed forces or civilian services;
- civil servants.

Under the new co-ordination rules, if you work simultaneously in two or more member states, you are subject to the legislation of the member state of residence if you pursue a substantial part of your activities in that member state.[52]

If you are subject to the legislation of the UK either because you last worked in the UK or you are resident in the UK, you remain subject to the legislation of the UK until:

- you start to work in another EEA member state;
- you move to another state and start to receive a pension from another EEA member state;
- you move to another EEA member state and become resident there.

Note: see p204 for the meaning of 'resident'.

The old co-ordination rules: Regulation 1408/71

You are subject to the legislation of the UK under Regulation 1408/71 if you have worked in the UK and paid NI contributions, or you are a family member of a person who has worked or paid NI contributions. However, see below for some exceptions.

Exceptions to the general rule

Regulation 1408/71 describes specific situations in which you are not subject to the legislation of the member state in which you last worked.

- If you have stopped work in a member state and have subsequently moved to another member state, you become subject to the legislation of the state of residence rather than the state of employment.[53] This appears to allow member states to impose residence requirements for continued entitlement to benefit.
- You work temporarily in another member state for a UK employer.
  - If the company that employs you sends you to work in another member state for less than a year, you remain subject to the legislation of the original member state. However, if you are replacing another employee whose period of posting is ending, you are subject to the legislation of that member state.[54]
  - If you are being sent from the UK to another member state to work for less than a year, you should obtain Form E101 from the DWP before you go abroad. This certifies that you remain covered by UK legislation. If the job is extended for up to a year because of unforeseen circumstances, you can apply for an extension using Form E102. Your employer must apply for this extension before the end of the first 12-month period.[55]
- You are temporarily self-employed in another member state.
  - The same rules apply if you are self-employed and go to work in another member state for less than 12 months.[56] If you go from the UK to take up temporary self-employment in another member state you pay self-employed earner's contributions (Class 2 and 4) as if you were still in the UK. You do not have to contribute to the other member state's insurance scheme.[57]
  - You are normally accepted as self-employed if you have been self-employed for at least 12 weeks during the last two tax years or since then, although it may be possible to classify you as self-employed even if you do not fully meet this condition. To clarify the position you should contact the National Insurance Contributions Office (see Appendix 3).
  - People working in the German construction industry have, in the past, experienced difficulties when registering as self-employed in Germany. If you go to work in the construction industry in Germany, you must register at the local office of the Chamber of Handicrafts (Handwerkskammer), taking Form E101 with you. In order to register with the Handwerkskammer, you must prove that you are qualified in your trade. You must provide a 'certificate of experience', which you can obtain from the British Chamber of Commerce. If you do not register with the Handwerkskammer, you are not allowed to be self-employed in Germany.

- You are employed in two or more member states.[58] If you are employed in two or more member states, unless you are an international transport worker (see below), you are insured under the UK scheme if:
  - you normally live in the UK, and the UK is one of the member states in which you work; *or*
  - you work for several companies that are based in different member states; *or*
  - you do not normally live in any member state in which you work, but your employer is based in the UK.
- If, when you start work, you are sent abroad immediately by an employer or agency, you usually carry on paying UK NI contributions.
- If you are taken on while abroad, you are normally insured under that member state's scheme.

There are special rules if an agency hires you to work for a client in the Netherlands or Germany. You may have to pay UK NI contributions for up to nine months if you are in Germany and six months if you are in the Netherlands. After this period, you are insured in the member state in which you are working. Your employer needs to obtain Form E101 to inform the social security authority in the other member state that you remain insured in the UK, and Form CZ3822 to inform the UK National Insurance Contributions Office (see Appendix 3).

International transport workers
If you are an international transport worker and work in two or more member states, you are insured under the UK scheme if:
- your employer's registered office is in the UK; *or*
- your employer's registered office is in another member state and you work for a branch office in the UK; *or*
- you live in the UK and work mainly in the UK even if your employer does not have an office here.

If none of the above applies, you are insured under the scheme of the member state in which your employer has its main office.

Special arrangements
In some circumstances, it may be to your advantage to remain insured in the UK even if you are working in another member state.[59] If so, the UK National Insurance Contributions Office and its counterpart in the other member state must agree to this. You should write to the UK National Insurance Contributions Office to find out about your position.

Special rules also apply to mariners, civil servants, diplomatic or consular staff and people called up for service in the armed forces. You should get advice from the appropriate authority – ie, the National Insurance Contributions Office in the UK (see Appendix 3).

For how long does the United Kingdom remain the competent state

If you last worked in the UK, you should remain subject to the legislation of the UK under the old rules until:

- you start to work in another member state; *or*
- you start to receive a pension from another member state; *or*
- you live in another member state and become resident in that member state.

UK guidance states that you continue to be subject to the legislation of the UK when you go abroad if: [60]

- you work in the UK or pay NI contributions in the UK because of your work, but leave the UK to live in another member state or Switzerland and become a frontier or posted worker;
- you have paid enough NI contributions to be able to claim a UK contributions-based sickness benefit;
- you are in receipt of state pension, industrial injuries benefit, incapacity benefit (IB), contributory employment and support allowance (ESA) or bereavement benefits from the UK. These are referred to as 'relevant benefits';
- you are a family member (spouse, civil partner or someone dependent on a parent) of someone who works in the UK or has paid enough NI contributions to be able to get a UK contribution-based sickness benefit, or is in receipt of short-term IB or the assessment-phase rate of contributory ESA

If you are a family member of:

- someone who is working in the UK, your benefit will be paid for as long as that person continues to work in the UK, or the duration of your award if shorter;
- someone who has paid enough NI contributions for her/him to be able to claim a contributions-based sickness benefit, your benefit will be paid for as long as that person remains insured from her/his contributions, or the duration of your award if shorter;
- someone who is in receipt of short-term IB or the assessment-phase rate of contributory ESA, your benefit will be paid for as long as that person remains in receipt of that benefit, or the duration of your award if shorter.

In CPAG's view, this guidance does not entirely comply with Regulation 1408/71. It is our view that, under the old co-ordination rules, if you last worked in the UK you remain subject to the legislation of the UK as long as you do not work in another member state or start to receive another benefit from another member state. Under the new rules, this has changed and you become subject to the legislation of a member state where you are resident.

5. **Equal treatment**

If you are covered by the co-ordination rules, you are entitled to the same benefits under the legislation of the 'competent state' (see p171) as a national of that state. This is often referred to as the '**equal treatment**' provisions. Equal treatment is one of the fundamental rights of European Union (EU) law and the principle of non-discrimination prohibits any form of discrimination, direct or indirect, based on your nationality.

Direct discrimination arises when one person is treated less favourably than another. Indirect forms of discrimination are not so easy to identify but arise in rules which, although apparently neutral and non-discriminatory, have, in practice, a greater adverse impact on those who are not nationals of the competent state. For example, the habitual residence test and right to reside test in United Kingdom (UK) law (see Chapter 8) would appear to be a rule, which applies equally to all European Economic Area (EEA) nationals. However, British and Irish citizens are far more likely to satisfy the test than other EEA nationals. Therefore, the rule could be indirectly discriminatory. Commissioners and the upper courts have considered this matter and have accepted that there is discrimination, but presently the caselaw suggests that the discrimination is justified.[61]

A difference in treatment can be justified, but only if it is based on objective considerations that are independent of the nationality of the people concerned and proportionate to the legitimate aim of the national provisions.[62] In one case, the European Court of Justice (ECJ) held that a French national who had worked for only one day in Belgium should not be excluded from claiming unemployment benefits simply because she had not completed a specified period of employment. It said that to do so would be contrary to the equal treatment rules under Article 3 Regulation 1408/71 and Article 39 (now Article 45) of the Treaty.[63]

The non-discrimination principle has also been used to extend the rights of EEA claimants and their families in relation to widows' rights,[64] disabled people's allowances,[65] allowances for large families[66] and non-contributory old age allowances.[67]

Regulation 883/04 refers to equality of treatment in respect of benefits, income, facts or events. Specifically:

- if, under the legislation of the state from which you are claiming benefit, the receipt of a social security benefit and other income has certain legal effects, any equivalent benefits or income under the legislation of another member state will be treated in the same way; *and*
- if, under the legislation of the member state from which you are claiming benefit, certain events or facts are taken into account, the member state also has to take into account similar events or facts as though they had happened in that member state.

For example, if a UK benefit would passport a person onto another benefit, the same principle must now be applied to equivalent benefits from another member state. Equally, where UK income is disregarded or events might trigger a particular entitlement, they must be treated as though they occurred in the UK.

6. **Aggregation**

The aggregation and apportionment of insurance periods for the purpose of acquiring and calculating entitlement to benefit are key co-ordinating mechanisms.

'**Aggregation**' means adding together periods of national insurance (NI) contributions, residence or employment in all the member states in which you have lived or worked. This may be necessary if the entitlement, retention or recovery of benefits depends on your fulfilling a certain period of residence, employment or insurance. For example, if you want to claim a United Kingdom (UK) contribution-based benefit such as employment and support allowance (ESA), but you have paid insufficient NI contributions, you can rely on contributions that you have paid in other European Economic Area (EEA) states in order to satisfy the UK contribution rules. What constitutes a period of residence, employment or insurance is determined by the legislation of the member state in which it took place.[68]

The principle is that you should not lose out if you choose to exercise your rights to move within the EEA. If you were to be at a disadvantage should you need to claim benefit, this may deter you from moving. The principle of aggregation effectively lifts internal borders within the EEA in respect of residence and contribution conditions. Therefore, when deciding whether or not you are entitled to benefits, all the contributions you have made to all the social security schemes in any member state in which you have been insured are taken into account. In addition, periods of residence or employment in any state should be taken into account as if they were completed in the member state in which you are seeking benefit.

Example
Pilar is a Spanish national who has worked for many years in Spain. She arrives in the UK and works for two weeks. She may rely on the contributions paid in Spain to claim contribution-based benefits such as jobseeker's allowance or ESA. S/he may also rely on the periods of residence in Spain to meet any residence conditions – eg, for child benefit or disability living allowance.

The aggregation rule can be particularly helpful for A8 and A2 nationals (see p147) who may be excluded from benefits under the UK's right to reside test (see p116).

Example

Teresa, a Polish national, has worked for 10 months in the UK. She is pregnant and has a pregnancy-related illness. She has recently lost her job and she claims income-related ESA, which is refused under the right to reside test (see p116). However, Teresa worked in Poland for many years before coming to the UK and, by relying on the aggregation rules, she can meet the conditions for entitlement to contributory ESA. The same principle can be applied to maternity allowance, where instead of aggregating contributions, the periods of work can be aggregated.

Each type of social security benefit to which aggregation provisions are applied has its own rules and you need to take account of these when claiming.[69] These are covered in Chapter 12.

Apportionment

'**Apportionment**' means that two, or more, EEA member states pay a proportion of your benefit. It is a technique used in relation to longer-term entitlements such as old age and survivors' benefits and some other types of invalidity benefits.

Apportionment is often coupled with aggregation. For example, if you have contributed to the state pension scheme in a number of member states, each state must pay a proportion of the rate to which you would have been entitled if you had spent your whole working life in that state. The proportion is calculated by dividing your working life by the length of time actually worked in each member state.

To avoid duplication of benefit entitlement, only the 'competent state' (see p171) carries out the aggregation exercise, and you only receive a pro rata amount of any aggregated benefit.[70]

7. **Exporting benefits**

European co-ordination rules allow you to 'export' certain social security benefits to another state if you cease to be resident in the member state in which the entitlement arose.

This means that certain benefits may not be reduced, modified, suspended, withdrawn or confiscated just because you go to live in a different member state.[71] The rules for exporting vary according to the benefit concerned. There are also differences between benefits that can be exported under the new co-ordination rules of Regulation 883/04 and those under the old rules of Regulation 1408/71. Under Regulation 1408/71 fewer benefits could be exported.

Exporting benefits under Regulation 883/04

Under Regulation 883/04, all benefits other than those deemed special non-contributory benefits (see p166) are exportable. The extent to which you can export a benefit depends on the type of benefit concerned. For example, a benefit like retirement pension can be exported indefinitely, whereas a benefit such as contribution-based jobseeker's allowance may be exported for a maximum of three months.

You should check the individual category of benefit in Chapter 12 to see whether that benefit can be exported and, if so, what steps you need to take before and after you go abroad.

Exporting benefits under Regulation 1408/71

Under Regulation 1408/71, certain benefits are fully exportable, some may be exportable on a temporary basis, and some are not exportable at all.

Fully exportable benefits

The following benefits are fully exportable:
- invalidity benefits;
- old age benefits;
- survivors' cash benefits;
- pensions for accidents at work or occupational diseases;
- death grants.

The above can be exported indefinitely.

Benefits with limited exportability

The following benefits can be exported for a limited period or subject to certain restrictions:
- unemployment benefits, sickness and maternity benefits;
- family allowances.

The exporting of sickness benefits has become a significant issue in the UK, following a judgment of the European Court of Justice.[72] This held that attendance allowance, disability living allowance care component and carer's allowance are all sickness benefits and consequently can be exported in some limited circumstances (see p210).

Benefits that cannot be exported

- special non-contributory benefits (see p166);
- family benefits.

You cannot export special non-contributory benefits; they are paid only in the state in which you are resident.[73]

Family benefits generally cannot be exported, but you can claim family benefits for family members who are living apart from you in another member state. The only exception to this is for certain family allowances which can be exported if a person receives a pension. Child benefit is classified as both a family benefit and family allowance and, in some limited circumstances, can be exported. The rules on exporting benefits vary according to the benefit concerned and are covered in Chapter 12.

8. **Overlapping benefits**

A general principle of the European Union (EU) rules on co-ordination is that a claimant should not use one period of compulsory insurance to obtain more than one benefit derived from that period of insurance.[74] In general, you are only insured in one European Economic Area (EEA) member state for any one period,[75] so you cannot use insurance from that one period to obtain entitlement to benefits of the same kind from two member states. Usually, benefits are adjusted to ensure that either only one state (the 'competent state' – see p171) pays the benefit, taking into account periods of insurance in other EEA member states; or that the benefit is paid pro rata according to the lengths of periods of insurance in different member states. Aggregation or portability provisions apply, but not both.

Member states can introduce provisions to prevent 'double recovery'. In the United Kingdom (UK) these are contained in the regulations on overlapping benefits.[76] For more information, see CPAG's *Welfare Benefits and Tax Credits Handbook*.

In certain cases, however, you may be paid both the full level of a UK benefit and a proportion of the benefit from another member state, accrued as a result of having paid insurance contributions there. Following a decision of the European Court of Justice,[77] member states are not allowed to apply provisions preventing the overlapping of their own benefits with those of other member states if it would have the effect of reducing what you would have received from your years of contributions in the first member state alone.

For benefits, like old age and death benefits, which are paid pro rata by different member states depending on the length of the period of insurance in each member state, the overlapping provisions do not apply if they would 'adjust' benefits downwards. Each member state must pay you either the benefit you have earned under its system pro rata, or the rate payable under its own legislation for the years worked, whichever is higher. In such cases, the single state rule does not apply.

Example

In the UK, if you have been employed for 90 per cent of the qualifying years of your working life, you are entitled to a basic rate state retirement pension at the full rate. If you have spent the remaining 10 per cent of your working life in another member state, you can receive your full UK pension as well as the 10 per cent *pro rata* pension to which you are entitled from the other member state.

There are further detailed exceptions to the overlapping provisions for benefits paid for invalidity, old age, occupational disease or death.[78] Broadly speaking, a member state is not allowed to apply its overlapping provisions to reduce benefits of the same kind that you receive from that state just because you are receiving other benefits in respect of those risks from another member state.

Notes

2. Who is covered by the co-ordination rules

1 Art 87(8) EU Reg 883/04
2 Art 2 EU Reg 883/04
3 Art 87(8) EU Reg 883/04
4 *Bestuur de Bedrijfsvereniging voor de Metaalnijverheid v Mouthaan* C-39/76 [1976] ECR 1901 (ECJ)
5 Art 1(l) EU Reg 883/04
6 *Hoekstra (ne Unger)* C-75/63 [1964] ECR 177 (ECJ); *De Cicco* C-19/68 [1968] ECR 473 (ECJ) (under EU Reg 3, the predecessor to EU Reg 1408/71)
7 Art 1(a) EU Reg 1408/71
8 Contrast *Levin v Staatssecretaris van Justitie* C-53/81 [1982] ECR 1035 (ECJ) with *Heissische Knappschaft v Maison Singer et fils* C-44/65 [1965] ECR 965 (ECJ)
9 *Bestuur de Bedrijfsvereniging voor de Metaalnijverheid v Mouthaan* C-39/76 [1976] ECR 1901 (ECJ)
10 *Hoekstra (ne Unger)* C-75/63 [1964] ECR 177 (ECJ)
11 *Bestuur van het Algemeen Ziekenfonds Drenthe-Platteland vs G Pierik* C-117/77 (ECJ)
12 Students were added to the list by EU Reg 1408/71 in 1999; EU Reg 307/99

13 Although students fall within the scope of the Regulation, this does not mean they can override UK rules which exclude students from accessing certain benefits. These exclusions apply to all students and therefore are not in breach of EU Reg 1408/71. However, exclusion of students from income-based JSA has been found to breach EC Dir 79/7 by discriminating against women. See CJSA/1920/1999 (*65/00).
14 *Kits van Heijuningen* C-2/89 [1990] ECR 1753 (ECJ)
15 *Nolte* C-317/93 [1995] (ECJ)) suggests that a lower earnings limit cannot be displaced as constituting indirect sex discrimination, contrary to Directive 79/7, because it can be justified by objectives of social policy.
16 Art 1 EU Reg 1408/71
17 Art 11(b)(iv) EU Reg 987/09
18 Art 1(d) EU Reg 1408/71; Art 1(g) EU Reg 883/04
19 Art 1(e) EU Reg 1408/71; Art 1(h) EU Reg 883/04
20 Art 1(f)(i) EU Reg 1408/71; Art 1(i)1(i) EU Reg 883/04
21 s137 SSCBA 1992

22 Art 1(f) EU Reg 1408/71; Art 1(i)1(i) EU Reg 883/04

23 See *Cristini* C-32/75 [1975] ECR 1085 (ECJ)

24 *Kermaschek* C-40/76 [1976] ECR 1669 (ECJ), and see paras 23-24 and 34 of *Cabanis-Issarte* C-308/93 (ECJ)

25 *Gul v Dusseldorf* C-131/85 [1980] ECR 1573 (ECJ), [1987] 1 CMLR 501; *Echternach* C-389 and C-390/87 [1989] ECR 723 (ECJ); *Diatta v Land Berlin* C-267/83 [1985] ECR 567 (ECJ), [1986] 2 CMLR 164. The inconsistent decision of the House of Lords in *Re Sandler, The Times*, 10 May 1985, is probably wrong and should have been referred to the ECJ.

3. **Which benefits are covered by the co-ordination rules**

26 *Gillard* C-9/78 [1978] ECR 1661, para 12 (ECJ); *Piscitello* C-139/82 [1983] ECR 1427, para 10 (ECJ); *Stanton-Newton v CAO* C-356/89 (ECJ)

27 *Scrivner and Cole* C-122/84 [1986] 1 ECR 1027 (ECJ)

28 *Stanton-Newton v CAO* C-356/89 (ECJ)

29 Art 4(2) EU Reg 1408/71

30 Art 4(2) EU Reg 1408/71

31 Art 4(2a) EU Reg 1408/71

32 *Beerens* C-35/77 [1977] ECR 2249 (ECJ); *Stanton-Newton* C-356/89 (ECJ)

33 Resolution 2001/C44/06 of the Administrative Commission, 29 June 2000

34 Art 4(1)-(2a) EU Reg 1408/71

35 *Scrivner and Cole* C-122/84 [1986] 1 ECR 1027 (ECJ)

36 Art 5 EU Reg 1408/71; the declarations are published in the *Compendium of European Social Security Law*

37 Annex IIa EU Reg 1408/71

38 *Beerens* C-35/77 [1977] ECR 2249 (ECJ); *Stanton-Newton* C-356/89 (ECJ)

39 This case involved a claim under EC Dir 79/7 on the equal treatment between men and women in social security. *Hockenjos v Secretary of State for Social Security* [2001] EWCA Civ 624, CA and CJSA/1920/1999 (*65/00)

40 *Beerens* C-35/77 [1977] ECR 2249 (ECJ)

41 In *Stanton Newton* C-356/89 (ECJ), the UK government said that mobility allowance was not a social security benefit because it was not in its declaration and was more akin to social assistance. The ECJ said that it had more of the characteristics of social security.

42 Art 4(1) EU Reg 1408/71; Art 3 EU Reg 883/04

43 Paternity benefits are included under the new rules only from 1 May 2010; Art 3 EU Reg 883/04

44 Pre-retirement benefits are included under the new rules only from 1 May 2010; Art 3 EU Reg 883/04

45 From 1 May 2010, for people covered by the new rules; Art 3 EU Reg 883/04

46 Before June 1992, AA and DLA were considered to be invalidity benefits and therefore exportable. However, from 1 June 1992, they are listed as special non-contributory benefits and are no longer exportable: *Partridge*; *Snares* CDLA/913/94. However, those eligible for benefit before this date retain the right to export these benefits; Art 95 EU Reg 1408/71

47 *Fossi v Bundesknappschaft* C-79/76 [1977] ECR 667 (ECJ)

48 *Piscitello v INPS* C-139/82 [1983] ECR 1427 (ECJ)

4. **The 'competent' state**

49 Art 13 EU Reg 1408/71; Art 11 EU Reg 883/04

50 Contained in Art 13 EU Reg 1408/71; Art 11(2) EU Reg 883/04

51 Art 14(c) EU Reg 1408/71

52 Art 13 EU Reg 883/04

53 Art 13(2)(f) EU Reg 1408/71; *Kuusijrvi* C-275/96 [1998] ECR I-3419 (ECJ)

54 Art 14(1)(a) EU Reg 1408/71

55 Art 14(1)(b) EU Reg 1408/71

56 Art 14a(1)(a) EU Reg 1408/71

57 Art 14a(1)(a) EU Reg 1408/71

58 Art 14(2) EU Reg 1408/71

59 Art 17 EU Reg 1408/71

60 DMG memos 14/08 and 17/09

5. **Equal treatment**

61 *Patmalniece v SSWP* [2009] EWCA Civ 621. This case was due to be heard by the Supreme Court on 29 November 2010.

62 Art 3 Reg 1408/71; *O'Flynn* C-237/94 [1996] ECR I-2617, para 19 (ECJ); *Collins* C-138/02 [2004] ECR I-2703, para 66 (ECJ)

63 *Chateignier* C-346/05 (ECJ)

64 *Vandeweghe* C-130/73 [1973] ECR 1329 (ECJ)

65 *Costa* C-37/74 [1974] ECR 1251 (ECJ)

66 *Palermo* C-237/78 [1979] ECR 2645 (ECJ)

67 *Frascogna* C-256/86 [1987] ECR 3431 (ECJ)

6. **Aggregation**
68 *Mura* C-22/77 [1977] ECR 1699 (ECJ), [1978] 2 CMLR 416; but see also *Frangiamore* C-126/77 [1978] ECR 725 (ECJ) and *Warmerdam-Steggerda* C-388/87 [1989] ECR 1203 (ECJ)
69 Sickness and maternity (Art 18 EU Reg 1408/71), invalidity (Art 38), old age, death (survivors) and certain other invalidity benefits (Art 45(1)-(4)), occupational disease (Art 57), death grants (Art 64), unemployment (Art 67(1) and (2)), family benefit (Art 72).
70 The general overlapping provisions are contained in Arts 12 and 46 EU Reg 1408/71.

7. **Exporting benefits**
71 Art 10(1) EU Reg 1408/71; Art 7 EU Reg 883/04
72 C-299/05 (ECJ)
73 Art 10a EU Reg 1408/71

8. **Overlapping benefits**
74 Arts 12 and 48 EU Reg 1408/71; see also specific provisions in relation to particular benefits: Arts 19(2), 25(1)(b), 34(2), 39(2) and (5), 68(2), 71(2), 76 and 76(3) EU Reg 1408/71
75 Art 13 EU Reg 1408/71
76 SS(OB) Regs
77 *Petroni* C-24/75 [1995] ECR 1149 (ECJ)
78 Arts 46a, 46b and 46c EU Reg 1408/71

Chapter 12

. . . .

The co-ordination rules for categories of benefits

This chapter covers the co-ordination rules for the various categories of social security benefits. It contains:

1. Introduction (below)
2. Invalidity benefits (p185)
3. Old age benefits (p189)
4. Survivors' benefits (p194)
5. Benefits for accidents at work and occupational diseases (p195)
6. Unemployment benefits (p196)
7. Family benefits (p201)
8. Special non-contributory benefits (p204)
9. Death grants (p206)
10. Sickness, maternity and paternity benefits (p207)

Chapter 11 outlines the general conditions that must be met in order to be able to rely on the co-ordination rules. This chapter outlines the specific benefit rules for the particular category or 'risk' under the co-ordination rules. It lists the United Kingdom benefits that fall within Regulations 1408/71 (the old rules) and 883/04 (the new rules) and explains how these benefits are affected by the co-ordination rules. It also highlights any differences between the old and the new co-ordination rules.

Note: housing benefit and council tax benefit are not covered by the co-ordination rules.

---

1. Introduction

European Union (EU) law does not define the category in which a benefit should be. Instead, each member state declares which benefits fall within each category. This should be done by considering:[1]

• the purpose of the benefit; *and*
• the conditions of entitlement to the benefit; *and*
• who is entitled to claim that benefit;

Consequently, a benefit, such as income support, paid in a range of different circumstances does not fall within any of the risk categories, whereas a benefit, such as state pension, is clearly only for people of pension age and therefore falls within the category of old age benefit.[2]

It does not necessarily matter if a member state does not consider a benefit is covered by a particular risk. You can argue that a United Kingdom (UK) benefit should fall within a particular risk if you believe the purpose, conditions and claimants would all fall within that risk. For example, the UK currently lists income-based jobseeker's allowance (JSA) as a special non-contributory benefit rather than an unemployment benefit. Yet arguably the characteristics of income-based JSA are those of an unemployment benefit.

From 1 May 2010, member states must ensure that people covered by the co-ordination rules receive a timely response to any enquiries relating to their entitlements under the co-ordination rules.[3] At the very latest, a response must be provided within national time limits. Member states without any such time limits are encouraged to introduce them. The UK has target times for dealing with claims, but in areas of EU law claimants often have to wait months before receiving a decision. If you are in this situation, you should get advice on whether you have grounds for a complaint or a judicial review.

Under the new rules (see p161), if there is a dispute about which member state is responsible for paying you benefit, you should be temporarily affiliated to a social security scheme until a decision is made about which state is responsible for you.[4]

2. Invalidity benefits

In European Union (EU) law, benefits categorised as 'invalidity benefits' are treated very differently from those categorised as sickness benefits. In the United Kingdom (UK), traditionally benefits for invalidity (such as incapacity benefit (IB) and invalidity benefit) were earnings-replacement benefits for total incapacity to work. In EU law, however, invalidity benefits are more like a disability benefit paid according to the level of your disability, similar perhaps to industrial disablement benefit. Invalidity benefits may change to retirement pension at different times in different states because of the different pension ages in each state.

Invalidity benefits available in the UK under the co-ordination rules are:

- contributory employment and support allowance (ESA). Only ESA paid after the initial assessment phase is considered by the UK to be an 'invalidity benefit'. The assessment phase of ESA is classified as a sickness benefit (see p207) and income-related ESA is categorised as a special non-contributory benefit (see p204);

- ESA in youth; the government has never stated which category this benefit falls within. However, severe disablement allowance (SDA) was initially replaced by non-contributory IB and more recently by ESA in youth. Given the similarity between ESA in youth and SDA, it is arguable that ESA in youth should be treated as an EU invalidity benefit;
- long-term IB;
- attendance allowance (AA), disability living allowance (DLA) care and mobility components and carer's allowance (CA) if you have been receiving them since before 1 June 1992 (see p211). If you claimed after this date, see p211.

Note: adult dependency increases can be paid with the above benefits (if available) for family members, even if they are living in another member state.[5] However, such increases are classed as 'family benefits' rather than invalidity benefits (see p201).

Types of invalidity benefits

There are two basic types of long-term invalidity benefits paid by European Economic Area (EEA) states. These are referred to as 'Type A' and 'Type B' benefits.
- **Type A benefits.** The amount of benefit is not related to the duration of the period of insurance. Typically, with Type A benefits, you must be insured at the time the risk insured against materialises. UK benefits, such as contributory ESA, are Type A benefits.
- **Type B benefits.** The amount of benefit depends on the duration of the period of insurance you have completed. Typically, with Type B benefits, it is not necessary for you to be insured at the time the risk insured against materialises. Instead, the periods of insurance are 'stored' and you can claim the benefit at a later date when the risk materialises.

Examples

Ralf works for many years, paying national insurance (NI) contributions, and is insured during that period against any invalidity. He then becomes ill. The amount of benefit to which he is entitled does not depend on the number of years he has worked. The benefit is therefore a Type A benefit.

Shamira works for a number of years, paying NI contributions, and is insured against any invalidity. With each year that passes, the amount of benefit to which she would be entitled if she fell ill increases. The benefit is therefore a Type B benefit.

The UK and Ireland both operate a Type A system of long-term benefits, but most other EEA states operate Type B systems. Some states have Type A schemes for certain groups or benefits.

Rights under the co-ordination rules

The main principles of aggregation (see p177) and exportation (see p178) apply to invalidity benefits. Therefore, periods of insurance in any member state must be taken into account, if necessary, in order for you to qualify for benefit. In practice, this means that if you have worked, even briefly, in the UK before falling ill, you can rely on NI contributions paid in the UK as well as elsewhere in the EEA in order to qualify for benefit.

Similarly, if entitlement depends on incapacity for work or receiving a sickness benefit for a certain period of time, account can be taken of periods in receipt of another state's benefit.[6]

There are no restrictions for A8 or A2 nationals.

Example
Eva is a Polish national and came to the UK to work. She previously worked for many years in Poland. After only three months of registered work, she is diagnosed with cancer and dismissed from her job. Eva is able to claim contributory ESA under the co-ordination rules by relying on the contributions she has paid in Poland before coming to the UK.

Claims

Generally, there are no special claim forms; you simply claim benefit in the appropriate way either to the competent institution (see p171) or to the state in which you reside. The date of your claim is the date of receipt by either authority or the date your entitlement to a sickness benefit ends, whichever is the later.[7]

How you are paid

If you have only worked in states with Type A invalidity benefits

With Type A invalidity benefits, the amount of benefit you receive does not depend on the amount of contributions paid. It is paid at a standard rate.[8] ESA is a Type A invalidity benefit.

If you have only worked and paid NI contributions in member states with Type A invalidity benefits, you are entitled to invalidity benefit under one member state's legislation only. Which member state is responsible depends on:
- where you became sick; *and*
- whether you worked in that member state or, if not, the member state in which you were last employed.

Invalidity benefit is paid by the state in which you were insured at the time incapacity began. The only exception to this is if an unemployment benefit is being paid by the country of residence, rather than employment. In this case, the state of residence pays invalidity benefits.[9] If you receive an invalidity benefit from the state of residence, it is not paid by any other state under EU law.

However, if you are not entitled under this state, there may be entitlement in one of the other states in which you were insured. If you are eligible in more than one state, the state where you were most recently insured should pay.[10]

Claims can be made either to the competent institution (see p171), which is liable to pay you, or to the social security authority in the state of residence, which will forward it to the competent institution. Your date of claim is the date that it is received by either authority, or the date when entitlement to sickness benefits expired, whichever is later.[11]

If entitlement depends on incapacity for work or receiving a sickness benefit for a certain period of time, account can be taken of periods during which you received another state's benefit.[12]

If you have only worked in states with Type B invalidity benefits

The rate of your invalidity benefit depends on the amount of contributions that you have paid.[13] You may be able to get Type B invalidity benefit from two or more EEA member states if you have paid insurance contributions in any of the following member states: Austria, Denmark, Finland, France (but only under the French miners' insurance scheme, or if you were self-employed in France), Germany, Greece (except under the agricultural insurance scheme), Iceland, Italy, Liechtenstein, Luxembourg, Norway, Portugal or Sweden.

How much you get from each member state is worked out according to a formula. It is calculated by two different methods and you get whichever is higher.[14]

Invalidity benefit from each state is worked out as follows.

Step one
- Assess under national law alone.

Step two
- Add up total insurance in all member states and work out the amount of benefit this would give.
- Work out the proportion of years in each state to decide the pro rata amount which is then payable by each state.

Step three
- The two rates of benefit produced in steps one and two are compared and you receive the higher of the two.

If you paid contributions in any one of the above states and you are getting benefit from only one of these, you should ask the benefit authority there to send your details to the other member states in which you have been subject to the legislation/paying contributions. You may be entitled to a higher level of benefit.

If you have worked in states with Type A invalidity benefits and in states with Type B invalidity benefits

If you were insured in a country where the amount of invalidity benefit is not dependent on your NI contributions when your incapacity begins, benefit can be paid as above (Type A), provided there is no entitlement under an insurance-related scheme and you have not yet claimed retirement pension.

Exporting invalidity benefits

Once you are entitled to an invalidity benefit, you can 'export' (see p178) that benefit to another member state, whatever your reason is for going there.[15] Such benefits can continue to be paid indefinitely while you are abroad, provided you continue to meet the general rules of entitlement. Your benefit will also be uprated annually, in the same way as it would if you were in the UK.

The state from which you claim benefit is the one that determines your degree of invalidity, but medical reports from other states must be taken into account. In some circumstances, a state can insist on your being examined by a doctor of its own choice. This is rare, however, and the general rule is that any checks and medicals take place in the state in which you are living, rather than the one that pays you benefit. The reports are then sent to the paying state.[16] There are special rules that apply if your condition worsens.[17] These vary according to your situation but, in general, if your condition gets worse, this should be taken into account in the assessment of your benefit. You should raise the matter with the 'competent institution' (see p171) or the relevant social security department of the state in which you are living.

Under the old co-ordination rules (see p161), if an invalidity benefit is suspended (eg, because you fail to attend a medical) but then resumed, the same state continues to pay. If it is withdrawn but further invalidity arises, the question of who pays is decided afresh.[18] There is no equivalent provision in the new co-ordination rules.

3. Old age benefits

Old age benefits available in the United Kingdom (UK) that are covered by the co-ordination rules are:

- state retirement pension;
- additional pension;
- graduated retirement benefit;
- winter fuel payments;[19]
- adult dependency increases in retirement pension;
- Christmas bonus;
- bus passes for pensioners.[20]

Category A, B C and D retirement pensions are all covered.

Category A and B retirement pensions are contributory, while Category D carries a residence test and is paid in very limited circumstances. Category C pension is no longer relevant as it only applies to people who were of pension age in 1948. For further details of the general rules for entitlement to these benefits, see CPAG's *Welfare Benefits and Tax Credits Handbook*.

Rights under the co-ordination rules

If you have worked in more than one member state, your insurance record is preserved in each of those states until you reach pension age. You will get a contribution to your retirement pension from each member state in which you worked for a year or more, based on your insurance record in that member state or, if residence counts for benefit purposes, the length of your residence in that member state.

This means that you can be entitled to a pension under European Union (EU) law, even if you do not qualify for a pension under the national legislation of the country in which you are resident. Therefore, if you have paid contributions in the UK for a short period and you do not qualify for a Category A or B pension under British legislation, but you have worked in another European Economic Area (EEA) state, you may qualify for a retirement pension when those contributions are taken into account.

Increases of retirement pension for child dependants are family benefits, not old age benefits (see p201).

Your retirement pension is worked out using a complex formula (see p192). If a pension depends on periods of residence in a particular state, any periods of residence in other member states are taken into account to help you qualify.

The age at which you may be entitled to a retirement pension differs from member state to member state. Because of this, you may be entitled to an old age benefit in one member state before you reach retirement age in another. Similarly, if you have been incapable of work before you reached pension age you may be entitled to pro rata invalidity benefits in the member state where you have not yet reached pension age.

Category D retirement pension

You may be entitled to this if you are 80 years of age or over, but it is paid only in limited circumstances. Residence in another EEA member state can count towards satisfying the 10-year residence conditions for a Category D pension provided that either:

- residence in the other EEA member state counts towards entitlement to old age benefits in that member state; *or*
- you were insured in the other member state and you have at some time been subject to UK legislation – eg, you have been liable to pay UK Class 1 or Class 2 national insurance contributions.

If you satisfy these conditions, the period of residence in the other EEA member state is added to the periods of residence in the UK and pro rata Category D retirement pension is awarded. The UK pays the percentage of benefit which is equivalent to the number of years of residence in the UK used to satisfy the 10-year residence condition.

Winter fuel payments

Winter fuel payments from the social fund are considered to be old age benefits under the co-ordination rules and therefore should be fully exportable in the same way as a state retirement pension.[21] However, the practice of the Department for Work and Pensions (DWP) has been to allow a winter fuel payment to be exported only if it has already been awarded to you at least once while you were living in the UK. If you have already moved to another EEA state, you cannot subsequently make a first claim for a winter fuel payment.

The reason for this seems to be that the wording of Article 10(1) of EU Regulation 1408/71 states that 'benefits for old age acquired under the legislation of one or more member states shall not be subject to any reduction, modification, suspension, withdrawal or confiscation by reason of the fact that the recipient resides in the territory of a member state other than that in which the institution responsible for payment is situated.'

The DWP interprets this as meaning that a person has to first receive the benefit in the UK. It seems to be the use of the word 'acquired' which that has caused the problem. The new co-ordination rules do not use the word 'acquired' and so if you are covered by the new Regulation 883/04, it may now be easier to make a claim for a winter fuel payment from abroad as long as the UK remains the competent state (see p171).[22]

However, for people who are only covered by the old co-ordination rules, it is still possible to argue that a first claim for a winter fuel payment is possible from abroad. There is caselaw from the European Court of Justice (ECJ) which makes clear that the scope of Article 10(1) is not confined to the right to export benefits already acquired and that it is unlawful to make the acquisition of old age benefits dependent on residence in a member state.

This was the position taken by the ECJ in *Smieja*[23] and confirmed in *Carraciolo*,[24] in which a claim for invalidity benefit under Belgium law was made by a person resident in Italy. Benefit was refused because the claimant was not present in Belgium. The ECJ, referring back to its judgment in *Smieja*, held that:

> ... the aim of the provision contained in Article 10 is to promote the free movement of workers by insulating those concerned from the harmful consequences which might result when they transfer their residence from one member state to another. It is clear from that principle not only that the person concerned retains the right to receive pensions and benefits acquired under the legislation of one or more member states even after taking up residence in

another member state, but also that he may not be prevented from acquiring such a right merely because he does not reside in the territory of the state in which the institution responsible for payment is situated.

In later cases, the ECJ confirmed its earlier rulings stating that:[25]

> Article 10 of Regulation No 1408/71 must be interpreted as meaning that a person may not be precluded from acquiring or retaining entitlement to the benefits, pensions and allowances referred to in that provision on the sole ground that he does not reside within the territory of the member state in which the institution responsible for payment is situated.

Calculating your pension

The following rules apply wherever you are in the EEA. If you have been subject to the legislation of more than one member state, each must calculate your pension entitlement as follows.

Step one
Each member state should calculate the pension to which you are entitled (if any) under its own legislation.[26] For example, if you have been insured in the UK for 20 years, you will be entitled to a UK pension of approximately 50 per cent of the standard rate. On the other hand, under UK domestic legislation, if you have only worked for eight years in the UK you will have no entitlement.

Step two
Each member state should then calculate a theoretical pension as if your entire career in the EEA had been spent in that state.[27] This theoretical amount is then reduced in proportion to the actual time you worked in that state compared with the time worked in the EEA as a whole. The resulting amount is known as your pro rata entitlement.

Step three
Each member state then pays you whichever is the greater of the amount to which you are entitled under its own domestic legislation, and the pro rata amount of its benefit to which you are entitled from that member state calculated in accordance with the co-ordination rules.[28]

Example

Mr Coiro from Italy has worked for 43 years in different member states:

– 8 years in the UK;
– 15 years in Italy;
– 20 years in Ireland.

His entitlement in the UK based on UK domestic legislation (based on periods of insurance) amounts to nothing. However, if his entitlement to a UK pension were calculated as if his entire EEA career of 43 years' work had been carried out in the UK, he would be eligible for 100 per cent of the UK rate of retirement pension (this is his 'theoretical entitlement'). He can therefore claim the pro rata amount of this entitlement in respect of his years of work in the UK.

His pro rata entitlement is worked out as follows:

The theoretical rate x the UK period of insurance divided by the EEA period of insurance =

$$100\% \times \frac{8 \text{ years}}{43 \text{ years}} = 19\%$$

So Mr Coiro will be entitled to the pro rata rate of 19 per cent of the UK standard rate. Since the alternative amount which he could claim from the UK based on his eight years' contributions is nil, the pro rata amount is the higher of the two possible entitlements to a UK pension and that is what Mr Coiro can claim.

In this example, Italy and Ireland would perform similar calculations and Mr Coiro would receive a pension from each on the same basis. It could be that, for either or both of these member states, the calculation based on their domestic legislation turned out to be higher, and Mr Coiro would receive that larger pension.

Because of the way the calculation rules work for UK pensions, entitlement under domestic legislation alone will almost invariably be equal to or higher than the pro rata amount calculated in accordance with the co-ordination rules.[29]

If you have worked for a period of less than one year in an EEA member state, your pension is calculated differently and you receive no pension from that state.[30] However, the period is included in the calculation of your total period of employment in the EEA.[31]

Graduated retirement benefit in the UK is not included in the pro rata rate calculation, but your UK entitlement is added on after the calculation under the co-ordination rules has been carried out.[32]

The pro rata equation is not recalculated when benefits are uprated, although the rate of retirement pension is increased.[33]

Claims

In general, you make a claim for your pension in the state in which you are resident. If you have never been insured in that state, your claim will be forwarded to the member state in which you were last insured.[34] Alternatively, when you approach pension age, you could apply directly to the 'competent state' (see p171) to claim your pension. That state will pass details of your claim to any other EEA member state in which you have been insured, so that each can do its calculation. The competent state will inform you whether you will be better off under domestic law alone or with your entitlement calculated under the co-ordination rule.[35]

Each member state decides how to pay your pension and pays it itself.

How you are paid

You can be paid a UK pension in any other EEA member state at the same rate as you would get if you were living in the UK.[36] Your pension may be paid directly into a bank in the member state in which you are living or in the UK.

You may have claimed a means-tested benefit, such as income support (IS), while waiting for your retirement pension to be calculated and paid from another member state. Any arrears of pension will usually be sent directly to you. However, you should bear in mind that you will have to repay any IS you received when your pension arrives. Similarly, if you have been getting an IS-type benefit in another EEA member state while waiting for your UK retirement pension, you may have to repay that amount when your UK pension arrives.

Exporting old age benefits

Retirement pensions are fully exportable. This means that your retirement pension is paid to you regardless of where you live or stay in the EEA without any reduction or modification.[37]

4. **Survivors' benefits**

Survivors' benefits available in the United Kingdom (UK) under the co-ordination rules are all bereavement benefits apart from bereavement payment – ie:[38]

- widowed mother's allowance;
- widowed parent's allowance;
- bereavement allowance;
- industrial death benefit.

Your rights under the co-ordination rules for survivors' benefits mirror those for old age benefits (see p189). Periods of insurance, residence and employment can be aggregated in order to qualify for benefit.

Exporting survivors' benefits

Survivors' benefits are fully exportable. This means they must be uprated in line with UK increases and continue indefinitely unless you are no longer eligible.

Chapter 12: The co-ordination rules for categories of benefits
5. Benefits for accidents at work and occupational diseases

12

5. Benefits for accidents at work and occupational diseases

Benefits for accidents at work and occupational diseases available in the United Kingdom (UK) under the co-ordination rules are:

- disablement benefit;
- constant attendance allowance (which you may receive if you are getting 100 per cent disablement benefit and need somebody to look after you);[39]
- exceptionally severe disablement allowance (which you may receive if you are getting constant attendance allowance at one of the two highest rates, and your need for constant attendance is likely to be permanent);[40]
- reduced earnings allowance (which you may receive if you are assessed at at least 1 per cent for disablement benefit and your accident occurred or your disease started before 1 October 1990, and you cannot do your normal job as a result).[41]

Rights under the co-ordination rules

Your rights under the co-ordination rules for industrial injuries benefits are very similar to those for old age benefits (see p189).[42] Periods of insurance, residence and employment can be aggregated in order to qualify for benefit, and industrial injury benefits are fully exportable.

Although European Union (EU) Regulation 1408/71 and Regulation 883/04 apply to both employed and self-employed people, you should remember that UK industrial injuries benefits are only available to employed earners and not to self-employed people.[43]

A person who has had an industrial accident or contracted an occupational disease and who goes to stay temporarily in another member state can continue to get benefits.[44] This also applies if you go to another member state for medical treatment.

Under the old co-ordination rules, accidents while travelling abroad in another member state could be deemed to have occurred in the state liable to pay industrial injuries benefit. This also applied while in transit between member states.[45] This is strengthened under the new co-ordination rules, which make clear that any events or facts arising in one member state must be taken into account as though they had happened in the member state of residence.[46]

If you have worked in two or more European Economic Area (EEA) states in a job that gave you a prescribed industrial disease, you will only get benefit from the member state in which you last worked in that job.

Under the old co-ordination rules, previous accidents or diseases that arose in other member states could be taken into account when deciding the extent of the disablement for industrial injuries benefits. Similarly, later accidents or diseases could affect the assessment of disablement if:

12

Chapter 12: The co-ordination rules for categories of benefits
5. Benefits for accidents at work and occupational diseases

- no industrial injuries benefit was payable for the original accident or disease; *and*
- there was no entitlement in the state in which the subsequent accident occurred.[47]

This provision has also been improved under the new co-ordination rules to make clear that there must be equal treatment in respect of benefits, income, facts or events which take place in another EEA state.[48]

Claims

Generally, claims should be made to the 'competent institution' (see p171). However, you should be able to claim from any of the member states who must then forward your claim to the correct institution.

How you are paid

If you live in a state different to the one liable to pay you benefit, you can nevertheless claim from abroad and be paid.[49]

If you were insured in another EEA member state, you will be paid directly by the appropriate institution of that state according to its rules for determining whether or not you are eligible and how much you should be paid. That institution may arrange for the Department for Work and Pensions to make your payments, but this will not alter the amount you receive.

If your condition deteriorates and you are getting, or used to get, benefit from an EEA member state, that state is responsible for carrying out any necessary further medical examinations and paying any additional benefit.

Exporting benefits for accidents at work and occupational diseases

Industrial injury benefits are fully exportable if you go to another EEA member state. If you are intending to travel, you should consult the office that pays you benefit well in advance so that arrangements can be made for payment in the other member state.

---

6. Unemployment benefits

The only unemployment benefit that the United Kingdom (UK) government considers to be a European Union (EU) unemployment benefit is contribution-based jobseeker's allowance (JSA).[50]

Arguably, income-based JSA should also be treated as an unemployment benefit as it is a benefit paid only to people who are unemployed. In addition, the UK already lists contribution-based JSA as an unemployment benefit and under the co-ordination rules it is not possible to have a benefit categorised as two different types of benefit.[51]

A commissioner and, in a separate case, the Court of Appeal have held that income-based JSA is also an unemployment benefit for the purposes of European Community Directive 79/7.[52] This Directive specifies that there must be equal treatment in social security between men and women. Although the decision relates to a different area of EU law, there are clearly some grounds to argue that income-based JSA is also an unemployment benefit. The European Commission has also stated that income-based JSA is an unemployment benefit.[53]

There may also be grounds to argue that employment and support allowance (ESA) should also be considered an unemployment benefit.

Rights under the co-ordination rules

The general rules of aggregation apply (see p177). Contribution-based JSA requires you to have paid contributions in the two years prior to your claim. You can use periods of insurance or employment completed as an employed person under the legislation of any other member state to satisfy the contribution conditions, provided you were subject to UK legislation immediately before claiming contribution-based JSA. Each week of employment completed as an employed person in any other member state is treated as a contribution paid into the UK scheme on earnings of two-thirds of the present upper earnings limit for contribution purposes.

If you become unemployed while working abroad and are insured in that member state's unemployment insurance scheme, you will be subject to the legislation of the state in which you are working and that member state is responsible for paying you unemployment benefit. If you were previously insured in the UK, you are normally able to use periods during which you paid national insurance and aggregate them with periods of insurance in the member state in which you last worked to enable you to get the unemployment benefit of the member state where you have been working.[54]

If members of your family are living in another European Economic Area (EEA) member state and the amount of your unemployment benefit is determined by the number of people in your family, they are taken into account as if they were living in the member state that pays your benefit.[55] If your dependant lives in another member state, you need Form E302 from the employment institution of the member state in which your dependant lives.

How you are paid

You are paid an unemployment benefit by the member state in which you were last employed.[56] An exception to this general rule is if you reside in one member state but you are working or paying contributions in another. In this case, you can claim from either the member state in which you reside or the member state in which you pay contributions.

If you are potentially entitled to an unemployment benefit from both the member state in which you last worked and the member state in which you reside, you must choose where to register for work and claim the benefit.[57]

Exporting unemployment benefits

There is a limited provision for 'exporting'unemployment benefits. If you are receiving an unemployment benefit from one member state and you go to another member state, you continue to be entitled to the unemployment benefit from the competent state for a period of up to three months. The new co-ordination rules allow for unemployment benefits to be exported for a maximum of six months. However, member states can elect to restrict exporting to three months and the UK has elected to do this.[58]

After three months, you must return to the competent state to continue receiving the unemployment benefit.

If you are going to look for work in another EEA member state, you are entitled to contribution-based JSA abroad if:[59]

- you satisfy the conditions for contribution-based JSA before you leave the UK.[60] You qualify even if you have claimed contribution-based JSA but no decision has yet been made on your entitlement, but you are getting JSA hardship payments pending the decision; *and*
- your entitlement to contribution-based JSA arises from aggregating insurance payments you have made in different member states.[61] Your entitlement to contribution-based JSA must not arise as a result of a reciprocal agreement between the UK and a state that is not a member of the EEA;[62] *and*
- you are going to the other EEA member state to seek work.[63] You are not entitled to exportable contribution-based JSA if you are going on holiday, visiting a sick relative or accompanying your partner. If you give up work to accompany your partner on a posting abroad, it is very unlikely that you will be able to export your UK contribution-based JSA. In order to establish entitlement you must show that:
  – there was just cause for voluntarily leaving your employment; *and*
  – you were capable of, available for and actively seeking work.
  Usually it is accepted that if you left work to accompany your partner on a foreign posting, you have just cause provided you left no earlier than was reasonable to organise your affairs before travelling.[64] However, you may still lose entitlement because you will find it difficult to establish that you were available for work during this time. If, on the other hand, you were already unemployed and you accompany your partner abroad to seek work, you may be accepted as satisfying this condition; *and*

- you have been registered as available for work for at least four weeks in the UK.[65] In exceptional circumstances, you may be allowed to leave the UK before the four weeks have expired and still qualify. You must get authority in advance to do so from Pensions and Overseas Benefits Directorate in Newcastle; *and*
- you are registered for work in another EEA member state.[66] If you are looking for work in another member state, you must register for work there within seven days of leaving the UK and comply with that member state's regulations unless there are exceptional circumstances;[67] *and*
- the employment services of that member state will pay contribution-based JSA in accordance with its own legislation. This includes the method and frequency of payment.[68] The requirement to sign on at Jobcentre Plus is satisfied if:
  - you attend at an equivalent office in the other member state; *or*
  - you comply with that member state's control procedures, showing that you are available for work as its rules require.

The member state to which you have moved carries out checks on entitlement to JSA in accordance with its own procedures. If there is doubt about whether you meet the registration and availability conditions of the member state in which you are living this will be reported to the Department for Work and Pensions (DWP) in the UK. On the advice of the other EEA state, the DWP will make a decision about whether or not you continue to be entitled. While the question is referred to the DWP, your benefit may be suspended by the other state. It is important that the decision is made in the UK because you have the right to appeal. In some EEA states there is no right of appeal against the decision of a decision maker.

On request, a statement will be issued by the DWP for you to give to the employment services of the member state where you are going to look for work.[69] The statement will give:

- the rate of contribution-based JSA that is payable;
- the date from which JSA can be paid;
- the time limit for registration in the other EEA member state;
- the maximum period of entitlement;
- any other relevant facts that might affect your entitlement.

You can export JSA to more than one EEA member state during the same period of absence from the UK.

Under the old co-ordination rules, JSA could only be exported once from the UK during any one period of unemployment. Under the old co-ordination rules you could not return to the UK and then go abroad a second time in the same period until you had worked and paid more contributions in the UK.[70] This has changed under the new co-ordination rules and it is possible to go abroad more than once and export your unemployment benefit in any one period of unemployment. However, as UK contribution-based JSA is limited to a maximum payment period of six months, this extension of rights may not be of significant benefit to those receiving JSA unless it is accepted that income-based JSA is also exportable.

If you have not found a job within three months and return to the UK before the three-month period has expired, you will continue to get contribution-based JSA in the UK, assuming that the six-month period for which JSA can be paid is not exhausted.[71]

Under the old co-ordination rules, if you are sick or become pregnant while looking for work in another EEA member state, you may be entitled to ESA or a UK maternity benefit but only for the period until your contribution-based JSA entitlement runs out.[72] For example, if you have already received JSA for four months in the UK, you are only entitled to two months' contribution-based JSA abroad.

There is no equivalent provision in the new co-ordination rules.

If you are entitled to receive JSA while in another EEA member state, you should get a letter from Jobcentre Plus to help register for work in the other member state.

If you are going to look for work in Austria, Belgium, Finland, France, Germany, Greece, Iceland, Italy, Norway, Portugal, Spain or Sweden, you will be given Form E303. If you are going to look for work in another EEA member state, Form E303 will be sent directly to that member state.

If you come to the United Kingdom and are unemployed

If you are a returning resident or an EEA national coming to the UK to work or to seek work, the following applies to you.

If you have worked and paid insurance contributions under the legislation of another EEA member state, the periods of insurance in that state may count towards your entitlement to contribution-based JSA on your return to the UK. This will apply if, after your return to the UK, you get employment, pay Class 1 contributions but then become unemployed again.[73] You are then subject to UK legislation (ie, the UK is the competent state) and the UK is responsible for paying you the appropriate amount of contribution-based JSA.

If you were not subject to another member state's legislation while abroad (because you were an exception to the rule that the competent state is the state where you work – see p173), the unemployment insurance you paid while abroad may nevertheless still be taken into account when assessing your entitlement to contribution-based JSA if it is decided that, while you were abroad, you remained 'habitually resident' in the UK (see p110).

If you are coming to or returning to the UK to look for work and have been insured in another EEA member state, you may be able to get the other member state's unemployment benefit for up to three months if:[74]

- you were getting that member state's unemployment benefit immediately before coming to the UK;[75] *and*
- you have been registered as available for work for four weeks (or less if the member state's rules allow) in the other member state;[76] *and*
- you register and claim UK JSA within seven days after you were last registered in the other member state;[77] *and*
- you satisfy the UK's availability for work rules.[78] The DWP will carry out checks and pay benefit where an unemployment benefit has been exported from another EEA member state to the UK. However, it cannot decide whether or not there is entitlement to the other state's unemployment benefit. If a doubt arises about your continuing entitlement, the DWP will inform the employment authorities of the other state and, if appropriate, may suspend payment of your unemployment benefit while waiting for a reply. Before you leave the other member state, you must get Form E303.[79]

Example

Ildiko, a Hungarian national, is a lone parent working in the UK in registered work. After three months, she is dismissed. Her claim for JSA is rejected under the right to reside test. However, under the co-ordination rules, Ildiko can sign on for JSA, relying on the contributions she has paid in Hungary to qualify for contribution-based JSA.

7. **Family benefits**

The family benefits available in the United Kingdom (UK) under the co-ordination rules are:

- child benefit;
- child tax credit (CTC);
- guardian's allowance.

Rights under the co-ordination rules

The general principle of aggregation applies to family benefits (see p177). Under the old co-ordination rules, this is limited to aggregating periods of insurance or employment. No mention is made of aggregating periods of residence. Under the new co-ordination regulations, family benefits are treated in the same way as any other social security benefit. Periods of employment, self-employment, insurance or residence can be taken into account as though they were periods completed in the UK.[80] The distinction between family benefits and family allowances (see p170) has been abolished. You can therefore:

- export family benefits such as child benefit, CTC and guardian's allowance if you go to live in another member state. Under the old co-ordination rules, it was not generally possible to export family benefits unless you were receiving

a UK pension (this could include state pension and employment and support allowance);
- claim family benefits in the UK for family members living in another state. For example, a Spanish person working in the UK can claim child benefit for her/his children living in Spain.

Overlapping benefit rules

Migrant workers may be separated from family members while they search for work or establish themselves in another member state. This, combined with the fact that different member states have different conditions for benefits (some based on residence, some on employment, others on contributions), means that there is scope for duplication of payments. Therefore, European Union (EU) law has rules to prevent a person from claiming family benefits from more than one state.

If you are entitled to family benefits under the legislation of more than one state, you will receive the highest amount provided for, topped up if necessary by the paying state.[81] You cannot receive family benefits twice for the same family member. The state that pays benefits based on employment or self-employment takes precedence over the state that pays benefits based on a pension or residence. If you are entitled to benefits from more than one state on the same basis, the priority is:[82]
- if family benefits are based on employment/self-employment in both states, the state where the children reside if the parent works there, otherwise the state that pays the highest amount;
- if family benefits are based on receipt of a pension in both states, the state where the children reside if that state also pays the pension, otherwise the state where you have been insured or resided for the longest period;
- if family benefits are based on residence, the state where the children reside.

Claims

Claims should be made to the state liable to pay on the appropriate claim form for that benefit. A certificate proving that the children are your dependants must be obtained. There is a duty to notify any changes in the size of your family, the fact that you have moved to a different state, that your partner is working and due to get family benefits from another member state and any other change that might affect entitlement.[83]

If you do not use a family benefit for the benefit of the family, it can be paid to another person who will use it in this way.[84]

How you are paid

Generally, you are entitled to a family benefit from the state in which you are working or you last worked. However, there are exceptions to this.

If you are employed

If you are employed in a member state, you claim from the state in which you are working even if your family is living in another member state.[85] Therefore, it is possible to claim a benefit such as child benefit even though the child is not living with you.

If you are unemployed

If you were previously employed or self-employed and you are getting an unemployment benefit from a European Economic Area (EEA) member state, you are entitled to family benefits from that member state for members of your family who are living in any EEA member state.[86] Therefore, it is possible to claim benefits even though your child does not reside with you.

If you are wholly unemployed, you are entitled to family benefits from your state of residence *only* for members of your family who are residing with you if:[87]

- you are unemployed; *but*
- you were previously employed; *and*
- during your last period of employment you were resident in a different EEA member state to the one in which you were working; *and*
- you are receiving unemployment benefit from the member state where you are living.

Family benefits for children of pensioners

If you are getting your pension from only one EEA member state, family benefits are payable by that member state regardless of where in the EEA you or your children live.

If you are receiving a pension from more than one member state, family benefits are payable by the member state where you live, provided there is entitlement under that member state's scheme. If there is no entitlement under its scheme, the member state to which you have been subject to the legislation for the longest period and under which you have entitlement to family benefits, is responsible for paying you.[88]

Exporting family benefits

Under the new co-ordination rules you can export family benefits such as child benefit, CTC and guardian's allowance if you go to live in another member state. Under the old co-ordination rules, it was not generally possible to export family benefits. The exception to this was if you were receiving a UK pension (this could include state pension and employment and support allowance).

8. Special non-contributory benefits

Each member state is required to list the benefits it considers as being 'special non-contributory benefits' in an annex to the Regulations. This list is often out of date. The United Kingdom (UK) lists the following benefits as special non-contributory benefits in Regulation 883/04:[89]

- disability living allowance (DLA) mobility component;
- income support (IS);
- income-based jobseeker's allowance (JSA);
- pension credit (PC).

Income-related employment and support allowance (ESA) is not listed by the UK as a special non-contributory benefit.[90] However, UK guidance states that it is a special non-contributory benefit, although arguably, it should be considered as a sickness or invalidity benefit rather than a special non-contributory benefit.

Rights under the co-ordination rules

Special non-contributory benefits are subject to the principle of aggregation. A member state whose legislation makes entitlement to its own special non-contributory benefits subject to the completion of periods of employment, self-employment or residence must treat periods of employment, self-employment or residence completed in another member state as though they were completed in its own.

However, this only applies once it is established that you are habitually resident in the member state where you want to claim benefit (see below).

Once it is decided that you are habitually resident in a member state, you may rely on the co-ordination provisions to satisfy any residence or contribution conditions. Therefore, if you need to claim benefit, the state in which you are habitually resident must add together periods of residence or employment in other member states in order for you to qualify for benefit. However, you cannot use residence in other states to show that you are habitually resident in the state where you are claiming benefit.

Habitual residence

Old co-ordination rules

There is no detailed definition in Regulation 1408/71 (the old co-ordination rules) of 'habitual residence' and there is some confusion about what habitual residence means, both for the co-ordination rules and for entitlement to certain UK benefits (see p110). Habitual residence for European Union purposes is slightly different from the habitual residence test for certain UK benefits, but there is some overlap between the two.

Consequently, there has been a significant amount of caselaw on this. In *Snares*, the European Court of Justice (ECJ) held that entitlement to special non-contributory benefits was not conditional on the claimant having previously been subject to the social security legislation of the state in which s/he applies for the benefit.[91] The crucial factor for this type of benefit was the place of habitual residence.

The House of Lords, however, has given a definition on habitual residence for domestic law purposes which does not precisely follow caselaw from the ECJ. In *Nessa*, the House of Lords held that, in order to satisfy the habitual residence test, a person must satisfy a period of residence.[92] This follows earlier caselaw that held that it was necessary to complete an appreciable period of residence in the country before you became habitually resident.

However, you do not have to have completed any period of residence to show you are habitually resident for the purpose of relying on the co-ordination rules. The leading judgment on habitual residence in respect of the co-ordination rules is the case of *Di Paolo*, which held that the key factors in determining a person's habitual residence are:[93]

> ... the length and continuity of residence before the person concerned moved, the length and purpose of his absence, the nature of the occupation found in the other member state and the intention of the person concerned as it appears from all the circumstances.

This case was concerned with unemployment benefits and is more concerned with past rather than future events. For this reason, a commissioner warned that caution should be used in terms of applying this definition.[94] However, later judgments of the ECJ have cited *Di Paolo* as authoritative.

In the case of *Swaddling*, the ECJ considered both the UK and EU habitual residence test. It cites the *Di Paolo* test as being authoritative for both tests and found that an employed person who went to another member state to work, who then returns to her/his country of origin and has no close relationships or ties in the state which s/he has left, is habitually resident in her/his country of origin. Consequently, Mr Swaddling was habitually resident in the UK.

Once it is established that someone is habitually resident and covered by the co-ordination rules, s/he may claim a special non-contributory benefit. In this case, Mr Swaddling could not be refused benefit because he failed to satisfy the appreciable period under the UK habitual residence test.

Although the *Swaddling* case involved a British citizen, the decision can also apply to other European Economic Area nationals.

In theory, therefore, a person who is covered by the co-ordination rules who has been refused a benefit such as income support (IS) under the right to reside test (see p116) may be able to access IS under the co-ordination rules.

The UK courts, however, have not been convinced by this argument, consistently holding that, in order to claim a special non-contributory benefit under the co-ordination rules, a person must be habitually resident in the UK and this requires a person to have a right to reside or, in other words, be economically active or have a retained or permanent right of residence. See Chapter 13 for more details on the rights of residence for EEA nationals.

New co-ordination rules

Unlike Regulation 1408/71, Regulation 883/04 (the new co-ordination rules) sets out factors which may be used to help determine your place of habitual residence.

The following factors may be used to help determine your place of habitual residence for the purposes of the co-ordination rules:[95]

- the duration and continuity of presence in the state(s) concerned;
- your personal situation including:
  - the nature and specific characteristics of any activity pursued, in particular the place where such activity is habitually pursued, the stability of the activity, and the duration of any work contract;
  - your family status and family ties;
  - any unpaid activity such as voluntary work;
  - if you are a student, the source of your income;
  - your housing situation, in particular how permanent it is;
  - the member state in which you are deemed to reside for taxation purposes.

If there is still a dispute about your place of residence, consideration must be given to your intentions, especially the reasons that led you to move. This will be decisive in establishing your actual place of residence.

If you are refused benefit under the right to reside test, you could argue that you qualify for benefits such as IS under the co-ordination rules. However, the Department for Work and Pensions is unlikely to accept this argument. If you are in this position, you should appeal and obtain specialist help. Under the new rules, you are treated as temporarily affiliated to a member state during a dispute. You should therefore ask for interim payments to be made pending the outcome of your appeal.

Claims

Claims should be made to the state liable to pay on the appropriate claim form for that benefit.

9. Death grants

There are no death grants available in the United Kingdom under the co-ordination rules.

10. **Sickness, maternity and paternity benefits**

Benefits for sickness, maternity and paternity include the following.
- **Benefits in kind.** These comprise health and welfare services, so, for example, medical treatment would fall under this category. They also cover cash payments to reimburse the cost of these services if you have already been charged for them.
- **Cash benefits.** These are social security benefits paid as compensation for loss of earnings, and so include social security benefits such as employment and support allowance (ESA) in the assessment phase.[96]

The benefits for sickness, maternity and paternity available in the United Kingdom (UK) under the co-ordination rules are:
- attendance allowance (AA);
- carer's allowance (CA);
- disability living allowance (DLA) care component;
- statutory maternity pay (SMP) – but see below;
- maternity allowance (MA);
- statutory sick pay (SSP) – but see below;
- statutory paternity pay (SPP) – but see below;
- ESA in the assessment phase.

The rules on this category of benefits are particularly complex and some benefits (AA, DLA and CA) have, in the past, been classified as different risks.

Paternity benefits have only been included in the co-ordination rules since 1 May 2010 and are only available for people covered by Regulation 883/04.

There is a question about whether SSP, SMP and SPP are covered. Guidance from the Department for Work and Pensions (DWP) suggests they are outside the scope of the co-ordination rules because they are contractual pay, not social security benefits.[97] However, despite being paid by employers, all these benefits are social security benefits and would appear to fall within the broad definition of those benefits that should be included. Furthermore, UK legislation for all these benefits allows for aggregation of periods of employment in other member states to be treated as though they were completed in the UK.[98] Consequently, you should be entitled to have periods of work in other member states treated as though they were periods of work in the UK to establish your entitlement.

Rights under the co-ordination rules

If a member state makes entitlement to a particular sickness or maternity benefit conditional on completing periods of insurance, residence and employment, it must take into account any periods completed in other states.[99] This means that a person (including A2 and A8 nationals) who has worked briefly in the UK, but who worked in another member state before coming to the UK, can rely on the work undertaken or contributions paid in that other member state in order to qualify for UK sickness and maternity benefits.

You should not be excluded from claiming cash benefits from the state in which you are insured simply because you reside elsewhere. However, if you are sick or pregnant, you may also have to make use of health or welfare services – eg, antenatal care. It may be unrealistic to expect you to receive such treatment from the state in which you were last insured if you are resident elsewhere. In such cases, the state of residence provides the treatment or service.

The state with whom you were last insured is liable to bear the cost of the benefit, whether it is cash or in kind. This applies, even if you receive treatment or benefit in another member state.

In addition to these general principles, there are specific rules, which vary according to whether you are employed (see below) or unemployed (see p209) and whether or not you are a pensioner (see p209).

Claims

In general, you make a claim for benefits on the usual claim form provided for that benefit by the competent institution. The competent institution is the DWP in the UK and its equivalent in any other state. If you are unsure from which state you should claim, you should start your claim in the state in which you are living and it will be passed to the competent institution. There are, however, some forms that may be useful to obtain. Again these are generally available from the competent institution.

If you have been working in another member state, you should try to obtain Form E104, which is a record of the social insurance that you have paid in that member state, before returning to the UK. This will help with any claims for benefit. It is not essential to have this form, and if you provide evidence of your work to the DWP it will check your insurance record with the other member state. You should be able to obtain this from the competent institution of the state in which you have been working, or you could ask for a copy from the DWP prior to going abroad.

You should use Form E119, available from the competent institution, to obtain benefits in kind and submit evidence of incapacity to substantiate the claim.

How you are paid and

If you are employed or self-employed

If you are working in, and insured for sickness in, another European Economic Area (EEA) state and you fall sick, you may need to claim benefit for short-term sickness under that state's social security scheme. Periods of insurance contributions in the UK may be aggregated with periods of insurance in that member state and count towards your entitlement to such a benefit.[100] It is sometimes possible to claim benefit from a state other than the one in which you were last insured.

If you go temporarily to another EEA member state, you can claim sickness and maternity benefits from that state if your condition 'necessitates immediate benefits'.[101] This includes both cash benefits and benefits in kind. This could include reimbursement of medical and pharmaceutical expenses, treatment or medication, as well as weekly cash benefits. Your sickness or pregnancy does not, of itself, necessitate immediate benefit, but requiring medical treatment would.

You may wish to go to another member state for treatment because it is more effective or to avoid a lengthy waiting list. If you are already entitled to benefit and go to another member state for treatment, you can continue to receive benefit. You must get authorisation from the DWP in order to do this. Authorisation cannot be withheld because your home state provides the treatment necessary, if the treatment cannot be provided within a reasonable time, taking into account your current state of health. If you are going abroad, you should give the DWP plenty of advance warning to enable it to advise you on procedures and make the necessary arrangements on your behalf.

If you have been working in and are insured in another EEA member state and become ill, you may wish to return to the UK. In these circumstances, you may be entitled to the other member state's sickness benefit in the UK. However, in order to benefit, you should make your claim before you leave the other member state. If you are entitled to benefit and want to move to another member state or return to the state in which you normally live, you can get benefit there if you are authorised by the DWP. Such authorisation can only be refused if removal would be prejudicial to your health. It does not have to be obtained prior to departure, but not having it is likely to lead to problems with your claim.

If you live in a state other than the competent state (see p171), you can nevertheless claim and receive benefit from the state in which you were last insured.[102]

If you are unemployed

If you are unemployed and receiving an exportable unemployment benefit (jobseeker's allowance in the UK) while looking for work in another member state and you become sick or the maternity allowance period begins, you no longer get the unemployment benefit, but sickness or maternity benefit. This is paid for the remainder of the unemployment benefit period of three months.

If you are eligible for one state's unemployment benefit because you live in that state rather than having last worked there, you are also eligible for that state's benefit while sick or pregnant.

Pensioners

If you receive an old age benefit from more than one member state, including a pension from the state in which you reside, you receive sickness or maternity benefit from the state in which you are resident, rather than the state in which you were last insured.[103]

If you are entitled to a pension from more than one member state but you do not receive a pension from the state in which you reside, you can get sickness or maternity benefit from the member state that pays you a pension.[104]

If you are eligible for a pension in one state but are resident in another and you are waiting for the pension claim to be processed, you are entitled to receive benefits in kind, which will be paid by the state of residence. Once the pension claim is processed and it is established who is responsible for paying sickness benefits, that state will reimburse the state that has paid for your benefits in kind.[105]

Exporting sickness, maternity and paternity benefits

The rules relating to the export of sickness, maternity and paternity benefits are very complex. Generally, these benefits are not fully exportable and you will only be able to export them if you meet particular rules. You will need to check firstly whether the UK is the competent state in your case and then whether you fit within the rules which allow for exporting your benefit.

AA, DLA and CA have been subject to different categorisations in the past. At various points they have been invalidity benefits, allowing full exportation, then treated by the UK as special non-contributory benefits, which were not exportable at all and, more recently, AA, CA and DLA care component have been categorised as sickness benefits. DLA mobility component remains a special non-contributory benefit, although this is now subject to a legal challenge.[106] Because of all the changes, the rights you have under European Union (EU) law depend on when you made your claim.

- If you were entitled to AA, DLA care or mobility component or CA before 1 June 1992, you have the right to export these benefits as an EU invalidity benefit (see p211).

- If you claimed on or after 1 June 2002 and are currently in receipt of AA, DLA care component or CA, you can export these benefits under the rules which allow EU sickness benefits to be exported (see p211). These are more limited than for invalidity benefits (see p211).

- If you were in receipt of AA, DLA care component or CA after 1 June 1992 and you went abroad after 8 March 2001 and your benefit ceased because you were no longer living in the UK, you may be able to ask for a reconsideration, revision or supersession depending on the circumstances of your case. If an appeal is in place, benefit can be paid from the date of the appeal.

- If you moved to live in Switzerland, the relevant date is 1 June 2002 because the EU rules only became applicable to Switzerland from that date.

- If you moved to an A8 state, Malta or Cyprus, the relevant date is 1 May 2004 when these countries joined the EU.

- If you moved to an A2 state, the relevant date is 1 January 2007, when those two countries joined the EU.

CPAG's view is that AA, DLA care component and CA should not have been treated as special non-contributory benefits from 1 June 1992 and, therefore, some people may have been wrongly refused benefit while they were in another EEA state. The European Court of Justice (ECJ) has stated this to be the case[107] and this view has been confirmed by the Upper Tribunal.[108]

However, there are two major difficulties that you may face in exporting your benefit.

Firstly, sickness benefits are not fully exportable benefits under EU law. Instead, they are payable only if the special rules in the co-ordination rules allow it. These rules are extremely complex and do not sit well with the UK rules on AA, DLA or CA. The complexity of the sickness benefits rules is partly because cash sickness benefits are linked to benefits in kind – ie, healthcare. The co-ordination rules must take into account the fact that when a person needs healthcare abroad, s/he may also need cash benefits, which are linked to the healthcare being provided.

Secondly, the UK time limits for appeals, revisions and supersessions mean that, even though you may have been wrongly denied the right to export your benefit, practically it will be difficult (although not impossible) to challenge this decision. See p214 for further details on how to challenge a decision.

Entitlement before 1 June 1992

If you were entitled to AA, either component of DLA or CA before 1 June 1992, your benefit is fully exportable. This is because before this date all these benefits were classified as invalidity benefits under the co-ordination rules, and as such they were fully exportable on an indefinite basis.

This position was confirmed in *Newton*, in which the ECJ held that mobility allowance (the predecessor of DLA mobility component[109]) was an invalidity benefit for the purpose of Regulation 1408/71 and was fully exportable.[110] However, this changed in 1992 when these benefits were reclassified by the UK as special non-contributory benefits, which are only payable in the place of residence.

There is transitional protection, so if you were entitled to AA, DLA (either component) or CA before 1 June 1992, you can export your benefit if go to live in another EEA member state, provided:

- you satisfy all the other conditions of entitlement, except the 'residence' and 'presence' conditions; *and*
- the UK is the competent state (see p171).

Entitlement from 1 June 1992 to 5 May 2005

The co-ordination rules were amended on 1 June 1992 to include a new category of 'special non-contributory' benefits (see p166).[111] Member states were required to list the benefits they considered fell within this category in an annex to Regulation 1408/71.[112] The UK included AA, DLA and CA as special non-contributory benefits.[113] Consequently, if you became entitled to AA, DLA or CA from 1 June 1992, you could not export these benefits, other than under the circumstances outlined in UK regulations, which allow for these benefits to be paid for a maximum of six months when you are temporarily abroad. They were payable only in, and at the expense of, the member state of 'habitual residence'.

The change in classification was the subject of a number of legal challenges.[114] Initially, these challenges failed, with the ECJ holding that DLA and AA were special non-contributory benefits and not exportable.[115]

However, in a number of subsequent decisions, the ECJ changed its position. In *Jauch*, the ECJ rejected a submission that the listing of a benefit in the Annex to Regulation 1408/71 was conclusive of its nature as a special non-contributory benefit.[116] The ECJ held in *Jauch* that an Austrian care allowance was not a 'special non-contributory benefit', even though it had been listed as such in the Annex.

Shortly after the *Jauch* decision, the ECJ held that the inclusion of a maternity allowance by a member state in the Annex was invalid.[117] The same point was made by the ECJ in the case of *Hosse*.[118]

In the light of the developing caselaw, the European Commission brought a case to the ECJ.

In this case, the ECJ held that AA, DLA care component and CA all fell within the category of sickness benefits and, therefore, it was possible to export them in line with the conditions for sickness benefits under the co-ordination rules.[119]

This decision makes it clear that these benefits are exportable from 5 May 2005, the date on which Regulation 1408/71 was amended.

In guidance, the DWP has accepted that people who had their entitlement to AA, DLA care component or CA terminated following a move to another EEA state between 8 March 2001 (the date of the decision in the *Jausch* case) and 18 October 2007 (the date of the ECJ decision) can have it reinstated from the date of the request. You can have your benefit reinstated from an earlier date if the decision to terminate your benefit is being appealed, the UK is the competent state (see p171) and you meet all the other conditions of entitlement.[120]

The DWP may say that it cannot change a decision to terminate your award from a date before 18 October 2007, or from the date you request. If you think you should get paid from an earlier date, seek advice.

Disability living allowance mobility component

The ECJ did not consider the position of DLA mobility component, apparently because it considered the mobility component to be a benefit intended to replace or supplement a social security benefit and to have the nature of social assistance justified on economic and social grounds. This meant that DLA mobility component has the characteristics of a special non-contributory benefit rather than a social security benefit in EU law.

Arguably, the rulings in *Jauch* and the other cases before the ECJ which led to the action by the Commission apply as much to the mobility component as to the care component. Therefore, claimants could try to argue that the mobility component is also exportable. The Upper Tribunal has recently made a reference to the ECJ on the position of the mobility component.[121] Other similar cases will be stayed pending the outcome of this. If you are in this situation, you appeal and wait for the judgment of the ECJ. This is unlikely to be determined until 2011 at the earliest.

The ECJ has made it clear that, although it did not reclassify DLA mobility component as a sickness benefit, the issue had to be revisited. This is because DLA mobility component is not a separate benefit from DLA care component. To avoid the UK being forced to allow the export of DLA mobility component, the ECJ unusually allowed its judgment to be of temporary effect. In doing so, it is allowing the UK a 'reasonable period' in which to take appropriate measures to resolve the problem. The most likely solution would be for the UK to separate the two components into separate benefits. What constitutes a 'reasonable period' is not defined, but the decision is already some years old.

Entitlement from 5 May 2005

From 5 October 2005, DWP guidance outlines when you can export AA, DLA care component or CA to another EEA state and the circumstances in which the UK is the competent state (see p171).[122] You must be:

- in receipt of a contribution-based UK benefit, or in receipt of severe disablement allowance or DLA mobility component that was paid before 1 June 1992; *or*
- a person who is not receiving a contribution-based benefit but who has paid sufficient national insurance contributions to qualify for contributory employment and support allowance or short-term incapacity benefit; *or*
- a family member of one of the above.

The guidance states that the UK will be the competent state for:

- posted workers and their family members;
- frontier workers who work in Great Britain, and their family members;
- family members of workers living and working in Great Britain.

The guidance states that the UK remains the competent state unless the person:

- stops being entitled to a UK benefit; *or*
- starts work in another state; *or*
- starts to receive an EU sickness benefit either in cash or in kind, or starts to receive an old age or invalidity benefit, or other pension from the state of residence.

If the claimant is in receipt of an old age or invalidity benefit or other pension from both Great Britain and another EEA member state which is not the state of residence, the competent state is the one whose legislation the claimant was subject to for the longest period of time.

Challenging refusals to export sickness benefits

If you satisfy the conditions for AA, CA or DLA care component but for the fact that you are living in another member state, you should challenge the decision. Whether this is done by appeal, revision or supersession depends on the circumstances of the individual case.

Once a decision awarding benefit has been made it is final. If the DWP decides to terminate your benefit when you go to another member state, it has to revise or supercede your award.

It is only possible to revise or supersede an earlier decision if certain grounds set out in regulations are met.[123]

Before 24 September 2007, it was only possible to revise a decision awarding AA or DLA on the grounds of ignorance of, or mistake as to, a material fact relating to a 'disability determination'. Any decision about residence or presence conditions is not a 'disability determination'. Consequently, the DWP could not revise your AA or DLA on residence grounds before this date. The rules were amended and, from 24 September 2007, it is now possible to revise a decision in these circumstances.

Even if there are grounds for revision or supersession, it is also necessary to establish the effective date of the revising or superseding decision. For revisions, this is straightforward. The effective date of the revising decision will be the same as that of the original decision unless one of the reasons for the revision is that the effective date of the original decision is incorrect.

Supersessions are more difficult. A decision takes effect (with certain exceptions) from the date on which it is made.[124]

However, before 10 April 2006, a decision on DLA and AA could only be superseded on the grounds that there had been a relevant change of circumstances, unless that change affected a 'disability determination' and a decision about residence and presence conditions is not a disability determination. Consequently, if you were awarded AA or DLA and then went to live abroad, your benefit could only be superseded from the date of the superseding decision, not from the date you failed to satisfy those conditions for going abroad.

It is not clear whether the changes to the supersession regulations from 10 April 2006 are retrospective. If the changes are not retrospective, the Secretary of State can supersede from 10 April 2006, but not from any earlier date. This issue is currently being considered by the Upper Tribunal.[125]

Notes

1. Introduction
1 *Gillard* C-9/78 (ECJ)
2 Joined cases *Jackson* C-63/91 and *Cresswell* C-64/91 [1992] (ECJ)
3 Preamble 7 EU Reg 987/09
4 Preamble 10 EU Reg 987/09

2. Invalidity benefits
5 Art 39(4) EU Reg 1408/71; Arts 5 and 44 EU Reg 883/04
6 Art 40(3) EU Reg 1408/71; Arts 5 and 46 EU Reg 883/04
7 Art 35(1) EU Reg 574/72; Art 81 EU Reg 883/04
8 Art 37 EU Reg 1408/71; Art 44 EU Reg 883/04
9 Art 39 EU Reg 1408/71; Arts 5 and 44 EU Reg 883/04
10 Art 39(2) and (3) EU Reg 1408/71; Arts 5 and 44 EU Reg 883/04
11 Art 35(1) EU Reg 574/72; Art 81 EU Reg 883/04
12 Art 40(3) EU Reg 1408/71; Arts 5 and 46 EU Reg 883/04
13 Art 45(1) EU Reg 1408/71; Arts 6 and 51 EU Reg 883/04
14 Art 46(3) EU Reg 1408/71; Art 52 EU Reg 883/04
15 Art 10(1) and Annex VI O(12) EU Reg 1408/71; Art 7 EU Reg 883/04
16 Art 40(4) EU Reg 1408/71; Arts 40 and 51 EU Reg 574/72; Arts 5 and 44 EU Reg 883/04
17 Arts 40(4) and 41 EU Reg 1408/71; Arts 5 and 46 EU Reg 883/04
18 Art 42 EU Reg 1408/71(there is no corresponding provision in EU Reg 883/04)

3. Old age benefits
19 *R v Secretary of State for Social Security ex parte Taylor* C-382/98 (ECJ)
20 *R v Secretary of State for Social Security ex parte Taylor* C-382/98 (ECJ)
21 CIS/488/2004; CIS/1491/2004
22 Art 7 EU Reg 883/04
23 C-51/73 (ECJ)
24 C-92/81 (ECJ)
25 *Giletti and others* C-379 to C-381/85 and C-93/86 (ECJ)

26 Art 46(1) EU Reg 1408/71; Art 52 EU Reg 883/04
27 Art 46(2) EU Reg 1408/71; Art 52 EU Reg 883/04
28 Art 46(2) EU Reg 1408/71; Art 52 EU Reg 883/04
29 Art 46(1) and (2) EU Reg 1408/71; Art 52 EU Reg 883/04
30 Art 48 EU Reg 1408/71; Art 57 EU Reg 883/04
31 Art 46(2) EU Reg 1408/71; Art 52 EU Reg 883/04
32 Annex VI O(8) EU Reg 1408/71
33 Art 51(1) EU Reg 1408/71; Art 59 EU Reg 883/04
34 Art 36(1) EU Reg 574/72
35 Arts 36 and 41 and Annex 3 (O) EU Reg 574/72; *Balsamo Institut National d'Assurance Maladie Invalidité* C-108/75 [1976] ECR 375 (ECJ); R(S) 3/82
36 Art 10(1) and Annex VI O(12) EU Reg 1408/71; Arts 5 and 7 EU Reg 883/04
37 Arts 1(h) and (i), 10(1) and Annex VI O(12) EU Reg 1408/71; Art 7 EU Reg 883/04

4. Survivors' benefits
38 para 070160 DMG

5. Benefits for accidents at work and occupational diseases
39 s104(1) and (2) SSCBA 1992
40 s105 SSCBA 1992
41 Sch 7 para 11(1) SSCBA 1992
42 Art 10(1) EU Reg 1408/71
43 s95(1)-(4) SSCBA 1992
44 Art 55(1) EU Reg 1408/71; Art 36 EU Reg 883/04
45 Art 56 EU Reg 1408/71; Art 5 EU Reg 883/04
46 Art 5 EU Reg 883/04
47 Art 61(5) and (6) EU Reg 1408/71; Arts 5 and 40 EU Reg 883/04
48 Art 5 EU Reg 883/04
49 Arts 52 and 63 EU Reg 1408/71; Arts 36 and 41 EU Reg 883/04

6. Unemployment benefits

50 Arts 67-71 EU Reg 1408/71; Arts 5, 61, 64 and 65 EU Reg 883/04

51 *Commission of the European Communities v European Parliament and Council of the European Union* C-299/05 (ECJ)

52 *Hockenjos v Secretary of State for Social Security* [2001] EWCA Civ 624, CA; CJSA/1920/1999 (*65/00)

53 s1(2)(i) JSA 1995. In a letter to the TUC, November 1996, Allan Larsson of the EC said that both contribution-based and income-based JSA would be treated as falling within the scope of EU Regs 1408/71 and 574/72. Income-based JSA is a special non-contributory benefit under Arts 4(2a) and 10(a) and Annex IIa EU Reg 1408/71 although, given current domestic caselaw, this probably has little significance.

54 Art 67 EU Reg 1408/71

55 Art 68(2) EU Reg 1408/71; Arts 5 and 62 EU Reg 883/04

56 Art 13 EU Reg 1408/71; Art 11 EU Reg 883/04; *Caisse Primaire d'Assurance Maladie de Rouen v Guyot* C-128/83 (ECJ); *Gaetano d'Amico v Landesversicherungsanstalt Rheinland-Pfalz* C-20/75 [1975] ECHR 891 (ECJ); R(U) 4/84

57 *Francis Aubin v ASSEDIC and UNEDIC* C-227/81 [1982] ECR 1991 (ECJ)

58 Art 64 (3) EU Reg 883/04

59 Art 69(1) EU Reg 1408/71; Art 64 EU Reg 883/04

60 Art 69(1) Reg 1408/71; Art 64(1) EU Reg 883/04

61 Arts 67(1)-(3) and 71(1)(a)(ii) and (b)(ii) EU Reg 1408/71; Arts 61(1)-(3) and 65 EU Reg 883/04

62 Annex VI sO(7) EU Reg 1408/71

63 Art 69(1) EU Reg 1408/71; Art 64(1) EU Reg 883/04

64 R(U) 2/90

65 Art 69(1)(a) EU Reg 1408/71; Art 64(1) EU Reg 883/04

66 Art 69(1)(b) EU Reg 1408/71; Art 64(1)(b) EU Reg 883/04

67 Art 69(1)(b) Reg 1408/71; *Gaetano d'Amico v Landesversicherungs-anstalt Rheinland-Pfalz* C-20/75 [1975] ECHR 891. Some EEA member states have more stringent conditions than the UK and may require people with children to have formal childminding arrangements in place, including a contract, before the unemployed person is treated as available for work.

68 Art 55(3) EU Reg 883/04; Art 83(3) EU Reg 574/72

69 Art 55(1) EU Reg 883/04; Art 83(1) EU Reg 574/72; R(U) 5/78

70 Art 69(3) EU Reg 1408/71

71 Art 69(2) Reg 1408/71; Art 64(2) EU Reg 883/04; s5 JSA 1995

72 Art 25 EU Reg 1408/71

73 Art 67 Reg 1408/71; Art 61 EU Reg 883/04

74 Art 69(1)(a) EU Reg 1408/71; Art 65 EU Reg 883/04

75 Art 69(1) EU Reg 1408/71; Art 65 EU Reg 883/04

76 Art 69(1)(a) EU Reg 1408/71; Art 65 EU Reg 883/04

77 Art 69(1)(b) EU Reg 1408/71; Art 65 EU Reg 883/04; *d'Amico* C-20/75 (ECJ)

78 Art 69(1) EU Reg 1408/71; Art 65 EU Reg 883/04

79 Art 69(1)(c) EU Reg 1408/71; Art 65(1)(c) EU Reg 883/04

7. Family benefits

80 Art 6 EU Reg 883/04

81 Art 68(1)(b) EU Reg 883/04

82 Art 68(1)(b) EU Reg 883/04

83 Arts 86, 88, 90 and 91 EU Reg 574/72

84 Art 75(2) EU Reg 1408/71; Art 68a EU Reg 883/04

85 Art 73 EU Reg 1408/71; Art 67 EU Reg 883/04

86 Art 74 EU Reg 1408/71; Art 67 EU Reg 883/04

87 Art 72a EU Reg 1408/71; Art 6 EU Reg 883/04

88 Arts 77(2)(b)(i) and (ii) and 79(2) EU Reg 1408/71

8. Special non-contributory benefits

89 Annex IIa EU Reg 1408/71; Annex X EU Reg 883/04

90 Annex X EU Reg 883/04

91 *Snares* C-20/96 (ECJ)

92 *Nessa v CAO* [1999] WLR 1937 (reported as R(IS) 2/00)

93 *Di Paolo* C-76/76 (ECJ)

94 R(IS) 2/2000

95 Art 11 EU Reg 987/09

10. Sickness, maternity and paternity benefits

96 C-61/85 (ECJ)

97 This is based on the decision of the ECJ in *Gillespie* C-342/93. This case related to an equal pay claim rather than the co-ordination rules.

98 **SSP** SSP(MAPA) Regs
SMP SMP(PAM) Regs
SPP/SAP SPPSAP(PAM) Regs

99 Art 18 EU Reg 1408/71; Art 6 EU Reg 883/04

100 Art 18 EU Reg 1408/71; Art 6 EU Reg 883/04

101 Art 22 EU Reg 1408/71; Arts 19, 20 and 21 EU Reg 883/04

102 Arts 19(1) and 21 EU Reg 1408/71; Arts 17 and 21 EU Reg 883/04

103 Arts 27 and 31 EU Reg 1408/71; Arts 23, 29 and 33 EU Reg 883/04

104 Art 28 EU Reg 1408/71; Arts 24 and 29 EU Reg 883/04

105 Art 26 EU Reg 1408/71; Art 22 EU Reg 883/04

106 *JS v SSWP* [2009] UKUT 81 (AAC) (CDLA/ 2078/2005), paras 10-11

107 *Commission of the European Communities v European Parliament and Council of the European Union* C-299/05 (ECJ)

108 *JS v SSWP* [2009] UKUT 81 (AAC) (CDLA/ 2078/2005), paras 10-11

109 Mobility allowance was replaced by DLA in April 1992 but the rules were virtually unchanged.

110 *Newton* C-356/89 (ECJ)

111 EU Reg 1247/92 introduced Arts 4(2)(a) and 10a. Art 5 was also amended to provide that member states were to list the benefits considered to fall within this category in Annex IIa to EU Reg 1408/ 71.

112 Annex IIa EU Reg 1408/71 and now listed in Annex X EU Reg 883/04

113 The UK has also listed IS and income-based JSA as being special non-contributory benefits.

114 *Snares* C-20/96 (ECJ)

115 *Partridge* C-297/96 (ECJ)

116 *Jauch* C-215/99 (ECJ)

117 *Leclere and Deaconescu* C-43/99 (ECJ)

118 *Hosse* C-286/03 (ECJ)

119 *Commission of the European Communities v European Parliament and Council of the European Union* C-299/05 (ECJ)

120 Memo DMG 28/10

121 *JS v SSWP* [2009] UKUT 81 (AAC) (CDLA/ 2078/2005)

122 Memos DMG 14/08, 17/09 and 28/10, available online at www.dwp.gov.uk/ publicationsspecialist-guides/decision-makers-guide/#memos

123 Regs 3 and 6 SS&CS(DA) Regs

124 Reg 7 SS&CS(DA) Regs

125 CIS/3041/2008

Chapter 13

· ·

Using European Union law to claim benefits

This chapter covers:
1. Rights under European Union law (below)
2. Right of residence and access to benefits (p223)
3. Workers (p229)
4. Workseekers (p233)
5. Self-employed people (p234)
6. Students (p235)
7. People who are self-sufficient (p235)
8. Service providers and users (p236)
9. Retired or permanently incapacitated workers and self-employed people (p238)
10. A8 and A2 nationals (p239)
11. Family members (p241)
12. Primary carers of children in education (p243)
13. People who are economically inactive (p244)

If you are a European Economic Area (EEA) national (or a family member of an EEA national) who can rely on European Union (EU) law, you are in a privileged position compared with other migrants to the United Kingdom (UK). If you are covered by the EU Treaty, you are entitled to a range of social rights, including having a right to reside in the UK and to access benefits on the same terms as British citizens.

---

1. Rights under European Union law

Who can rely on European Union law

In order to rely on European Union (EU) law you must be:
- a European Economic Area (EEA) national (see p145); *or*
- a family member of an EEA national (see p241); *or*
- a national from a country that has an agreement with the EU (see Chapter 14); *or*

- a British citizen who has moved to another EEA state to exercise a Treaty right (see p222).

If you are a United Kingdom (UK) national and working in the UK, you and your family members cannot rely on EU law unless:[1]
- you have travelled to another EEA state; *and*
- you went to that member state to exercise an EU Treaty right there; *and*
- you later returned to the UK to exercise an EU Treaty right here.

Some people in the UK may have dual nationality (eg, Irish and British), even though they have always lived in the UK. Caselaw from the European Court of Justice (ECJ) has established that, if you are a dual national with the nationality of another EEA state (eg, Ireland), you and your family members can rely on EU law, even if you have never moved within the EEA.[2]

Principles of European Union law

There are a number of important principles underlying EU law:
- proportionality (see below);
- effectiveness (see p220);
- non-discrimination on grounds of nationality (see p220);
- protection of fundamental human rights (see p220).

The EU Treaty (see p149) sets out the fundamental principles of EU law. It was amended and renumbered by the Treaty of Lisbon, with effect from 1 December 2009, and provides for:
- freedom of movement for workers (Article 45, ex 39);
- freedom of movement for self-employment (Article 49, ex-59);
- freedom of movement for service providers (Article 49, ex-59);
- freedom of movement and residence subject to limitations and conditions (Article 21, ex-18);
- the right not to be discriminated against on grounds of your nationality (Article 18, ex-12);
- citizenship of the Union (Article 20, ex-17).

Proportionality

The principle of '**proportionality**' requires that the means employed to achieve a given end must be no more restrictive than is necessary to achieve that end. Therefore, in order to establish whether an EU law provision or national law measure implementing an EU law obligation is proportionate, it is 'first necessary to establish whether the means it employs to achieve its aim correspond to the importance of the aim and, in the second place, whether they are necessary for its achievement'.[3]

In respect of free movement and residence rights of EU citizens, the ECJ has consistently held that the principle of proportionality requires an assessment of the consequence of the decision for the person concerned and, if relevant, for the members of her/his family, regarding the loss of the rights enjoyed by every EU citizen. It is therefore necessary to establish whether that loss is justified.[4]

In the case of *Baumbast*, the ECJ employed the principle of proportionality to find that Mr Baumbast had a right to rely on Article 21 (ex-18) and therefore had a right of residence in the UK.[5] Although Mr Baumbast did not have comprehensive sickness insurance (see p236), the ECJ held that this limitation must be subjected to the test of proportionality. After taking into account Mr Baumbast's personal circumstances, the ECJ held that it would be a disproportionate interference to his right of free movement and residence to insist on strict compliance with the sickness insurance requirement. The application of the principle of proportionality therefore provided Mr Baumbast with a right of residence in the UK, where previously it was thought there was none.

Effectiveness

The idea of effectiveness is connected with the principle of proportionality. It means there must be effective protection and enforcement of EU law, not just by the institutions of the EU but also by the legal systems of the member states. In the ECJ cases of *Van Gend en Loos* and *Costa v ENEL* the principle of effectiveness was used to find and justify the ideas of the supremacy of EU law and the principle of 'direct effect' (see p149).[6] 'Effectiveness' is therefore also a route by which you can protect and assert your individual rights as an EU national, or family member of an EU national.

Non-discrimination

Article 18 (ex-12) EU Treaty protects against discrimination on the grounds of nationality, and Article 19 (ex-13) protects against other forms of discrimination. The prohibition of discrimination on the grounds of nationality applies where the provisions of the EU Treaty apply. The principle of equality means, in its broadest sense, that people in similar situations should not be treated differently – unless the difference in treatment can be objectively justified. Increasingly, the EU has passed legislation in the area of equality (eg, Directive 2000/43) to combat both direct and indirect discrimination on the grounds of racial or ethnic origin in the areas of employment, social provision, education and access to services.

Protection of fundamental human rights

Respect for fundamental rights has long been a principle of EU law. The obligation on the EU to respect fundamental rights is set out in Article 6 of the Treaty on European Union. Further protection has been achieved by enshrining the Charter of Fundamental Rights into primary EU law.[7] These rights are protected by the ECJ.

However, you can only rely on the protection of fundamental rights when the issue in dispute falls within the scope of EU law.[8]

The protection of fundamental rights extends to the acts of member states when implementing their obligations under EU law. A recent opinion of an Advocate General reiterates that fundamental rights cannot be invoked as a free-standing right independent of any link to EU law,[9] but this limitation will not be a problem in any case where an EU national moves to and resides in another member state, as a sufficient link to EU law will be established simply by exercising the right to free movement.[10]

Fundamental rights are important in the context of freedom of movement as they can have a powerful effect on your rights. In the case of *Konstantinidis*, the ECJ held that all EU nationals and their family members exercising free movement rights had the full protection of the European Convention on Human Rights (ECHR).[11] Therefore, an EU national who goes to another member state is entitled to be:[12]

> ... treated in accordance with a common code of fundamental values... In other words, he is entitled to say *'civis corpeus sum'* (I am a citizen of Europe) and invoke that status in order to oppose any violation of his fundamental freedoms.

This extends to all the fundamental freedoms protected by the ECHR, including the following, all of which may be relevant for EU nationals and their family members in benefits cases:

- Article 3: prohibiting inhuman and degrading treatment;
- Article 8: the right to respect for private and family life;
- Article 14 prohibiting discrimination;
- Article 1 to the First Protocol: protection of property;
- Article 2 to the First Protocol: right to education.

From December 2009, the Charter of Fundamental Rights of the European Union has the same legal value as the Treaties of the EU.[13] Title IV to the Charter is called 'solidarity'. Article 34 in this section addresses social security and social assistance. Article 34(2) provides that everyone 'residing and moving legally within the European Union is entitled to social security benefits and social advantages in accordance with Union law and national laws and practices'. Article 34(3) proclaims that in order to combat exclusion and poverty the:

> Union recognises and respects the right to social and housing assistance so as to ensure a decent existence for all those who lack sufficient resources, in accordance with the rules laid down by Union law and national laws and practices.

The UK has attempted to secure an opt-out to the above rule. However, the Secretary of State conceded before the Court of Appeal that 'the fundamental rights set out in the Charter can be relied on as against the UK'.[14] It therefore remains to be seen the extent to which the Charter will assist EU nationals seeking to access benefits in the UK.

Freedom of movement to enter and reside

All EEA nationals, including A8 and A2 nationals, and their family members have a right of entry to any other EEA state.[15] On entry to the UK, all EEA nationals have a right of residence, but the type and length of residence depends on what you are doing in the UK.

You may have one of the following types of residence.

- **Initial right of residence.** All EEA nationals have a right to initial residence in another member state for a period of up to three months. This residence does not depend on your working or being economically active in any way (see p224).
- **Extended right of residence.** This applies to EEA nationals who are workers, self-employed, self-sufficient or students (see p225).
- **Permanent residence.** If you have been resident for five years, you can acquire permanent residence. If you have worked, but have become permanently incapable of work or reached retirement age, you may be able to acquire permanent residence before five years (see p225).
- **Residence as a family member of an EEA national.** Your residence will usually be the same as the EEA family member and, therefore, this can be initial, extended, retained or permanent residence, as above. There are special rules in cases of divorce or death (see p242).

See Chapter 4 for more details.

Exercising economic Treaty rights

Before the creation of citizenship of the EU in 1992, free movement and residence rights were closely connected to economic activity. Thus, you could only use EU law to benefit from the free movement rules above if you were exercising Treaty rights, or had done so in the past. Generally, you are exercising an EU Treaty right if you are:

- employed (see p229);
- looking for work and signing on for jobseeker's allowance (see p233);
- self-employed (see p234);
- a student who is self-supporting at the start of your studies (see p235);

- not economically active, but you can support yourself from your own resources (see p235);
- receiving or providing services – eg, as a tourist or paying for education or healthcare (see p236).

If you had never exercised a Treaty right, you could not rely on EU law unless you were the family member of a person who had exercised an EU Treaty right. Economically inactive EU nationals were often referred to as not exercising EU rights because they were not within the personal scope of EU law.

However, citizenship of the EU was introduced by the Maastricht Treaty in 1992. By granting the right to move and reside freely within the EU to every citizen, the EU began the process of separating free movement rights from economic activity. In a landmark case, *Martinez Sala*, the ECJ used what are now Articles 20 and 21 of the EU Treaty to hold that, simply by virtue of citizenship of the EU and the exercise of the right of free movement, Ms Martinez Sala fell within the personal scope of the Treaty and could thus rely on EU law.[16] In 2001, the ECJ went further and declared that citizenship of the EU was 'destined to become the fundamental status of nationals of the member states' when exercising their rights of free movement and residence.[17] This phrase has often been reiterated by the ECJ and is enshrined in EU Directive 2004/38. This states that citizenship of the EU 'confers on every citizen of the Union a primary and individual right to move and reside freely within the territory of the member states' and that 'free movement of persons constitutes one of the fundamental freedoms of the internal market'. Article 3 of the Directive states that the Directive applies to 'all Union citizens who move to or reside in a member state other than that of which they are a national'.

All EU nationals and their family members who move to or reside in the UK or any other member state can therefore rely on EU law.

Note: in the case of *Ruiz Zambrano* the Advocate General has suggested that Article 21 of the EU Treaty creates two rights: one to move and another, independent, right of residence. This would mean that a UK national who had not moved elsewhere in the EU would have an EU right of residence. However, in another case (*McCarthy*), the Advocate General reached the opposite view. At the time of writing, judgment of the ECJ is awaited in both cases.[18]

2. **Right of residence and access to benefits**

To be entitled to the following benefits in the United Kingdom (UK), you must satisfy certain residence conditions, including the right to reside test (see p116):[19]

- income support (IS);
- income-based jobseeker's allowance (JSA);
- income-related employment and support allowance (ESA);

- pension credit (PC);
- housing benefit (HB);
- council tax benefit (CTB);
- child benefit;
- child tax credit (CTC);
- health in pregnancy grants.

For child benefit (see p87), CTC (see p86) and health in pregnancy grants, the right to reside test is part of the existing presence test for those benefits. For the other benefits listed above, it is part of the habitual residence test (see p77).

Some people automatically have a right to reside in the UK – eg, British citizens, Irish citizens or people with indefinite leave. If you have been admitted to the UK with limited leave, you will also have a right of residence under the UK Immigration Rules, although if you fall into this group, you are likely to already be excluded from accessing benefits as a 'person subject to immigration control' (see p55).

The main group of people affected by the residence rules are, therefore, European Economic Area (EEA) nationals. This makes the UK right to reside test, in particular, complex because EEA nationals have rights of residence under European law, which must be considered in addition to the UK rules.

In most cases, if you have a right of residence under European Union (EU) law, you are entitled to equality of treatment in terms of access to benefits with nationals of the state in which you are living.

From 30 April 2006, most (but not all) rights of residence are set out in EU Directive 2004/38. This has been incorporated into UK law in the Immigration (European Economic Area) Regulations 2006. If these conflict with, or do not completely incorporate, Directive 2004/38, the Directive takes precedence.

Before 30 April 2006, residence rights were contained in a variety of EU Directives, EU Regulations and in the Treaty itself.[20] EU Directive 2004/38 repealed all the existing residence Directives and amended EU Regulation 1612/68. EU Regulation 1251/70 was also subsequently repealed.[21] Directive 2004/38 largely consolidates the earlier secondary legislation and incorporates caselaw from the European Court of Justice (ECJ).[22] Although the Directive refers only to EU nationals, the UK applies it to all EEA nationals.

Note: the new Directive did not change the existing rights of residence outlined in the EU Treaty.[23] Its purpose was to strengthen residence rights and the European Court of Justice (ECJ) has interpreted it in this light.[24]

Initial right of residence

All EEA nationals have an unconditional right of entry to any member state.[25] EEA nationals also have an initial right of residence in any member state for the first three months of their stay. This initial right of residence is given whether or not you are working, seeking work or carrying out any other economic activity.

During this initial three-month period, you can benefit from the general right to equality of treatment, but each member state can decide whether or not to grant you access to social assistance.[26]

This means that, if social security rules exclude an EEA national from entitlement to benefit, you cannot rely on the equal treatment rules in the Directive in order to overcome them. However, if the benefit rules do not bar those in the initial period of residence, you may be able to claim that benefit.

UK regulations exclude you from entitlement to IS, income-related ESA, PC, HB and CTB if your only right of residence is on the basis of the initial three-month period. If you are within your first three months in the UK and you have a right of residence on another basis (eg, as a worker), you may be able to claim any benefits for which you qualify.

For CTC, child benefit and health in pregnancy grants, the rules simply state you must have a right to reside and are silent in respect of the three-month period.[27] This means that if you are an EEA national and within your initial three-month period of residence in the UK, you can claim CTC, child benefit and a health in pregnancy grant during this three months, even if you are not exercising a Treaty right.[28] However, you will not be entitled after the first three months, unless you have an extended right of residence (see below).

Extended right of residence

EU Directive 2004/38 provides what the UK refers to as an 'extended right of residence' to a:[29]

- worker (see p229) or someone who retains her/his rights as a worker (see p231);
- workseeker (see p233);
- self-employed person (see p234);
- someone receiving or providing services (see p236);[30]
- student (see p235);
- self-sufficient person (see p235);
- family member of any of the above (see p241);
- primary carer of a child in education if either you are, or the child's other parent is, an EU national who has worked in the UK (see p243).

Permanent right of residence

The key question that arises in respect of the right of permanent residence is what it means to have **'resided legally'** in a member state.

The UK's Immigration (EEA) Regulations 2006 that seek to implement the right of permanent residence stipulate that to acquire the right of permanent residence a person must have 'resided in the UK in accordance with these regulations for a continuous period of five years'.[31] Residence in accordance with the previous 2000 Regulations also counts.[32] The UK took the view that the right of residence in Article 16 of EU Directive 2004/38 was not retrospective.

However, in the case of *Lassal,* the ECJ held that continuous periods of five years' residence in accordance with earlier EU law completed before the date of Directive 2004/38 do count for the purpose of acquiring the right of permanent residence.[33] The ECJ's judgment makes clear that absences from a host member state of less than two consecutive years that occurred before the Directive came into force do not affect the right of permanent residence if it had already been acquired.

However, the *Lassal* case did not address whether 'legally residing' means only residence in accordance with EU or whether it extends to lawful residence in accordance with domestic law. The answer to this question is significant for EEA nationals who have been living in the UK for many years, but whose residence has not been in accordance with the requirements of EU law. The vast majority of these EU nationals have not been subject to any removal decisions by the UK authorities. In fact, many have been supported by the UK's benefit system. Even though they are not 'qualified persons' as defined by the UK's Immigration (EEA) Regulations, these EEA nationals are nevertheless lawfully present in the UK. A number of court decisions confirm this, including Court of Appeal judgments on the right to reside test for means-tested benefits.[34]

If it is decided that the terms 'lawfully present' and 'resided legally' mean the same thing, all EEA nationals who have lived continuously in the UK for five years without becoming subject to an expulsion measure will have acquired the right of permanent residence.

At the time of writing, the question of the meaning of 'resided legally' has been referred to the ECJ.[35]

Note: as it currently stands, the UK's caselaw is clear that lawful residence in accordance with UK law alone is not sufficient to acquire a right of permanent residence. If you are an EEA national or family member of an EEA national who has lived in the UK for more than five years but are refused benefits, you should seek specialist advice

Note also: time spent in prison by a person convicted of a criminal offence cannot be treated as residence when calculating the period towards permanent residence.[36]

- -

Example

Simone is a French national who came to the UK in May 2003. She worked from May 2005 to August 2007 and then studied on a childcare course until June 2008. She then claimed JSA until September 2008, when she got a job in a nursery. She worked in the nursery until June 2010, when she stopped work because of pregnancy. She claims IS.

Simone had an extended right of residence as a worker for the 27 months from May 2005 to August 2007. She retained her right of residence as a worker while studying on a vocational course (see p227) and while signing on for JSA.[37] She also had a right of residence as a worker while working in the nursery. Simone has therefore accrued over five years' residence in the UK and now has a permanent right of residence. She no longer has to be economically active to retain a right to reside. Instead, she is entitled to be treated on an equal basis to a UK national, and can claim IS on the grounds that she is pregnant.

Continuity of residence

When calculating your periods of residence towards permanent residence, only 'continuous residence' can be taken into account. However, your continuity of residence is not affected by temporary absences of up to six months in a year, or 12 months for military service. Longer absences do not affect your continuity of residence if they are for an important reason – eg, pregnancy and childbirth, serious illness, study or vocational training, or a posting in another member state or a third country.[38] The wording of the Directive implies that the temporary absence relates to periods abroad. However, it may be possible to argue that temporary absences from the labour market for reasons such as pregnancy should also not affect your continuity of residence.

Any periods of absence that are not temporary are not counted towards the five-year period required for permanent residence (see p225).[39]

Example

Carlos is a Portuguese national who has been living and working in the UK for two years. He leaves the UK to deal with a family illness in Portugal and remains away from the UK for five months. On his return to the UK, he has not lost the two years' work and residence that he had acquired and this can count towards his permanent residence. However, he will need to complete another three years of residence before he can acquire permanent residence.

Residence permits, cards and registration certificates

EU Directive 2004/38 changed the administrative formalities and residence card requirements for EEA nationals. During the initial three-month period, there are largely no formal requirements. For periods of residence longer than three months, member states can require you to comply with national administrative measures. If these are met, you must be issued a residence certificate. Family members of EEA nationals who are not themselves EEA nationals have greater administrative formalities, and states are also required to issue residence cards to non-EEA nationals who are family members.

EEA nationals do not require any documentation or permission to be in the UK. However, a document can be provided by the Home Office which confirms the EEA national's status. These documents must be provided promptly and free of charge. These residence documents include the following.
- **Residence permits.** Before the introduction of Directive 2004/38, an EEA national exercising Treaty rights could receive a residence permit.[40] These no

longer exist, but some people will have valid five-year residence permits issued before April 2006. Residence permits have now been converted into residence certificates.

- **Residence certificates.** Directive 2004/38 replaced the old residence permit system and all valid and existing residence permits have been converted into residence certificates.
- **Residence cards.** Family members of EEA nationals who are not themselves EEA nationals can apply for a residence card. The card is generally valid for five years. Again, such a card is confirmation of your right to be in the UK.
- **Permanent residence certificates and cards.** These are valid for 10 years. Certificates can be given to an EEA national who has a permanent right of residence. A permanent residence card can be given to a non-EEA family member who has permanent residence. These types of documents are likely to help with benefit claims.
- **Worker registration certificates.** These are issued by the Worker Registration Scheme on payment of a fee of £90 to A8 nationals who take up registered work for an authorised employer (see p239). While you are working for the authorised employer, the certificate is evidence of your right of residence in the UK. When you have worked for the authorised employer for 12 months, you are no longer required to register your work.
- **Accession worker card.** These are issued to A2 nationals who are in authorised work (see p239). While you are working for an authorised employer, the card is evidence of your right of residence in the UK. Once you have worked for the authorised employer for 12 months, you are no longer required to get your work authorised.

In terms of welfare benefits, the key issue is whether the possession of EU residence documents provides proof of an existing right of residence that is binding on the Department for Work and Pensions. In respect of residence permits, this question is currently before the ECJ in the case of *Dias*.[41]

The Court of Appeal, which made the reference to the ECJ, strongly doubted that a residence permit issued under the old rules continues to confer a right of residence when its holder no longer satisfies the underlying conditions of entitlement. The commissioner whose decision was the subject of the appeal had decided that the residence permit remained valid unless or until it expired or was revoked.[42]

The Upper Tribunal has ruled that a registration certificate does not provide proof of an ongoing right of residence. Its reasoning is based on a literal interpretation of the UK's immigration regulations, which define a residence certificate as 'proof of the right of residence as of the date of issue'.[43] The Upper Tribunal interpreted this as meaning a registration certificate only proves a right of residence as of the date of issue and nothing more. There is ECJ caselaw which contradicts the Upper Tribunal decision. In the case of *Trojani*, the ECJ held that possession of a valid permit issued under domestic law entitled the person to claim social assistance.[44] There is little or no reason to suggest that a residence certificate issued by the Home Office does not have at least the same effect.

For family members who are not EEA nationals, the Upper Tribunal has held that a valid registration card does confer a right of residence.[45]

3. Workers

If you are a 'worker':

- you have a right of residence under Directive 2004/38 and Article 45 (ex-39) of the European Union (EU) Treaty;
- you are exempt from the right to reside test (see p116);
- you are exempt from the habitual residence test (see p110);
- you have the right to the same tax and social advantages as nationals – eg, to benefits, housing and employment (see p229);
- you can be joined by family members, whatever their nationality (see p241);
- your child(ren) can enter education and remain in education even if you become involuntarily unemployed or leave the United Kingdom (UK). If this is the case, the primary carer of your child(ren) will also gain a right of residence.[46]

Tax and social advantages

If you have worker status, you are entitled to the same 'tax and social advantages' as nationals of the state in which you are working. These rights stem from Article 45 of the EU Treaty and the detailed rules are found in EU Regulation 1612/68.[47] This is one of the many equal treatment rules in EU law. It means that a person who is a 'worker' cannot be discriminated against in terms of access to any social security benefits or tax credits and UK regulations are normally drafted to recognise these rights.

The term 'social advantage' has been interpreted widely by the European Court of Justice (ECJ). It covers all types of social security benefits, but could also include items such as transport fare reduction cards, education grants and hospital treatment. Anything that can be construed as a social advantage should be covered.

Who is a worker

Sometimes it will be clear that someone is a worker – eg, because s/he is employed full time and has been in work for a significant period of time. However, there may be difficulties in showing that you are a worker if the work is part time or if you have only worked for a short period. It is clear that you can retain worker status during temporary interruptions of work if you remain in the labour market.

However, even if you have removed yourself from the labour market, you can continue to benefit from the effects of your former worker status for a period (see p231).

There is a significant amount of caselaw on the meaning of the term 'worker' and the ECJ often interprets the term generously.

The ECJ has never laid down a minimum period you must work in order to gain worker status. Each case must be looked at on its own merits. Some general principles, however, have been established.

- A worker is anyone who pursues 'effective and genuine work' that is more than 'marginal or ancillary'.[48] The following activities have been considered to be genuine and effective work giving worker status:
  - teaching music for 12 hours a week;[49]
  - work for 60 hours over 16 weeks under a contract with no fixed hours, but which required the person to be available to work;[50]
  - training over the summer in a hotel school;[51]
  - working as an au pair for 13 hours a week for £35 and board and lodging;[52]
  - working for two weeks as a steward at Wimbledon and receiving £789.86 net for those two weeks.[53]
- Agency work is not necessarily marginal and ancillary, and a person undertaking work through an agency can be a worker.[54]
- There must be an employment relationship, in which the employee accepts directions from another and the work is carried out in return for remuneration.[55] In the case of *Martinez Sala*, the ECJ held that a person who, for a certain period of time, performs services for (and under the direction of) another person in return for remuneration must be considered to be a worker.[56]
- You can be a worker if engaged only in part-time work, even if topped up with benefits.[57] The concept of 'worker' covers part-time workers on less than the minimum wage.[58] Neither the level of productivity nor the origin of the funds for paying the person concerned are relevant to the question as to whether you are a worker.[59]
- If you are in voluntary work, you are not a worker.[60] However, if you do not receive any remuneration, but receive some form of pay in kind, such as board and lodging, you can be considered to be a worker.[61] If you do some unpaid work for a period of time under an agreement that is intended to lead to payment, you may be a worker, but this does not apply if your work is simply therapeutic or for your rehabilitation.
- If you are a European Economic Area (EEA) national who has worked in other EEA states but not in the United Kingdom (UK), you do not have worker status in the UK. However, unless you are an A8 or A2 national (see p239), signing on for jobseeker's allowance (JSA) will usually give you the status of 'workseeker'.[62]
  Note: a commissioner has held that a person who has not worked in the UK cannot be exempt from the habitual residence test.[63] The commissioner

followed earlier caselaw that confirmed that a person only has rights as a worker under EU law in the UK once s/he has worked in the UK.[64]

Retaining worker status

Before looking at whether a person who has acquired worker status retains that status, it is first necessary to consider the possibility that s/he, in fact, remains a worker for the purposes of Article 45 (ex-Art 39). For example, if you remain under a contract of employment but are not working because of illness or pregnancy, you remain a worker for the purposes of Article 7(1) of EU Directive 2004/38.[65] The Upper Tribunal has also held that a person remains a worker while on a period of leave from work, even if that leave is unpaid.[66]

The ECJ has held that, once the contract of employment has ended, the status of worker is generally lost, but having had the status of worker can continue to produce certain effects.[67] It is therefore possible that the right to rely on Article 7(2) EU Regulation 1612/68 (the right to equal treatment in respect of social advantages) is not lost immediately on the termination of your employment.

Following the implementation of EU Directive 2004/38, the retention of worker status is now governed by Article 7(3). You can retain your worker status if:[68]

- you are temporarily incapable of work as the result of an illness or accident (see p231);[69] *or*
- you are involuntarily unemployed (see p232), but have registered as a jobseeker with Jobcentre Plus and:
  - you were employed for at least a year before becoming unemployed. When this applies, you retain worker status indefinitely while signing on for JSA;[70] *or*
  - you have been unemployed for less than 12 months and are signing on. In this situation, you retain worker status for as long as you are genuinely seeking work; *or*
- you are involuntarily unemployed (see p232) and on vocational training (see p233); *or*
- you have voluntarily stopped work and are on vocational training (see p233) related to your previous employment.

The above list has been held to be a complete list of the circumstances in which worker status can be retained. All attempts to argue that it is not exhaustive have failed.[71]

If you are pregnant, see p232.

Temporary incapacity for work

The test of your incapacity to work is an EU test, not a UK test such as that for employment and support allowance. The test is whether you can be fairly described as unable to do the work you were doing or the sort of work you were seeking.[72] It must be the worker who is ill, not her/his child or other family member. Therefore, if you give up work to care for a sick child or other relative, you do not retain your worker status.[73]

The Upper Tribunal has held that a temporary incapacity is one which has a certainty of recovery.[74] Even if you have a condition which may be permanent, it does not follow that the incapacity is also permanent. It is the fact that you have a temporary incapacity for work that is significant, not whether you have a permanent condition. For example, a person may have a long-term mental health condition, with episodes that result in an incapacity for work. Although the condition may be permanent, the incapacity for work is temporary.

Involuntary unemployment

'**Involuntary unemployment**' is when you have left one job (ie, the employment relationship has ended), but you are available to take another.[75] The term 'involuntary' relates to your ongoing connection to the labour market, not the circumstances in which your original job was lost.[76]

Article 7(3) of EU Directive 2004/38 refers to a person being in 'duly recorded involuntary unemployment' and 'having registered as a job-seeker with the relevant employment office'.[77] These requirements can clearly be satisfied by claiming JSA. The difficulty that arises is if you claim income support or fall within a category of person who is unable to claim JSA – eg, because of your age. The Upper Tribunal has held, however, that claiming JSA is not the only method by which a person can satisfy the requirement to register as a jobseeker.[78] At the time of writing, this decision is being appealed to the Court of Appeal.

Gaps between leaving a job and signing on

A commissioner has held that you can retain your worker status during a gap between losing your job and seeking work again.[79] However, a gap of two years would be too long. The commissioner stated that the reasons for the gap must be considered in order to decide whether you have withdrawn from the labour market. [80]

Pregnancy and childbirth

EU Directive 2004/38 is silent on the rights of workers who are unable to work because of pregnancy or childbirth. If you are unable to work because of pregnancy or childbirth, you are still a worker and have a right of residence if:

- you are still under your contract of employment. You are still a worker while on maternity leave and can claim income support, subject to meeting the other conditions of entitlement.[81] This includes A8 and A2 nationals;[82] *or*
- you are self-employed and you stop work for a period of maternity leave. You do not lose your status as a self-employed worker (see p234);[83] *or*
- you are a family member of a person with a right of residence (see p241); *or*

- you have a permanent right of residence (see p225); *or*
- you have been working, but you become ill because of your pregnancy.[84] It has been held, however, that pregnancy, in itself, is not an illness. Therefore, if you were forced to give up work during pregnancy, you do not retain your worker status on the basis of being temporarily unable to work as a result of an illness.[85] However, if you have a pregnancy-related illness that prevents you from working, you can retain your worker status.[86]

If you are in the final stages of pregnancy and you have been dismissed from work, or you are a casual or agency worker and you do not retain any employment rights, and you are unable to work because you are pregnant, the Upper Tribunal has ruled that you are treated as having lost your worker status.[87] This decision is being appealed to the Court of Appeal. If you are in this situation, seek advice.

Vocational training

If you are a worker, you can retain worker status if you take up vocational training.[88] Vocational training refers to training linked to your former work, retraining you to find reasonably equivalent employment.

4. **Workseekers**

The right of residence of workseekers arises directly from Article 45 of the European Union (EU) Treaty.[89] It is only obliquely set out in EU Directive 2004/38 (Articles 14 and 24). Article 45 provides for free movement of workers. This means that a person looking for work can enter any member state and, while looking for work, has a right of residence in that state. Although workseekers have a right of residence, however, they do not automatically satisfy the habitual residence test (see p110).

If you are an EU national and you claim jobseeker's allowance (JSA), you should be considered to have a right of residence as a workseeker.[90] You will then be able to claim other benefits on the same basis. If you claim income support, you will generally need to show you have a right of residence on another basis, as the rules of entitlement exclude workseekers.

If you are accepted as a workseeker by signing on for JSA, you have residence throughout the period that you are seeking work. Consequently, it can count towards the period needed for a permanent right of residence (see p225).[91]

Member states can currently limit the access of nationals from the accession states (see p147) to their labour markets. The United Kingdom (UK) has decided that A8 and A2 nationals (see p239) do not have rights of residence as workseekers. A8 and A2 nationals are required to have their work registered or authorised (see p33).

However, the exception to this is if a person can rely on the co-ordination rules to claim contribution-based JSA (see p196). For instance, nationals of Iceland, Liechtenstein, Norway and Switzerland cannot rely on Article 45 of the EU Treaty as workseekers, as they are not EU nationals, but they have the same rights under an agreement made between the EU and these countries. This agreement is known as the European Economic Area Agreement.[92] The UK regulations treat nationals of these countries in the same way as EU nationals for this purpose.

5. Self-employed people

If you are a self-employed European Economic Area (EEA) national in the United Kingdom (UK), you have a right to reside in the UK under the European Union (EU) Treaty and under Directive 2004/38.[93] There is no minimum period of residence or work. There are no special rules for self-employed A8 or A2 nationals. They have the same rights of residence and entitlement to benefit as other self-employed EEA nationals.

The rights and the rules on residence are equivalent to those for workers (see p229). Thus, if you are temporarily unable to pursue self-employment because of an illness or accident, you retain your status as a self-employed person.[94] You also retain your right of residence if you are temporarily unable to carry out your work as a self-employed person because you are on maternity leave.[95]

It is relatively simple to register as self-employed in the UK. You need to notify HM Revenue and Customs (the Revenue) that you are self-employed and then seek contracts. This could be achieved by advertising in shops or leafleting local houses or businesses. You can fall within this category while searching for self-employment and are covered even if the work is part time.[96] If you have taken preparatory steps to offer services, you count as self-employed.[97] It is not essential for you to have registered your self-employed status with the Revenue in order to be a self-employed person.[98]

The position of EEA nationals whose self-employment has come to an end, but who seek to retain their status as self-employed, has been controversial. The UK courts and the Upper Tribunal have held that a former self-employed person cannot retain her/his status through registering and looking for work.[99] The issue has been heard by the Court of Appeal and a judgment is awaited. This causes particular problems for A8 and A2 nationals who have not completed 12 months' registered or authorised work, as they do not have a right to reside in the UK simply as jobseekers. If you are a former self-employed person in this position, you should seek specialist advice.

6. Students

You have an extended right of residence (see p225) if you are a European Economic Area student and you:[100]
- are enrolled as a student in a college accredited by the host member state;
- have comprehensive sickness insurance (see p236);
- provide an assurance at the start of your studies that you have sufficient resources for yourself and your family members not to become a burden on the social assistance system of the host member state during the period of residence (see below).

A student only has to provide an assurance that s/he is self-supporting at the beginning of her/his studies. There have been a number of cases in which students have been able to use Article 18 of the European Union Treaty to gain access to social assistance.

7. People who are self-sufficient

You have an extended right of residence (see p225) as a self-sufficient person if you have: [101]
- sufficient resources for yourself and your family not to become an unreasonable burden (see p236) on the social assistance system of the host member state; *and*
- comprehensive sickness insurance (see p236).

Sufficient resources

The European Union (EU) Directive 2004/38 states that:[102]

> Member states may not lay down a fixed amount which they regard as 'sufficient resources', but they must take into account the personal situation of the person concerned. In all cases this amount shall not be higher than the threshold below which nationals of the host member state become eligible for social assistance or, where this criterion is not applicable, higher than the minimum social security pension paid by the host member state.

Some decision makers, in particular local authorities, have taken the approach that the term 'sufficient resources' means the total of the person's applicable amount for income support (IS), income-based jobseeker's allowance (JSA), income-related employment and support allowance (ESA) or pension credit (PC) (including any premiums for which s/he might qualify) plus the amount of housing benefit (HB) and council tax benefit (CTB) for which s/he would qualify. This view has been supported by the Upper Tribunal, which has held that 'sufficient resources' means the appropriate IS applicable amount together with the amount that would be paid toward rent.[103]

However, this contradicts European caselaw (in particular *Kempf* and *Levin*). The Directive refers to the 'threshold below which nationals of the host member state become eligible for social assistance'. In our view, this means the applicable amount for IS, not a combined total of a person's benefit.

An unreasonable burden

In *Grezelczyk*, the European Court of Justice (ECJ) held that the right of residence is only lost once a person becomes an 'unreasonable burden' on the state.[104] This requires investigation into the particular circumstances of the person and implies that there will be situations in which people who are not economically active can claim benefits. The ECJ also held that this condition does not preclude an EU national from being entitled to benefit.

The notion of 'unreasonable burden' is flexible and, according to the ECJ, implies that Directive 2004/38 accepts a degree of financial solidarity between the member states in assisting each other's nationals residing lawfully on their territory.

Comprehensive sickness insurance

In order to have residence either as a self-supporting European Economic Area (EEA) national or an EEA student (see p235), you are required to have comprehensive sickness insurance.

The United Kingdom courts have said that payment of national insurance contributions as an employee is not sufficient to provide a person with comprehensive sickness insurance. They have also implied this means private health insurance.[105]

However, European Commission guidance states that any insurance cover, private or public, contracted in the host state or elsewhere, is acceptable in principle, as long as it provides comprehensive coverage and does not create a burden on the public finances of the host state.[106] The guidance goes on to make clear that an EEA national can fulfil the conditions of comprehensive sickness insurance cover under the co-ordination rules. This means that a person who is covered by EU Regulation 1408/71 and now Regulation 883/04 (see p161) should count as having sickness insurance. Provided the UK would be able to claim any NHS costs for treating you from another state, you will satisfy the requirements for comprehensive medical insurance.[107]

8. Service providers and users

Before 30 April 2006, people receiving or providing services were treated in the same way as self-employed people for benefit purposes and were exempt from the habitual residence test and right to reside test (see Chapter 8). United Kingdom (UK) legislation no longer recognises the residence rights of providers or users of services.[108]

Directive 2004/38 makes no express reference to services. A person who comes under the services provisions has a direct right of residence under Article 55 of the European Union (EU) Treaty and a consequent right to equal treatment with nationals of the state in which s/he receives or provides those services.[109]

The European Court of Justice (ECJ) has confirmed that Article 55 can be relied on by those providing or receiving services. The ECJ also held that Article 55 is directly effective and does not need secondary legislation for it to be relied on.[110]

Providing services

The category of services is a residual category and does not apply if you can rely on any other parts of the Treaty relating to freedom of movement – eg, as a self-employed person or worker (see p229). Under Article 55 of the EU Treaty, 'services' are defined as services that are normally provided for remuneration.

Services include:
- industrial activities;
- commercial activities;
- activities of craftsmen and women;
- activities of the professions.

There is some overlap between services and self-employment. However, it may not be essential to clarify whether the person is providing services or is self-employed, provided s/he is involved in some economic activity. The ECJ held in *Royer* that a residence permit should be granted, even if it is uncertain whether a person involved in some economic activity fell under the provisions for 'workers', self-employed people or service providers.[111]

Receiving services

Article 55 is expressed in terms of providing services, but has been extended by the ECJ to include people who are receiving services. Any European Economic Area (EEA) national who falls within this category has a right of residence.[112]

The ECJ has held that recipients of services, include tourists, people receiving medical treatment and people travelling for the purposes of education and business are covered, provided there is a commercial aspect to the service received. In short, if you pay for the service, you are covered.[113]

The right to reside in the UK continues for as long as the services are being received.

Receiving services includes:
- tourism,[114] but this must be more than visiting friends;[115]
- education, except for that provided as part of the national education system;[116] *and*

- medical treatment.[117]

The references to medical treatment and education apply only where there is some payment for these.

The ECJ was asked to consider whether the term 'recipient of services' included someone who has no fixed abode and no money or luggage, on the basis that there is an assumption that, if s/he is in an another member state, s/he is a tourist, and that services associated with short-term residence, such as accommodation and the consumption of meals, are received.[118]

Unfortunately, the ECJ failed to address this point. However, it does open up the issue of whether apparently non-economically active EEA nationals are, in fact, service users. Many EEA nationals who are not in work come to the UK with savings, may be paying for accommodation, eating in restaurants or simply paying for other services. Such activity may well mean they are covered by Article 49.

This area of EU law is complex and largely untested, so it is always advisable to rely on another area of EU law if possible. However, if you are only able to rely on the category of service providers and users, you should appeal any refusal and get specialist advice.

---

9. **Retired or permanently incapacitated workers and self-employed people**

If you previously had worker status or were self-employed and you are now retired or permanently incapable of work, in some circumstances you can retain the rights of a worker and gain permanent residence in the host state.[119] These rights extend to your family members and, therefore, can be crucial – eg, if your spouse is not a European Economic Area (EEA) national. The rights of your family members to benefit from your former worker status can continue even if you die.

You retain your rights as a worker or self-employed person and gain a right to permanent residence if:

- you have reached retirement pension age in the host member state;[120] *and either:*[121]
  - you had worked in the host state for at least the last 12 months before retirement and resided continuously in the United Kingdom (UK) for more than three years; *or*
  - your spouse or civil partner is a British citizen (or s/he lost that citizenship because s/he married or entered into a civil partnership with you);[122] *or*
- you stopped working because of permanent incapacity *and either:*[123]
  - at the date you stopped working you had resided continuously in the UK for more than two years; *or*

- your incapacity was caused by an industrial injury or disease; *or*
- your spouse or civil partner is a British citizen (or lost that citizenship because s/he married you).[124]

When working out your period of 'continuous residence', include:[125]
- absences from the UK of up to six months in a year;
- longer absences because of your country's rules about military service;
- longer absences for important reasons, such as pregnancy, childbirth or a serious illness.

When working out your period of employment, ignore:[126]
- days of unemployment (even if you were not paid jobseeker's allowance – eg, because of an inadequate contribution record);
- absence from work because of illness or an accident.

10. **A8 and A2 nationals**

Nationals from the accession states (see p147), referred to in this *Handbook* as A8 and A2 nationals, are European Economic Area (EEA) nationals. However, the Treaties of Accession for the A8 and A2 states restrict some European Union (EU) rights. The intention of these restrictions is to enable member states to limit accession state nationals from the labour market if they wish. How member states do this is largely up to individual member states. **Note:** it is only in terms of access to the labour market that the rights of A8 and A2 nationals are restricted.

If you are an A8 national, you can work in the United Kingdom (UK) provided your work is registered for the first 12 months with the Worker Registration Scheme. There is a fee of £90. If you are an A2 national, you must obtain a work authorisation document before you can take up employment. You will then be issued with an accession worker card.

If you are an A8 or an A2 national whose work has to be registered or authorised, you do not have a right to reside as a workseeker or as a worker until you are either in registered or authorised work, or you have completed 12 months' registered or authorised work (see below).

If you are an A8 national who is in registered work or an A2 national who is in authorised work, you are a 'worker' and you have the full range of rights available to workers, including the right of residence and to the same tax and social advantages under Article 7 of EU Regulation 1612/68 (see p229).[127] However, if you become unemployed and have not yet completed 12 months' registered or authorised work, you no longer have worker status and you do not have a right of residence.[128]

If you are an A8 or an A2 national and your work does not have to be registered or authorised (see p240), you are treated in the same way as any EEA national.

This means that if you lose your job and sign on or become temporarily incapable of work because of an illness or accident, you retain your right of residence as a worker.

If you are an A8 national, the main circumstances in which your work does not have to be registered are if:

* on 30 April 2004, you had leave to enter or remain in the UK under the Immigration Act 1971, which was not subject to any condition restricting your employment; *or*
* you were working legally in the UK on 30 April 2004 and had worked legally for 12 months before this date; *or*
* you have worked legally (ie, for periods before accession as above, and for periods after accession in accordance with the Worker Registration Scheme) without an interruption of more than 30 days for a continuous period of 12 months.

If you are an A2 national, the main circumstances in which your work does not have to be authorised are if:

* on 31 December 2006, you had leave to enter or remain in the UK under the Immigration Act 1971, which was not subject to any condition restricting your employment; *or*
* you were working legally in the UK for 12 months up to and including 31 December 2006; *or*
* you have legally worked for at least 12 months beginning either before or after 31 December 2006; *or*
* you are the spouse/civil partner of a UK national or of a person settled in the UK.

If you are an A8 national who is required to register, you have a right of residence if you are working for an authorised employer. The main circumstances in which an employer is authorised are if:

* you were legally working for that employer on 30 April 2004 and have not ceased working for that employer;
* you are within the first month of employment for that employer;
* you applied for a registration certificate within the first month of your employment, but you have not yet received it;
* you have a valid registration certificate in respect of that employer.

If you are an A2 national who is required to authorise your work and you are not in authorised work, you are treated in the same way as an A8 national who is required to register but not in registered work. If you are in this situation and you work in unauthorised or unregistered work, you do not have a right of residence in the UK.[129]

11. **Family members**

Family members of a European Economic Area (EEA) national can gain a right of residence through that EEA national if s/he has a right of residence.[130] This applies to family members whether or not they are EEA nationals themselves.

Family members are defined in European Union (EU) Directive 2004/38 as:

- a spouse;
- a civil partner;
- direct descendants under the age of 21;
- direct descendants over the age of 21 if dependent;
- descendants of a spouse or civil partner under the age of 21;
- descendants of a spouse or civil partner over the age of 21 who are dependent;
- direct relatives in the ascendant line (parents, grandparents) and those of a spouse or civil partner who are dependent.

Note: the rights exist irrespective of the nationality of the EEA national's family member.

In addition, some extended family members have rights through the EEA national. These are:

- a partner with whom the EEA national has a durable relationship;
- any other family members who do not fall within the definition above, who are dependants of the EEA national, or members of her/his household, in the country from where they have come;
- any other family member who requires personal care by the EEA national on serious health grounds.

The Court of Appeal has held that, for relatives in the ascending line (the same reasoning is likely to apply to relatives in the descending line), dependence is a matter of fact shown by material support provided by the EEA national who has a right of residence. Dependence is not lost if the family member claims and receives benefit.[131] Dependence can arise in the host member state.

Family members who are not European Economic Area nationals

If you are a non-EEA national and you have a right to remain in the United Kingdom (UK) as a family member of an EEA national (see p241), you do not require leave to remain. Consequently, you are not a 'person subject to immigration control' for benefit purposes (see p56).[132] This applies whether or not you have an EEA residence document. A family member who has resided in a member state for five years acquires the right of permanent residence in that member state.

If you are under 21 and you are estranged from your parent who is working in the UK, you still have a right to reside as her/his family member since you do not need to show that you are dependent on her/him.

Extended family members

Under Directive 2004/38, member states must facilitate the entry and residence for extended family members in accordance with national law.[133] For this purpose, 'extended family members' are the people listed on p241.

If you are an extended family member and you obtain a residence certificate or card, you count as a family member (see p241). A commissioner has held that, if you do not have the required residence documentation, you do not have a right of residence. This is because the right does not arise under the Directive, but is only something the UK is required to facilitate.[134] If you are in this situation, you should get specialist advice.

Family members who separate, divorce or end their civil partnership

A family member of an EEA worker does not necessarily lose her/his right of residence if the couple separate or divorce, or if the civil partnership comes to an end. Residence is not lost if:

- before the initiation of the divorce or termination of the civil partnership, the marriage or civil partnership lasted at least three years, including one year spent in the host member state; *or*
- the spouse or partner who is not a national of a member state has custody of the EEA national's child(ren); *or*
- the spouse or partner who is not a national of a member state has custody of the EEA national's child(ren) or has the right of access to a child under 18, provided a court has ruled that such access must be in the host member state and for as long as is required; [135] *or*
- this is warranted by particularly difficult circumstances, such as having been a victim of domestic violence.

However, before acquiring the right of permanent residence, you must show that you are a worker, or a self-employed or self-sufficient person.

Family members of retired or permanently incapacitated workers or self-employed people

If you have a right of residence as a worker or self-employed person who has retired or is permanently incapacitated, these rights are extended to your family members, even after your death and regardless of their nationality.[136]

If a worker dies during her/his working life before having acquired the right of residence, members of her/his family are entitled to remain in the particular member state, provided that:

- at the date of her/his death, the worker had resided continuously in that state for at least two years; *or*
- her/his death resulted from an accident at work or an occupational disease; *or*
- the surviving spouse or civil partner is a national of the state of residence or lost the nationality of that state by marriage to the worker.[137]

12. **Primary carers of children in education**

A child of a worker or former worker has a right to reside in the country in which s/he is pursuing her/his education.[138] This right is set out in Article 12 of European Union (EU) Regulation 1612/68, which states:

> The children of a national of a Member State who is or has been employed in the territory of another Member State shall be admitted to that State's general educational, apprenticeship and vocational training courses under the same conditions as the nationals of that State, if such children are residing in its territory. Member States shall encourage all efforts to enable such children to attend these courses under the best possible conditions.

The right continues until the child's education (which can include higher education) is completed.[139] However, the term 'general education' does not include nursery education.[140]

While exercising this right, the child also has the right to have her/his parent or primary carer remain in the host state to care for her/him. Therefore, this part of EU law also gives the primary carer of the child a right to reside.

The European Court of Justice (ECJ) has held that this right of residence extends to primary carers who are not European Economic Area (EEA) nationals.[141]

However, the United Kingdom (UK) applied a literal interpretation to the ECJ's judgment and applied it only to non-EEA family members. This meant that a non-economically active EEA national in this situation would not have a right to reside as a primary carer, but a non-EEA national would. The ECJ has confirmed in two judgments that a national of an EEA state who is the primary carer of a child in education does have a right of residence while the child completes her/his education.[142] **Note:** these rights only arise if at least one of the parents/carers has worked in the UK.

The ECJ held that the right of residence will usually continue until the child reaches the age of majority. However, it went on to say that the right of residence of the primary carer can extend beyond the age of majority if the child continues to need her/his presence and care in order to be able to pursue and complete her/

his education.[143] Earlier caselaw from the ECJ also held that this provision extends to higher education.[144]

The parent or carer does not have to be self-sufficient, and neither must s/he have been in work at the time the child enters education. One of the parents/carers, however, must have worked in the UK.

The Department for Work and Pensions has now issued guidance following the judgments, which confirms that a claimant has a right to reside if, at the date of claim: [145]

- s/he is the parent (or step-parent) and primary carer of a child; *and*
- s/he or the child's other parent is a citizen of another EEA state; *and*
- either s/he or the child's other parent is working or has worked as an employed person in the UK; *and*
- that child is still in general education in the UK and is under 18.

In CPAG's view, the guidance is wrong to limit this provision to the age of 18 as the judgments from the ECJ do not apply such a limit.

In EU law, a **'child'** is defined as a person under the age of 21 rather than 18. The right to education extends to higher education, so the date a child completes her/his education may be after the age of 'majority', which in the UK is 18.

A8 and A2 nationals

A8 and A2 nationals who have been in registered or authorised work can also obtain a right of residence if they have a child in education.[146]

Self-employed European Economic Area nationals

The caselaw relating to primary carers covers only employees or former employees. However, it is arguable that self-employed EEA nationals can obtain a right of residence if they have a child in education, as described above. This is because the ECJ has consistently held that the rights of self-employed people are identical to those of workers, even when the legislation is different.[147]

Gaining permanent residence as a primary carer

EU law allows you to gain permanent residence once you have been lawfully resident in a member state, usually for a period of five years years (see p225). If you have been resident on the basis of being the primary carer of a child in education, you should acquire a permanent right of residence on this basis after five years. However, this is being challenged by the UK.

13. **People who are economically inactive**

Some European Economic Area (EEA) nationals and their family members who are not economically active and not self-supporting do not have a right of residence under either European Union (EU) law or the United Kingdom (UK) Immigration Rules and will, most likely, be refused benefit. **Note:** if you are in, or you are deemed to be in, this category, you have fallen into one of the most controversial areas of UK social security law. If you have claimed a social benefit or tax credit and it has been refused on the basis that you do not have a right to reside, you should seek specialist help.

You may have had, at some point, an extended right of residence but you no longer satisfy the EU or UK residence requirements on the date of your benefit claim, or you may never have acquired an extended right of residence and have had only had the three-month right of residence, but have subsequently remained in the UK.

The legality of the UK's 'right to reside' test for social assistance benefits has not yet been tested in the European Court of Justice (ECJ). However, it continues to be argued in the UK courts and virtually all the challenges based on citizenship of the EU, freedom of movement and the principle of equal treatment have been rejected.[148]

Nevertheless, until there is an authoritative ruling by the ECJ, arguments based on EU law remain important. If you are an EEA national, you can rely on EU law and the principles outlined in this *Handbook*.

A series of judgments from the ECJ suggests that entitlement to social security benefits and social assistance for EEA nationals and their family members flows from the fact of their EU citizenship, coupled with their lawful residence in the host member state, and that 'lawful residence' means residence that is lawful under either EU or domestic law. The ECJ's caselaw does make it clear, however, that over-reliance on social assistance could lead to an EEA national and her/his family members losing rights of residence by becoming an 'unreasonable burden' on social assistance (see p236).[149]

It is also arguable that EU Directive 2004/38 prohibits a blanket ban on access to social assistance regardless of the claimant's personal circumstances. Support for this argument can be found in Article 24, the equal treatment provision. This makes it clear that an EEA national or family member who has attained an extended right of residence 'enjoys equal treatment with the nationals of the member state within the scope of the Treaty', provided s/he does not become an unreasonable burden on the social assistance system' of the host state.

It is therefore arguable that EU Directive 2004/38 provides that, in terms of access to social assistance, an EEA national does not have to prove s/he has an ongoing right to reside as a precondition to claiming social assistance. Rather, the Directive makes clear that, ultimately, recourse to social assistance for persons who are not economically active may cause the right of residence to be lost.

If you are in this situation, you should seek specialist advice.

Notes

1. Rights under European Union law

1   *Surinder Singh* C-370/90 [1992] ECR I-4265 (ECJ); *Eind* C-219/05 (ECJ)
2   *Micheletti* C-369/90 [1992] ECR I-4239 (ECJ); *Gullung* C-292/86 [1988] ECR 111 (ECJ). See also CPC/1013/2008, and *McCarthy* C-434/09 awaiting judgment of the ECJ.
3   *Fromancias v Forma* [1983] ECR, para 8 as cited in *Zalewska v Department for Social Development* [2008] UKHL 67
4   *Rottman* C-135/08 (ECJ)
5   *Baumbast and R v Secretary of State for the Home Office* C-413/99 (ECJ)
6   *Van Gend en Loos* C-26/62 [1963] ECR1 (ECJ); *Costa v ENEL* C-6/64 [1964] ECR 585 (ECJ)
7   Art 6(1) and Protocol No. 8 to Art 6(2) Treaty on European Union
8   *Rutili* C-36/75 [1975] ECR 1219 (ECJ) and *Heylens and Others* C-222/86 [1987] ECR 4097 (ECJ)
9   *Gerado Ruiz Zambrano* C-34/09 (ECJ)
10 *Singh* C-370/90 [1992] ECR I-4265, para 23 (ECJ)
11 *Konstantinidis* C-168/91 [1993] 3 CMLR (ECJ)
12 *Konstantinidis* C-168/91 [1993] 3 CMLR (ECJ), opinion of Advocate General Jacobs
13 Art 6 Treaty on European Union
14 *R (Saeedi) v Secretary of the Home Department* [2010] EWHC 705 (Admin). The case is not yet recorded by the Court of Appeal but it recorded the concession on 12 July 2010
15 Nationals of Norway, Iceland and Liechtenstein have rights of free movement and associated rights by virtue of the EEA Agreement. The EC Switzerland Agreement provides similar rights to nationals of Switzerland.
16 *Martinez Sala* C-85/96 (ECJ), para 59
17 *Grzelczyk* C-184/99 [2001] ECR I-6193 (ECJ), para 31
18 *Ruiz Zambrano* C-34/09 and *McCarthy* C-434/09.

2. Right of residence and access to benefits

19 **IS** Reg 21AA(3) IS Regs
    JSA Reg 85A JSA Regs
    ESA Reg 70 ESA Regs
    PC Reg 2 SPC Regs
    HB Reg 20 HB Regs
    CTB Reg 7 CTB Regs
    CB Reg 23 CB Regs
    TC Reg 3 TC(R) Regs
    HPG Reg 4 HPG(EA) Regs
20 These were EU Dirs 64/221, 68/360, 72/194, 73/148, 75/34, 75/35, 90/364, 90/365 and 93/96
21 EU Dir 635/2006
22 This is made clear in the preamble to the Directive.
23 For example, Art 39 gives rights of residence to workseekers and Art 49 to those receiving or providing services.
24 *Blaise, Baheten, Metock and Others v Minister for Justice* C-127/08 (ECJ)
25 In fact the Directive only refers to EU nationals, but the UK has extended its scope to all EEA nationals.
26 Art 24 EU Dir 2004/38
27 **CB** Reg 23(4) CB Regs
    TC Reg 3(5) TC(R) Regs
    HPG Reg 4 HPG(EA) Regs
28 This is subject to meeting all the other general conditions of entitlement.
29 Art 24 EU Dir 2004/38
30 Art 49 EU Treaty; *Mary Carpenter v Secretary of State for the Home Department* C-60/2000 [2002] ECR 006279 (ECJ)
31 Reg 15 I(EEA) Regs
32 Sch 4, para 6 I(EEA) Regs
33 *SSWP v Lassal* C-162/09 [2010] ECR (ECJ)
34 *Abdirahman v SSWP, Abdirahman v Leicester City Council etc* [2007] EWCA Civ 657 and *Kaczmarek v SSWP* [2008] EWCA Civ 1310
35 *McCarthy* C-434/09
36 *HR (Portugal) v Secretary of State for the Home Department* [2009] EWCA Civ 371, 5 May 2009

37 CIS/4304/2007 and *SSWP v IR* [2009] UKUT 11 (AAC) confirm you can move from one of the grounds to another and retain worker status.
38 Art 16 EU Dir 2004/38
39 CIS/2258/2008
40 Residence permits were issued in accordance with EU Dir 68/360 (workers) or EU Dir 71/143 (self-employed people or service providers/users)
41 *Dias v SSWP* [2009] EWCA Civ 807
42 CIS/185/2008
43 Reg 2 I(EEA) Regs
44 *Trojani* C-456/02 (ECJ)
45 *EM and KN v SSWP* [2009] UKUT 44 (AAC), para 16

3. Workers
46 Art 12 EU Reg 1612/68; *London Borough of Harrow v Nimco Hassan Ibrahim* and *Secretary of State for the Home Department and Teixeira v Lambeth LBC* C-310/08 and C-480/08 [2008] EWCA Civ 1088 (ECJ)
47 Art 7(2) Reg 1612/68
48 *Levin v Staatssecretaris van Justitie* C-53/81 (ECJ)
49 *Kempf* C-139/85 [1986] ECR 1741 (ECJ)
50 *Raulin v Minister van Onderwijs en Wetenschappen* C-357/89 [1994] ECR I-1027, 1 CMLR 227 (ECJ)
51 *Le Manoir* C-27/91 (ECJ)
52 CIS/12909/1996, paras 14-15
53 *Barry v London Borough of Southwark* [2008] EWCA Civ 1440, CA, 19 December 2008
54 CIS/1502/2007
55 *Lawrie-Blum v Land Baden-Württemberg* C-66/85 [1986] ECR 2121, [1987] 3 CMLR 389, [1987] ICR 483 (ECJ)
56 *Martinez Sala* C-85/96 [1988] ECR I-2691 (ECJ)
57 *Kempf* C-139/85 (ECJ). In CH/3314/05 and CIS/3315/05 the commissioner suggested a person should be earning an amount which, with tax credits, exceeds her/his IS applicable amount plus the level of her/his rent. Arguably, this conflicts with *Kempf*. See also CJSA/1475/2006, which restricted the application of the test to a claimant who was not in work and who had placed restrictions on his/her availability. In CIS/4144/2007, the commissioner declined to follow the approach in CH/3314/05 and CIS/3315/05.
58 *Levin* C-53/81 (ECJ)

59 *Bettray* C-344/87 (ECJ)
60 CIS/868/2008; CIS/1837/2006
61 *Steymann* C-196/87 [1988] ECR 6159 (ECJ)
62 *Centre Public d'Aide Social, Courcells v Lebon* C-316/85 [1987] ECR 2811 (ECJ)
63 CIS/4521/1995, para 15
64 CIS/4521/1995, para 14; *Lair* C-39/86 [1988] ECR 03161 (ECJ) and *Raulin* C-357/89 [1992] ECR 1-01027 (ECJ)
65 *CS v SSWP* [2009] 16 (AAC)
66 *BS v SSWP* [2009] UKUT 16 (AAC)
67 *Martinez Sala* C-85/96 [1988] ECR I-2691 (ECJ)
68 Art 7(3) EU Dir 2004/38
69 CIS/3890/2005
70 CIS/601/2008
71 CIS/339/2009; *SSWP v Dias* [2009] EWCA Civ 807, para 21
72 CIS/4304/2007
73 CIS/3182/2005. See, however, *Drake v Chief Adjudication Officer* C-150/85 (ECJ) which holds that 'working population' for Dir 79/7 includes someone who gives up work to care for a sick child.
74 CIS/3890/2005
75 R(IS) 12/98
76 CH/3314/2005 and R(IS) 12/98
77 Art 7(3)(b) and (c) EU Dir 2004/38
78 *SSWP v FE* [2009] UKUT 287 (AAC)
79 CIS/1934/2006
80 *SSWP v IR* [2009] UKUT 11 (AAC)
81 CIS/185/2008, para 8
82 CIS/4237/2007
83 CIS 1042/2008
84 CIS/731/2007
85 CIS/4010/2006
86 CIS/731/2007
87 *SSWP v JS(IS)* [2010] UKUT 131 (AAC), although this is being appealed.
88 Art 7(3) EU Reg 1612/68

4. Workseekers
89 *Collins* C-138/02 [2004] ECR 1-02703 (ECJ)
90 Although if you stay on JSA for a very long time, it could be terminated on the basis that you do not have a reasonable prospect of finding employment. See *Antonissen* [1991] ECR 1-745 (ECJ)
91 CIS/4299/2007. This case was appealed to the Court of Appeal, which referred it to the ECJ as *Lassal* C-162/09. The Secretary of State conceded before the Court of Appeal that the claimant was a worker, so the issue of whether residence as a workseeker could count towards a permanent right of residence was not pursued before the ECJ.

92 Art 28 EEA Agreement

5. Self-employed people
93 Art 7(1)(a) para 1 EU Dir 2004/38
94 Art 16(3) EU Dir 2004/38; reg 6(3)
    I(EEA) Regs
95 CIS/1042/2008
96 R(IS) 6/00
97 CIS/3559/1997
98 CIS/3213/2007
99 R (on the application of Tilianu) v Social
    Fund Inspector and SSWP [2010] EWHC
    213 Admin and SSWP v RK [2009] UKUT
    209 (AAC)

6. Students
100 Art 7.1(c) EU Dir 2004/38; regs 6(1)(d)
     and 14 I(EEA) Regs

7. People who are self-sufficient
101 Art 7.1(b) EU Dir 2004/38; regs 6(1)(d)
     and 14 I(EEA) Regs
102 Art 8(4) Dir 2004/38
103 CH/3314/05 and CIS/3315/05
104 Grzelczyk C-184/99 (ECJ)
105 W(China) and X(China) v Secretary of
     State for the Home Department [2006]
     EWCA Civ 1494
106 www.statewatch.org/news/2009/jul/
     eu-com-family-members-com-313.pdf
107 SG v Tameside MBC [2010] UKUT 243
     (AAC)

8. Service providers and users
108 In the past, rights for service providers
     and receivers were contained in the
     same residence Directive as those for
     self-employed people and, therefore, UK
     legislation usually provided them with
     an exemption from restrictions to
     benefits. This is no longer the case, but a
     person covered by the services
     provisions should rely instead on Art 49
     EU Treaty to gain a right of residence
     and access to benefits.
109 Mary Carpenter v Secretary of State for the
     Home Department C-60/2000 [2002]
     ECR 1-006279 (ECJ)
110 Van Binsberg v BBM C-33/74 (ECJ)
111 Royer C-48/75 (ECJ)
112 Art 7 EU Dir 2004/38

113 The point was originally raised in Watson
     and Belmann, in which the Commission
     suggested that the freedom to move
     within the Community to receive
     services was the necessary corollary to
     the freedom to provide services. This
     was approved by the ECJ in Luisi v
     Ministero del Tesoro, in which it was held
     that recipients of services included
     tourists, people receiving medical
     treatment and people travelling for the
     purposes of education and business, so
     far as there is a commercial aspect to the
     service provided.
114 Cowan C-186/87 [1989] ECR 195 (ECJ)
115 Tisseyre, UKIAT
116 Humbel C-263/86 [1988] ECR 5365
     (ECJ)
117 Luisi C-286/82 and Carbone C-26/83
     [1988] ECR 5365 (ECJ)
118 Oulane C-215/03 (ECJ)

**9. Retired or permanently incapacitated
workers and self-employed people**
119 Art 17 EU Dir 2004/38
120 s122(1) SSCBA 1992, 'pensionable age'
121 Art 17(1) EU Dir 2004/38
122 Art 17(2) EU Dir 2004/38
123 Art 17(1) EU Dir 2004/38
124 Art 17(2) EU Dir 2004/38
125 Art 17(1) EU Dir 2004/38
126 Art 17(2) EU Dir 2004/38

10. A8 and A2 nationals
127 Zalewska v Department for Social
     Development [2008] UKHL 67
128 Zalewska v Department for Social
     Development [2008] UKHL 67
129 Zalewska v Department for Social
     Development [2008] UKHL 67

11. Family members
130 Arts 2 and 7 EU Dir 2004/38
131 Pedro v SSWP [2009] EWCA Civ 1358
132 s115(9) IAA 1999
133 Art 3 EU Dir 2004/38
134 CIS/612/2008
135 Art 13(2) EU Dir 2004/38
136 Art 17(3) EU Dir 2004/38
137 Art 17(2) EU Dir 2004/38

**12. Primary carers of children in
education**

138 Teixeira v London Borough of Lambeth C-480/08 (ECJ); Ibrahim v London Borough of Harrow C-310/08 (ECJ); Baumbast v Secretary of State for the Home Department C-413/99 [2002] ECR I-7091 (ECJ); see also DMG Memo 30/10 and HB/CTB Circular A10/2010; Echtenach C-389/87 and Moritz C-390/87 (ECJ)
139 Echtenach C-389/87 and Moritz C-390/87 (ECJ)
140 CIS/3960/2007
141 Baumbast v Secretary of State for the Home Department C-413/99 [2002] ECR I-7091 (ECJ)
142 Teixeira v London Borough of Lambeth C-480/08 (ECJ); Ibrahim v London Borough of Harrow C-310/08 (ECJ)
143 Teixeira v London Borough of Lambeth C-480/08 (ECJ)
144 Echtenach C-389/87 and Moritz C-390/87 (ECJ)
145 Memo DMG 30/10
146 The exclusions apply to Arts 1-6 EU Reg 1612/68. The rights of the primary carer stem from Art 12 EU Reg 1612/68.
147 This is to be considered in CIS/2357/2009

13. People who are economically inactive
148 For example, Abdirahman and Another v SSWP and Another [2008] EWCA Civ 657 (R(IS) 8/07); Kaczmorek v SSWP [2008] EWCA Civ 1310 (R(IS) 5/09)
149 Grezelczyk C-184/09 (ECJ) and Trojani C-456/02 (ECJ)

Chapter 14

. . . .

International agreements

This chapter covers:
1. Reciprocal agreements (below)
2. Council of Europe conventions and agreements (p256)
3. European Union co-operation and association agreements (p257)

1. Reciprocal agreements

A reciprocal agreement is a bilateral agreement made between the United Kingdom (UK) and one other country. They are part of UK law and their purpose is to protect your entitlement to benefits if you move from one country which is a party to the agreement to the other.[1] Like European Union (EU) law (see p149), a reciprocal agreement can help you qualify for certain benefits by allowing periods of residence and contributions paid in each of the two countries to be aggregated. Furthermore, they often specify that you must receive equal treatment with nationals of the country to which you have moved.

The scope of reciprocal agreements differs greatly, not only in terms of the benefits covered and the provisions made, but also in respect of the people covered. It is therefore crucial to check the individual agreement. You can find the agreements in volumes 9 and 10 of the *Law Related to Social Security* at www.dwp.gov.uk.

This chapter gives an outline of the benefits covered and the general principles relating to the agreements. You can find a list of all the countries and the benefits covered in Appendix 6.

Note: the following benefits are *not* covered by any of the agreements:
- child tax credit;
- working tax credit;
- social fund payments;
- contributory employment and support allowance (ESA);
- income-related ESA;
- ESA in youth;
- income-based jobseeker's allowance (JSA); *and*
- income support (IS).

Agreements with non-European Economic Area countries

The UK has reciprocal agreements with some countries outside the European Economic Area (EEA).

Each reciprocal agreement is different in terms of who is covered and which benefits are included.

For a full list of the countries and the type of reciprocal agreement see Appendix 6.

Agreements with Northern Ireland, the Isle of Man and the Channel Islands

Technically, the rules relating to most social security and tax credits apply only to Great Britain – ie, England, Wales and Scotland. It does not include Northern Ireland, the Isle of Man or the Channel Islands, which have their own social security legislation. However, there are reciprocal agreements between all of these to ensure you do not lose out if you move between these countries.

Agreements with European Economic Area states

The UK has reciprocal agreements with all the established EEA member states, except Greece. Of the newer member states, only Cyprus, Malta and Slovenia have agreements. Reciprocal agreements can only be relied on by EEA nationals if EU provisions do not apply.[2]

You cannot qualify for benefits using reciprocal agreements if you:
- fall within the personal scope of the co-ordination rules (see p161);[3] *and*
- acquired your right to benefit on, or after, the date EU provisions applied.[4]

If you are not covered by the co-ordination rules, you may be able to get benefits using the reciprocal agreements. Appendix 6 lists the countries with which the UK has social security agreements, and the benefits covered by each. Agreements between EEA member states continue to apply if you do not fall within the personal scope of the co-ordination rules but you do fall within the scope of the reciprocal agreement.[5]

Agreements between EEA member states can also continue to apply if:
- the provisions of an agreement are more beneficial to you than the EU provisions; *and*
- your right to use the reciprocal agreement was acquired before:
  - EU provisions applied to the UK on 1 April 1973; *or*
  - the other member state joined the EU/EEA.[6]

Note: the UK's agreement with Denmark applies in both the Faroes and Greenland as they are not part of the EU/EEA. Greenland left the EU on 1 February 1985.

People covered by the agreements

Some of the agreements cover nationals of the contracting countries, while others apply to 'people going from one member state to another'. This may be particularly significant if you are a non-EEA national who has worked in two or more EEA member states but cannot benefit under the co-ordination rules (see p161). Of the member states that now form the EEA (see p145), the agreements with Belgium, Denmark, France, Italy and Luxembourg are confined to nationals only.[7] The convention with the Netherlands extends to all people moving from one member state to the other who fall within its scope.

The reciprocal agreements define who is counted as a national for the purpose of the agreement where nationality is an issue. In all of these, a UK national is defined as a 'Citizen of the United Kingdom and Colonies'.[8]

The category of people termed 'Citizens of the United Kingdom and Colonies' disappeared on 1 January 1983 when the British Nationality Act 1981 came into force. From this date, a person who had previously held citizenship of the UK and colonies became:

- a British citizen;
- a British dependent territories citizen;
- a British overseas citizen; *or*
- a British subject.

See Chapter 1 for further details on nationality.

For the purposes of the UK social security 'nationals-only' conventions with Belgium, Denmark, France, Italy and Luxembourg, a national in relation to the UK now includes anyone in one of the above four categories.

The definition of nationality contained in the agreements with Denmark, Italy and Luxembourg is simply that of a 'Danish' or 'Italian' or 'Luxemburger' national.[9] These agreements confer no rights if you are not a national of one of these member states. The agreement with Belgium, however, covers a 'person having Belgian nationality or a native of the Belgian Congo or Ruanda-Urundi'. The agreement with France refers to 'a person having French nationality' and 'any French-protected person belonging to French Togoland or the French Cameroons'.

When these agreements came into force in 1958, the Belgian Congo and Ruanda-Urundi and French Togoland and the French Cameroons were Belgian and French territories respectively. The question concerning who is presently covered by these agreements, insofar as Belgian and French nationals are concerned, is a matter for the Belgian and French authorities. If you come from one of these countries (present-day Democratic Republic of Congo, Rwanda, Burundi, Togolese Republic and the Republic of Cameroon), enquire whether you are covered by these agreements with the Belgian or French authorities.

The agreements give equal treatment to the nationals of the contracting countries, stating that a 'national of one contracting party shall be entitled to receive the benefits of the legislation of the other contracting party under the same conditions as if he were a national of the latter contracting party'.[10]

The agreements with Finland, Iceland, Ireland, Portugal, Spain and Sweden are not confined to nationals but give rights to:

- 'people who go from one country to another' (Ireland);
- 'a person subject to the legislation of one contracting party who becomes resident in the territory of the other party' (Portugal);
- 'a national of one contracting party, or a person subject to the legislation of that party, who becomes resident in the territory of the other contracting party' (Spain); *and*
- 'a national of the state and person deriving their rights from such nationals and other people who are, or have been, covered by the legislation of either of the states and people deriving their rights from such a person' (Sweden).

The agreements with Austria and Norway have nationality restrictions which apply to the protocol on benefits in kind (eg, medical treatment) but not to social security contributions and benefits. A national of the UK is defined as anyone who is recognised by the UK government as a UK national, provided that s/he is 'ordinarily resident' in the UK. A person can be treated as ordinarily resident from the first day of her/his stay in the UK (see p72 for more information).

The agreement with Germany is not restricted to nationals of either agreement member state insofar as social security benefits are concerned. However, a nationality provision applies to the Articles relating to contribution liability.

Even if you are not a national of one of the contracting parties to these agreements, you may still be able to benefit from their provisions.

Benefits covered by the agreements

The following benefits are covered by some of the reciprocal agreements. See Appendix 6 for a full list of which benefits apply to which countries.

Unemployment benefits

The relevant benefit in the UK is contribution-based JSA.

None of the agreements allow you to receive unemployment benefits outside the country in which you paid your national insurance (NI) contributions. However, a number do allow NI paid in one country to count towards satisfying the conditions of entitlement in another. This is the case with the UK agreements with Austria, Cyprus, Finland, Iceland, Malta, New Zealand and Norway.

Sickness benefits

In the UK, the relevant sickness benefit is short-term incapacity benefit (IB).

Note: from 27 October 2008 IB was abolished for new claims and replaced with ESA, but the Government has stated that the reciprocal agreements in the UK will not be amended to include ESA. Therefore, ESA of any type is not covered by reciprocal agreements.

If you are entitled to sickness benefits, some of the agreements allow you to receive your benefit in another country. In other cases, contributions that you have paid under one country's scheme may be taken into account to help you satisfy the conditions of entitlement in another.

Maternity benefits

In the UK, the relevant maternity benefit is maternity allowance (MA). If you are entitled to maternity benefits, some of the agreements allow you to receive your benefit in another country. You may be entitled to MA, or continue to be paid MA, if absent from the UK, under the reciprocal agreements with: Barbados, Cyprus, the Isle of Man, Jersey and Guernsey, Switzerland, Turkey and the former Republic of Yugoslavia. The circumstances under which you may be able to claim or retain MA differ from agreement to agreement.

Invalidity benefits

The relevant benefit in the UK is long-term IB.

Note: from 27 October 2008 IB was abolished for new claims and replaced by ESA. The Government has announced that the reciprocal agreements in the UK will not be amended to include ESA. However, people who continue to be entitled to IB after the introduction of ESA will still be covered by the reciprocal agreements.[11]

A number of agreements allow you to receive invalidity benefits in another country. The agreements with Austria, Cyprus, Iceland, Norway and Sweden allow you to continue to receive your long-term IB in these countries, subject to medical controls being undertaken in the agreement country. Correspondingly, you are able to receive the other country's invalidity benefits in the UK. The agreement with Barbados allows a certificate of permanent incapacity to be issued, permitting you to receive long-term IB without medical controls.

Benefits for industrial injuries

The relevant benefits in the UK are disablement benefit (including any additional components), reduced earnings allowance and retirement allowance.

Most of the agreements include industrial injuries benefits. The arrangements determine which country's legislation will apply to new accidents or diseases, depending on where you are insured at the time. Many of the agreements allow you to combine the industrial injuries incurred in each country when assessing the degree of your latest injury. Furthermore, if you work in one country and remain insured under the other country's scheme and you have an industrial injury you can be treated as though the injury arose in the country in which you are insured. Most agreements include arrangements to allow you to receive all three of the UK benefits for industrial injuries indefinitely in the other country.

Retirement pensions and bereavement benefits

All the agreements include retirement pensions and bereavement benefits. In the UK, the relevant benefits are retirement pensions, bereavement allowance and widowed parent's allowance. In most cases, you can receive a retirement pension or bereavement benefit in the agreement country at the same rate as you would be paid in the country where you are insured. This is the case under all of the agreements except those with Canada and New Zealand, which do not permit the uprating of these benefits. If you go to live in one of these countries, your retirement pension (and any other long-term benefit) will be 'frozen' at the rate payable either when you left the UK, or when you became entitled to your pension abroad.

If you do not qualify for a retirement pension or bereavement benefit from either country, or you qualify for a pension or bereavement benefit from one country but not the other, the agreements with the following countries allow you to be paid basic old-age and bereavement benefits on a pro rata basis, with your insurance under both schemes taken into account: Austria, Barbados, Bermuda, Cyprus, Finland, Iceland, Israel, Jamaica, Malta, Mauritius, Norway, the Philippines, Sweden, Switzerland, Turkey, the USA and the former Republic of Yugoslavia.

Family benefits

In the UK, the relevant family benefits are child benefit and guardian's allowance. The provisions concerning these two benefits enable periods of residence and/or presence in the other country to be treated as residence and/or presence in Great Britain. The extent to which reciprocity exists varies, however, according to the particular agreement. For example, residence or contributions paid in the following countries count towards your satisfying UK residence conditions for guardian's allowance: Cyprus, Israel, Jamaica, Jersey/Guernsey, Mauritius and Turkey.

If you are covered by a reciprocal agreement for child benefit, you are exempt from the definition of a 'person subject to immigration control' in the UK for child benefit purposes (see p55) and are eligible, subject to meeting all the other conditions of entitlement.

Dependants' benefits

In the UK a dependant's benefit is an increase of benefit covered by the agreement. Dependants' increases can be paid if the dependant is in either country to the agreement.

2. Council of Europe conventions and agreements

There are numerous European conventions and agreements. These are prepared and negotiated within the Council of Europe. The most famous is perhaps the European Convention on Human Rights. The purpose of these conventions is to address issues of common concern in economic, social, cultural, scientific, legal and administrative matters and in human rights. However, such agreements and conventions are not legally binding in the United Kingdom (UK) unless or until they incorporated into UK law or legislation is enacted in order to give specific effect to the Treaty obligations in question – eg, the UK Human Rights Act in respect of the European Convention on Human Rights. They are statements of intent of the individual countries that are signatories. The UK is a signatory to a number of these agreements, two of which are significant for social security.

The European Convention on Social and Medical Assistance

The European Convention on Social and Medical Assistance (ECSMA) has been in force since 1954. It requires that ratifying states provide assistance in cash and in kind to nationals of other ratifying states, who are lawfully present in their territories and without sufficient resources, on the same conditions as their own nationals. It also prevents ratifying states repatriating lawfully present nationals of other ratifying states simply because the person is in need of assistance.

The countries that have signed this agreement are all the European Economic Area (EEA) countries (see p145) plus Macedonia and Turkey.

However, European Union (EU) rules are more generous than this Convention, so it would not usually need to apply to EEA nationals.

You can only benefit from the Convention if you are 'lawfully present' in the UK. The House of Lords has held that an asylum seeker on temporary admission is 'lawfully present' and, therefore, could potentially claim benefit under this agreement.[12] However, a person who is lawfully present could still be excluded from benefit on the basis that s/he does not have a right to reside (see p116 for more details).[13]

The rights given are recognised in UK law and, if you are a person who is covered by the Convention, you are not defined as a 'person subject to immigration control' (see p56) for means-tested benefits. However, the Court of Appeal has held that a Turkish national who was lawfully resident and who was a beneficiary of this Convention nevertheless had to satisfy the right to reside test.[14]

The 1961 Council of Europe Social Charter

This agreement is similar to the ECSMA agreement. The signatory states are all EEA countries (see p145) plus Macedonia, Croatia and Turkey. If you are a national of one of these states and you are lawfully present you are not a 'person subject to immigration control' for means-tested benefits.

It is only this 1961 Charter that gives access to UK social security benefits. If you are a national of a country that has signed a later charter only, you are not exempt from the definition of 'person subject to immigration control'.

Although the Council of Europe agreements stem from Europe, they are not part of EU law. Therefore, they are of little practical use unless recognised and incorporated into UK law.

3. **European Union co-operation and association agreements**

The European Union (EU) Treaty provides for agreements to be made with so-called 'third countries' outside the EU.[15] These co-operation and association agreements are of far more significance than the agreements outlined on pp250-256. This is because they are part of EU law and therefore have the potential to override United Kingdom (UK) rules.

At present, the only agreements which directly affect benefits in the UK are those with Algeria, Israel, Morocco, San Marino, Tunisia and Turkey.

All of these agreements contain provisions which specify that there must be equal treatment for those covered by the agreement in matters of 'social security'. The UK regulations go some way to recognising these rights, but they do not fully recognise them.

UK regulations specify that if you are a national of one of these states and you are lawfully working in the UK, you are exempt from the definition of 'person subject to immigration control' (see p55) for the purposes of:

- attendance allowance;
- carer's allowance;
- child benefit;
- child tax credit (CTC);
- disability living allowance;
- employment and support allowance in youth;
- health in pregnancy grants;
- payments from the social fund.

However, the EU agreements offer equal treatment to a wider range of benefits. In *Surul*, the European Court of Justice (ECJ) equated the Turkish agreement with EU Regulation 1408/71 and held that the benefits covered were the social security benefits in EU Regulation 1408/71. Social security in this context has a distinct meaning. It refers to certain benefits intended for the risks of unemployment, sickness, maternity, old age, bereavement, industrial injury and death (see p169 for a full list of these benefits). It is clear that these benefits are covered and it has been established that income-based jobseeker's allowance (JSA) is an unemployment benefit for EU purposes.[16] **Note:** housing benefit and council tax benefit are *not* covered by EU Regulation 1408/71 or EU Regualtion 883/2004 and consequently do not fall within the scope of the co-operation and association agreements.

Furthermore, there is caselaw to support the view that all the benefits covered by EU Regulation 1408/71 or Regulation 883/2004 also fall within the scope of some of the co-operation and association agreements. In *Babahenini*, the ECJ considered whether a disability allowance was a benefit within the scope of the Algerian agreement.[17] As in earlier caselaw, its decision was based on the principle that EU Regulation 1408/71 should be looked to for guidance.

Who is covered

To benefit from the agreements, you must be within their 'personal scope' – ie, you must be a national of Algeria, Israel, Morocco, Tunisia, San Marino or Turkey and you must be lawfully working. This has been equated with being an 'insured person'. An insured person has the meaning given in EU Regulations 1408/71 amd 883/2004 (see p161). In broad terms, this means that you must have worked in the UK and have (or you ought to have) paid national insurance contributions. In one case, a commissioner held that an asylum seeker who had worked in the UK was covered by the Turkish Association Agreement and was therefore eligible for family credit as a family benefit under that agreement.[18]

Notes

1. **Reciprocal agreements**
   1 s179(2) SSAA 1992
   2 Art 6 EU Reg 1408/71; Art 8 EU Reg 883/04
   3 Art 2 EU Reg 1408/71; Art 2 EU Reg 883/04
   4 *Walder v Bestuur der Sociale Verzekeringsbank* C-82/72 [1973] 599 (ECJ) and *Jean-Louis Thévenon and Stadt Speyer-Sozialamt v Landesversicherungsanstalt Rheinland-Pfalz* C-475/93 [1995] (ECJ)
   5 Art 2 EU Reg 1408/71; Art 2 EU Reg 883/04; *Galinsky v Insurance Officer* C-99/80 [1981] 503 (ECJ); R(P) 1/81
   6 *Ronfeldt* C-227/89 [1991] ECR I-323 (ECJ); *Jean-Louis Thévenon and Stadt Speyer-Sozialamt v Landesversicherungsanstalt Rheinland-Pfalz* C-475/93 [1995] (ECJ)
   7 Art 3 to each of the relevant reciprocal agreements
   8 Art 1 to each of the relevant reciprocal agreements
   9 Art 1 to each of the relevant reciprocal agreements
   10 Art 1 to each of the relevant reciprocal agreements
   11 Memo DMG 38/08

2. Council of Europe conventions and agreements

12 *Szoma v SSWP* [2005] UKHL 64, [2006] 1 All ER 1 (reported as R(IS) 2/06)
13 R(IS)3/08
14 *Yesiloz v London Borough of Camden and Department for Work and Pensions* [2009] EWCA Civ 415

3. European Union co-operation and association agreements

15 Art 310 EU Treaty
16 *Hockenjos v Secretary of State for Social Security* [2001] EWCA Civ 624, [2001] 2 CMLR 51, *Times Law Report,* 17 May 2001; CJSA/1920/1999 (*65/00)
17 C-113/97 – in a commissioner's decision, however, the commissioner held that the Turkish Agreement did not apply to income support.
18 CFC/2613/1997

Part 4

Support for asylum seekers

Chapter 15

· ·

Support for asylum seekers

This chapter covers:
1. Support for asylum seekers: overview (below)
2. Who is entitled to asylum support (p266)
3. Exclusions from asylum support (p269)
4. When asylum support can be suspended or discontinued (p270)
5. Temporary asylum support (p272)
6. Who is entitled to Section 4 support (p272)
7. When Section 4 support can be suspended or discontinued (p282)
8. Other forms of support (p284)

---

1. Support for asylum seekers: overview

Types of support for asylum seekers

There are three main types of government support for people who have made a claim for asylum in the United Kingdom (UK):

- **asylum support** for the period until a final decision on an asylum application is made;[1]
- **temporary** (often called **emergency**) **support**, available to asylum seekers waiting for an asylum support decision;[2]
- **Section 4 support** (previously known as **hard cases support**), available to failed asylum seekers who meet certain criteria.[3]

Note: the phrase '**asylum support**' is sometimes used to refer to all three types of support. This can be confusing and, therefore, in this chapter 'asylum support' is used only when referring to support provided until a final decision is made on an asylum application.

The UK Border Agency

Over recent years, the role of providing financial and other support, including housing, to asylum seekers has passed between different Home Office agencies. Until April 2006 the support scheme for asylum seekers and failed asylum seekers was administered by the National Asylum Support Service (NASS). In April 2006,

NASS ceased to exist and its role was taken over by the Border and Immigration Agency (BIA), but the BIA was very short-lived.

On 7 April 2008, the UK Border Agency (UKBA) was formed, taking over the support role of the BIA. It also took over the immigration and asylum functions of the Immigration and Nationality Department (IND). From that point, BIA and IND no longer existed. Thus, the support role and the immigration and asylum functions have been combined into the work of the single agency, UKBA. This means UKBA deals not only with support for asylum seekers, but also asylum claims.

Despite this, many people (including many UKBA officials themselves) still (incorrectly) refer to NASS or NASS support when intending to refer to the support role of UKBA.

UKBA is based in Croydon in South London and has a number of regional offices. All new claims for asylum made after April 2007 are dealt with by the UKBA under the 'New Asylum Model' (known as NAM) and are allocated to a 'caseowner'. This caseowner is responsible for all issues concerning the asylum seeker until s/he is granted refugee status or leaves the United Kingdom (UK). Thus, the caseowner also has responsibility for deciding whether or not the asylum seeker should receive asylum support. This is very different to the former system, where NASS dealt only with asylum support and the asylum claim was dealt with elsewhere in the Home Office.

A separate part of the UKBA, the **Case Resolution Directorate** (CRD), deals with all issues relating to those individuals who made their original claim for asylum before 1 April 2007. Thus, the CRD deals with the asylum claim, appeals, further representations and all support matters until the individual obtains permission to remain or leaves the UK. These cases have been called 'legacy cases' and the CRD has often been called the 'legacy directorate'. It is based in Croydon, but with a number of regional teams around the UK. It was intended for the CRD to have dealt with all legacy cases by July 2010 and so it may have no further role.

One-stop agencies

The Home Office has contracts with certain voluntary sector agencies, under which the agencies take on the responsibility of assisting asylum seekers to submit claims for asylum support. These agencies are collectively known as '**one-stop agencies**' and include the Refugee Arrivals Project, Refugee Action, the Refugee Council and the Scottish and Welsh Refugee Councils (see Appendix 2 for addresses).

Background to the system of support

Before 5 February 1996 asylum seekers without funds received income support at the urgent cases rate of 90 per cent, and housing benefit. Those without accommodation and in 'priority need' were entitled to local authority housing under the homelessness legislation. In February 1996 the Government decided that providing benefits was a factor that attracted asylum seekers to the UK and withdrew state benefits, leaving nothing in their place. Asylum seekers, therefore, sought the safety-net provisions from local authorities, in particular relying on s21 National Assistance Act 1948 and also ss17 and 20 Children Act 1989.

From 6 December 1999, the Immigration and Asylum Act 1999 restricted the ability of asylum seekers and other migrants to access support from local authorities. These restrictions have been extended,[4] so they now apply to the following local authority support:

- ss21 and 29 National Assistance Act 1948;
- s2 Chronically Sick and Disabled Persons Act 1970;
- s21 and Schedule 8 National Health Service Act 1977;
- ss17, 23C, 24A and 24B Children Act 1989;
- s2 Local Government Act 2002.

Note: the exclusions do not prevent a local authority from providing support under the above provisions, if failing to do so would result in a breach of an asylum seeker's human rights.

The Immigration and Asylum Act 1999 retained the general exclusion of asylum seekers and others from state benefits and other welfare provisions on the basis that they are 'persons subject to immigration control' (see p55).[5] From 3 April 2000, asylum seekers were to be provided with asylum support by NASS (or with 'interim support' by local authorities as a temporary measure while NASS support was being introduced and which was entirely withdrawn in 2006).

The system introduced in April 2000 remains the current system of asylum support, now managed by the UKBA. At that time it was administered by NASS and later (from 2006 to 2007) by its short-lived replacement, the BIA (see above) until the UKBA took on the role on 7 April 2007. Although NASS has now been wound up, the phrase 'NASS support' is still frequently (although incorrectly) used.

Section 4 support

Until early 2005, failed asylum seekers could only receive 'hard cases support' under s4 Immigration and Asylum Act 1999, provided entirely at NASS's discretion. On 31 March 2005, regulations were introduced, specifying entitlement to support under this section for certain failed asylum seekers and their dependants (see p272).[6]

Community care support

If an asylum seeker (or a non-European Economic Area national) is destitute and 'in need of care and attention' because of age, pregnancy, disability, mental health needs or other special reasons, s/he may be able to obtain assistance as community care from the local authority under s21 National Assistance Act 1948.

The local authority can be asked to carry out a community care assessment to determine whether s/he needs support from the local authority.[7] Community care is restricted for asylum seekers and support from a local authority may not be provided if the person's need for care and attention arises solely from the effects, or anticipated effects, of being destitute (see pp268 and 284).[8]

Unaccompanied minors

Unaccompanied asylum seekers who are children, often referred to as unaccompanied minors (ie, up to the age of 18 and, exceptionally, over 18), continue to be supported by social services (see p287).

2. **Who is entitled to asylum support**

You are entitled to asylum support (see p263) if:[9]
- you are an asylum seeker or the dependant of an asylum seeker; *and*
- you are destitute or likely to become destitute; *and*
- unless you made your claim before 8 January 2003, you have made your claim for asylum 'as soon as reasonably practicable'.[10]

See p272 for who is entitled to temporary support. The criteria are similar, but it must appear that you are actually destitute, not simply likely to become destitute.

Who is an asylum seeker for support purposes

For the purposes of asylum support, you are an asylum seeker if:[11]
- you are over 18 years; *and*
- you have made a claim for asylum; *and*
- the claim has been recorded by the Secretary of State; *and*
- the claim has not been determined.

The **asylum claim** may be made either under the 1951 Convention (Refugee or Geneva Convention – see p3) or under Article 3 of the European Convention on Human Rights. If you have made a different type of claim, such as an Article 8 claim or a claim for indefinite leave to remain (see p10), you cannot claim asylum support. For further details on asylum claims, see p17.

For support purposes, you continue to be treated as an asylum seeker for 28 days after one of the following events:[12]
- your claim for asylum is granted;
- you are granted leave to remain; *or*
- your asylum appeal is allowed.

Alternatively, you continue to be an asylum seeker for 21 days after your asylum claim has been refused by the Home Office or, if there is an appeal, for 21 days after that appeal is finally dismissed (see p267).

The '**recording**'of an asylum claim is not a process clearly defined by Home Office rules or regulations. It appears that this could be a simple statement or action by the Secretary of State, acting through the UK Border Agency (UKBA), in recognition that a claim for asylum (as defined by immigration law) has been made.

First claims are generally recorded at the time they are made, or at a 'screening interview' conducted by the Home Office.[13] However, it is arguable that a first asylum claim has also been 'recorded' by the Secretary of State when representations are submitted, claiming that a person's removal would breach Article 3 of the European Convention on Human Rights or the Refugee Convention.[14]

In practice, whether or not a claim has been 'recorded' is more of an issue when a 'fresh claim' is made after the first asylum claim has failed (see p21). A fresh claim (ie, a subsequent claim) is not 'recorded' until the Home Office accepts that the representations constitute a fresh claim – ie, they do not simply repeat arguments and facts previously presented.

An asylum claim remains undetermined during the time allowed for any appeal to be made and during any appeal lodged within that time (or any appeal accepted out of time) whether to an immigration judge in the First-tier Tribunal (Immigration and Asylum), or a further appeal. However, an application for judicial review of an immigration decision does not have the same effect; an asylum claim is not considered undetermined while the judicial review is outstanding.

An asylum seeker with a dependent child whose claim for asylum has been determined is treated as continuing to be an asylum seeker for support purposes until the child's 18th birthday, providing s/he remains in the United Kingdom (UK).[15] **Note:** this only applies if you had a dependent child under 18 years old in the UK when you were still an asylum seeker. The Asylum Support Adjudicators (as the appeal tribunal was called at that time) has held that, if an asylum seeker had a dependent child with her/him in the UK, but was not claiming asylum support at the relevant time (ie, up to 21 days after the date her/his claim is finally determined), these extended support provisions do not apply.[16] This decision relies on the word 'continuing' in s94(5) Immigration and Asylum Act 1999 which says: 'He is to be treated (for the purposes of this Part) as continuing to be an asylum-seeker.'

This interpretation, however, is challengeable as it can be argued that the word 'continuing' means that the person continues to be an asylum seeker for support purposes, not that there must be some pre-existing support, which will be continued.[17]

The birth of a child after an asylum claim has failed and all appeal rights are exhausted does not create entitlement to asylum support. In any event, you should be aware that the UKBA can withdraw support from failed asylum-seeker families who, in the opinion of the Secretary of State, have not taken steps to leave the UK voluntarily.[18] This means that you are expected to demonstrate that you are taking steps to arrange your departure from the UK to return home. This power was piloted across the UK in 2005, but has not been adopted as general practice. If the UKBA decides to withdraw your support because it says that you are not taking steps to leave the UK with your family, you have the right to appeal against this decision to the First Tier Tribunal (Asylum Support) (see Chapter 18).

Who is a dependant of an asylum seeker for support purposes

Support is provided for an asylum seeker and her/his dependants, so long as they are destitute. A dependant is:[19]

- the spouse or civil partner of the asylum seeker;
- a child aged under 18 years of the asylum seeker or her/his spouse/civil partner who is dependent on her/him;
- a child aged under 18 years of the close family of the asylum seeker/spouse/ civil partner (the child does not have to be dependent on her/him);
- a child aged under 18 years who has lived in the asylum seeker's household for six out of the last 12 months, or since birth;
- someone now over 18 years old, but who was under 18 years and within the above categories when the asylum support claim was made or when s/he entered the UK;
- a close family member or someone who has lived with the asylum seeker for six out of the last 12 months (or since birth) who is disabled and in need of care and attention from a member of the household;
- a partner who was living with the asylum seeker as an unmarried couple for at least two of the three years before the support claim or before entering the UK;
- a member of the household who was previously receiving support under s17 Children Act 1989 immediately before 6 December 1999;
- someone who lodges a claim with the Home Office to remain on the basis of being a dependant of the asylum seeker.

The definition of destitute

Under s95(3) Immigration and Asylum Act 1999, a person is destitute if:

(a) he does not have adequate accommodation or any means of obtaining it (whether or not his other essential living needs are met); *or*
(b) he has adequate accommodation or the means of obtaining it, but cannot meet his other essential living needs.

The Nationality, Immigration and Asylum Act 2002 was passed with the intention to alter this part of the 1999 Act, so that you would only be regarded as 'destitute' if you did not have 'adequate accommodation, *and* food *and* other essential items' – ie, you would have to be without all three to qualify as destitute. However, as this has still not come into force at the time of writing, it is doubtful if it ever will. (If it were to be brought into force, it appears that the 'financial support only' option for asylum support would disappear and it would only be possible to accept the complete package of accommodation and support).

When you make an application for asylum support, you are regarded as destitute if there is a likelihood of destitution within 14 days.[20] If you already receive asylum support, you will continue to be regarded as destitute if there is a likelihood of destitution within 56 days.

See Chapter 16 for what income and assets are taken into account when deciding whether or not you are destitute.

3. Exclusions from asylum support

Even if you meet the definition of a person eligible for asylum support, you can be excluded from getting support if:[21]

- you are not excluded from getting social security benefits because of your immigration status (see p55);
- you are not being treated as an asylum seeker (see p266) or the dependant of an asylum seeker (see below) for immigration purposes;
- you apply for support as part of a group and every person is excluded under either of the above rules.

You can also be excluded if you did not claim asylum 'as soon as reasonably practicable' on entering the United Kingdom (UK).[22] **Note:** this currently only applies to asylum seekers without dependent children.

There is no statutory definition of the term '**as soon as reasonably practicable**' and this led to substantial numbers of in-country asylum seekers (ie, people who did not claim asylum at the port of entry, but only after they had entered UK) being refused support and a flood of judicial review cases in the High Court when the rule was first implemented. The Home Office subsequently issued a policy stating that any claim made within three days of arrival is treated as made 'as soon as reasonably practicable'.[23]

Asylum support should not be withheld if a refusal of support would be in breach of a person's human rights.[24] There have been many legal challenges on this issue, the result of which is that asylum support should only be withheld from applicants who have an alternative source of support.

Dependants of asylum seekers

If you make an application for asylum support for yourself alone as the dependant of an asylum seeker, you cannot get asylum support if the Home Office does not treat you as a dependant of the asylum seeker for immigration purposes.[25]

There is a difference between those who are treated as dependants of asylum seekers for asylum support purposes (see p268)[26] and those who the Home Office generally treats as dependent on an asylum claim. The spouse and minor children of an asylum seeker who accompany her/him to the UK are considered by the Home Office to be dependants of the asylum claim unless they claim in their own right.[27] A dependent child who reaches age 18 before a decision is made on the application continues to be treated as a dependant pending the decision and during any appeal. The Home Office also has a discretion to treat other relatives and those who do not arrive at the same time as the principal applicant as dependants, provided there has not yet been a decision on the asylum application.

Other exclusions

Some people are excluded from asylum support (and also excluded from community care under the National Assistance Act 1948 – see p284).[28] However, a child cannot be excluded from support. Nor can an adult be excluded if the provision of support is necessary to avoid a breach of human rights.[29] Those excluded from asylum support are:

- people with refugee status granted by a European Economic Area (EEA) state and their dependants;[30]
- EEA nationals and their dependants.[31]

4. **When asylum support can be suspended or discontinued**

If you have been granted support, the UK Border Agency (UKBA) has the power to discontinue or suspend it in specified cases.[32] **Note:** a 'power' means a discretion which the UKBA must exercise lawfully. Support can be suspended or discontinued if:

- the UKBA has reason to believe that you or your dependant has committed a serious breach of the rules of the accommodation, if accommodated in 'collective accommodation' – eg, a hostel or shared house.[33] Each accommodation provider is likely to have a set of 'house rules', which every person must follow – eg, to be respectful of other residents and not to make any noise late at night;
- the UKBA has reason to believe that you or your dependant has committed an act of seriously violent behaviour;[34]
- you or your dependant has committed a criminal offence under Part VI of the Immigration and Asylum Act 1999.[35] This includes making a false claim to get support and failing to report a change of circumstances to the UKBA – eg, not informing the UKBA about a change in your financial resources;
- you fail within five working days to provide the UKBA with information about an application for, or receipt of, support;[36]

- you fail without reasonable excuse to attend an interview relating to your dependant's support;[37]
- you fail within 10 working days to provide information regarding your dependant's asylum application;[38]
- the UKBA has reason to believe that you or your dependant has concealed financial resources and unduly benefited from asylum support;[39]
- you or your dependant fail to comply with reporting requirements;[40]
- the UKBA has reason to believe that you or your dependant have made, or attempted to make, a second claim for asylum before the first claim is determined;[41]
- there are 'reasonable grounds' to suspect that you have abandoned the 'authorised address' (see p306) without first informing the UKBA or without the UKBA's permission.[42] Even if you have only asked the UKBA for financial support and not accommodation (eg, because friends have offered to let you stay with them), you must inform the UKBA of your address for support purposes and this becomes your authorised address. You must tell the UKBA if you need to leave this address and you are not allowed to leave the address for more than 14 days.

Discontinuation or suspension can only take effect if you are already being supported by the UKBA.[43] Suspension, by its very nature, is temporary and is used when the UKBA requires time or more information to decide whether to discontinue support – ie, to terminate support entirely. If it is satisfied that there has been a breach of conditions, when deciding whether to continue to provide support the UKBA must take into account the extent of the breach of any conditions upon which support has been granted. Even if the grounds for suspension or discontinuation are established, you can still retain entitlement to support if you can show you are destitute and require support to avoid a breach of your human rights.

If you apply for support again after it has been discontinued, the UKBA may refuse to consider the application if:[44]

- there has been no 'material change in circumstances' since the original decision to suspend or discontinue the support. This means a change of any of the circumstances which you must notify to the UKBA (see p298);[45] *and*
- there are no 'exceptional circumstances' that justify considering the your application for support. New evidence that you are destitute would constitute a basis for making a new application.

If the UKBA decides to consider your application for support in these circumstances, it may still refuse support.[46]

A decision to suspend or discontinue asylum support can be appealed to the First-tier Tribunal (Asylum Support) (see p316).

5. Temporary asylum support

While the UK Border Agency (UKBA) is considering an application for asylum support from an asylum seeker, it can, and usually does, provide a temporary form of support to her/him or her/his dependant(s).[47] This 'temporary support' is commonly called 'emergency support'.

Temporary asylum support can be provided if it appears that the applicant *may* be destitute at the time of the application – ie, even if there is some uncertainty.[48] 'Destitution' is defined for the purposes of temporary support in the same way as it is for ordinary asylum support (see p293),[49] except there is no power to provide temporary support solely on the basis that an applicant is likely to become destitute within 14 days (as there is with asylum support[50]).

Temporary support may be provided subject to conditions, which must be given in writing. It can only be provided until the UKBA decides whether or not asylum support is to be provided. If the UKBA refuses asylum support, temporary support ends at the same time.

There is no appeal to the First-tier Tribunal (Asylum Support) (see p316) against a refusal or withdrawal of temporary support.[51] The only method of challenging such a decision is by judicial review proceedings.

Exclusion from temporary support

You are excluded from temporary support if:[52]
- you are not excluded from getting social security benefits because of your immigration status (see p55);
- you apply as a dependant, but you are not being treated as a dependant of an asylum seeker for immigration purposes;
- you apply as part of a group and every person in the group is excluded under either of the above rules.

6. Who is entitled to Section 4 support

Failed asylum seekers who have reached the end of the appeal process and exhausted any appeal rights are not generally entitled to support from the UK Border Agency (UKBA) and the Home Office expects them to return to their country of origin. If, for some reason, a failed asylum seeker is unable to leave the United Kingdom (UK), s/he may be able to claim support under s4 Immigration and Asylum Act 1999. This is known as 'Section 4 support' (formerly known as 'hard cases support').

To get Section 4 support you must:
- be destitute; *and*
- meet one of the five criteria for support; [53] *or*

- be applying for accommodation to support an application for bail or release from immigration detention (see p18).

Section 4(1) of the Immigration and Asylum Act 1999 also gives the Home Office an additional power to provide Section 4 support to 'persons temporarily admitted to the UK'. This is very rarely, if ever, provided as it is only a power and not a duty and has no related regulatory framework. It appears that the Home Office considers that it need not provide this support because an applicant will normally have the choice to leave the UK and, if not, s/he can apply for support under other provisions – eg, asylum support as an asylum seeker or Section 4(2) support as a failed asylum seeker (see below).

The definition of destitute

This is the same test as for asylum support (see p293).[54] If you apply for Section 4 support within 21 days of your asylum support ending, the UKBA automatically accepts that you are destitute. However, if you have not recently had asylum support, the UKBA usually insists that it is up to you to prove you are now destitute and requires detailed information on how you have survived without social security benefits and how your situation has now changed to leave you destitute. In these circumstances, the UKBA asks you to provide evidence, such as letters from friends, family and charities, explaining:
- what support they have given you in the past; *and*
- why that cannot continue.

If this evidence cannot be obtained, you will need to tell the UKBA (and the First-tier Tribunal in any appeal) why this is the case – eg, the friendship may have now deteriorated because you have overstayed your welcome.

It is also important to remember the test of destitution as it is set out in the regulations on p268. An asylum seeker or failed asylum seeker who relied on friends and relatives may still have been destitute within the regulations, even while receiving that help – eg, s/he may have spent nights sleeping on various friends' floors without a key to gain access, and walking the streets during the day, or has had no money and/or little food. Such an individual has been destitute under the regulations throughout this period as s/he has not had adequate accommodation and/or has been unable to meet her/his essential living needs. It is important when applying for Section 4 support in these circumstance to give full details about what support has been made available in the past.

Criteria for support

To qualify for Section 4 support, you must also prove that you fall into one of the following situations.

You are taking all reasonable steps to leave the United Kingdom

You must be taking all reasonable steps to leave the UK, including, if relevant, applying for a travel document.[55] Initially, signing up for voluntary return with the International Organization for Migration (IOM) is usually regarded as sufficient to satisfy this requirement.[56] However, thereafter, you are required to show that you have diligently pursued the aim of leaving the UK. This includes regularly contacting the IOM to establish the progress of what is being done to help you leave. You are also expected to continue with attempts to get travel documents – eg, by visiting your embassy. The UKBA reviews such cases every six weeks or so after granting Section 4 support and will ask you for documentary proof of what you have done. It is advisable to keep a diary of the steps you take and it is important to keep copies of all letters and emails, and notes of telephone calls and visits to, for example, the IOM and your embassy.

In June 2009, the UKBA amended its policy on the criterion of 'taking all reasonable steps'. Its new policy relates to claims made to the IOM after 8 June 2009 for assistance with voluntary return.[57] The policy states that support will not be provided for longer than three months if applied for on these grounds. It is the UKBA's view that a three-month period of support is sufficient for most individuals to be able to arrange their departure from the UK. UKBA policy says that Section 4 support will only continue in exceptional circumstances if the initial claim to the IOM for assisted voluntary return is not successful within three months of being made. This policy may not be lawful as it does not reflect the test laid out in the regulations which refers to whether the failed asylum seeker 'is' taking all reasonable steps to leave the UK. Thus, the question is what steps you are currently taking and not solely what have you done in the past. A mere statement of policy by the Secretary of State cannot, of course, restrict the scope of regulations. It is likely, therefore, that this policy change will be challenged by judicial review. In the meantime, any refusal of support on this basis should be appealed to the First-tier Tribunal (Asylum Support) (see p316).

In any event, Section 4 support is often withdrawn on the grounds that an applicant has not taken *all* reasonable steps. It could be argued that the UKBA's view in this respect is often unrealistic, bearing in mind that applicants are destitute, desperate and may speak little English. However, on appeal, the First-tier Tribunal (Asylum Support) seems to take the view that, if any reasonable step can be identified that has not been taken by a person, even if not previously thought of by her/him, s/he will not have satisfied the requirement and will be refused support.

The UKBA is aware that a few foreign embassies refuse to co-operate in issuing travel documents to failed asylum seekers, making it impossible for individuals to return to their country of origin. Palestinians have particular difficulty, as travel documents are only issued within Palestine and only to people registered as residents within certain districts. Specialist advice should be sought in these cases – eg, from the Asylum Support Appeals Project (see Appendix 2 for the address).

You are unable to leave the United Kingdom because of illness or a disability

This means you are unable to travel – ie, to make a single journey from the UK to your country of origin, because of 'a physical impediment'.[58]

In order to get support under this criterion, the UKBA says that you must provide medical evidence from a medical professional (such as a GP, consultant or psychiatrist). This report must indicate whether you are likely to be able to travel in the future and, if so, when.

While the report should explain your medical problems, it is crucial that it states that those problems physically (or mentally) render you *unable* to travel. The test is *not* whether you should be allowed to stay in the UK – eg, because there is no medical treatment available in your own country or because it would be preferable for you to remain in the UK to continue a course of treatment.

In July 2009, together with a new Section 4 application form (see p300), the UKBA also introduced a form of medical certificate, to be completed by a medical professional which should accompany an application for Section 4 support under this ground.[59]

When asking the medical professional for a report, you should point out the method of travel (eg, by plane) and how many hours it will take to travel to, and wait at, the UK international airport, as well as the number of hours to travel by air to your country of origin and home area. When deciding whether to grant Section 4 support, the UKBA will not consider any opinion of your doctor that you should be allowed to stay in the UK – eg, on compassionate grounds or to get treatment for medical problems. Indeed, if your doctor says this, it might prejudice your claim, as the UKBA might discount the report believing that your doctor has applied the wrong test.

The UKBA accepts that a woman cannot travel during the period of 'around' six weeks before the expected date of giving birth and six weeks after the birth.[60] With your Section 4 application form you must provide medical documentation (usually Form MATB1 issued by your GP or midwife) to confirm the pregnancy and expected date of birth or the birth certificate. The UKBA recognises that a woman may be unable to travel for a longer period if there are particular medical problems with the pregnancy. To establish this, you must provide further medical evidence. In any event, according to the NHS, 'the length of a normal pregnancy varies between about 37 and 42 weeks' although the expected delivery date is 'calculated at 40 weeks from the first day of your last period'.[61] Only 5 per cent of babies, however, are born on their due date. This means that, in practice, a substantial number of babies are born up to three weeks before the expected due date. The First-tier Tribunal (Asylum Support) has, on at least one occasion, accepted this as evidence of the need to provide support earlier than six weeks before the expected date of delivery.

You are unable to leave the United Kingdom because there is no viable route of return

To qualify under this criterion, the Secretary of State must have made a declaration that, in her/his opinion, there is no viable route to a particular country.[62]

At the time of writing, there is no country to which this applies. Irrespective of your personal circumstances, therefore, you will not succeed in claiming support under this criterion unless, by the time of your application, the Secretary of State has made a declaration that there is no safe route to your country. In January 2005, the Secretary of State did say there was no viable route to Iraq, but then withdrew the statement six months later.[63] If your claim under this ground is refused, you might be able to argue in judicial review proceedings that this is a breach of your human rights (see below).

You have applied for judicial review

You must have lodged with the court an application for judicial review to challenge a decision refusing your claim for asylum and, in England and Wales, you must have been granted permission to proceed (or leave to proceed in Northern Ireland).[64] Simply lodging a judicial review claim at court in Scotland is sufficient as there is no permission/leave stage in Scotland.

If you are waiting for the court to consider a claim for judicial review that you have lodged in England or Wales, you may be able to receive support to avoid a breach of your human rights (see below).

Section 4 support is necessary to avoid a breach of human rights

You will qualify for Section 4 support if you can show that the provision of accommodation is necessary to avoid a breach of human rights.[65] The arguments you may be able to rely on include:

- you have lodged fresh representations with the Home Office (see below);
- you have made an 'out-of-time' appeal to the First-tier Tribunal (Immigration and Asylum) (see p280);
- you have no safe route of return (see p281);
- other human rights arguments (see p281).

You have lodged fresh representations with the Home Office

This is the most usual situation in which a failed asylum seeker is given support to avoid a breach of human rights. You must show that:

- you have made a further application to the Home Office to remain in the UK. The application is usually by way of 'fresh representations' (sometimes called fresh submissions) that you want the Home Office to accept as a fresh asylum claim. It can, however, include an application under Article 8 (see p266);
- this application is still outstanding – eg, the UKBA has not yet decided whether it amounts to a fresh asylum claim (see p277);

- it would be a breach of your human rights (Article 3 and/or Article 8) to require you to leave the UK until that application is decided by the UKBA and to refuse you support in the meantime.

The High Court has stated that support should be provided in the above circumstances.[66]

It used to be the case that, if you had fresh representations that you wanted the Home Office to accept as a fresh asylum claim, it was sufficient to lodge them with the Home Office by post to establish that you were entitled to Section 4 support (provided that you could also show that you were destitute).

In October 2009, however, without any prior notice, the UKBA brought in a new process to deal with fresh representations. In practice, this involves a delay of many weeks before any support is provided, if at all. Although there has been no change in statute or the regulations, the UKBA policy is to refuse to consider any application for Section 4 support unless the new process is followed by applicants.

Many advisers believe this new process to be unlawful. At the same time, however, most immigration lawyers advise their clients to follow it as the most likely way to make any progress with the Home Office and the fresh representations. There have been a few challenges by way of judicial review, but no case has yet come to a full hearing. This means there is great uncertainty.

The UKBA has said that, from October 2009, it will not consider any application for Section 4 support based on fresh representations unless the applicant:

- books by telephone an appointment to attend the UKBA office in Liverpool which deals with fresh representations;
- attends that appointment to lodge the fresh representations with other documents, including up-to-date photographs;
- waits while the UKBA decides whether or not to accept the fresh representations as a fresh asylum claim.

Applicants have, at times, found it impossible to get through by telephone to the Liverpool office to make an appointment. Those who have been successful have been given appointments some weeks after the telephone call was made. (At one stage, a three-week wait was usual, but the UKBA has been making changes to the process). No time limit has been fixed by the UKBA for decisions to be made. In the meantime, no financial support (under Section 4 or otherwise) is provided by the UKBA, even though applicants are destitute and require Section 4 support to avoid a breach of their human rights – or lack the finances to travel to Liverpool to lodge the fresh representations.

Since introducing the new process, the UKBA has responded to criticisms by stating that, in exceptional cases involving health difficulties, fresh representations can be lodged by post, but this is subject to the agreement of the UKBA. It has said it believes it will usually be able to arrange an appointment and make a decision on the fresh representations within a certain period of the telephone call booking the appointment in Liverpool. Unfortunately, the UKBA has not been clear on how this 'certain period' is calculated, but it is apparently around 21 to 28 days. Nevertheless, the UKBA has adopted an express blanket policy to delay consideration of any claim received for Section 4 support until a period of around 28 days has passed since the original telephone call. The UKBA has said that the only exception to this policy is with those cases where it is clear to the UKBA that it cannot come to a decision on the fresh representations within the certain period. In these cases, it will consider the application for Section 4 support immediately.

The situation is clearly unsatisfactory. Legal challenges under immigration law are awaited on the UKBA's refusal to accept fresh representations made by post and without an appointment in Liverpool. Separate legal challenges are awaited to the UKBA's refusal to consider applications for Section 4 support until the fresh representations are lodged in Liverpool and considered by UKBA.

In the meantime, it is advisable to submit an application for Section 4 support at the earliest opportunity if you are destitute and wish to lodge fresh representations. It would appear that a claim for Section 4 support should have a good prospect of success, if it is argued that there will be a breach of your human rights if you are not immediately granted Section 4 support while you are attempting to follow the onerous process that the UKBA has created for applicants to lodge fresh representations. This could be the case where you have further fresh representations prepared and ready to lodge, but have been unable to make an appointment in Liverpool by telephone or unable to go to Liverpool because of lack of finances. Section 4 support might also be required because you have to wait a number of days or weeks until the date of the appointment in Liverpool in circumstances where you are destitute. You should immediately seek legal advice to challenge by judicial review any delay or refusal by the UKBA to consider the Section 4 application. If you receive a decision from the UKBA refusing Section 4 support because it is still waiting to receive, or is still considering, the fresh representation, an appeal should be lodged immediately with the First-tier Tribunal (Asylum Support).

Unless and until the courts confirm the legitimacy of the UKBA's new policy for the submission of fresh representations, it is advisable to take the following steps immediately, once the fresh representations have been prepared.

- Make an application for Section 4 support explaining you require Section 4 support on the basis of fresh representations being lodged. It is a good idea to include a copy of the fresh representations with the application form if possible.
- Post the fresh representations to the UKBA in any event by 'recorded, signed for' (which has replaced recorded delivery).
- Telephone the UKBA Liverpool office and make an appointment to lodge the fresh representations in person.

Although the UKBA's policy is not to accept the fresh representations by post and it says that it will delay consideration of the Section 4 support application, by taking the above steps you are putting yourself into a position where you may be able to take legal action against the UKBA for any such refusal or delay. You will need to take legal advice on this.

It is not enough simply to show that you have sent the fresh representations to the Home Office. You need to establish that they have been *received*. The Home Office should acknowledge receipt, but sometimes loses track of correspondence and maintains it has not received any fresh representations at all. In theory, you should only have to establish that it is more likely than not that your further representations have been received – eg, by pointing out that, despite complaints about the post, the vast majority of letters do get delivered. This type of argument may succeed on appeal at the First-tier Tribunal (Asylum Support) but, if at any stage, the UKBA denies receipt, you should provide a copy of the fresh representations, pointing out that they have previously been submitted. In any event, to help avoid these problems, it is always advisable to:

- send any representations regarding a claim for asylum by 'recorded signed for';
- attach a copy of the fresh representations to the Section 4 application that you submit to the UKBA. On appeal against any refusal of support, the First-tier Tribunal will accept that such representations have in this way been received by the UKBA with the Section 4 claim, if not before.

Before the introduction of the New Asylum Model in April 2007 (see p264), Section 4 support officers at the Home Office sometimes decided that the fresh representations were bound to fail on their merits as an asylum claim and so refused Section 4 support. This has been held to be unlawful, as it is only immigration officers appointed by the Secretary of State who have the delegated power and experience to make a decision about an asylum (as opposed to a support) claim. In judicial review proceedings, however, the High Court has accepted that a Home Office worker without immigration experience or delegated powers is able to recognise whether fresh representations have any new material in them. The Court agreed that, in cases showing no new evidence or legal argument, applications for Section 4 support could be refused by Section 4 support officers.

This means that those UKBA employees who are only responsible for support decisions (and not immigration and asylum matters) can only refuse Section 4 support if:

- the fresh claim or representations contain no detail whatsoever – eg, if you write to the UKBA stating that you are still fearful of returning to your country of origin, but do not give any further information or simply state that you will send new information later;
- the evidence or arguments that you have submitted as part of your fresh claim have already been seen and rejected by the Secretary of State or rejected on

appeal and they do not rely on any change in the law since the previous refusal.

Under the New Asylum Model (see p264), the UKBA 'caseowners' are trained in immigration law, have appropriate delegated powers and have responsibility for asylum claims as well as support decisions. Nevertheless, if a caseworker refuses support on *a preliminary assessment* of the fresh representations, it is still arguable on appeal to the First-tier Tribunal (Asylum Support) that support should not be denied on the basis of a cursory view of the fresh representations. You should argue that you are entitled to have your representations containing fresh evidence considered fully before support is denied.

A fresh claim for these purposes may raise new grounds or evidence for an asylum claim (ie, a claim under Article 3 of the European Convention on Human Rights) or raise other human rights issues – eg, if removal would constitute a breach of your family and/or private life which would not constitute an asylum claim.

As a matter of legal argument, it would appear that a failed asylum seeker would additionally have to show that being left without support would constitute a breach of her/his human rights under Article 3 of the European Convention of Human Rights – eg, by being left street-homeless.[67] In fact, the UKBA (and sometimes the First-tier Tribunal) accepts that support should be given to a failed asylum seeker who has made fresh representations and who falls within the statutory definition of destitute without her/him having to bring further evidence to establish a breach of Article 3.

Once the UKBA has looked at any fresh representations, you will be informed in writing if they have been accepted as a new asylum claim. If accepted, a fresh asylum claim will be recorded. At this point, you become an asylum seeker again and should re-apply for asylum support under Section 95 (see p266). If your representations are not accepted as an asylum claim, your Section 4 support will be withdrawn unless you can prove that you meet one of the other criteria for support.

You have made an 'out-of-time' appeal to the First-tier Tribunal

If you are a failed asylum seeker and want to appeal against the refusal of your asylum claim but the time for appealing has expired, you must ask the First-tier Tribunal (Immigration and Asylum) for permission for your 'out-of-time' appeal to proceed. In these circumstances, the UKBA and the First-tier Tribunal (Asylum Support) usually grant Section 4 support, considering that it would be a breach of your human rights to expect you to leave the UK in the meantime.

You are still considered to be an asylum seeker if you appeal within the prescribed time limits (see p317) and so you may still be eligible for asylum support under Section 95 (see p266). If the First-tier Tribunal (Immigration and Asylum) gives you permission to appeal out of time, you again become an asylum seeker and are again eligible for Section 95 support (and, at that stage, no longer eligible for Section 4 support).

You have no safe route of return

In the case *of M Ahmed v Asylum Support Adjudicator and the Secretary of State,* Mr Ahmed argued that there was no safe route for him to return to his home in Iraq and, therefore, he could not leave the UK and so should be given Section 4 support to avoid a breach of his human rights.[68] The judicial review application to the High Court was dismissed in October 2008 as he did not have sufficient evidence to establish that the route back to his home was so dangerous that it would be a breach of his human rights to require him to leave the UK. The Secretary of State, however, agreed that there may be cases in which this argument could succeed and the judge in the case agreed that such an argument might well succeed if there were sufficient evidence to support it. The judge also said, however, that the UKBA (or the First-tier Tribunal (Asylum Support)) would be entitled to conclude that the risks to an applicant of a return journey would have been considered when the asylum claim was refused, and so the applicant would have to show that circumstances had changed since the asylum claim was refused (or from the time any asylum appeal failed). The judge also indicated that when applying for Section 4 support under this criterion, the failed asylum seeker might alternatively wish to argue, with supporting evidence, that the asylum decision maker was incorrect in deciding there was a safe route of return. But this latter remark was made in passing and could have such wide implications that the position will not be clear until there is a further judicial review decision on the issue.

Other human rights arguments

Many cases will depend on their own particular facts. For example, it might be a breach of your human rights under Article 8 of the European Convention of Human Rights to expect you to leave the UK when you have a partner and/or child who has British nationality who is settled in the UK.

On one occasion, the First-tier Tribunal (Asylum Support) decided that a failed asylum seeker could not be expected to leave the UK while on probation and subjected to reporting requirements and medical tests because of drug offences. Leaving the UK would have meant he could not comply with the probation order made by the court. In this particular case, the applicant would have been street homeless in the UK, which would have constituted a breach of Article 3 because, as with most asylum seekers and failed asylum seekers, he was not entitled to work to support himself.

7. **When Section 4 support can be suspended or discontinued**

Certain individuals are **excluded** from Section 4 support. They are the same people who are excluded from asylum support under Section 95 (see p269). Section 55 of the Nationality and Immigration Act 2002 applies in the same way to Section 4 eligibility as it does to Section 95.

However, the list of grounds for suspension or termination of Section 4 support is different.

When support can be suspended

The UK Border Agency (UKBA) has no power to **suspend** Section 4 support. This may have been an oversight in drafting the regulations or it may have been thought that, as the nature of the support is in theory temporary, it can simply be terminated.

When support can be discontinued

The UKBA will **discontinue** your support if it believes you are no longer eligible – eg, because you are not taking all reasonable steps to leave the UK or an application for judicial review has failed.

It is, therefore, the UKBA's policy to review Section 4 support:[69]

- two weeks after it is granted on the basis that you are taking all reasonable steps to leave the UK and you have indicated on the application that you intend to apply for assisted voluntary return through the International Organization for Migration (see p274);
- six weeks after you have applied for assisted voluntary return and every six weeks thereafter;
- six weeks after the birth of a baby (if you have received support on the basis of late pregnancy or birth of a baby; the UKBA accepts that a mother cannot travel six weeks before or six weeks after giving birth);
- at the end of the period estimated by the UKBA medical adviser, or your doctor, as the period within which you should recover sufficiently from an illness or disability that has prevented you from travelling earlier.

Until November 2008 the UKBA usually sent you a 'review enquiry letter', asking you to state if you believed there were still grounds for you to received Section 4 support. In the absence of a satisfactory response justifying the continuance of Section 4 support, the UKBA would send a further letter terminating support.

In November 2008, the UKBA decided to act immediately on cases where some time had past without any review or contact and now issues letters stating that it has made a decision to withdraw support and giving 21 days' notice of withdrawal. If you receive one of these letters, it is crucial that you:

- respond immediately, giving any grounds that justify your Section 4 continuing; *and at the same time*
- appeal to the First-tier Tribunal (Asylum Support) in case the UKBA does not accept what you say in your letter.

If you have breached the conditions of support

As with asylum support, Section 4 support can be granted subject to certain conditions. The conditions for Section 4 support must be given to you in writing and must involve:[70]
- specified standards of behaviour; *or*
- a reporting requirement; *or*
- a requirement:
  - to reside at an authorised address; *or*
  - if absent from an authorised address without the UKBA's permission, to ensure that that absence is for no more than seven consecutive days and nights or for no more than a total of 14 days and nights in any six-month period; *or*
- specified steps to facilitate your departure from the UK.

If the UKBA believes you have breached a condition of your Section 4 support, it must write to you, giving details of the alleged breach, explaining the consequences of breaching support conditions and inviting you to provide an explanation. It is important to respond promptly or support will be withdrawn. The UKBA's written policy gives some examples on how it will treat certain breaches and when it will consider it appropriate to terminate support.

There have been recent cases where the UKBA has simply, and incorrectly, terminated support, alleging a breach of a condition without first inviting comments from the recipient – eg, where it appeared that a reporting requirement had not been complied with, but the reporting requirement had not been communicated to the failed asylum seekers. If this occurs, you should appeal immediately as appeal times are extremely short (see p316). You could also telephone the UKBA immediately and try to get your support reinstated to allow time for a response. If this is not successful, you should also make a complaint, pointing out the UKBA's stated policy of inviting comments before withdrawing support.

A refusal or termination of Section 4 support can be appealed to the First-tier Tribunal (Asylum Support) (see p316).

8. **Other forms of support**

Community care

Asylum seekers (and other non-European Economic Area (EEA) nationals) who have a need for care and attention may qualify for community care from local authority social services departments under s21 National Assistance Act 1948. If someone is entitled to this support, any potential or actual asylum support or Section 4 support received must be ignored by the local authority when deciding whether or not to give support and at what level.[71]

You are not eligible for community care support if you fall into a list of excluded groups, unless to exclude you would constitute a breach of human rights (see below). The excluded groups are:

- people with refugee status granted by an EEA state or their dependants;[72]
- EEA nationals and their dependants;
- failed asylum seekers and their dependants who fail to comply with removal directions;[73]
- people who are not current asylum seekers and are in the United Kingdom (UK) unlawfully – ie, in breach of the immigration laws. The courts have confirmed that a failed asylum seeker is lawfully in the UK if s/he applied for asylum at the port of entry (as s/he would then have been granted temporary admission) and has abided by the terms of his/her temporary admission. A failed asylum seeker is usually unlawfully present if s/he only applied for asylum later – ie, 'in-country';[74]
- failed asylum seekers with children who the Secretary of State has stated have failed without reasonable excuse to take reasonable steps to leave (or place themselves in a position to leave) the UK (called Section 9 cases).[75] Although the Home Office has retained the right to apply this exclusion, it is rarely used.

Human rights

The above exclusions do not apply if Section 21 support is necessary to avoid a breach of human rights. In particular, failed asylum seekers and other migrants in need of care and attention who are unlawfully in the UK, but who have made a fresh claim for asylum or for permission to remain in the UK on the basis of the European Convention on Human Rights (ECHR), may be able to argue that a local authority should provide community care support in order to avoid a breach of their human rights while their claim is outstanding with the Home Office. If this could apply to you, you should argue that you cannot be expected to leave the UK while the further application to the Home Office remains outstanding and, if refused support, you would be street homeless or your situation in the UK would be in breach of Article 3 of the ECHR in some other way.[76]

In need of care and attention

To be eligible for community care support you must have a need for 'care and attention' which is not otherwise available to you. The need has to arise from one of the following:

- age;
- physical or mental illness;
- disability;
- some other reason (destitution alone is not enough – see below).

Pregnant women and breastfeeding mothers who are in need of care and attention can apply for support but the local authority has a discretion whether or not to provide it. The High Court considered this issue in 2008 and decided that breastfeeding mothers should be supported by the UK Border Agency (UKBA), not local authority social services departments unless there are particular difficulties that give rise to the need for care and attention.[77]

'**Care and attention**' had been given a wide interpretation by case law until the judgment of the House of Lords in the leading case of *M v Slough*.[78] 'M' was HIV positive, but had no significant symptoms that impacted on his daily life. He could live independently, and was physically and mentally able to carry out all everyday personal functions. The House of Lords decided that he was not in need of care and attention because he did not need 'looking after'. He needed warm and secure accommodation with a refrigerator for his medication, but this was not 'care and attention'. He needed some medical monitoring or treatment, but any such medical care was not within the care role of social services, but was the responsibility of the NHS. It recognised that his health might well deteriorate at some time in the future to a point where he would need care and attention (ie, someone to provide him with some social care), and at that point Section 21 services would be appropriate. This case makes it clear that the relevant test is not the presence of a serious illness, but whether there is a need to be 'looked after'.

'Destitution plus'

The need for 'care and attention' (or to be 'looked after') must arise not just from being destitute (or from the anticipated effects of being destitute).[79] There must be some additional reason why you need to be looked after. Because of this, the test has become known as the 'destitution plus' test. The courts have said that if someone has poor health or a disability, it has to be shown that, if made destitute, s/he would be likely to suffer more acutely than an 'able-bodied' applicant.

How to apply for support

The usual community care process is followed. The social services department carries out a community care assessment and, on the basis of this, decides whether or not to provide a service to meet an unmet need under s21 National Assistance Act 1984.

Social services have a duty to carry out an assessment of needs of anyone who comes to their attention and is over 18 years old and may be in need of community care services, such as Section 21 services.[80] Strictly, it is not even necessary to make a written application, but apart from very straightforward cases (eg, an application from an elderly person for a bus pass), a community care assessment will need to be in writing in order to reflect adequately the situation.

The social services department in the area where you 'reside' has the responsibility to assess you. Many asylum seekers, failed asylum seekers and other migrants do not 'reside' in any particular area. In these situations, the social services department that has the responsibility to assess you is the department which covers the area where you happen to be on the day or where you spent the previous night. There are special procedures that local authorities must follow to resolve arguments between themselves about who must assess and provide any community care support.[81] In the meantime, assessments must be carried out and appropriate support must be provided.

You should ask social services to:

- carry out a community care assessment of your needs under s47(1) National Health Services and Community Care Act 1990;
- provide you with a written copy of the assessment once completed;
- provide you with temporary support and accommodation until the assessment has been completed.[82]

There is extensive government guidance on how a local authority social services department should carry out an assessment. It is worth noting that this requires social services to discuss the proposed outcome with the individual to obtain her/his views on the proposals and to record them in the assessment. Most assessment forms also have a space at the end for the signature of the individual being assessed. If you have not been asked your views on the draft assessment or have not been offered the chance to sign the assessment, you can argue that the assessment process under s47(1) has not been completed and the temporary community care support under s47(5) should continue. You should refuse to sign the form if you disagree with it, but remember that the social services department does not have to obtain your agreement; it only has to seek your views.

The process must include a financial assessment to see if you can buy support for yourself – if so, the service would 'otherwise be available' to you without social services help. Note, however, that social services must ignore any accommodation and financial or other support available from the UKBA. The courts have made this absolutely clear in a number of cases since *NASS v London Borough of Westminster* in the House of Lords.[83] If social services refuse you support, telling you it is the UKBA's duty to support you, you should remind the department of the decision in this case, which is well known to local authorities. If it still refuses to carry out a community care assessment, you should obtain advice from an experienced community care adviser on taking judicial review proceedings to force the local authority to make an assessment. You should also obtain legal advice if you are refused temporary support pending an assessment or if you are provided with a written assessment that does not sufficiently or accurately record your situation.

If you are eligible for support under s21 National Assistance Act 1948, it is the duty of social services to support you, not the UKBA. In a household where one or more adults are eligible for Section 21 support, but the children do not have community care needs, accommodation for the family should be provided by the local authority along with support for the eligible adult(s). Support for the children is provided by the UKBA by arrangement with social services.[84]

This is a complex area of law. For example, it is not straightforward to assess whether the denial of support to an excluded person may amount to a breach of her/his human rights that could be averted by her/his departure from the UK.[85] If you believe that you have grounds to receive Section 21 support, you should seek expert advice from a community care adviser. See also CPAG's *Paying for Care Handbook* for more information about community care.

Support under the Children Act 1989

Children who are dependent on a parent's asylum claim will themselves be entitled to asylum support (or Section 4 support if the claim failed and the eligibility criteria are met). Generally, asylum seekers are excluded from help under the Children Act 1989 if they are eligible for UKBA support.[86]

Asylum seekers with children who have been excluded from asylum support (eg, because they have breached the conditions of their support) may be able to get help from social services under the Children Act 1989. Social services only have a duty to provide support to a child and to act in her/his interests, but may have to provide support to the parent(s) of that child if this is in the best interests of the child and/or failing to do so would result in a breach of the right to respect for family and private life contrary to Article 8 of the European Convention on Human Rights.

Children under the age of 18 years who arrive in the UK alone and claim asylum (often referred to as 'unaccompanied minors') are the responsibility of the local authority. As this placed a great burden on social service departments in the area of UK ports and airports (eg, Dover and Heathrow), unaccompanied asylum seeker children are dispersed to various social service departments around the country. They are placed with foster carers or have other suitable accommodation arrangements made for them.

A young person who is aged 16 or 17 who has been looked after for 13 weeks or more under the Children Act 1989 is entitled to protection under the Children (Leaving Care) Act 2000. This allows for a needs assessment and potential support up to the age of 21 or 24 if still in education.

When an unaccompanied asylum-seeker child applies for asylum, the UKBA will refer her/him to social services for support unless it strongly believes s/he is over 18 years old. If the social services department has any doubt about an applicant's age, it will carry out an age assessment to decide whether it is likely that s/he is under 18 years. In 2005 in the *Merton* case a High Court judge laid down a number of guidelines on the steps that social services must take in carrying in out an age assessment.[87] However, there is no accurate scientific test that can ascertain an individual's age[88] and it is always more difficult to assess the age of an individual from another culture or someone who has experienced great trauma, as is the case with many asylum-seeking children.

Social security benefits and tax credits

Most asylum seekers are now excluded from all social security benefits and tax credits. See Chapter 7 for more details.

Notes

1. Support for asylum seekers: overview
1 s95 IAA 1999
2 s98 IAA 1999
3 s4 IAA 1999
4 Sch 3 para 1 NIAA 2002
5 s115(9) IAA 1999
6 IA(POAFAS) Regs; see also www.ukba.homeoffice.gov.uk/ sitecontent/documents/policyandlaw/ asylumprocessguidance/asylumsupport
7 under s47 National Health Services and Community Care Act 1990
8 *London Borough of Westminster v NASS* [2002] UKHL 38

2. Who is entitled to asylum support
9 ss94(1) and 95(1) and Sch 9 paras 1-3 IAA 1999; regs 2(1) and 3 AS Regs
10 s55 NIAA 2002
11 ss94(1) and 95(1) and Sch 9 para 1(1)(2) IAA 1999; reg 3(1) AS Regs
12 s94(3) IAA 1999; regs 2 and 2A AS Regs

13 s44 NIAA 2002 was passed by Parliament to amend s94(1) IAA 1999 so as to require a claim for asylum to be made at a 'designated place'. At the time of writing, however, this provision had still not been brought into force. Nevertheless, for support purposes an asylum claim must have been made in compliance with immigration law, and s113 NIAA 2002 requires an asylum claim relying on Art 3 ECHR to be made at a designated place. Thus, in order to rely on an Art 3 asylum claim for support purposes it must be made in a designated place. In practice, the UKBA acts as if it has a discretion and will usually accept that an asylum claim can be submitted by post if the individual cannot personally attend (eg, because of ill health), and regularly accepts submission of further (ie, fresh) claims by post from asylum seekers whose first claims have failed.

14 The real question is whether the claim should be regarded as a claim for asylum; see *R Nigatu (on the application of) v Secretary of State for the Home Department* [2004] EWHC 1806 (Admin), 9 July 2004, available at www.bailii.org/ew/cases/EWHC/Admin/2004/1806.html

15 s95(4) IAA 1999

16 ASA/02/02/1877

17 As a matter of statutory interpretation and logic, the word 'continuing' in s94(5) provides that the person continues to be an asylum seeker for support purposes, not that there must be some pre-existing support to continue. There is no ambiguity and, even if there were, no logical reason for requiring earlier support. Clearly the intention of the provision is to ensure that former asylum seekers with children will not be left destitute between refusal and removal/departure and that the responsibility for ensuring this falls on the Secretary of State, as opposed to local authorities. Further, this is incongruent with (former) asylum appeal tribunals' treatment of the question of whether the relevant child must be a dependant of the person at the time the person ceased to be an asylum seeker under s94(5), where the use of the word 'continuing' is said to require the person to continue to be an asylum seeker (ASA/05/09/10091). It may be ambiguous whether the provision that s/he is to be treated as 'continuing to be an asylum seeker' requires that s/he must continuously meet that definition, but we prefer the interpretation that continuity is not a requirement as, again, the intention of the provision is to ensure that former asylum seekers with children will not be left destitute between refusal and removal/departure and that the responsibility for ensuring this falls on the Secretary of State as opposed to local authorities.

18 s9 AI(TC)A 2004

19 s94(1) IAA 1999; reg 2 (4) AS Regs

20 Reg 7 AS Regs

3. **Exclusions from asylum support**

21 s95(2) IAA 1999; reg 4 AS Regs

22 s55 NIAA 2002

23 UKBA *Policy Bulletin* 75, para 3.5

24 s55 IAA 1999

25 The wording relates to people who have not made a 'claim for leave to enter or remain in the United Kingdom or for variation of any such leave' in which they are being considered an asylum seeker or her/his dependant. A claim for asylum or to be the dependant of an asylum seeker, provided it is accepted as such, in immigration terms is simultaneously a claim for leave in such capacity (see paras 327-28, 330, 335, 349 IR, HC 395 and see paras 31-33 IR, HC 395 absolving asylum seekers from the requirement to apply for leave on a prescribed Home Office form); reg 4(2) and (4)(c) AS Regs. This provision also excludes people who the Home Office is not treating as asylum seekers for immigration purposes. It is doubtful that this adds anything to the general requirement that those applying as asylum seekers must have made a 'claim to asylum' which has been 'recorded by the Secretary of State' (see s94(1) IAA 1999). However, the exclusion does operate to prevent support being provided to the potentially large group of people who fall within the definition of 'dependant' for support purposes (reg 2(4) AS Regs), but are not treated by the Home Office as dependent on the asylum claim for immigration purposes.

26 Reg 2(4) AS Regs

27 para 349 IR, HC 395

28 Sch 3 NIAA 2002

29 Sch 3 paras 2 and 3 NIAA 2002

30 Sch 3 para 4 NIAA 2002

31 Sch 3 para 5 NIAA 2002

4. **When asylum support can be suspended or discontinued**

32 Reg 20(1) AS Regs provides that support 'may' be suspended or discontinued

33 Reg 20(1)(a) AS Regs

34 Reg 20(1)(b) AS Regs

35 Reg 20(1)(c) AS Regs

36 Reg 20(1)(e) AS Regs

37 Reg 20(1)(f) AS Regs

38 Reg 20(1)(g) AS Regs

39 Reg 20(1)(h) AS Regs

40 Reg 20(1)(i) AS Regs

41 Reg 20(1)(j) AS Regs

42 Reg 20(1)(d) AS Regs

43 See the wording of reg 20(1) AS Regs, which refers to support for a 'supported person' or her/his dependants. Such a person is defined as an asylum seeker or the dependant of an asylum seeker who has applied for support and for whom asylum support has been provided (s94(1) IAA 1999), and indeed the regulation refers to the 'suspension' or 'discontinuation' of the existing support, which presupposes the current provision of that support.

44 Reg 21(1) AS Regs; UKBA *Policy Bulletin* 84

45 Reg 21(1)(c) and (2) AS Regs, with reference to reg 15 AS Regs

46 Reg 21(3) AS Regs

5. Temporary asylum support

47 s98 IAA 1999

48 s98(1) IAA 1999; UKBA *Policy Bulletin* 73

49 s98(3) IAA 1999 applying s95(11)

50 As compared with the position relating to ordinary asylum support (see s95(1) IAA 1999)

51 This is because s103 IAA 1999, which deals with appeals, does not refer to s98 support.

52 Reg 4(8)(9) AS Regs

6. Who is entitled to Section 4 support

53 Reg 3(1)(a) IA(POAFAS) Regs

54 These are listed in reg 3(2)(a-e) IA(POAFAS) Regs

55 Reg 3(1)(b) and (2)(a) IA(POAFAS) Regs; ASA 06/03/12859

56 The assisted voluntary return package is often referred to as AVR or VAARP (voluntary assisted returns and reintegration programme).

57 Incorporated into Section 4 instructions and review instructions, available at www.ukba.homeoffice.gov.uk

58 Reg 3(1)(b) and (2)(b) IA(POAFAS) Regs; *R (Secretary of State for the Home Department) v ASA and Osman, Yillah, Ahmad and Musemwa (interested parties)* [2006] EWHC 1248

59 Available with the Section 4 application form at 'Looking for a Form' at www.ukba.homeoffice.gov.uk/asylum/support/apply/section4

60 Section 4 policy instructions, available at www.ukba.homeoffice.gov.uk

61 See www.nhs.uk

62 Reg 3(1)(b) and (2)(c) IA(POAFAS) Regs

63 *R (Rasul) v ASA* [2006] EWHC 435; ASA 06/03/12859

64 Reg 3(1)(b) and (2)(d) IA(POAFAS) Regs

65 Regs 3(1)(b) and (2)(e) IA(POAFAS) Regs

66 *R (Nigatu) v Secretary of State for the Home Department* [2004] EWHC 1806 (Admin), para 20

67 See House of Lords decision in the case of *Limbuela* [2005] UKHL 66

68 *M Ahmed v Asylum Support Adjudicator and the Secretary of State* [2008] EWHC 2282 (Admin): judgment given 2 October 2008

7. When Section 4 support can be suspended or discontinued

69 Section 4 instructions and review instructions available at www.ukba.homeoffice.gov.uk/sitecontent/documents/policyand law/asylumprocessguidance/asylumsupport

70 Reg 6 IA(POAFAS) Regs

8. Other forms of support

71 *R (Westminster) v NASS* [2002] UKHL 38

72 Sch 3 para 4 NIAA 2002

73 Sch 3 para 6 NIAA 2002

74 *R (AW) v Croydon London Borough Council* [2005] EWHC 2950

75 Sch 3 para 7A NIAA 2002, as amended by s9 AI(TC)A 2004

76 *Secretary of State for the Home Department v Limbuela and Others* [2004] EWCA Civ 540

77 *R (Gnezele) v Leeds City Council and Anor* [2007] EWHC 3275 (Admin), 11 December 2007

78 *R (M) v Slough Borough Council* [2008] UKHL 52

79 By the addition of s21(1A) NAA 1948

80 s47(1) National Health Services and Community Care Act 1990

81 S24 NAA 1948

82 Under s47(5)

83 *R (Westminster) v NASS* [2002] UKHL 38

84 *R (Westminister) v NASS* [2002] UKHL 38; *R(O) v Haringey LBC* [2004] EWCA Civ 535

85 See *PB (Claimant) v Haringey LBC* [2006]
EWHC 2255, *Gordon Binomugisha v
Southwark LBC* [2006] EWHC 2254 and
M v Islington LBC [2004] EWCA Civ 235.
In these cases it was accepted that
support may need to be provided by the
local authority to avoid a breach of the
applicant's human rights. See also *R(K) v
Lambeth LBC* [2003] EWCA Civ 1150 and
Lambeth LBC v Grant [2004] EWCA Civ
1711 – in both the latter cases it was not
accepted that the denial of support
(beyond temporary short-term support
in the *Grant* case) would breach the
applicant's human rights.
86 See UKBA *Policy Bulletins* 29 (on when
minors become adults) and 33 (on age-
disputed cases)
87 *Merton* [2005] EWHC 1753 (Admin)
88 *Croydon* [2009] EWHC 939 (Admin)

Chapter 16
Applications

This chapter covers:
1. Applying for asylum support (below)
2. Deciding if you are destitute (p293)
3. Applying for Section 4 support (p300)

1. Applying for asylum support

If you are either an asylum seeker or a dependant of an asylum seeker for support purposes, you can apply for asylum support to the UK Border Agency (UKBA).[1] The application can be for you alone or for yourself and your dependants.[2] As with social security benefits, you must use a particular form to apply for asylum support.[3] At the time of writing, this was still called Form NASS1 and the form itself still referred to the National Asylum Support Scheme, even though this ceased to exist from April 2007 (see p263).

The application form is available from one-stop agencies (see p264) and from the UKBA website (www.ukba.homeoffice.gov.uk/asylum/support/apply). Even if the application is for both yourself and your dependants, you only need to complete one form. If you wish to obtain support as the dependant of a person who is already being supported by the UKBA, it is not necessary to complete the application form again. The UKBA will consider providing additional support for you if notified of your existence in writing.[4] Nevertheless, it is advisable for a separate application form to be completed by the dependant to be added. In this way the dependant appears to have the right of appeal against any refusal which seems is not the case if the asylum seeker simply applies for the extra support by letter.[5]

One-stop agencies will help you fill in the form and submit it to the UKBA. It is strongly advised to seek assistance from a one-stop agency if you are able to travel to a local office. You must complete the form in full and in English.[6] There are detailed notes that accompany the application form, which give further information about the application procedure and guidance on how to fill out the form.

The form asks for details of the stage your asylum claim has reached, the kind of support you need, your current accommodation, any other kind of support you receive (including support from friends or relatives, details of cash, savings, investments or other property you own, any employment you have and state benefits you receive) and details of any disabilities or special needs you have. You must send documents to confirm the information you give. You must also supply four passport-size photographs. For your application to be considered as soon as possible, the form can be faxed to the UKBA (the one-stop agencies will do this for you); otherwise it can be sent by post. If you send the form by fax, you should also send the original by post.[7]

The UKBA may ask you for further information on any of the details contained in the application form.[8]

2. **Deciding if you are destitute**

If you apply for support for yourself, the UK Border Agency (UKBA) must be satisfied that you are 'destitute'. If you apply for support for yourself, together with dependants, the UKBA will decide whether the group as a whole is destitute.[9]

'**Destitute**' includes if you are 'likely to become destitute within 14 days'.[10] You are destitute if, either:[11]

- you do not have 'adequate accommodation' (see p294) or any means of getting adequate accommodation; *or*
- you cannot meet your essential living needs (even if you do have adequate accommodation).

The UKBA must follow special rules that set out what is and what is not relevant in deciding these questions. These rules apply when you make an application for support and at any stage if there is a question of whether you should continue to be provided with support.

When considering whether you are destitute (both in terms of whether you have adequate accommodation and whether you can meet your essential living needs), the UKBA must take into account any of the following that are available to you or to any of your dependants:[12]

- any income you have, or which you may reasonably be expected to have;
- any other support that is available, or which may reasonably be expected to be available to you;
- any of the following assets that are available to you, or which might reasonably be expected to be available to you:
  - cash;
  - savings;
  - investments;
  - land;
  - vehicles;
  - goods for trade or business.

This might include support from friends and relatives in the United Kingdom (UK) or from voluntary sector organisations. Land may include property, such as a house and other outbuildings. Investments include business investments, income bonds, life assurance policies, pension schemes, stocks and shares and unit trusts (but not jewellery[13]).

The UKBA may provide you with support on a limited basis to allow you time to sell items of property – eg, six months if it is a house. The UKBA treats the money received from the sale as cash or savings and takes it into account when deciding whether or not to provide support. If you do not consider it reasonable that you should have to sell your property, you should give your reasons for this at the time you send in your application form.[14]

In addition, when deciding whether you have adequate accommodation and whether you can meet your essential living needs, the UKBA must ignore any:

- assets that you or your dependants have which are not listed above;[15]
- UKBA support or temporary support that you or your dependants presently have or may be provided with.[16]

The UKBA has confirmed that it ignores items of personal clothing, bedding and medical or optical items – eg, wheelchairs.[17] Although jewellery is excluded, you should disclose in your application for support any items of jewellery or watches belonging to you or your dependants that are worth over £1,000 at the current market value, and inform the UKBA immediately if any of these items are subsequently sold and for how much they were sold.[18] The intention is that the money you have received as a result of the sale may be taken into account.

Adequate accommodation

If you are applying for support but you have some form of accommodation, the UKBA must decide whether your existing accommodation is 'adequate'. Similarly, if you are already being financially supported by the UKBA but your accommodation is not being provided by the UKBA (as previously you did not require it), you can ask the UKBA for accommodation. In this case, the UKBA must consider whether your current accommodation is adequate or whether it should provide you with accommodation in addition to the financial support. In deciding either[19] of these questions, UKBA must take into account whether:[20]

- it is 'reasonable' for you to continue to occupy the accommodation;
- you can afford to pay for the accommodation;
- you can gain entry to the accommodation;
- if the accommodation is a houseboat, a caravan or some other moveable structure that can be lived in, whether there is somewhere you can place it and have permission to live in it;
- you can live in the accommodation with your dependants;
- you or your dependants are likely to experience harassment, threats or violence if you continue to live in the accommodation.

Accommodation may be considered inadequate, for example, if you are staying with a friend and sleeping on the floor, or you cannot gain entry to it during the day or if it is unsuitable for you because of your health needs or a physical disability.

If you have told the UKBA that you want to stay in your current accommodation and only want financial assistance, the factors listed above will not be taken into account in deciding whether you are destitute,[21] except for the question of whether you can afford the accommodation.

Is it reasonable for you to continue to occupy the accommodation?

The UKBA must consider whether it is 'reasonable' for you to continue to occupy the accommodation.[22] In considering this, it may have regard to the general housing circumstances that exist in the district[23] of the local government housing authority in which the accommodation is situated.[24] So if your accommodation is worse or more overcrowded than the other accommodation generally found in the area in which you live, it may not be reasonable for you to continue to live there.[25]

Can you afford to pay for the accommodation?

The UKBA must consider whether you can afford to pay for your existing accommodation.[26] It must take into account:[27]

- any income or assets (see p293) other than from UKBA support or temporary support, available to you or any of your dependants, or which might be expected to be available to you or your dependants;
- the costs of living in the accommodation;
- your other reasonable living expenses.

Do you have access to the accommodation?

Your accommodation is not adequate if you have been illegally evicted from the accommodation or squatters have unlawfully moved into the accommodation.

Is there harassment, threats or violence?

The UKBA must consider whether it is 'probable' that your continued occupation of the accommodation will lead to domestic violence against you or any of your dependants.[28] The domestic violence must be:[29]

- from a person who is, or who has been, a 'close family member'; *and*
- in the form of either actual violence, or threats of violence that are likely to be carried out.

There is no definition of 'close family member' but, depending on the circumstances, it may cover married or unmarried partners and ex-partners, those to whom you have a blood relationship, in-laws, relatives of your partner and others who live (or have lived) in your household. **Note:** the family member does not have to live with you.[30] You may fear that, because your address is known to the person, your continued occupation of that accommodation is likely to lead to domestic violence.

Although the asylum support rules only expressly refer to domestic violence, it must be the case that other forms of violence or threats which you have had from anyone not normally associated with you must be relevant when deciding whether your current accommodation is adequate.[31] This treatment may be in the form of racial harassment or attacks,[32] sexual abuse or harassment, and harassment because of your religion or for other reasons.

Your essential living needs

For the purposes of deciding whether you can meet your essential living needs,[33] certain items are not treated as essential and your inability to provide for yourself any of the following items is not relevant when deciding whether you are destitute:[34]

- the cost of sending or receiving faxes, photocopying or buying or using computer facilities;
- travelling expenses.

Although the above expenses cannot be taken into account at this stage, if you are found to be destitute, they can be relevant if the UKBA has to consider the expenses incurred in connection with your asylum claim or if your case is exceptional (see below).

Although the rules appear to exclude the cost of any travel, the regulations exempt from this exclusion the costs of your initial journey from any place in the UK (where you happen to be) to accommodation which is being provided for you by the UKBA, or your journey to accommodation not being provided by the UKBA where you are intending to live, the address of which you have given to the Home Office or the UKBA.[35] This is normally accommodation at which it is a condition of your temporary admission to the UK that you reside (see p18). Although the rules do not expressly state that these journeys are to be taken into account when considering whether you are destitute, the fact that they are exempt from being excluded indicates that the UKBA should take them into account and, if it finds that you do not have the means to pay for this travel, should provide support in order that you can travel to your accommodation.

If you have another need that is not referred to in these rules, it does not necessarily mean that need is an 'essential living need'.[36] The UKBA must decide for itself whether that need is essential. In determining this question, the individual circumstances of applicants are important.

Clothing

When deciding whether you can meet your essential living needs in terms of clothing, the UKBA cannot take into account your personal preferences.[37] This rule is designed to prevent complaints based on your inability to provide for yourself particular clothing which is more expensive than that which is reasonably required – eg, particularly fashionable clothes or designer wear. However, the UKBA can take into account your individual circumstances when deciding whether you can meet your clothing requirements.[38] The following factors are all relevant when deciding whether you can meet this essential living need:

- whether you can afford to provide for yourself clothes suitable for the different weather conditions in the UK;
- whether you have enough changes of clothes required for cleanliness; *and*
- whether you have clothes that are suitable for any particular health or other individual needs you have.

Decisions and support pending a decision

Although the regulations do not require the UKBA to make a decision within any particular time, the Government intends that it should make a decision within two working days of receiving the application, but this target is often missed. If no decision has been made within seven days of making the application, the UKBA should write to you, explaining why there is a delay.[39]

You are required to respond to any enquiry made by the UKBA about your application within five working days. It will not consider the application if you fail to complete the application form properly or accurately or fail to provide evidence requested without reasonable excuse within this period.[40]

While you are waiting for a decision on your application, you should be provided with temporary support.[41] This is provided to you directly by a voluntary agency, but paid for by the UKBA.

If the UKBA decides to provide you with support, it will inform you in writing that your application has been accepted and about the package of support that will be provided. Although there are no rules requiring it to give reasons for its decisions, the Government intends that it will give you a written explanation if you are refused all support and will give you details about how you can appeal (see p319).[42]

Conditions attached to the support

The UKBA may provide you with support, subject to certain conditions.[43] No examples or limits are given in the regulations on the extent of these conditions, but they must be reasonable. The conditions might include, for example, that the accommodation is not sub-let or that noise is kept down to a reasonable level in the interests of neighbours, or that you must live at the address the UKBA has provided and inform it of any changes in your circumstances. Conditions must be in writing[44] and given to the person who is being supported.[45]

The UKBA may take into account any previous breach of conditions when deciding whether or not to provide support, whether to continue to provide support, and in deciding the level or kind of support that is to be provided.[46]

Dispersal

It is the general policy of the Home Office to provide support and accommodation outside London.[47] Under this 'dispersal' policy, most people who are entitled to support will be provided with accommodation outside London and the South East unless they can show a very strong reason for staying where they are living. It is very difficult to succeed in arguing against dispersal. As a matter of policy,[48] the UKBA used to accept that people receiving treatment from the Medical Foundation for the Care of Victims of Torture and the Helen Bamber Foundation should be accommodated in London (they had to be a patient of either organisation and not simply be at the referral/assessment stage). These organisations are based in London and have expertise in assisting victims of torture, so it was a sensible policy to accept that their patients should not be dispersed. In 2009, without notice or consultation, the UKBA withdrew this policy and said that each case will now be considered on its merits. There has been strong pressure on the UKBA to reinstate the earlier exemptions from dispersal.

There are special provisions for women who are in the late stages of pregnancy. In particular, you are not expected to travel to a dispersal area within a minimum of two weeks of giving birth.[49] If you are receiving other medical treatment (eg, for HIV), before dispersal takes place, the UKBA medical officer must liaise with the relevant medical professional in the receiving area to secure continuing treatment.[50]

Health benefits

If your application for asylum support is accepted, the UKBA will also issue you with a certificate (HC2) enabling you to get free NHS prescriptions, dental treatment, sight tests and wigs. You may also be able to get vouchers towards the cost of glasses and contact lenses. The HC2 certificate itself tells you how to use it and what you can use it for. If you have already paid for any of the above items or travel to and from hospital for NHS treatment, you may be able to claim the money back.

Change of circumstances

If you are provided with support, you are required to notify the UKBA of certain relevant changes in your circumstances.[51] These are if you (or any of your dependants):[52]
- are joined in the UK by a dependant;

- receive or obtain access to any money or savings, investments, land, cars or other vehicles, goods for the purposes of trade, or other business which has not previously been declared to the UKBA;
- become employed;
- become unemployed;
- change your name;
- get married;
- begin living with another person as if you are married to her/him;
- get divorced;
- separate from a spouse or from a person with whom you have been living as if married;
- become pregnant;
- have a child;
- leave school;
- begin to share your accommodation with another person;
- move to a different address or otherwise leave your accommodation;
- go into hospital;
- go to prison or some other form of custody;
- leave the UK;
- die.

If there is a relevant change of circumstances, a decision may be made to change the nature or level of the existing support or to provide or withdraw support for different individuals.

Eviction from accommodation

The usual law on security of tenure does not apply to UKBA accommodation.[53] The regulations allow tenancies or licences created when UKBA support is provided to come to an end when asylum support is terminated – ie, if:[54]

- asylum support is suspended or discontinued (see p270) because there has been a breach of conditions, a criminal offence, intentional destitution, absence from the address without permission, or if you have ceased to reside at the address;
- your claim for asylum has been determined;
- you are no longer destitute;
- you move to be supported in other accommodation.

In any of the above circumstances, any tenancy or licence which you have obtained during the period of support will be terminated at the end of the period (minimum of seven days) specified in a 'notice to quit' which is given to you.[55]

Further applications for support and appeals

If you are refused support, in most cases there is nothing to prevent you from making a further application for support at any time and your application must be considered by the UKBA. The exception to this is when your support was suspended or terminated because of a breach of conditions of support.[56] In this case, the UKBA 'need not entertain' the fresh application unless there has been a 'material change of circumstances' as defined in the regulations[57] or if there are 'exceptional circumstances' since your support was terminated. The words 'need not' means that the UKBA has a discretion, and so a material change of circumstances is not always necessary. There are indications that the UKBA will be stricter in allowing fresh applications than it was in the past. The prescribed list of material change of circumstances is the same list of changes in circumstances that a recipient of asylum support must notify to the UKBA (see p298).

You may appeal against a negative decision by the UKBA. For more information, see Chapter 18.

3. Applying for Section 4 support

The procedure for claiming Section 4 support is very similar to applying for asylum support under s95 Immigration and Asylum Act 1999 (see p292). The prescribed forms can be obtained from the one-stop agencies or the UK Border Agency (UKBA) website (www.ukba.homeoffice.gov.uk/asylum/support/apply).

It is crucial to submit all the necessary information and documentation with your Section 4 application form. If you supply insufficient or ambiguous information, the claim will be rejected or the UKBA will write to you requesting more information, which will delay the provision of support. There is no interim or emergency support available under Section 4.

The UKBA says it has a target of making a decision on a Section 4 application within two days (but see p276 for when this does not apply to applications for support based on lodging fresh representations).

In practice, advice agencies have regularly experienced delays of seven to 14 days and sometimes longer. The delay in making a decision was challenged in the case of *R (Matembera) v Secretary of State for the Home Department*.[58] The Court made an interim (ie, emergency) order requiring the UKBA to give Mr Matembera accommodation and support until the Court could hear the application for permission to proceed. By the time of the hearing, his immigration status had changed and so the judge ordered that the case could not proceed, but he did say: 'In my judgement, it is incumbent on the Secretary of State to put in place a system which deals specifically with the problem [of delays].'

The UKBA says its two-day target only starts to run when it has all the information. It used to maintain that delays occurred because it often did not receive all the necessary information with the application form that was in use until July 2007 (the new form is referred to below) and needed to make enquiries of the applicant. While it would appear that the UKBA has an obligation to provide support as soon as eligibility is established, it is clear that there is further delay after it has made a decision to provide support and before the support is provided. It is UKBA policy to give accommodation providers five to nine days to provide accommodation. In fact, the UKBA (through its regional accommodation providers) sometimes takes weeks to find vacancies and arrange dispersal. In the meantime, you are left without support. It is to be hoped that these delays will be challenged in judicial review proceedings as soon as possible.

There is one form of support for people who are detained (or were detained) under the Immigration Acts and want to apply for support and an address for bail (Section 4(1)) and another (which, in fact, has two minor variations) for failed asylum seekers who cannot leave the United Kingdom (Section 4(2)). In July 2009, the UKBA replaced the Section 4(2) application form with a new 16-page form. Although the form is now longer and appears more cumbersome, it is hoped that by asking for more details at the outset, all relevant information will be supplied with the application form and so a decision on entitlement for support can be made more quickly.

The Section 4(1) application form for detainees is very simple and consists of a single page. This is because the destitution test and other detailed criteria relevant to Section 4(2) do not apply. If you are currently detained by the immigration authorities and have made an application for your release or are intending to make an application for bail, you may make an application for an accommodation address and support in the expectation of your release.[59] The form should be marked 'Priority A' (as you are detained) and faxed to the UKBA.

If you are a failed asylum seeker and you want to apply for Section 4(2) support, you need to know whether you have a UKBA 'caseowner'. This is because there are two versions of the form to be submitted. The forms are almost identical, but in the heading one states that you have a caseowner and the other states that you do not. They are sent to different departments depending on whether you have a caseowner or not. If you claim asylum after 5 March 2007 you have a UKBA caseowner who is responsible for all stages of the asylum claim and support. Regional UKBA teams deal with these claims. People who claimed asylum before 5 March 2007 will be absorbed gradually into the scheme and will be allocated caseowners. If you claimed asylum before 5 March 2007 and do not have a caseowner (or are not sure if you have a caseowner), you should submit your claim to the Section 4 team in the Case Resolution Department in Croydon. When the UKBA has decided that you should receive Section 4 support and has made the necessary arrangements with an accommodation provider, you will be notified of the travel arrangements to the dispersal area (see p306).

Notes

1. Applying for asylum support

1. Reg 3(1) AS Regs
2. Reg 3(2) AS Regs
3. Reg 3(2) AS Regs
4. Reg 3(6) AS Regs
5. See wording of s103 IAA 1999
6. Contained in ASGN to Form NASS1, found on the UKBA website
7. ASGN
8. Reg 3(5) AS Regs

2. Deciding if you are destitute

9. s95(4) IAA 1999; reg 5(1) AS Regs
10. Reg 7 AS Regs
11. s95(3) IAA 1999
12. s95(5) and (7) IAA 1999; reg 6(4)-(5) AS Regs
13. ASGN, 'Cash, savings and assets'
14. ASGN, 'Property'
15. Reg 6(6) AS Regs
16. Reg 6(3) AS Regs
17. ASGN, 'Cash, savings and assets'
18. ASGN, 'Jewellery'
19. That these rules apply to either situation is set out in reg 8(1)(a)(b) AS Regs
20. s95(5)(a) IAA 1999; reg 8(1)(a)-(b) and (3) AS Regs
21. Reg 8 (2) AS Regs
22. Reg 8(3)(a) AS Regs
23. Reg 8(6)(b) AS Regs. 'District' for these purposes is given the same meaning as in s217(3) Housing Act 1996.
24. Reg 8(4) AS Regs
25. ASGN, 'General housing circumstances'
26. Reg 8(3)(b) AS Regs
27. Reg 8(5)(a)-(b) AS Regs
28. Reg 8(3)(g) AS Regs
29. Reg 8(6)(a) AS Regs; UKBA *Policy Bulletin* 70
30. Although the ASGN accompanying Form NASS1 ask for information about people who 'normally stay with you' (under 'Domestic violence')
31. ASGN, 'Violence or threats of violence'
32. See UKBA *Policy Bulletin* 81
33. s95(7)-(8) IAA 1999
34. Reg 9(3)(4) AS Regs
35. Reg 9(5) AS Regs
36. Reg 9(6) AS Regs
37. s95(7)(b) IAA 1999; reg 9(1)(2) AS Regs

38. Reg 9(2) AS Regs
39. ASGN, 'How long will an application take'
40. s57 NIAA 2002; reg 3(5A-5B) AS Regs; see also UKBA *Policy Bulletin* 79
41. s98 IAA 1999
42. ASGN, 'What happens next?'
43. s95(9) IAA 1999
44. s95(10) IAA 1999
45. s95(11) IAA 1999
46. Reg 19 AS Regs
47. UKBA *Policy Bulletin* 31, 'Dispersal guidelines'
48. UKBA *Policy Bulletin* 19, now withdrawn from UKBA website
49. UKBA *Policy Bulletin* 61
50. UKBA *Policy Bulletin* 85, 'Dispersing asylum seekers with healthcare needs', para 9
51. Reg 15(1) AS Regs
52. Reg 15(2) AS Regs
53. They are 'excluded tenancies' under s3A (7A) Protection from Eviction Act 1977
54. Reg 22(2) AS Regs
55. Reg 22(1) AS Regs
56. Reg 21(1) AS Regs
57. Regs 15 and 21(2) AS Regs

3. Applying for Section 4 support

58. *R (Matembera) v Secretary of State for the Home Department* [2007] EWHC 2334 (Admin), September 2007
59. This is the case even though s4(1) refers to an individual who has already been released. See ASGN, 'Do you live in any other kind of accommodation?'

Chapter 17

Payment and accommodation

This chapter covers:
1. Asylum support (below)
2. Contributions and recovery (p309)
3. Section 4 support (p311)

---

1. Asylum support

The legal framework

Part VI of the Immigration and Asylum Act 1999 creates the framework for asylum support. Most of the details are contained in the Asylum Support Regulations 2000, as amended.[1]

The standard weekly rates of financial asylum support are fixed each year by regulations, usually taking effect from around the beginning of April. The Secretary of State for the Home Department also issues policy bulletins, which allow for support to be provided in specific situations – eg, maternity payments.[2] From 2008, these policy bulletins are gradually being replaced by 'Instructions and Guidance' issued by the UK Border Agency (UKBA) for its staff and which are available on the UKBA website.[3]

In 2003, the European Community issued the Reception Directive 2003/9. This sets out minimum standards for the reception of asylum seekers and was a key step towards establishing a common European asylum system as intended on the coming into force of Treaty of Amsterdam in May 1999. European Directives are binding on member states and are relevant in interpreting national law. The Directive should therefore be considered if a challenge is to be mounted against a refusal of, or the inadequacy of, support for asylum seekers (or failed asylum seekers).

If you are a supported asylum seeker, you can be provided with:[4]
* support for the essential living needs of yourself and your dependants;
* accommodation that is adequate for your and your dependants' needs;
* expenses, other than legal expenses, in connection with your asylum claim;
* expenses that you or your dependants have in attending bail hearings if you or your dependants are detained for immigration purposes;

- services in the form of education, English language lessons, sporting or other developmental activities;[5]
- if the circumstances of your particular case are exceptional, any other form of support which the UKBA thinks is necessary.[6]

In deciding the level and kind of support to make, the UKBA takes into account:[7]
- any income that you or any of your dependants have or might reasonably be expected to have;
- any support which might reasonably be expected to be available to you or any of your dependants;
- any assets (see p293) in the United Kingdom (UK) or elsewhere which are, or may reasonably be expected to be, available to you or any of your dependants.

The UKBA may also take into account whether you have complied with any conditions on which the support has been, or is being, provided (see p297).[8] For example, if you have deliberately damaged any property provided to you as part of your support, it may take your conduct into account when deciding what further support to provide.[9] The meaning of 'compliance with conditions' for this purpose is the same as for the purpose of excluding you from support entirely (see p269).[10] When deciding whether to alter the level of your support on this basis and, if so, by how much, the UKBA must take into account how serious or trivial the breach of your conditions was.[11] In practice, however, we do not know of any incident where the UKBA has reduced the level of financial support because of a person's past conduct (as opposed to suspending and/or terminating it completely – see p270). Furthermore, in view of the low level of asylum financial support, it is doubtful that it could be reduced without constituting degrading treatment and risking a breach of Article 3 of the European Convention on Human Rights.

The UKBA can disregard any preference that you or your dependants may have as to how the asylum support will be provided or arranged.[12]

Note: while the Immigration and Asylum Act 1999 gives the Secretary of State for the Home Department the *power* to provide asylum support and lays out the general rules, the Secretary of State (through the UKBA) has a legal *duty* to provide asylum support in accordance with the Asylum Support Regulations.[13]

Support for your essential living needs

If the UKBA decides that you need support for your essential living needs, the general rule is that you will be provided with cash on a weekly basis.[14]

Amount of support

The weekly amount of support provided from 12 April 2010 is set out in the table on p305.[15] In the past, it has been increased every 12 months (except once – see p305). If the application includes a person in more than one of the categories listed, the amounts must be added together to work out the total value of weekly support.[16] For example, if a couple apply for support for themselves and their 14-year-old daughter, the total value of their support would be £121.71.

Weekly amount	
Couple	£70.34
Lone parent aged 18 or over	£42.62
Single person aged 25 or over who was granted support and reached 25 before 5 October 2009	£42.62
Any other single person aged 18 to 24	£35.52
16/17-year-olds (unless part of a qualifying couple)	£38.60
Under 16	£51.37

A **married couple** is a man and a woman who are married to each other and who are members of the same household.[17]

An **unmarried couple** is a man and a woman who, although not married, are living together as though they are married.[18]

A **lone parent** is a person who is not a part of a married or unmarried couple who is the parent of child under 18 *and* support is being provided for that child.[19]

A **single person** is someone who is *neither* a member of a married or unmarried couple *nor* the parent of a child under 18 for whom support is being provided.[20]

There are additional payments of:[21]

- £3 a week for pregnant women;
- £5 a week for babies under one;
- £3 a week for children between the ages of one and three.

The amounts in the above table are reduced if the UKBA is providing you with accommodation as part of your support and some provision for your essential living needs is included with it.[22] For example, if you are being provided with bed and breakfast accommodation, the above amount of support is reduced by an amount corresponding to the cost of your breakfasts.

The standard rates of support used to be based on the equivalent of 70 per cent of the applicable amount of income support (IS), without any premiums, to which an adult would otherwise be entitled if s/he qualified for IS and had no other income.[23] See CPAG'S *Welfare Benefits and Tax Credits Handbook* for more details. Since its introduction in 2000, the rates have increased in April every year. However, the expected increase in April 2009 was delayed to July 2009 and there was no increase in the rate for a single adult. It is therefore difficult to predict how the rates of support may change in future. The level of support was originally deliberately set at less than the rate of IS in recognition of the intention that it is to be provided temporarily and, therefore, the cost of replacement items (eg, furnishings or clothing) over time is not taken into account.[24] In reality, however, it is not uncommon for some people to remain reliant on asylum support for a number of years.

If the UKBA accepts that your case is exceptional, it can decide to provide additional support, in cash or otherwise.[25] You could, therefore, apply for additional asylum support if you can show that there are special circumstances. In practice, however, it will be difficult to persuade the UKBA to agree.

Maternity payment

The UKBA also pays a one-off maternity payment of £300.[26] You must apply in writing between one month before the expected birth and two weeks afterwards, enclosing evidence – eg, a birth certificate, Form MAT B1 from your GP or some other original formal evidence. A payment can also be made if you are a supported parent or a parent applying for support and you have a child under three months old who was born outside the UK. It is important to make this application in time. If made late, it is likely to be refused. The policy bulletin does not say that it is possible to make a late claim, but it may be worth trying if you can give good reasons for the delay.

Accommodation ('dispersal')

The majority of claims for asylum and asylum support are made in South East England. The UKBA has a strict policy of 'dispersal'.[27] This means that, apart from a few exceptions, the accommodation and support it provides (as asylum support and Section 4 support) are outside London and the South East.

The UKBA does not own and provide accommodation itself. It makes arrangements with private contractors and local authorities, who provide the support and accommodation throughout the UK.[28] These arrangements, which include transport, are a crucial part of the dispersal scheme.

When deciding the location and nature of the accommodation you will be given, the UKBA must consider:[29]

- the fact that you are only being provided with accommodation on a temporary basis until your claim for asylum has been dealt with (including any period during which you are appealing);
- the fact that it is desirable to provide accommodation for asylum seekers in areas where there is a good supply of accommodation. For example, this includes some areas outside London, as it is the Government's view that there is an acute shortage of accommodation in the London area.[30]

The UKBA will not take into account your preferences on:

- the area in which you wish the accommodation to be located;[31]
- the nature of the accommodation which is to be provided;[32]
- the nature and standard of the fixtures and fittings in the accommodation.[33]

However, when deciding the accommodation to be provided, the UKBA may still take into account your individual circumstances as they relate to your accommodation needs.[34] These include:[35]

- your ethnic group and/or religion. The UKBA should identify an area where there is an existing community of people of similar culture, together with support organisations that are sensitive to your cultural background and needs;
- any special dietary needs you or your dependants may have;
- your or your dependants' medical or psychological condition, any disabilities you have and any treatment you are receiving for these.

The UKBA should provide accommodation that is appropriate to these needs.[36] The UKBA did have an express policy not to disperse people who were patients of the Medical Foundation for the Care of Victims of Torture and the Helen Bamber Foundation.[37] In 2009, without notice or consultation, it withdrew this policy from its website, saying that each case will now be considered on its merits. There has been strong pressure on the UKBA to reinstate the earlier exemptions from dispersal.

Note: it is the UKBA that must apply the above criteria when determining how and where support is to be provided, even though a private contractor or local authority is making the actual arrangements.

Expenses in connection with your asylum claim

The UKBA may meet some of your expenses connected with your asylum claim.[38] These do not include 'legal' expenses. It will not, for example, meet the costs of paying your lawyer to prepare your case and represent you.

Eligible expenses include costs of preparing and copying documents and travelling to UKBA interviews,[39] and appear to include the costs of the following items associated with your claim for asylum:

- sending letters and faxes in order to obtain further evidence;
- medical reports and expert reports on your country of origin;
- your travel expenses (or those of your witnesses) to attend your appeal;
- medical or other examinations in connection with your claim.

Although the cost of faxes, computer facilities, photocopying and travel expenses are expressly excluded[40] from being 'essential living needs' for the purposes of determining whether or not you are 'destitute',[41] if you are, in fact, found to be destitute, these expenses can still be met when providing support.

There is no prescribed way of claiming these expenses (except travel expenses) from the UKBA.[42] In practice, the difficulties and bureaucratic nature of dealing with the UKBA often make the process of claiming overwhelming and uneconomic.

Although not paid as asylum support, the cost of your fares incurred in travelling to comply with any immigration reporting requirements can be reclaimed from the UKBA if you live more than three miles from the reporting centre. The claim must be made at the reporting centre. It is only possible to claim the travel costs for your next reporting date (ie, in advance) and not the costs already incurred. Some reporting centres are very strict in applying the wording of the guidance which says the test is a three-mile 'radius', interpreted as the straight-line distance between the travel centre and your accommodation and not whether the distance that you must travel is over three miles. The UKBA has, however, been pressed to interpret the guidance more sensibly. The cost of fares can be reclaimed by anyone who has to report. It is not necessary to be in receipt of asylum support.

Backdating support

There is often some delay after you have applied for support and before it is paid. This can be serious if you are without support in the meantime. With other welfare benefits (eg, housing benefit), regulations normally stipulate the start date of the particular benefit. This is not the case with asylum support as there are no express rules in the legislation that identify the date from when support must be provided. It is, therefore, unclear whether you are entitled to support from, for example, the date the UKBA receives your application or the date it makes a decision.

In the absence of legislation stating otherwise, it is arguable that support should be payable from the date the UKBA receives a full and valid claim – ie, a claim which shows that you are destitute and eligible for support. This should be the case, no matter what delays are caused by the UKBA or the appeal procedure.

In practice, the UKBA usually only awards support from the date it makes the original decision. We consider this is to be unacceptable.

In its *Policy Bulletin* 80 and *Asylum Process Guidance*, the UKBA recognises that awards of asylum support under Section 95 should be 'backdated' if there is a delay on the part of the UKBA and the applicant has not caused the delay.[43] However, these policies relate to missed payments of support after a favourable decision on eligibility has already been made. They do not relate to delays by the UKBA in processing the initial application for support and before a favourable decision has been made.

These written policies also recognise that the First-tier Tribunal (Asylum Support) has the power to award backdated support. See p327 for details.

Services

The UKBA may provide the following services to someone who is receiving UKBA support:[44]

- education (including English language lessons);

- sporting or other developmental activities.

The UKBA has the power to provide these services, but it is not under a duty to do so. In addition, the services may only be provided in order to 'maintain good order' among supported asylum seekers.[45] This does not mean that 'good order' must have broken down before these services are provided, but it is necessary that the UKBA is, at least, able to anticipate that 'good order' is less likely to be maintained without the stimulation of education, language lessons and developmental activities, and general access to, and integration into, the wider community.

2. **Contributions and recovery**

Contributions to support

In deciding what level of support to provide to you as a destitute asylum seeker, the UK Border Agency (UKBA) must take into account the income, support and assets that are available, or might reasonably be expected to be available, to you (see p293).[46] However, if you have income and/or assets, it can decide that, instead of reducing the level of support to be provided, you will be required to make a contribution to the cost of your support.[47] In these circumstances, you will be notified of the amount and must make payments directly to the UKBA.[48] If you are required to make a contribution to your support, the UKBA may also make it a condition of your support that you pay your contributions promptly.[49] In practice, however, we are not aware of any such contributions ever having been required.

Recovery of support

There are four circumstances in which you may be required to repay your asylum support. **Note:** there is no equivalent process of recovery for Section 4 support.

The UKBA may require you to repay support it has provided if:
- you had assets at the time of your application for support that you can now convert into money (see p293). This only applies to asylum support (under Section 95) not to temporary support (under Section 98);[50]
- you have been overpaid support as a result of an error (see p310).[51] This applies to both temporary support (under Section 98) and asylum support (under Section 95);[52]
- you have misrepresented or failed to disclose a material fact. This applies to both temporary support (under Section 98) and asylum support (under Section 95);[53]
- it transpires that the supported person was not destitute.[54]

In addition, the UKBA may try to recover asylum support provided to you from a person who has sponsored your stay in the UK.[55]

The UKBA can recover the support by deductions from your existing asylum support[56] or through the civil courts as though it were a debt.[57] Temporary support can only be recovered through the civil courts and not by deductions.[58] In both cases, UKBA has a discretion to waive recovery even if the relevant conditions are met.[59]

Convertible assets

Apart from any overpayments, the UKBA can require you to repay the value of any asylum support that has been paid to you if:[60]

- at the time of your application for asylum support, you had assets (eg, savings, investments, property or shares) either in the UK or elsewhere that you could not convert into money that is available to you; *and*
- you are now able to convert those assets into money that would then be available to you (even if you have not done so).

The UKBA cannot require you to repay more than either:[61]

- the total monetary value of all the support provided to you up to the date that it asks you to make a repayment; *or if it a lesser amount*
- the total monetary value of the assets which you had at the time of the application for support and which you have since been able to convert into money.

Overpayments of support as a result of an error

The UKBA may require you to repay any temporary support or asylum support that has been provided to you as a result of an 'error' by the UKBA.[62] Unlike recovery of overpayments of most social security benefits, you do not need to have been responsible for the overpayment in any way. In the asylum support scheme, it is the error on the part of the UKBA that enables recovery rather than prevents it.

For more details on the recovery of benefits, see CPAG's *Welfare Benefits and Tax Credits Handbook*.

The UKBA may recover the support from you whether or not you are still being supported.[63] It cannot recover more than the total monetary value of the support provided to you as a result of its error.[64]

Misrepresentation and failure to disclose

If the UKBA believes that you have received support as a result of a misrepresentation or failure to disclose a material fact by any person, it may apply to a county court for an order to require the person who made the misrepresentation or who was responsible for the failure to disclose to repay the support.[65] This means recovery is possible against people other than an asylum seeker or her/his dependant who received the support. The total amount that the court can order the person to repay is the monetary value of the support which has been paid as a result of the misrepresentation or failure to disclose and which would not have been provided if it had not been for that misrepresentation or failure to disclose.[66]

Recovery from a sponsor

Support may be recovered from a sponsor of a person who receives asylum support.[67] A 'sponsor' is a person who has given a written undertaking under the Immigration Rules to be responsible for the maintenance and accommodation of someone seeking to enter or remain in the UK (see p14).[68] This form of recovery is intended to deal with the situation in which a person obtains admission to the UK under a sponsorship agreement in a non-asylum capacity and then seeks to remain in the UK as a refugee and becomes entitled to asylum support during the process. The sponsor can only be made liable to make payments for the period during which the undertaking was in effect.[69] A sponsor should not, therefore, be liable for payments for any period of leave which was given subsequent to the original leave in relation to which the undertaking was given, unless a further undertaking was given, nor is the sponsor liable for payments during any period of residence without leave.

In order to recover, the UKBA must apply to a magistrates' court (or, in Scotland, a sheriff court) for an order that the sponsor make payments. The court may order the sponsor to make weekly payments to the UKBA of an amount which the court thinks is appropriate, having regard to all the circumstances of the case and, in particular, to the sponsor's own income.[70] The weekly sum must not be more than the weekly value of the support being provided to the asylum seeker.[71] The court can order that payments be made to cover any period before the time the UKBA applied to the court, but if it does so, it must take into account the sponsor's income during the period concerned rather than her/his current income.[72] The order can be enforced in the same way as a maintenance order.[73]

---

3. Section 4 support

Section 4 support is provided as a package of accommodation and vouchers or pre-payment cards which can be used to obtain food and goods at certain shops. Vouchers were used exclusively until 2009, when the UK Border Agency (UKBA) started to introduce (in stages throughout the United Kingdom) the use of a card, usually called an 'azure card' because of its colour. The card is held by the failed asylum seeker and credited on a weekly basis with the Section 4 support due. Vouchers are likely to be phased out completely in the near future.

No cash is paid to a failed asylum seeker at any stage. This is because Section 4 only refers to the provision of 'facilities for accommodation'. Although the Secretary of State has the power to make regulations for the provision of Section 4 support,[74] these cannot allow for the provision of cash.[75] Even if additional services are to be provided (see p313), they can only be made available by vouchers or the azure card.

Accommodation and vouchers

Some failed asylum seekers have friends or family who could provide them with accommodation and are not able to support them. Unfortunately the UKBA maintains that it cannot provide the financial element of Section 4 (in vouchers or with the azure card) without, at the same time, requiring the individual to occupy UKBA accommodation. The UKBA argument relies on the wording of s4 Immigration and Asylum Act 1999, which specifically refers to 'the provision of facilities for *accommodation*.'[76] It asserts that any Section 4 support can only be provided in relation to UKBA accommodation. Therefore, you have to take up the offer of UKBA accommodation in order to receive vouchers/azure card credits. In this way, the Section 4 system is fundamentally different to the asylum support (provided under Section 95) system, in which cash alone can be claimed and provided.

This situation can cause severe hardship and can seem absurd. You may have friends who will provide you with accommodation, companionship and social, psychological and moral support which may be crucial to you, and in this case it would be substantially less expensive for the Government simply to provide you with vouchers or the azure card without accommodation. Nevertheless, the UKBA will tell you this is not possible. You will be left with the stark choice of living with your friends but remaining destitute (with the risk that your friends may then refuse to accommodate you) or be dispersed – possibly far from your friends to a place where you know no one and, if you are a single person, where you may have to share a room with strangers.

The UKBA has split adults (ie, over 18 years old) from their families in this way when they have had separate asylum claims. It is therefore important that you obtain advice from your immigration lawyer on the inclusion of a family member in the asylum claim of another as a dependant.

It appears that the inflexibility of Section 4 support (or, at least, the interpretation of it by the UKBA) in this way constitutes a breach of Article 8 of the European Convention on Human Rights as an unnecessary and disproportionate interference with private and family life, and so is open to judicial review.

The value of vouchers and the azure card

The financial element of Section 4 support is not fixed in the legislation. It is decided by the Secretary of State for the Home Department. When the Section 4 support regulations were made in 2005, the value of the vouchers was set at £35 per individual – ie, for each adult and child. This was even lower than the rate of asylum support under Section 95. Only once since 2005 has this amount been increased – in early 2010 it was raised to £35.39 for each member of the household.

There has been severe criticism of the very low level of financial support provide under Section 4 and, in order to comply with a European Directive, the Government introduced additional Section 4 support in 2007.[77] This additional support can be claimed by failed asylum seekers (and/or their dependants) in prescribed circumstances. **Note**: this additional support is not provided automatically. You must submit a claim to the UKBA. There is no statutory application form and so, in theory, you could make an oral application. However, the UKBA has issued a particular form,[78] which it requires you to use and you will find it difficult to persuade the UKBA to provide extra support without using its form. An application form for extra support is also included with the new longer Section 4 application form, introduced in July 2009.

You can claim additional support:
- for the costs of travel to receive healthcare treatment where a 'qualifying journey' is necessary. A 'qualifying journey' is a single journey of not less than three miles, or of any distance if:
  - you are unable or virtually unable to walk a distance of up to three miles because of a physical impediment or for some other reason; *or*
  - you have one or more child dependants aged under five years; *or*
  - you have a child who is unable or virtually unable to walk a distance of up to three miles because of a physical impediment or for some other reason;
- for the costs of travel to register a birth;
- to obtain a child's full birth certificate;
- if you are age 18 or over, for telephone calls and letters (ie, stationery and postage) for medical treatment or care and to communicate with:
  - a 'qualified person' – ie, a solicitor, barrister or authorised immigration adviser;
  - a court or tribunal;
  - a voluntary sector partner;
  - a Citizens Advice Bureau;
  - a local authority;
  - an immigration officer;
  - the Secretary of State (including the UKBA);
- if you are pregnant (additional support up to the value of £3 a week);
- if have a child under one year (additional support up to the value of £5 a week);
- if have a child between one and five years (additional support up to the value of £3 a week);
- for clothing for a child under 16 years old (additional support up to the value of £5 a week);
- for exceptional specific needs. The UKBA must be satisfied that there is an exceptional need (which may not be met by the above) for travel, telephone calls, stationery and postage, or essential living needs.

Many failed asylum seekers and others in receipt of Section 4 support are required to sign at an immigration reporting centre each week and may be able to reclaim their travel costs.

Reductions, contributions and recovery

Unlike asylum support under Section 95, there are currently no specific legislative provisions for:

- the value of additional support provided to individuals under Section 4 to be reduced;
- contributions to be made by the recipient of Section 4 support;
- the recovery of the value of Section 4 additional support if it has been provided to someone who is not entitled to it.

Notes

1. Asylum support

1 AS Regs
2 Available on the UKBA website at www.ukba.homeoffice.gov.uk/asylumsupportbulletins/accesstosupport
3 www.ukba.homeoffice.gov.uk/sitecontent/documents/policyandlaw/asylumprocessguidance/asylumsupport
4 s96(1) IAA 1999
5 Sch 8 para 4 IAA 1999; reg 14 AS Regs
6 s96(2) IAA 1999
7 Reg 12(3) AS Regs
8 Reg 19(1) AS Regs
9 Vandalism is the example cited in the Explanatory Notes, para 284.
10 s95(9)-(11) IAA 1999
11 This is because reg 19(1) allows the Secretary of State to take into account the 'extent' to which conditions have been complied with.
12 s97(7) IAA 1999

13 Although the AS Regs often use the word 'may' in referring to the decision-making power of the Secretary of State/UKBA, the 'Wednesbury principles' (from the case of *Associated Provincial Picture Houses v Wednesbury Corporation* [1948] 1 KB 223) and (bearing in mind the destitution of most asylum seeker) the Human Rights Act 1990 inexorably create duties on the Secretary of State to provide support.
14 Reg 10(1)(2) AS Regs
15 Reg 10(2) AS Regs; the Asylum Support (Amendment) Regulations 2009, No.1388
16 Further definitions are contained in reg 10(3)(4) AS Regs
17 Reg 2(1) AS Regs
18 Reg 2(1) AS Regs
19 Reg 10(4)(b)(d) AS Regs
20 Reg 10(4)(c) AS Regs
21 Reg 10A AS Regs, introduced by the Asylum Support (Amendment) Regulations 2003, No.241; see also UKBA *Policy Bulletin* 78
22 Reg 10(5) AS Regs
23 Applicable amounts for IS purposes are provided pursuant to s124(4) SSCBA 1992

24 IAA 1999 Explanatory Notes, para 305
25 See s96(2) IAA 1999; reg 10 AS Regs
   states that the stated rates are what you
   can 'generally' expect to receive to meet
   your essential living needs.
26 UKBA *Policy Bulletin* 37
27 UKBA *Policy Bulletin* 31
28 ss94(2) and 99-100 IAA 1999
29 s97(1)(a) IAA 1999
30 IAA 1999 Explanatory Notes, para 303
31 s97(2)(a) IAA 1999
32 Reg 13(2)(a) AS Regs
33 Reg 13(2)(b) AS Regs
34 Reg 13(2) AS Regs
35 Notes to Form UKBA1 in Schedule to AS
   Regs, 'Accommodation'
36 UKBA *Policy Bulletin* 85
37 UKBA *Policy Bulletin* 19
38 s96(1)(c) IAA 1999
39 Expressly included in IAA 1999
   Explanatory Notes, para 300
40 s95(8) IAA 1999; reg 9(4) AS Regs, but
   see also s97(5)(6) IAA 1999 which treats
   such expenses as essential living needs
   for the specific purposes of limiting the
   amount of overall expenditure incurred
   by the Secretary of State to any
   particular person.
41 s95(3) IAA 1999
42 UKBA *Policy Bulletin* 28
43 'Back-payment of asylum support' at:
   www.ukba.homeoffice.gov.uk/
   sitecontent/documents/policyandlaw/
   asylumprocessguidance/asylumsupport
44 Sch 8 para 4 IAA 1999; reg 14 AS Regs
45 Reg 14(1) AS Regs

2. Contributions and recovery

46 Reg 12(3) AS Regs
47 Reg 16(2) AS Regs
48 Reg 16(3) AS Regs
49 Reg 16(4) AS Regs. Conditions may
   generally be imposed under s95(9)-(12)
   IAA 1999
50 Reg 17 AS Regs
51 s114 IAA 1999
52 s114(1) IAA 1999
53 ss112 and 114(1) IAA 1999
54 Reg 17A AS Regs
55 s113 IAA 1999
56 Regs 17(4) and 18 AS Regs
57 s114(3) and Sch 8 para 11(2)(a) IAA
   1999

58 This is because, despite the general
   wording of reg 18 AS Regs, s114(4) IAA
   1999 only enables the regulations to
   make provision for the recovery by
   deduction from support of support
   provided under s95 and not s98 IAA
   1999.
59 Note the word 'may' in s114(2) IAA
   1999 and reg 17(2) AS Regs. In
   particular, in the case of the latter, it is
   also clear that the UKBA has a discretion
   to recover less than the amount which is
   in fact recoverable. See reg 17(3) AS
   Regs '...a sum not exceeding'.
60 Sch 8 para 11 IAA 1999; reg 17(1) AS
   Regs. Note that it is unclear whether the
   UKBA can require a person who is no
   longer being supported to repay the
   value of the support. There is no
   equivalent wording in para 11 or reg 17
   to that in s114(2) IAA 1999, which
   expressly refers to both those who are
   and have ceased to be supported
   persons for the purposes of recovery as
   result of UKBA errors.
61 Reg 17(2)(3)(5) AS Regs
62 s114(1) IAA 1999; see UKBA *Policy
   Bulletin* 67
63 s114(2) IAA 1999
64 s114(2) IAA 1999
65 s112 IAA 1999
66 s112(2)(3) IAA 1999
67 s113 IAA 1999
68 s113(1)(a) IAA 1999
69 s113(1)(b) IAA 1999
70 s113(3) IAA 1999
71 s113(4) IAA 1999
72 s113(5) IAA 1999
73 s113(6) IAA 1999

3. Section 4 support

74 s4 (10) IAA 1999. This resulted in the
   Asylum and Immigration (Provision of
   Accommodation to Failed Asylum
   Seekers) Regulations 2005, No.930
75 s4(11) IAA 1999
76 s4(1) and (2) IAA 1999
77 The Immigration and Asylum (Provision
   of Services or Facilities to Failed Asylum
   Seekers) Regulations 2007, No.3627
78 The form should be available from one-
   stop agencies and can also be
   downloaded from
   www.ukba.homeoffice.gov.uk/
   sitecontent/applicationforms/asylum/
   asylumsection4provision.pdf

Chapter 18
....
Appeals

This chapter covers:
1. The right to appeal (p317)
2. Appeal procedures (p317)
3. Decisions the First-tier Tribunal can make (p325)

If you are dissatisfied with a decision made by the UK Border Agency (UKBA) about asylum support or Section 4 support, you may be able to appeal to the First-tier Tribunal (Asylum Support).

Before 3 November 2008, appeals were made to the Asylum Support Tribunal in Croydon. On 3 November 2008, a new unified tribunal system was created, consisting of a First-tier Tribunal and an Upper Tribunal. The appeal functions of most of the existing tribunals in the UK were transferred to this new structure and assigned to 'chambers' within the First-tier Tribunal according to subject matter. The Asylum Support Tribunal became the First-tier Tribunal (Asylum Support), which is part of the Social Entitlement Chamber. Since September 2009, it sits in East London.

Although the Upper Tribunal deals with appeals from some tribunals, this is not the case with appeals from the First-tier Tribunal (Asylum Support). Thus, any legal challenge of a decision of the First-tier Tribunal can only be by judicial review. This was previously the case with the Asylum Support Tribunal. The First-tier Tribunal (Asylum Support) does have a very limited power to set aside some of it own decisions.

The Tribunal Procedure (First Tier) (Social Entitlement Chamber) Rules 2008 (referred to as the 'Tribunal Rules' in this chapter) contain the rules for appeals in the Social Entitlement Chamber.[1] Most of these rules are common to all tribunals in the Social Entitlement Chamber, but a few refer solely to the First-tier Tribunal (Asylum Support).

In all asylum support appeals, a single judge considers the appeal and makes the decisions. Tribunal judges have no power to make an order relating to the parties' costs, so even if you lose your appeal, you cannot be ordered to pay any legal costs to the UKBA or to the First-tier Tribunal.

In this *Handbook* we refer to the First-tier Tribunal (Asylum Support) as the First-tier Tribunal.

1. **The right to appeal**

The circumstances in which you have the right to appeal to the First-tier Tribunal are limited. You may only appeal if you have been refused support by the UK Border Agency (UKBA) or your support has been stopped – ie:[2]

- you have made an application for asylum support under Section 95 or Section 4 and it has been refused; *or*
- your support under Section 95 has been stopped for some other reason than because you have ceased to be an asylum seeker (unless the UKBA has made a mistake and you are still an asylum seeker);[3] *or*
- your support under Section 4 is stopped for any reason.

Any other UKBA decision relating to your asylum support (such as the level of support or the place of dispersal) or *any* decision relating to temporary support can only be challenged by judicial review. Also, it is not possible to appeal a decision refusing you support if the reason for the refusal is that:

- you have failed to provide complete or accurate information in connection with your claim;[4] *or*
- you have failed to co-operate with enquiries made in respect of the support claim;[5] *or*
- you did not make your claim for asylum as soon as reasonably possible.[6]

These decisions must be challenged by judicial review, although the UKBA will reconsider an application if missing information is later provided.

2. **Appeal procedures**

The Tribunal Rules set out a timetable for appeals to the First-tier Tribunal, a summary of which is set out below.[7]

Day	Event
Day 1	Notice of appealable decision is received by you.
Day 4 (latest)	Notice of appeal must be received by First-tier Tribunal. Delivery of a notice of appeal at any time up to midnight on the relevant day is sufficient. If not lodged in time, you will need to submit an application for an extension of time – see below.
Day 4 or Day 5	First-tier Tribunal faxes notice of appeal to the UK Border Agency (UKBA).

Day 7 (latest)	UKBA sends response and documentation to First-tier Tribunal by fax/hand, and to you by first-class post or by hand.
Day 7 or thereafter 'with the minimum of delay'	First-tier Tribunal judge decides whether to hold an oral hearing and: if no oral hearing to be held, determines the appeal and sends notice of decision and statement of reasons for decision to you and UKBA; *or* if there is to be an oral hearing, fixes hearing date, giving both parties one to five days' notice. It is likely that, at the same time, directions will be given. If the judge believes appeal should be struck out (eg, if the First-tier Tribunal does not have jurisdiction), s/he must give you an opportunity to make representations. It is likely that a hearing date will be fixed when striking out will be considered first and the full hearing will follow immediately if the appeal is not struck out.
Day 9 or thereafter 'with the minimum of delay'	Oral hearing held. First-tier Tribunal judge notifies decision to you and UKBA at the end of the hearing or, if either not present, sends decision notice.
Within three days after an oral hearing	First-tier Tribunal judge sends statement of reasons for decision to you and UKBA.

Appeals to the First-tier Tribunal should be processed with the minimum of delay.[8] Before November 2008 under the earlier rules for the Asylum Support Tribunal, an appeal had to be listed for hearing within eight days of the Asylum Support Tribunal receiving the appeal notice. Under the 2008 Tribunal Rules, however, there is no fixed time within which the hearing must take place. As asylum seekers are arguing that they are destitute and so require support immediately (and bearing in mind that if support has been refused, no interim support pending an appeal is available), it is likely that the First-tier Tribunal will consider itself bound to list oral hearings close to the previous timescale because of the statutory requirement of minimum delay and Article 3 (prohibition of inhumane and degrading treatment) of the European Convention on Human Rights.

All notices or documents must be sent to the First-tier Tribunal by post, fax or given by hand unless it agrees otherwise – eg, if the First-tier Tribunal agrees to receive information by email.[9]

If a time limit would expire on a non-working day (Saturday, Sunday and bank holidays), it is treated as expiring on the next working day.[10]

Representation

You may be represented throughout the appeal procedure by a representative of your choice. S/he does not have to be legally qualified.[11] If you are being represented, the name and address of your representative must be given in writing to the First-tier Tribunal.[12] This can be done by including the details in the appeal notice. An adviser should *not* state that s/he is your representative if s/he is simply helping you to complete and submit the appeal form and perhaps acting as a mail box for you. In these circumstances, the adviser should write on the form that this is the limit of her/his involvement.

It is generally understood that 'representation' implies an ongoing responsibility for the prompt conduct of all stages of the appeal including:

- securing and preparing all available relevant evidence and submitting it to the First-tier Tribunal;
- dealing with all correspondence with the First-tier Tribunal and the UK Border Agency (UKBA);
- responding in writing to the directions given by the First-tier Tribunal;
- advising you on each of these steps and at every stage;
- representing you at the First-tier Tribunal;
- advising you on the outcome of the appeal and on any steps to be taken – eg, to secure support if the appeal has been successful or any further challenge (eg, by judicial review) if the appeal was unsuccessful.

If you state that you have a representative, the First-tier Tribunal must give the details of your representative to the UKBA. Any documents that the UKBA is required to serve must then be served on the representative (and need not be served on you).[13] Anyone else who accompanies you to the appeal hearing cannot assist in presenting your case without the First-tier Tribunal's approval.[14]

Although legal advice can be given on asylum support under the 'Legal Help' scheme by advisers who have the relevant legal aid contract with the Legal Services Commission, legal aid is not available for representation at the First-tier Tribunal. The vast majority of appellants are unrepresented.

The Asylum Support Appeals Project (ASAP) aims to attend the First-tier Tribunal Monday to Friday to provide free representation and advice to as many people as possible.[15] The Tribunal judge might not allow the ASAP to represent you, however, if the notice of appeal says that you are 'represented' by solicitors in the appeal, even if those solicitors never intended to attend the hearing.

Notice of appeal

If the UKBA decides to refuse your application for support or to terminate your support, it will give you a written decision with reasons. It also informs you in the decision letter if you have a right of appeal and, if so, provides an appeal form.

You can also get an appeal form from the First-tier Tribunal website at: www.asylum-support-tribunal.gov.uk/formsguidance.htm.

The UKBA does not always get this right. So if you want to appeal, but the UKBA says you do not have the right to appeal, you should seek legal advice immediately.

Although you are not required to use a prescribed appeal notice, the Tribunal Rules require certain information to be included with the notice of appeal.[16] In order to ensure you comply with this requirement you should use the standard notice of appeal form, which indicates the information that must be given.

The notice of appeal must be completed in English or in Welsh.[17]

You must state the grounds for your appeal. In other words, you must state why you disagree with the UKBA's decision. The First-tier Tribunal may strike out an appeal if there appears to be no reasonable chance of the appeal succeeding (see p321). You must include a copy of the decision you are appealing against. If the appeal notice does not include all the necessary information and/or is not accompanied by the written UKBA decision, the First-tier Tribunal will not accept it and any later attempt to appeal may be out of time.

If you have any further information or evidence which relates to your claim for support or your appeal, you should (if possible) send copies of the relevant documents to the First-Tier Tribunal with the notice of appeal.[18] However, you should not delay submitting your appeal in order to get any further evidence – this can be faxed to the First-tier Tribunal later. It is very important that you provide the First-Tier Tribunal with any evidence that proves you are entitled to support. For example, if the UKBA does not accept that you are destitute, you may have to provide letters from someone who has been providing you with support, but who cannot continue to do so, or from a voluntary agency who knows you are destitute.

The notice of appeal asks whether you want to attend or be represented at an oral hearing or whether you are content for the appeal to be decided on the papers submitted to the First-Tier Tribunal. An appeal can be decided on the papers without a hearing if both sides consent and the First-tier Tribunal believes it is able to make a decision without a hearing.[19] Even if you ask for a paper appeal without an oral hearing, the First-Tier Tribunal may still decide that there will be an oral hearing if there are issues to be explored that are raised, but not explained, in the papers (see p323). It is always advisable to attend the hearing in person (the UKBA will arrange and pay for fares and overnight accommodation in London for the appellant, dependants and witnesses if necessary – see p324). The First-tier Tribunal judge is likely to understand your appeal much better if you are present to explain your situation. In 'mixed households' (ie, where the partner of the asylum seeker is a British national or has leave to remain and is in receipt of state benefits) it is usually important for the partner to attend the appeal in order to be able to give full details of the benefits (with documentary evidence) and to explain why s/he cannot support the appellant.

In the notice of appeal, you must also state whether you will need an interpreter at that hearing and, if so, in what language and dialect. If you have any difficulties with the English language you should ask for an interpreter. If required, an interpreter is supplied by the Tribunals Service.

Once you have completed the appeal form, you[20] (or your representative[21]) must sign it.

You must send your notice of appeal to the First-Tier Tribunal so that it is received by it within three days after the day on which you received the notice of the decision.[22] If you receive the UKBA's decision letter more than two days after the date it was written, it is advisable to state in your appeal the date on which you received it to show that you are not (or not fully) responsible for any delay. You can submit it to the First-tier Tribunal by fax – the fax number is on the appeal form.

Extension of time limits

If you do not appeal in time, you should ask the First-Tier Tribunal in the notice of appeal to extend the time limit.[23] You should explain why you could not appeal earlier – eg, if you were ill and incapable of dealing with your affairs at the time you received the notice or you needed advice. The First-tier Tribunal judges recognise that the usual time limit to appeal is very short, and an extension of a two or three days is often granted, especially for destitute individuals who may not speak English and may be reliant for advice on a one-stop agency, which is only open at certain hours. As with all decisions, the judge must consider your application fairly and justly, including considering why you (or your representative) could not comply with the time limit.

If the First-tier Tribunal refuses to extend the time limit, your only alternative is to seek a judicial review of the UKBA decision and/or of the decision of the First-tier Tribunal to refuse to give you more time.[24]

Striking out an appeal

The First-tier Tribunal has the power in certain circumstances to decide that your appeal cannot continue even before a hearing takes place. This is called **'striking out'** your appeal. The First-tier Tribunal must strike out your appeal if it does not have jurisdiction to decide the matter.[25] For example, it cannot consider an appeal about how much money the UKBA should pay you each week in asylum support. The First-tier Tribunal may also strike out your appeal without a hearing if it considers your case has no reasonable prospect of success.[26]

In either case, before striking out your appeal, the First-tier Tribunal must give you the opportunity to make representations. As the usual timescale for asylum support appeals is so short, instead of creating a delay by waiting for further written representations, the First-tier Tribunal will usually fix a date for you and the UKBA to attend to make any representations and, if the appeal is not struck out, the appeal will then proceed to a full hearing the same day.

Response from the UK Border Agency

On the same day as the First-tier Tribunal receives your notice of appeal or, if that is not reasonably practicable, as soon as possible on the next day, it must fax to the UKBA a copy of your notice of appeal and any supporting documents that you sent with your appeal form.[27]

By the third day after the notice of appeal is received by the First-tier Tribunal, the UKBA must ensure the First-tier Tribunal receives:[28]

- a statement saying whether or not the UKBA opposes the appeal;
- a copy of the decision letter refusing or withdrawing support;
- any other evidence which the UKBA took into account when refusing you support;
- any other grounds and reasons for the decision which have not been included in the decision letter;
- copies of all documents the UKBA has that are relevant to the case.

At the same time, the UKBA must provide you (or your representative) with a copy of all the above information and documents.[29]

The hearing

Paper hearings

After it receives the UKBA's response, the First-tier Tribunal judge must consider all the documents and decide whether it is necessary to hold an oral hearing or whether the appeal can be determined simply by considering the papers. The First-tier Tribunal can only decide the appeal without a hearing if both parties agree, but it can decide that an oral hearing is necessary even if you ask for a paper appeal.

You may have stated on the notice of appeal form that you did not want an oral hearing, but may not have been aware of all of the information or evidence relied on by the UKBA until after you lodged your appeal – eg, new papers might subsequently be disclosed to you by the UKBA or the First-tier Tribunal. If, having seen any new material, you change your mind and decide that you want an oral hearing in order to make direct representations to the First-tier Tribunal, you should notify the First-tier Tribunal as soon as possible by fax or telephone. The judge must then take this into account when deciding whether to grant an oral hearing. If you want to make written representations to the First-tier Tribunal about this further evidence, you should do so as soon as possible.

Decisions

In all cases, the First-tier Tribunal must make a decision with minimum delay.[30] If no oral hearing is required, the First-tier Tribunal judge will proceed to decide the appeal. S/he must send a copy of the decision notice, together with the written statement of reasons for the decision, to both parties on the same day as the appeal is decided.[31]

Oral hearings

Hearing date

If an oral hearing is necessary, the First-tier Tribunal must promptly inform the parties of the time and date. Since 3 November 2008, there has been no set time within which the First-tier Tribunal must hear an appeal. Nevertheless, because of the desperate situation of many destitute asylum seekers, it is likely that the hearing will take place within 11 days or so of the First-tier Tribunal receiving the notice of appeal.

Directions

When sending out the notice of a hearing date, the First-tier Tribunal usually also sends 'directions' to both you and the UKBA – eg, to produce further evidence.[32] This may include evidence of your destitution, medical evidence or copies of a previous asylum determination. If possible, these documents should be faxed to the First-tier Tribunal before the hearing. Even if you do not have the time and opportunity to fax them, you should take the relevant documents to the appeal hearing. It is very important to comply with any directions because if you do not, the First-tier Tribunal may not have all the evidence needed to make a decision on your appeal. If an agency or solicitor has helped you complete the appeal form, the directions may be sent to her/him, so it is important to keep in close and regular contact to check that the directions have been received and whether the adviser/solicitor can help you respond.

Further evidence

If you decide that you want to submit more evidence in support of your appeal which you did not send with your notice of appeal, you may still send it to the First-tier Tribunal to be considered. In particular, you may wish to rely on evidence which shows a change in your circumstances after the date of the UKBA decision or which has only now come into your possession. You should send this evidence to the First-tier Tribunal judge before the time for her/him to determine the appeal. You should do this immediately and by fax if possible, especially if no oral hearing is to be held as the First-tier Tribunal will determine the appeal very quickly.

You should also send a copy of this further evidence to the UKBA.[33] Although the Tribunal Rules no longer require you to do so, the First-tier Tribunal judge will want to ensure that the UKBA has seen the further evidence. There is even the (very unlikely) risk that the judge will refuse to allow evidence that is provided late and which has not been seen by the UKBA.[34]

In any event, you should take copies of all the appeal papers, including your evidence and the UKBA's documents and any new evidence, to the appeal hearing as you may need to refer to them. You should also ensure, at the start of the hearing, that none of the papers have gone astray and that the judge has all your evidence.

The UKBA can also send further evidence to the First-tier Tribunal before the appeal is determined. It is likely that the UKBA and/or the First-tier Tribunal will send copies to you (or your representative) or, if there is not sufficient time, provide you with copies at the hearing. In any event, you must be provided with copies of any documents which the UKBA intends to rely on at the hearing and you must have time to consider them.

Travel to the hearing

You are usually sent tickets for your travel to and from the First-tier Tribunal, and overnight accommodation is arranged and paid for by the UKBA if you live some distance away.[35] If tickets are not sent, a travel warrant can be requested from the UKBA travel bureau.[36] The UKBA will also provide tickets for dependants and witnesses, if requested.

The hearing

In principle, oral hearings before the First-tier Tribunal take place in public, but it is extremely rare for the public to attend.[37] The First-tier Tribunal judge can decide that a hearing or part of it should be in private and has the power to exclude anyone who is likely to cause a disruption or defeat the purpose of the hearing. In practice, judges politely check who is in the hearing room in order to ensure that there is no one present who may intimidate you or otherwise hinder a fair hearing. If, for any reason, you feel that someone should be excluded from the hearing, you should tell the First-tier Tribunal either before or at the start of the hearing.

As there are no rules that set out the procedure which must be adopted at the oral hearing, the precise procedure is decided by the First-tier Tribunal judge.[38] S/he should explain this to you at the outset. There are no strict rules on evidence, and so hearsay and letters from third parties can be considered. You can provide oral evidence, call any witnesses to give oral evidence in support of your case and question any UKBA witnesses. You or your representative must also have the opportunity of directly addressing the First-tier Tribunal about the decision it should make and commenting on all of the evidence, documentary or oral. If witnesses are called, they may be required to give their evidence under oath or affirmation.[39]

If you have any evidence which has not been presented to the UKBA or to the First-tier Tribunal before the appeal, you should take it to the appeal. If either you or the UKBA attend the hearing with further evidence which has not previously been provided, the other party must be given the opportunity of photocopying and looking at it in order to make comments on it before the hearing proceeds. The judge has the power to exclude evidence that was not provided in the time allowed by an earlier direction given by the First-tier Tribunal. This is unlikely to happen if you have acted as promptly as can be expected – the power to exclude evidence is more likely to be applied to the UKBA, which has experience and the resources and should be expected to respect the First-tier Tribunal's directions.

If possible, take notes of what is said at the hearing. It is usual for the judge to make her/his own written record. If you later want to challenge the decision by judicial review, you can request a copy of this.

If you do not arrive at the hearing in time, it may go ahead without you (or in the absence of a UKBA representative) if the judge:[40]

- is satisfied that you/the UKBA have been notified of the hearing or that reasonable steps have been taken to notify you/the UKBA of the hearing; *and*
- considers that it is in the interests of justice to proceed.

Decisions

At the end of the hearing, the judge must tell you and the UKBA representative the decision that has been reached.[41] The judge may retire for a period in order to consider the decision before telling you the outcome.

The judge must give reasons for her/his decision in writing. S/he must provide both parties with a 'decision notice' (ie, without reasons) at the end of the hearing.[42] This simply states whether the appeal has been allowed, dismissed or remitted (see below). The notice is also sent on the same day to any party (ie, you or the UKBA) who was not present at the hearing of the appeal. In addition, whether or not you were at the hearing, the judge must send a statement containing the reasons for her/his decision to both parties within three days of the hearing.[43]

3. **Decisions the First-Tier Tribunal can make**

When deciding the appeal, the First-tier Tribunal judge can:[44]

- substitute her/his own decision for the decision which was made by the UK Border Agency (UKBA) and thus allow the appeal – meaning you are entitled to support; *or*
- dismiss the appeal, so that the decision of the UKBA stands; *or*
- require the UKBA to reconsider the matter. The First-tier Tribunal calls this 'remitting' the appeal.

The effect of remitting a decision is to set aside the decision of the UKBA. This requires the UKBA to reconsider and come to a new decision on whether you should be provided with support. This puts you back into the position you were in before the decision was made. So if you had been receiving support and the

UKBA's decision to withdraw your support is remitted by the First-tier Tribunal, the UKBA must immediately reinstate the support until it comes to a new decision. Of course, if you were previously without support and are appealing the UKBA's decision to refuse your application, a First-tier Tribunal decision to remit that refusal decision will leave you in your previous position of being without support, at least until the UKBA comes to a new decision.[45]

Cases come before the First-tier Tribunal where the appellants are not sure of their immigration status or it has changed since an appeal has been lodged. The First-tier Tribunal judge, however, can only deal with the particular decision appealed against. If you have applied for, but have been refused, Section 95 support, the judge cannot make a formal and binding decision that you are entitled to Section 4 support (and similarly cannot award Section 95 support in an appeal against a UKBA decision on Section 4 support). Instead, the appeal must be dismissed. You must re-apply to the UKBA for the appropriate support and the UKBA must issue a fresh decision on your entitlement to that type of support.

First-tier Tribunal judges decide issues of fact on a balance of probabilities. This simply means deciding which facts in your case are more likely than not to be true. In asylum support appeals against a *refusal* of an application for support, it is up to you to prove, on a balance of probabilities, that you are entitled to support and meet the relevant criteria. If you are appealing a decision of the UKBA to *withdraw* support, it is up to the UKBA to establish, on the balance of probabilities, that the support should be terminated.

Under the previous Tribunal Rules for the Asylum Support Tribunal (see p316), when reaching a decision, the Tribunal was specifically able to take into account any change of circumstances that took place between the date on which the decision of the UKBA was made and the date of the determination of the appeal.[46] It is expected that this will remain the practice of the First-tier Tribunal, even though it is not expressly provided for in the Rules.

A decision on an appeal by the First-tier Tribunal is legally binding and, if the appeal is allowed, the UKBA is obliged to provide support on that day. In practice, successful appellants are regularly left without support and accommodation for days or weeks as the UKBA is slow to implement the First-tier Tribunal decisions. Such delays by the UKBA are unlawful and, despite numerous representations made to the UKBA about this, the Secretary of State for the Home Department has still not set up a reliable system to provide support to successful appellants from the date of the hearing. As a minimum, the UKBA should provide provisional support while more appropriate arrangements are made. Since December 2008, the UKBA has taken some steps to do so by providing support immediately to successful Section 4 appellants on the day of the hearing (but not to successful Section 95 appellants). This accommodation is provided in London, until more long-term accommodation is arranged elsewhere. The UKBA refers to this accommodation as 'temporary' accommodation, but this is misleading. Legally, there is no form of 'temporary' Section 4 accommodation and so the UKBA is bound to provide Section 4 support and accommodation under the usual terms. Of course, the UKBA can use its powers to disperse the successful applicant from London, but it cannot simply withdraw the accommodation and support unless it follows the usual rules in terminating Section 4 support (see p282).

If there is any delay by the UKBA in providing Section 4 or Section 95 support immediately after a successful appeal, it is clearly acting unlawfully and should be challenged in judicial review proceedings.

Backdating support

There are two situations in which you may you may want to ask the First-tier Tribunal to backdate support if your appeal is successful – ie:

- the UKBA has granted support but its decision was delayed and it has refused to backdate the support to the date of your claim;
- when the First-tier Tribunal allows an appeal against a refusal of support.

The UK Border Agency refuses to backdate support

It is generally presumed that a refusal by the UKBA to provide backdated support cannot be appealed to the First-tier Tribunal (and we are not aware of any such appeal having been made). This may be because s103(1) and (2) Immigration and Asylum Act 1999 (which provides the right of appeal to the First-tier Tribunal) only provides for an appeal against:

- a decision that you do not qualify for support; *or*
- a decision to withdraw support.

It is accepted that this does not allow for an appeal against the actual amount of an award. However, this does not mean that you cannot appeal against the date used to calculate the commencement of support. If an appeal to the First-tier Tribunal is not possible on this point, it would mean that any decision granting support but refusing (or restricting) backdating could only be challenged by judicial review proceedings, which are cumbersome and relatively expensive in an individual case. (Although a successful judicial review application would be a very beneficial precedent for thousands of individuals who are affected.)

However, there is a good argument that a decision by the UKBA not to pay backdated support is, in fact, a decision that 'the applicant does not qualify for support' for the relevant period and so falls within the appeal jurisdiction of the First-tier Tribunal. Thus, it appears that an appeal could be made to the First-tier Tribunal to decide the date from which you qualify for support.

The First-tier Tribunal has allowed an appeal

It is extremely rare for the First-tier Tribunal to state in its decision that a successful appellant should receive support backdated to before the hearing. However, this is because backdated support is rarely asked for.

Section 103(5) of the Immigration and Asylum Act 1999 specifies the powers of the First-tier Tribunal judge and states that s/he may substitute her/his decision for the decision against which the appeal is brought. This means that the judge has the same decision-making powers that the UKBA had in arriving at the original decision. So if the UKBA can backdate an award (as argued on p327), a First-tier Tribunal judge can award backdated support.

It is therefore hoped that many more requests will be made to the First-tier Tribunal for backdated support – ie, to state in its decision that the date from when the successful appellant qualifies for support is the day the UKBA received a full and valid application for support.

After the hearing

There is no right of appeal against the decision of the First-tier Tribunal. If you are dissatisfied with the decision, in very limited circumstances you can ask the Tribunal to set it aside.[47] Otherwise, the only way of challenging the decision is by judicial review.

Setting aside a decision

The First-tier Tribunal can only set aside its own decision and make a new decision (or set aside and remake part of a decision) in the following circumstances:[48]

- the decision was a decision disposing of the proceedings – ie, a final decision or a decision to strike out the appeal; *and*
  - a document relating to the proceedings was not sent or was not received at an appropriate time by either party or their representative; *or*
  - a document relating to the proceedings was not sent to the First-tier Tribunal at an appropriate time; *or*
  - a party or representative was not present at a hearing; *or*
  - there has been some other procedural irregularity in the proceedings; *and*
- the First-tier Tribunal considers that it is in the interests of justice to do so.

You cannot, therefore, ask the First-tier Tribunal to set aside a decision simply because you do not agree with it. Remember that, even if one of these conditions does apply, the First-tier Tribunal may still decide that it is not in the interests of justice to set aside the decision. For example, even if you did not receive a relevant document at the appropriate time, the First-tier Tribunal may still consider that this did not make any difference to the decision that was eventually made and so it is not in the interests of justice to set it aside.

If you wish to apply to set aside a decision, your application must be in writing and received by the First-tier Tribunal no later than one month after the date on which it sent the decision to you.[49]

Judicial review

To be successful in judicial review proceedings you will almost certainly need help from a solicitor, as it is a very legalistic procedure. Judicial review is consideration by a judge in the High Court of the lawfulness of a decision of a public body, and this includes a decision of the First-tier Tribunal. There has to be an error in law for a judicial review application to succeed – it is not enough that you do not agree with the decision that the judge arrived at on the facts in your case (unless you can clearly show that no reasonable tribunal could have come to that decision).

An application for judicial review must be made promptly and, in any event, within three months of the decision complained of. It must be in writing, laying out the facts and legal arguments, and be accompanied by copies of all relevant documents.

You need to get the permission of a High Court judge to take judicial review proceedings. A judge will look at the papers you lodge to see if there is an arguable point of law and, if not, will refuse you permission to proceed. In any event, a judge has a discretion to refuse you permission (or to reject your case at the full hearing) if s/he does not think an order should be made. This means that judicial review proceedings are only appropriate in a very few cases. If you think judicial review might be appropriate in your case, you should immediately seek legal advice.

Decision to remit

If the First-tier Tribunal decides to remit the matter and the UKBA then makes a new decision refusing you support, you may appeal again to the First-tier Tribunal against the new decision.

Fresh claims for support

Following an unsuccessful appeal, the UKBA cannot consider any further application for support from you, whether under Section 4 or Section 95, unless it is satisfied that there has been a 'material change' of circumstances between the time of the appeal and the new application for support. A 'material change' is defined and includes a long list of events – eg, a change of address or separating from a partner.

Withdrawing the appeal

The Tribunal Rules allow either party to serve a written notice of withdrawal. So if at any stage before the hearing, you decide you do not wish to carry on with your appeal, you can give written notice of withdrawal.[50] The Rules do not specify the effect of serving this notice, but it is clear that if *you* withdraw your appeal, the proceedings come to an end because they were instigated by, and based on, your notice of appeal. It is the role of the First-tier Tribunal to decide your entitlement to support when you make an appeal, and it no longer has that role when you have withdrawn your appeal.

The UKBA withdraws its case in a high number of appeals.[51] If it serves a notice of withdrawal, the First-tier Tribunal will treat this as concluding the appeal proceedings, leaving the UKBA to make a fresh decision. It is arguable, however, that this approach is wrong. When an appeal is lodged, the UKBA is required to state whether it opposed the appeal.[52] It is arguable that by withdrawing its 'case', the UKBA is simply withdrawing this statement of opposition to the appeal. Of course, it is open to the UKBA to state at the same time whether it now believes that you are entitled to support or, perhaps for some new reason, you are still not entitled to support. This does not mean that the First-tier Tribunal is absolved from deciding whether you qualify for support. It is arguable that the appeal remains a live process, leaving the First-tier Tribunal to make that decision (which could be a formality if the UKBA agrees that you do qualify). If this argument is not correct, it means that you are deprived of a conclusive decision by the First-tier Tribunal, the UKBA could repeatedly serve notices of withdrawal of further negative decisions against which you have appealed to the First-tier Tribunal and you could be left without support while the UKBA repeatedly vacillates on your entitlement. It remains to be seen how these arguments will evolve. It is likely that, at some stage, there be a judicial review challenge to the practice of the Tribunal terminating an appeal on withdrawal by the UKBA.

Notes

1 TP(FT) Rules

1. The right to appeal

2 s103(1)-(3) IAA 1999
3 s103(2) IAA 1999. Note that the legislation provides a right of appeal where a decision is made to stop providing support 'before that support would otherwise have come to an end'. The wording is ambiguous, but the intention is to allow a right of appeal in any case where support is terminated before the asylum seeker has ceased to be an asylum seeker for the support purposes. See IAA 1999 Explanatory Notes, para 317.
4 s57 NIAA 2002

5 s57 NIAA 2002
6 s55 NIAA 2002

2. Appeal procedures

7 rr22(2)(a), (7)(a), 24(1)(a), 29, 33 and 34 TP(FT) Rules
8 s104(3) IAA 1999 requires the appeal regulations to provide for this
9 r13(1) TP(FT) Rules
10 r12(2) and (3) TP(FT) Rules
11 r11(1) TP(FT) Rules. Note also that asylum support law is not immigration law and so an adviser does not have to be registered with the Office of Immigration Service Commission.
12 r11(2) TP(FT) Rules
13 r11(6a) TP(FT) Rules
14 r11(7) TP(FT) Rules

15 The ASAP is contactable on 020 8686 1888 or for advice on 0845 603 3884 or advice@ASAProject.org.uk.
16 r22(3-5) TP(FT) Rules
17 r22(3) TP(FT) Rules
18 The standard appeal form itself indicates this.
19 r27(1) TP(FT) Rules
20 r22(3) TP(FT) Rules
21 r11(5) TP(FT) Rules
22 r22(2)(a) TP(FT) Rules
23 rr5(3)(a) and 22(6) TP(FT) Rules
24 Note that, in judicial review proceedings, the Court may refuse to interfere with the decision you wish to challenge where you have failed to exercise a right of appeal.
25 r8(2) TP(FT) Rules
26 r8(3) TP(FT) Rules
27 r22(7)(a) TP(FT) Rules
28 r24(2) and (4) TP(FT) Rules
29 r24(5) TP(FT) Rules
30 s104(3) IAA 1999
31 s103(4) IAA 1999; r34(1)(b) TP(FT) Rules
32 r15 TP(FT) Rules
33 Which used to be the case under r8(1)(2) ASA(P) Rules
34 r15(2)(b)(1) TP(FT) Rules
35 Since late 2008, in response to representations made by the ASAP, the UKBA has agreed that the overnight accommodation includes an evening meal on arrival in South London the night before, and breakfast and a packed lunch for the return journey.
36 s103(9) IAA 1999; UKBA *Policy Bulletin* 28. The UKBA travel bureau is contactable on 020 8633 0683 or fax 020 8633 0941.
37 r30(1) TP(FT) Rules
38 TP(FT) Rules
39 r15(3) TP(FT) Rules
40 r31 TP(FT) Rules
41 r33 TP(FT) Rules
42 r33 (2)a TP(FT) Rules
43 s103(4) IAA 1999 and r34(1)(a) TP(FT) Rules

3. **Decisions the First-Tier Tribunal can make**
44 s103(3) IAA 1999
45 In an application for s95 support you could, in theory, receive temporary support under s98 IAA 1999 until a new decision is made.
46 r10(2) ASA(P) Rules

47 Some other tribunals have the power to review their own decisions under r40 TP(FT) Rules, but the First-tier Tribunal is expressly excluded from doing so by r40(1). If an application is made to the First-tier Tribunal to review one of its own decisions, it can instead treat the application as a request for the decision to be set aside: r41 TP(FT) Rules.
48 r37(1) TP(FT) Rules
49 r37(3) TP(FT) Rules
50 r17(1) TP(FT) Rules
51 In 2009, over 20 per cent of appeals were concluded by withdrawal by the UKBA.
52 r24(2)(e) TP(FT) Rules

Appendices

Appendix 1

Glossary of terms

A2 national. A national of the European Union member states Romania and Bulgaria.

A8 national. A national of the European Union member states Czech Republic, Estonia, Hungary, Latvia, Lithuania, Poland, Slovakia and Slovenia.

Absent. Not physically in the United Kingdom. Absence does not necessarily imply that someone has been present at some time in the past.

Accession states. The new members of the European Union: Bulgaria, Cyprus, Czech Republic, Estonia, Hungary, Latvia, Lithuania, Malta, Poland, Romania, Slovakia and Slovenia.

Administrative removal. A legal mechanism, used to remove foreign nationals who have entered the UK illegally, including by deception, or those who have breached the conditions of leave to enter or remain, including overstaying their leave.

Applicable amount. A figure representing a person's weekly needs for the purpose of calculating her/his benefit. For income support, the applicable amount is the amount s/he is expected to live on each week. For housing benefit and council tax benefit, it is the amount used to see how much help s/he needs with her/his rent or council tax. For tax credits, it is a fixed amount. For full details, see CPAG's *Welfare Benefits and Tax Credits Handbook*.

Application registration card. The form of identification for those who have claimed asylum, replacing the standard acknowledgement letter.

Association agreement. A treaty signed between the European Union and a country outside the Union, giving nationals of that country preferential access to countries of the European Economic Area (mainly for business and self-employment purposes).

. . . .

Asylum. Leave to enter or remain in the UK given to a refugee for humanitarian protection under Article 3 of the European Convention on Human Rights and for subsidiary or temporary protection under the Refugee Qualification Directive.

Asylum seeker. A person who has applied for asylum and whose application has yet to be decided, or whose appeal against a refusal of such an application remains outstanding.

Asylum support. Support given to asylum seekers instead of social security benefits or support under the National Assistance Act 1948 until a final decision on their asylum application is made. **Temporary** (or **emergency**) **support** is also available to asylum seekers waiting for an asylum support decision.

Azure card. A credit card-type card given to failed asylum seekers in receipt of Section 4 support, which is credited by the UK Border Agency with weekly subsistence support. The card is then used by the holder to make purchases at designated shops.

Caseowner. The UK Border Agency's policy is to allocate one caseowner to deal with each asylum seeker. The caseowner is responsible for all decisions on her/his application for asylum and support. The caseowner deals with the outcome while the asylum seeker is in the United Kingdom, until s/he is granted leave to remain or s/he leaves or is removed.

Certificate of entitlement. A certificate of entitlement to the right of abode demonstrates that a person has the right of abode (ie, the right to travel freely to and from the UK). British citizens have the right of abode and can demonstrate this by producing their passports. However, a few Commonwealth nationals also have the right of abode and can obtain a certificate of entitlement, endorsed in their own national passport, to demonstrate this.

Certificate of sponsorship. A unique reference number that an employer of educational institution issues to a migrant to enable her/him to apply for entry clearance to enter or remain in the UK under the points-based system. Unlike a work permit, this is not an actual certificate or paper document.

Civil partnership. The Civil Partnership Act 2004 gives same-sex couples rights and responsibilities identical to civil marriage.

Common travel area. The UK, Republic of Ireland, Isle of Man and the Channel Islands, between which there are no immigration controls.

Commonwealth countries. Antigua and Barbuda, Australia, Bahamas, Bangladesh, Barbados, Belize, Botswana, Brunei Darussalam, Cameroon, Canada,

Cyprus, Dominica, Fiji Islands, Gambia, Ghana, Grenada, Guyana, India, Jamaica, Kenya, Kiribati, Lesotho, Malawi, Malaysia, Maldives, Malta, Mauritius, Mozambique, Namibia, Nauru, New Zealand, Nigeria, Pakistan, Papua New Guinea, Samoa, Seychelles, Sierra Leone, Singapore, Solomon Islands, South Africa, Sri Lanka, St Kitts and Nevis, St Lucia, St Vincent and the Grenadines, Swaziland, Tanzania, Tonga, Trinidad and Tobago, Tuvalu, Uganda, Vanuatu, Zambia, Zimbabwe.

Deportation. A legal mechanism used to remove foreign nationals on the recommendation of a criminal court following her/his conviction for a criminal offence, or when the Home Secretary has decided that the person's presence in the UK is 'not conducive to the public good' – eg, following a criminal conviction where the court has not recommended deportation. If an order has been signed to deport a foreign national, s/he may not return unless and until the order has been revoked.

Discretionary leave. Permission to enter or remain in the UK given to a person outside the Immigration Rules or to a person who is refused asylum but who cannot be removed under another Article of the European Convention on Human Rights or for other humanitarian reasons.

Enforcement. A term used to refer to any of the different ways in which a person can be forced to leave the UK for immigration reasons – ie, having been refused entry at a port, having been declared an illegal entrant, or having been notified that s/he is someone who is liable for administrative removal, or who is being deported.

Entry clearance officer. An official at a British post overseas who deals with immigration applications made to that post.

European Community. In this *Handbook* we refer to the legislation of the European Union (previously known as the European Community and before that the European Economic Community) as European Union law.

European Convention on Human Rights. An international instrument agreed by the Council of Europe. The rights guaranteed by it have now largely been incorporated into UK law by the Human Rights Act 1998.

European Convention on Social and Medical Assistance. An agreement signed by all the European Economic Area states, plus Malta and Turkey, requiring that the ratifying states provide assistance in cash and kind to nationals of other ratifying states, who are lawfully present in their territory and without sufficient resources, on the same conditions as their own nationals. It also prevents ratifying states repatriating a lawfully present national of another ratifying state simply because the person is in need of assistance. A person who is covered by the Convention is not a 'person subject to immigration control' for benefit purposes.

European Economic Area. Covers all European Union states plus Iceland, Liechtenstein and Norway. European Economic Area nationals have free movement within these and all European Union member states. From 1 June 2002, the right to free movement also applies to Switzerland.

European Union. Austria, Belgium, Bulgaria, Cyprus, Czech Republic, Denmark, Estonia, Finland, France, Germany, Greece, Hungary, Ireland, Italy, Latvia, Lithuania, Luxembourg, Malta, Netherlands, Poland, Portugal, Romania, Slovakia, Slovenia, Spain, Sweden and the United Kingdom (the UK includes Gibraltar for this purpose).

European Union/European Economic Area national. In this *Handbook* we use this term to describe citizens of European Union member states and European Economic Area countries.

Exceptional leave. This is now been replaced with discretionary leave.

Family. For benefit purposes, under British law a person's family is her/himself, her/his partner and any dependent children who are members of her/his household. Under European Union law, family members include a wider range of relatives, including children under 21 (sometimes older if dependent). Under European Union law, parents, grandparents and other dependent family members can be considered part of your family.

Habitual residence. In order to be entitled to income support, income-based jobseeker's allowance, income-related employment and support allowance, housing benefit and council tax benefit, a person must be habitually resident in the common travel area. Some people are automatically treated as habitually resident and are exempt from the test. The term 'habitually resident' is not defined in the benefit regulations and is therefore be determined by looking at all the circumstances in each case. Having a settled intention to stay in the United Kingdom is an important consideration, as is a person's employment record and period of actual residence. Habitual residence has a different meaning in European Union law.

Humanitarian protection. Permission to enter or remain in the UK given to a person who needs protection from harm by others, but whose case does not fit the criteria for refugee status.

First-tier Tribunal (Asylum Support). The tribunal that decides appeals against the refusal or termination of asylum support or Section 4 support. Currently, the Tribunal only sits in East London, but deals with all support appeals.

First-tier Tribunal (Immigration and Asylum). The tribunal that hears and determines appeals against decisions made by the Secretary of State for the Home Department regarding matters of asylum, immigration and nationality.

First-tier Tribunal (Social Entitlement Chamber). The tribunal that hears and determines appeals against decisions made by the Department for Work and Pensions and local authorities about benefit entitlement.

Home Office. The government department responsible for matters of asylum, immigration and nationality.

Illegal entrant. A person who immigration officials decide has entered the UK in breach of the immigration laws. This could be by deception.

Immigration judge. A person who determines appeals in the First-tier Tribunal (Immigration and Asylum Chamber) or Upper Tribunal (Immigration and Asylum Chamber).

Immigration officer. An official, usually stationed at a British port of entry, who decides whether to grant or refuse leave to enter. Immigration officers also, however, have responsibility for enforcing immigration control.

Immigration Rules. Rules made by the Home Secretary, setting out the requirements for granting or refusing entry clearance, leave to enter and leave to remain to people applying in the different categories.

Indefinite leave. Permission to enter or remain which has no time limit.

Lawful presence. This is not defined in social security law. However, for housing law it has been decided that a person is not lawfully present if s/he has been given temporary admission to the UK. It has yet to be decided whether or not this applies to social security.

Limited leave. Permission to enter or remain which is given for a certain period of time only.

Maintenance undertaking. A formal statement signed by a sponsor in the UK that s/he will support a relative or other person applying to come to or stay in the UK. The relative is not eligible to claim non-contributory benefits for five years after it was signed, or after the person has been given leave to enter or remain in the UK on this basis (whichever is the later), unless the sponsor dies.

Ordinarily resident. A person is ordinarily resident in the UK if s/he is normally residing here (apart from temporary or occasional absences), and that residence has been adopted voluntarily and for settled purposes as part of the regular order of her/his life for the time being. A person can be ordinarily resident in more than one country. There must be some degree of continuity and therefore people who spend most of their time living abroad and are occasionally in the United Kingdom would not be ordinarily resident in the United Kingdom.

Partner. A wife, husband, civil partner or cohabitee who is, or is treated as, a member of the same household as the claimant for benefit purposes.

Person from abroad. A statutory definition that refers to a person who has failed the habitual residence test or the right to reside test. It is not linked to a person's immigration status and even a British citizen can be termed a person from abroad for social security purposes.

Person subject to immigration control. A social security term. A person subject to immigration control is excluded from entitlement to most social security benefits.

Points-based system. The new system of controlling migration to the UK from outside the European Union for economic purposes or studies.

Present. Physically in the United Kingdom throughout the whole day – ie, from midnight to midnight.

Public funds. For immigration purposes these are: housing provided by local authorities, either for homeless people or allocated from its housing register; attendance allowance; carer's allowance; child benefit; child tax credit; council tax benefit; disability living allowance; income-related employment and support allowance, health in pregnancy grant; housing benefit; income support; income-based jobseeker's allowance; pension credit; severe disablement allowance; social fund payments; working tax credit.

Refugee. A person who satisfies the definition of those who need international protection under Article 1A(2) of the 1951 Convention Relating to the Status of Refugees.

Removal. The final procedure for sending a person refused entry, or who is being treated as an illegal entrant, or who is subject to the 'administrative' removal or deportation process, away from the UK.

Resident. A person is usually resident in the country where s/he has her/his home for the time being – where s/he has her/his usual abode. It is possible to be resident in more than one country at one time, but this is unusual. An intention to return to a country may allow a person to count that country as her/his place of residence, even if s/he is living elsewhere.

Right of abode. The right to enter, remain, leave and return freely to the UK without the need to obtain 'leave' from the immigration authorities. All British citizens have the right of abode. Some Commonwealth nationals also have the right of abode.

Right to reside test. Part of the habitual residence test, this was introduced in 2004 and applies to claims for income support, income-related employment and support allowance, income-based jobseeker's allowance, pension credit, housing benefit and council tax benefit. It also applies to child tax credit. A person's right of residence will depend on her/his nationality, immigration status and whether or not s/he has rights under European Union law.

Secretary of State for the Home Department (the Home Secretary). The government minister with primary responsibility for decisions made by the Home Office regarding immigration, asylum and nationality.

Section 4 support. Support available in very limited circumstances to some former asylum seekers whose claims for asylum have failed.

Settlement/settled status. Defined in immigration law as being 'ordinarily resident' in the UK without any restrictions on the time the person is able to remain here. Those with indefinite leave are generally accepted as being 'settled' in the UK.

Social Charter. The 1961 Council of Europe Social Charter has been signed by all the European Economic Area countries, plus Cyprus, the Czech Republic, Hungary, Latvia, Malta, Poland, Slovakia and Turkey. A national of one of these states who is lawfully present in the UK is not a 'person subject to immigration control' for means-tested benefits.

Subject to immigration control. People often use this term to refer to those who need 'leave' to enter or remain in the UK – and this is the definition given in the Asylum and Immigration Act 1996. However, the Immigration and Asylum Act 1999 gives the same phrase a different, narrower, definition, which is used to exclude people from non-contributory benefits and certain services provided by local authorities' social services departments. In this *Handbook*, we use the term as it is defined in the 1999 Act.

Temporary admission. A temporary licence given to people to be in the UK while they are waiting for a decision to be made on their immigration status or while they are waiting to be removed from the UK. The alternative to temporary admission, used particularly if a person is waiting to be removed, is detention.

Third country. Usually used to refer to a country to which the UK Border Agency wishes to send an asylum seeker for her/his application for asylum to be considered, other than that of which s/he is a national, rather than in the UK.

The United Kingdom. Comprises England, Wales, Scotland and Northern Ireland. The Channel Islands of Jersey and Guernsey, and the Isle of Man are Crown Dependencies and not part of the UK.

UK Border Agency. The Home Office agency that deals with immigration control.

Unmarried partners. A term used in the Immigration Rules to refer to couples (heterosexual or same-sex) who have been together for two or more years, who are in a relationship 'akin to marriage' and who cannot marry according to the law – eg, because they are of the same sex or one of them is already married. The Immigration Rules give unmarried partners some rights to enter and remain in the UK if one partner is settled in the UK or has limited leave to enter or remain here.

Upper Tribunal (Immigration and Asylum Chamber). The tribunal that hears and determines appeals against determinations made by the First-tier Tribunal (Immigration and Asylum Chamber).

Visa national. A person who must obtain entry clearance in advance of travelling to the UK for most purposes, unless s/he is a person with indefinite leave returning within two years or returning within a period of earlier leave granted for more than six months. For a list of countries covered, see Appendix 1 to the Immigration Rules at www.ukba.homeoffice.gov.uk/policyandlaw/immigrationlaw/immigra-tionrules/appendix1

Work permit. A document issued by the UK Border Agency to employers allowing them to employ a named individual in a particular job. This is different form the UK Border Agency giving permission to work to, for example, an asylum seeker, which is done by letter and removal of the condition on the asylum seeker's temporary admission document (IS96) that states s/he is prohibited from working.

Appendix 2

Information and advice

Independent advice and representation on immigration issues

If you need help with an immigration problem, you should seek advice from your local law centre, a solicitor specialising in immigration work or one of the agencies listed below.

Joint Council for the Welfare of Immigrants

115 Old Street
London EC1V 9JR
Tel: 020 7251 8708
info@jcwi.org.uk
www.jcwi.org.uk

Immigration Advisory Service

County House
190 Great Dover Street
London SE1 4YB
Tel: 0844 974 4000
www.iasuk.org.uk

There are other regional offices and offices at ports.

Afro-Asian Advisory Service

53 Addington Square
London SE5 7LB
Tel: 020 7701 0141

AIRE Centre (Advice on Individual Rights in Europe)

3rd Floor
17 Red Lion Square
London WC1R 4QH
Tel: 020 7831 4276
info@airecentre.org
www.airecentre.org

Greater Manchester Immigration Aid Unit

1 Delaunays Road
Crumpsall Green
Manchester M8 4QS
Tel: 0161 740 7722
www.gmiau.org

Asylum Aid

Club Union House
253–254 Upper Street
London N1 1RY
Tel: 020 7354 9631
info@asylumaid.org.uk
www.asylumaid.org.uk

Law Centres Federation

PO Box 65836
London EC4P 4FX
Tel: 020 7842 0720
Fax: 020 7842 0721
info@lawcentres.org.uk

Does not give advice, but can provide details of your nearest law centre.

Community Legal Advice

Tel: 0845 345 4345
www.communitylegaladvice.org.uk

Includes access to a directory of legal aid suppliers.

Refugee Action

The Old Fire Station
150 Waterloo Road
London SE1 8SB
Tel: 020 7654 7700
www.refugee-action.org.uk

Has one-stop services throughout the country.

Refugee Council

240–250 Ferndale Road
London SW9 8BB
Tel: 020 7346 6700
www.refugeecouncil.org.uk

Scottish Refugee Council

5 Cadogan Square
(170 Blythswood Court)
Glasgow G2 7PH
Tel: 0141 248 9799
info@scottishrefugeecouncil.org.uk
www.scottishrefugeecouncil.org.uk/contact

Welsh Refugee Council

Phoenix Huose
389 Newport Road
Cardiff CF24 1TP
Tel: 029 2048 9800
info@welshrefugeecouncil.org
www.welshrefugeecouncil.org/contact-us

Migrant Helpline

Charlton House
Dour Street
Dover CT16 1AT
Tel: 01304 203 977
www.migranthelpline.org.uk

Independent advice and representation on social security

It is often difficult for unsupported individuals to get a positive response from the Department for Work and Pensions. You may be taken more seriously if it is clear you have taken advice about your entitlement or have an adviser assisting you.

If you want advice or help with a benefit problem, the following agencies may be able to assist.

- Citizens Advice Bureaux (CABx) and other local advice centres provide information and advice about benefits and may be able to represent you.
- Law centres can often help in a similar way to CABx and advice centres.
- Local authority welfare rights workers provide a service in many areas and some arrange advice sessions and take-up campaigns locally.

- Local organisations for particular groups of claimants may offer help. For instance, there are unemployed centres, pensioners' groups and centres for disabled people.
- Claimants' unions give advice in some areas.
- Some social workers and probation officers (but not all) help with benefit problems, especially if they are already working with you on another problem.
- Solicitors can give some free legal advice. This does not cover the cost of representation at an appeal hearing, but can cover the cost of preparing written submissions and obtaining evidence such as medical reports. However, solicitors do not always have a good working knowledge of the benefit rules and you may need to shop around until you find one who does.

Appendix 3
Useful addresses

Immigration

UK Border Agency
Lunar House
40 Wellesley Road
Croydon CR9 2BY
Tel: 0870 606 7766
Textphone: 0800 389 8289
www.ukba.homeoffice.gov.uk.

Visa Services Directorate
Lunar House
40 Wellesley Road
Croydon CR9 2BY
www.ukvisas.gov.uk

Application Forms Unit
Tel: 0870 241 0645

Immigration Enquiry Bureau
Tel: 0870 606 7766
Textphone: 0800 389 8289
ukbapublicenquiries@
ukba.gsi.gov.uk

Nationality Contact Centre
Tel: 0845 010 5200
ukbanationalityenquiries@
ukba.gsi.gov.uk

European Enquiries Contact Centre
Tel: 0845 010 5200
ukbaeuropeanenquiries@
ukba.gsi.gov.uk

Sponsorship and Employers' Helpline
Tel: 0300 123 4699
sponsorshipPBSenquiries@
ukba.gsi.gov.uk

Work permits
Customer Contact Centre
UK Border Agency
PO Box 3468
Sheffield S3 8WA
Tel: 0114 207 4074
accessionenquiries@ukba.gsi.gov.uk

Asylum Support Customer Contact Centre
Tel: 0845 602 1739

Independent Chief Inspector of the UK Border Agency
5th Floor
Globe House
89 Eccleston Square
London SW1V 1PN

First-tier Tribunal (Immigration and Asylum Chamber)
PO Box 7866
Loughborough LE11 2XZ
Tel: 0845 600 0877
Fax: 01509 221403
Textphone: 0845 606 0766
www.tribunals.gov.uk/
immigrationasylum/index.htm

Upper Tribunal (Immigration and Asylum Chamber)

Arnhem Support Centre
PO Box 6987
Leicester LE1 6ZX
Tel: 0845 600 0877
Fax: 0116 249 4130
Textphone: 0845 606 0766
www.tribunals.gov.uk/immigration-asylum/utiac/index/htm

Office of the Immigration Services Commissioner

5th Floor
Counting House
53 Tooley Street
London SE1 2QN
Tel: 0845 000 0046
www.oisc.gov.uk

Solicitors Regulation Authority

Ipsley Court
Berrington Close
Redditch B98 0TD
Tel: 0870 606 2555
www.sra.org.uk

Legal Ombudsman

PO Box 15870
Birmingham B30 9EB
Tel: 0300 555 0333
www.legalombudsman.org.uk

For complaints about lawyers.

Identity and Passport Service

Globe House
89 Ecclestone Square
London SW1V 1PN
Tel: 0300 222 0000
www.ips.gov.uk

The Overseas Visitors Record Office

Brandon House
180 Borough High Street
London SE1 1LH
Tel: 020 7230 1208

European Commission Representation in the UK

8 Storey's Gate
London SW1P 3AT
Tel: 020 7973 1992
www.ec.europa.eu/unitedkingdom

Immigration Law Practitioners' Association

Lindsey House
40–42 Charterhouse Street
London EC1M 6JN
Tel: 020 7251 8383
www.ilpa.org.uk

Electronic Immigration Network

The Progress Centre
Charlton Place
Manchester M12 6HS
Tel: 0845 458 4151
Tel: 0845 458 4151
info@ein.org.uk
www.ein.org.uk

Asylum Support Appeals Project

18 Barclay Road
Croydon CR0 1JN
Tel: 020 8686 1888
Fax: 020 8686 1899
Advice Line: 0845 603 3884
www.asaproject.org

First-tier Tribunal (Asylum Support)

2nd Floor
Anchorage House
2 Clove Crescent
East India Dock
London E14 2BE
Tel: 020 7538 6171
Freephone: 0800 389 7913

Social security

Department for Work and Pensions (benefits)

Quarry House
Quarry Hill
Leeds LS2 7UA
Tel: 0113 232 4000
www.dwp.gov.uk

Department for Work and Pensions (Decision Making and Appeal Unit)

Quarry House
Quarry Hill
Leeds LS2 7UA
Tel: 0113 232 4000

Department for Work and Pensions (policy)

The Adelphi
1–11 John Adam Street
London WC2 6HT
Tel: 020 7962 8000

Department for Work and Pensions (solicitor)

The Adelphi
1–11 John Adam Street
London WC2 6HT
Tel: 020 7962 8000

Benefit Enquiry Line

2nd Floor
Red Rose House
Lancaster Road
Preston PR1 1HB
Tel: 0800 882 200
Textphone: 0800 243 355
bel-customer-services@
dwp.gsi.gov.uk

International Pension Centre

Tyneview Park
Whitley Road
Benton
Newcastle upon Tyne NE98 1BA
Tel: 0191 218 7777

Exporting Benefits Overseas

Room B120D
Warbreck House
Warbreck Hill Road
Blackpool FY2 0YE
exportability.team@dwp.gsi.gov.uk

Child Benefit Centre

Freepost NEA 10463
PO Box 133
Washington NE38 7BR
www.hmrc.gov.uk/childbenefit

England, Scotland and Wales

Tel: 0845 302 1444
Textphone: 0845 302 1474

Northern Ireland

Tel: 0845 603 2000
Textphone: 0845 607 6078

Helpline for advisers

0845 302 1411

Disability Contact Processing Unit

Attendance allowance and disability living allowance

Warbreck House
Warbreck Hill
Blackpool FY2 0YJ
Tel: 0845 712 3456
Textphone: 0845 722 4433
dcpu.customer-services@
dwo.gsi.gov.uk

NHS Business Services Authority

Sandyford House
Archbold Terrace
Jesmond
Newcastle upon Tyne NE2 1DB
Tel: 0845 850 1166
www.nhsbsa.nhs.uk/792.aspx

Department for Education

Sanctuary Buildings
Great Smith Street
London SW1P 3BT
Tel: 0870 000 2288
Textphone: 18001 0870 000 2288
www.education.gov.uk

HM Revenue and Customs (tax credits)

Tax Credit Office
Preston PR1 0SB
Tel: 0845 300 3900
Textphone: 0845 300 3909
www.hmrc.gov.uk/taxcredits

Helpline for advisers
0845 300 3946

HM Revenue and Customs (national insurance contributions)

Benton Park View
Newcastle upon Tyne NE98 1ZZ
Tel: 0845 302 1479
Textphone: 0845 915 3296
www.hmrc.gov.uk/nic

The President of the Appeal Service

The President's Office
5th Floor
Fox Court
14 Grays Inn Road
London WC1X 8HN
Tel: 020 3206 0640
www.tribunals.gov.uk

The Upper Tribunal (Administrative Appeals Chamber)

England
5th Floor
Chichester Rents
81 Chancery Lane
London WC2A 1DD
Tel: 020 7911 7085
www.osscsc.gov.uk

Wales
Civil Justice Centre
2 Park Street
Cardiff CF10 1ET
Tel: 02920 662 257

Scotland
George House
126 George Street
Edinburgh EH2 4HH
Tel: 0131 271 4310

• •

Northern Ireland
3rd Floor
Bedford House
16–22 Bedford Street
Belfast BT2 7FD
Tel: 028 9072 8736
www.courtsni.gov.uk/en-GB/
services/tribunals

Independent Review Service for the Social Fund
Centre City Podium
5 Hill Street
Birmingham B5 4UB
Tel: 0800 096 1926
Textphone: 0800 096 1929
sfc@irs-review.org.uk
www.irs-review.org.uk

The Parliamentary and Health Service Ombudsman
Millbank Tower
Millbank
London SW1P 4QP
Tel: 0345 015 4033
phso.enquiries@ombudsman.org.uk
www.ombudsman.org.uk

The Independent Adjudicator
The Adjudicator's Office
8th Floor
Euston Tower
286 Euston Road
London NW1 3US
Tel: 0300 057 1111
www.adjudicatorsoffice.gov.uk

Appendix 4
Useful publications

Many of the books listed here will be in your local public library. Stationery Office books are available from Stationery Office bookshops and also from many others. They may be ordered by post, telephone or fax from The Stationery Office, PO Box 29, Norwich NR3 1GN (tel: 0870 600 5522, fax: 0870 600 5533; email:customer.services@tso.co.uk; web: www.tso.co.uk). also has a website for further information at www.opsi.gov.uk. Many of the publications listed are available from CPAG – see below for order details, or order from www.cpag.org.uk. For social security information in electronic format see details of CPAG's online services given below.

1. General immigration, nationality and asylum

JCWI Immigration, Nationality and Refugee Law Handbook
6th edition, JCWI, 2006

Macdonald's Immigration Law and Practice
6th edition, Ian Macdonald and Nicholas Blake, Macdonalds, 2005

Best Practice Guide to Asylum and Human Rights Appeals
M Henderson, ILPA, 2003

2. Nationality

Fransman: British Nationality Law
3rd edition, Bloomsbury Professional, 2010

3. Refugees and asylum seekers

The Rights of Refugees Under International Law
James Hathaway, Cambridge University Press, 2005

The Refugee in International Law
2nd edition, Guy Goodwin-Gill, Clarendon, 1996

Support for Asylum Seekers
3rd edition, Willman and Knafler, Legal Action Group, 2010

4. Human rights

Blackstone's Guide to the Human Rights Act 1998
Oxford University Press, 2003

European Human Rights Law
Starmer, Legal Action Group, 1999

5. Children

Working with Children and Young People Subject to Immigration Control: guidelines for best practice
ILPA/Heaven Crawley, 2004

6. **European Economic Area nationals**

Free Movement of Persons in the Enlarged European Union
N Rogers, R Scannell, Sweet & Maxwell, 2005

7. **Social security caselaw and legislation**

Social Security Case Law – Digest of Commissioners' Decisions
D Neligan, Stationery Office (looseleaf in two vols)
Commissioners' decisions also at www.osscsc.gov.uk and on CPAG's online services.

CPAG's Online Information Services
These include all social security legislation, consolidated and updated throughout the year; decisions of the courts, commissioners and Upper Tribunal, many with CPAG commentary; the *Welfare Benefits and Tax Credits Handbook* updated throughout the year with links to the relevant legislation; CPAG's *Housing Benefit and Council Tax Benefit Legislation* (with commentary updated in line with the print version); the *Child Support Handbook* and child support legislation. Three different annual subscription packages are available (plus a basic one without legislation). For more information and to get a free trial, visit the online services homepage at http://onlineservices.cpag.org.uk.

The Law Relating to Social Security
Stationery Office (looseleaf, 11 vols). All the legislation but without any comment. Known as the 'Blue Book'. Vols 6, 7, 8 and 11 deal with means-tested benefits.

Social Security Legislation, Volume I: Non-Means-Tested Benefits
D Bonner, I Hooker and R White (Sweet & Maxwell). Legislation with commentary. 2010/11 edition (October 2010) available from CPAG if you are a member: £92 for the main volume.

Social Security Legislation, Volume II: Income Support, Jobseeker's Allowance and the Social Fund
J Mesher, P Wood, R Poynter, N Wikely and D Bonner (Sweet & Maxwell). Legislation with commentary. 2010/11 edition (October 2010) available from CPAG if you are a member: £92 for the main volume.

Social Security Legislation, Volume III: Administration, Adjudication and the European Dimension
M Rowland and R White (Sweet & Maxwell). Legislation with commentary. 2010/11 edition (October 2010) available from CPAG if you are a member: £92 for the main volume.

Social Security Legislation, Volume IV: Tax Credits, Child Trust Funds and Employer-Paid Social Security benefits
N Wikeley and D Williams (Sweet & Maxwell). Legislation with commentary. 2010/11 edition (October 2010) available from CPAG if you are a member: £92 for the main volume.

Social Security Legislation – updating supplement to Volumes I, II, III and IV (Sweet & Maxwell). The spring 2011 update to the 2010/11 main volumes, available from CPAG if you are a member (£59).

CPAG's Housing Benefit and Council Tax Benefit Legislation L Findlay, C George, R Poynter and S Wright (CPAG). Contains legislation with a detailed commentary. 2010/11 edition available from December 2010, priced £95 including Supplement from CPAG. This publication is also available online.

The Social Fund: Law and Practice T Buck (Sweet & Maxwell). Includes legislation, guidance and commentary. The 3rd edition (March 2009) is available from CPAG for £89 if you are a CPAG member.

Social Fund Directions Available on the IRS website at www.irssf.demon.co.uk/ssdir.htm

8. **Social security guidance**
Decision Makers Guide 12 volumes, memos and letters available at www.dwp.gov.uk/advisers

Handbook for Delegated Medical Practitioners (Stationery Office, 1988)

Housing Benefit and Council Tax Benefit Guidance Manual (Stationery Office, looseleaf) Also available at www.dwp.gov.uk/advisers

Industrial Injuries Handbook for Adjudicating Medical Authorities (Stationery Office, looseleaf)

Income Support Guide (Stationery Office, looseleaf, 8 vols) Procedural guide issued to DWP staff.

The Social Fund Guide (Stationery Office, looseleaf 2 vols) Also available at www.dwp.gov.uk/advisers

9. **Leaflets**
The DWP publishes many leaflets available free from your local DWP or Jobcentre Plus office. To order larger numbers of leaflets, or receive information about new leaflets, write to Publicity Register, Freepost NWW 1853, Manchester, M2 9LU, tel. 0845 602 4444; email publicity-register@dwp.gsi.gov.uk.

10. **Periodicals**
CPAG's *Welfare Rights Bulletin* is published every two months by CPAG. It covers developments in social security law, including commissioners' decisions. The annual subscription is £33 but it is sent automatically to certain categories of CPAG member. For subscription and membership details contact CPAG.

Articles on social security and immigration can also be found in *Legal Action* (Legal Action Group, monthly magazine), and on social security in the *Journal of Social Security Law* (Sweet & Maxwell, quarterly).

11. **CPAG handbooks**

Welfare Benefits and Tax Credits Handbook 2010/11
£39 (£9 for claimants) Also available online

Child Support Handbook 2010/11
£27 (18th edition, October 2010) (£8 for claimants). Also available online

Child Support: the legislation
£87 (9th edition, March 2010)

Child Support: the legislation: Supplement
£49 (9th edition, August 2010)

Paying for Care Handbook
£19.50 (6th edition, March 2009)

Council Tax Handbook
£17 (8th edition, November 2009)

Debt Advice Handbook
£22 (9th edition, September 2010)

Fuel Rights Handbook
£19 (15th edition, December 2010)

Student Support and Benefits Handbook: England, Wales and Northern Ireland 2010/2011
£13.50 (8th edition, November 2010)

Benefits for Students in Scotland Handbook 2010/11
£13.50 (8th edition, September 2010)

Personal Finance Handbook
£16.50 (3rd edition, December 2009)

Children's Handbook Scotland 2010/11
£13 (3rd edition, October 2010)

A Guide to Housing Benefit and Council Tax Benefit 2010/11
£26 (Shelter/CIoH, May 2010)

Tribunal Practice and Procedure
£40 (Legal Action Group, October 2009)

Disability Rights Handbook 2010/11
£27.50 (Disability Alliance ERA, May 2010)

Young Person's Handbook
£15.95 (4th edition, Inclusion, December 2009)

Welfare to Work Handbook
£22 (4th edition, Inclusion, February 2010)

For CPAG publications and most of those in Sections 6 and 10, contact:

CPAG, 94 White Lion Street, London N1 9PF, tel: 020 7837 7979, fax: 020 7837 6414. Order forms are also available at: www.cpag.org.uk/publications. Postage and packing is free for orders up to £10 in value; for orders £10.01–£100, add a flat rate charge of £3.99; for orders £100.01–£400, add £5.99; for orders £400+, add £9.99.

Appendix 5

Leave to enter endorsements

Endorsements

Type of visa	Cat	Endorsement	Code	+POL	Duration	Add endorsement field	ECG Chapter
Exempt Status and Courtesy Endorsements							
Heads of state and their households	D	EXEMPT		N	6 months		5
Diplomat on posting	D	EXEMPT (DIPLOMAT)		N	5 years		5
Unmarried diplomat dependant	D	TO ACC PARTNER (DIPLOMAT)	1	N	2 years	add initial, surname, Embassy/High Commission	5
Unmarried diplomat dependant	D	TO JOIN PARTNER (DIPLOMAT)	1	N	2 years	add initial, surname, Embassy/High Commission	5
Visiting Diplomat	D	EXEMPT (DIPLOMAT)		N	6 months		5
Non-diplomatic staff at mission	D	EXEMPT OFFICIAL		N	5 years		5
Embassy locally engaged staff	D	EXEMPT		N	Other	(Use 'Exempt Official'	5
Visiting government ministers	D	EXEMPT		N	2 years	(Use 'Exempt Official'	5
Employees of international organisations	D	EXEMPT INTERNATIONAL ORGANISATION		N	5 years		5

Type of visa	Cat	Endorsement	Code	+POL	Duration	Add endorsement field	ECG Chapter
Interns/ official visitors of international organisations	D	EXEMPT INTERNATIONAL ORGANISATION		N	Other		5
Commonwealth Armed Forces	D	EXEMPT - MEMBER OF ARMED FORCES OF COMMONWEALTH		N	Other		5
Foreign Nationals in HM Forces	D	EXEMPT HOME FORCES		N	Other		5
Overseas military personnel visiting	D	EXEMPT VISITING FORCES		N	Other		5
Overseas military training with HM forces	D	EXEMPT ARMED FORCES TRAINING		N	Other		5
Spouse/ CP of exempt member of armed forces	D	TO ACC SPOUSE/CP	1	N	up to 4 years	add initial and surname of spouse/ CP	5
Spouse/ CP of exempt member of armed forces	D	TO JOIN SPOUSE/CP	1	N	up to 4 years	add initial and surname of spouse/ CP	5
Child of exempt member of armed forces	D	TO ACC PARENT(S)	1	N	up to 4 years	add initial and surname of armed forces parent	5
Child of exempt member of armed forces	D	TO JOIN PARENT(S)	1	N	up to 4 years	add initial and surname of armed forces parent	5
Arms control personnel - Vienna doc '92	D	EXEMPT - VISIT ARMS CONTROL INSPECTOR		N	2 years		5

Type of visa	Cat	Endorsement	Code	+POL	Duration	Add endorsement field	ECG Chapter
Arms control personnel - Vienna doc '92*	D	EXEMPT - VISIT ARMS CONTROL OBSERVER		N	2 years	(Use 'Exempt' add Visit Arms Control Observer)	
Arms control personnel - Vienna doc '92*	D	EXEMPT - VISIT ARMS CONTROL TRANSPORT CREW		N	2 years	(Use 'Exempt' add 'Visit Arms Control Transport Crew)	
General Visitor	C	VISIT	3	N	6 months		VAT 1
Family Visitor	C	VISIT - FAMILY VISIT	3	N	6 months		VAT 2
Child Visitor	C	VISIT - CHILD ACCOMPANIED	3	N	6 months	add parent/ guardian names, passport nos	VAT 3
Child Visitor	C	VISIT - CHILD UNACCOMPANIED	3	N	6 months		VAT 3
Parent of a child at school	C	VISIT - CHILD AT SCHOOL	3	N	12 months		VAT 5
Visitors for marriage	C	VISIT - MARRIAGE/CP	3	N	6 months	add initial and surname of intended spouse/ CP	VAT 6
Visitors for private medical treatment	C	VISIT - MEDICAL TREATMENT	3	N	6 months		VAT 7
Transit	B	VISIT - IN TRANSIT	3	N	6 months	(leave to enter limited to 48 hours on each transit)	VAT 8

Type of visa	Cat	Endorsement	Code	+POL	Duration	Add endorsement field	ECG Chapter
Direct Airside Transit Visa (DATV)	A	DIRECT AIRSIDE TRANSIT	3	N	3 months		VAT 8
Student Visitor	C	VISIT - STUDENT	3	N	6 months		VAT 9
Prospective Student	D	PROSPECTIVE STUDENT	3	Y	6 months		VAT 10
Business Visitor	C	VISIT - BUSINESS	3	N	6 months		VAT 11
Film Crew	C	VISIT - FILM CREW	3	N	6 months		VAT 11
Academic Visitor	D	ACADEMIC VISITOR	3	Y	max 12 months		VAT 12
Visiting Professor	C	VISIT - VISITING PROFESSOR	3	N	6 months		VAT 13
Visiting Religious Worker	C	VISIT - RELIGIOUS WORKER	3	N	6 months		VAT 14
PLAB test	D	PLAB TEST	4	N	6 months		VAT 15
Clinical attachment	D	CLINICAL ATTACHMENT	4	N	max 6 weeks		VAT 16
Dental Observation	D	DENTAL OBSERVATION	4	N	max 6 weeks		VAT 16
Sports Visitor	C	VISIT - SPORTSPERSON	3	N	6 months		VAT 17
Entertainer Visitor	C	VISIT - ENTERTAINER	3	N	6 months		VAT 18

Type of visa	Cat	Endorsement	Code	+POL	Duration	Add endorsement field	ECG Chapter
Approved Destination Status Agreement (ADS) China	C	VISIT - ADS	3	N	30 days		VAT 19
MOD Training course for overseas forces	D	COURSE F	3	N	Other	(Up to 6 months)	VAT 20
MOD Training course for overseas forces	D	COURSE F	1	N	Other	(Over 6 months)	VAT 20
Parent accessing a child	D	RIGHT OF ACCESS TO A CHILD	1	N	1 year		VAT 23
Diplomatic Couriers	C	VISIT - DIPLOMATIC COURIER	3	N	6 months		
Entry for Studies - Dependants of students who obtained leave on or before 30 March under Rules in force on 30 March 2009 and prospective students							
Spouse/ CP/ Child of Student (where student has less than 12 months leave)	D	STUDENT DEPENDANT	3	Y	Other	add initial and surname 12 of principal student	
Spouse/ CP/ Child of Student (where student has 12 months or more leave)	D	STUDENT DEPENDANT	1	Y	Other	add initial and surname 12 of principal student	

Type of visa	Cat	Endorsement	Code	+POL	Duration	Add endorsement field	ECG Chapter
Settlement: Fiancé(e)s, Proposed Civil Partners, Spouses, Civil Partners, Unmarried and Same-Sex Partners							
Fiancé(e)/ Proposed Civil Partner	D	MARRIAGE/CP	3	N	6 months	add initial and surname of fiancé(e)/ proposed CP	13
Spouse/ CP view to settlement	D	SPOUSE/CP	1	N	27 months	add initial and surname	13
Settlement spouse/ CP for 4 years passed KOL	D	SETTLEMENT SPOUSE/ CP		N	ILE	add initial and surname of spouse/ CP	13
Settlement spouse/ CP for 4 years but need KOL	D	SETTLEMENT SPOUSE/ CP(KOL REQ)	1	N	27 months	add initial and surname of spouse/ CP	13
Settlement - partner less than 4 years	D	TO ACC PARTNER	1	N	27 months	add initial and surname of partner	13
Settlement - partner less than 4 years	D	TO JOIN PARTNER	1	N	27 months	add initial and surname of partner	13
Settlement - partner 4 years KOL taken	D	SETTLEMENT TO JOIN/ ACC PARTNER		N	ILE	add initial and surname of partner	13

Type of visa	Cat	Endorsement	Code	+POL	Duration	Add endorsement field	ECG Chapter
Settlement - partner 4 years but need KOL	D	SETTLEMENT TO JOIN/ ACC PARTNER (KOL REQ)	1	N	27 months	add initial and surname of partner	13
Settlement Entry for Children							
Child - mother present and settled in UK	D	SETTLEMENT ACC FATHER TO JOIN MOTHER		N	ILE	add initial and surname of mother	14
Child - father present and settled in UK	D	SETTLEMENT ACC MOTHER TO JOIN FATHER		N	ILE	add initial and surname of father	14
Child - parent(s) present and settled in UK	D	SETTLEMENT TO JOIN PARENT(S)		N	ILE	add initial and surname of parent(s)	14
Child - parent admitted for settlement	D	SETTLEMENT ACCOMPANYING PARENT		N	ILE	add initial and surname of parent	14
Child - relative present and settled	D	SETTLEMENT TO JOIN/ ACC RELATIVE		N	ILE	add initial and surname of relative	14
Child - view to settlement	D	TO ACC FATHER/CYR	1	N	27 months	add initial and surname of sponsor	14
Child - view to settlement	D	TO ACC MOTHER/CYR	1	N	27 months	add initial and surname of sponsor	14

Type of visa	Cat	Endorsement	Code	+POL	Duration	Add endorsement field	ECG Chapter
Child- view to settlement	D	TO ACC PARENT(S)/CYR	1	N	27 months	add initial and surname of sponsor	14
Child- view to settlement	D	TO JOIN FATHER/CYR	1	N	27 months	add initial and surname of sponsor	14
Child- view to settlement	D	TO JOIN MOTHER/CYR	1	N	27 months	add initial and surname of sponsor	14
Child- view to settlement	D	TO JOIN PARENT(S)/CYR	1	N	27 months	add initial and surname of sponsor	14
Child of fiancé(e)/proposed CP- view to settlement	D	TO ACC FATHER/CYR	3	N	6 months	add initial and surname of sponsor	14
Child of fiancé(e)/proposed CP- view to settlement	D	TO ACC MOTHER/CYR	3	N	6 months	add initial and surname of sponsor	14
Child of fiancé(e)/proposed CP- view to settlement	D	TO JOIN FATHER/CYR	3	N	6 months	add initial and surname of sponsor	14
Child of fiancé(e)/proposed CP- view to settlement	D	TO JOIN MOTHER/CYR	3	N	6 months	add initial and surname of sponsor	14

Type of visa	Cat	Endorsement	Code	+POL	Duration	Add endorsement field	ECG Chapter
Child coming to the UK to be adopted	D	FOR ADOPTION\360\HO	1	N	2 years	(Mandatory deferral)	14
Adopted child - view to settlement	D	TO ACC FATHER/CYR	1	N	12 months	add initial and surname of sponsor	14
Adopted child - view to settlement	D	TO ACC MOTHER/CYR	1	N	12 months	add initial and surname of sponsor	14
Adopted child - view to settlement	D	TO ACC PARENT(S)/CYR	1	N	12 months	add initial and surname of sponsor	14
Adopted child - view to settlement	D	TO JOIN FATHER/CYR	1	N	12 months	add initial and surname of sponsor	14
Adopted child - view to settlement	D	TO JOIN MOTHER/CYR	1	N	12 months	add initial and surname of sponsor	14
Adopted child - view to settlement	D	TO JOIN PARENT(S)/CYR	1	N	12 months	add initial and surname of sponsor	14
Entry for Settlement: Other Dependent Relatives							
Other dependent relatives - overage child	D	SETTLEMENT TO JOIN PARENT(S)		N	ILE	add initial and surname of parent(s)	15
Other dependent relatives - elderly parent	D	SETTLEMENT TO JOIN/ACC CHILD		N	ILE	add initial and surname of child	15
Other dependent relatives - grandparent	D	SETTLEMENT TO JOIN/ACC GRANDCHILD		N	ILE	add initial and surname of grandchild	15

Appendix 5: Leave to enter endorsements

Type of visa	Cat	Endorsement	Code	+POL	Duration	Add endorsement field	ECG Chapter
Other dependent relatives	D	SETTLEMENT TO JOIN/ ACC RELATIVE		N	ILE	add initial and surname of relative	15
Catch all for those joining relatives to settle	D	SETTLEMENT TO JOIN/ ACC		N	ILE	add initial and surname of sponsor	15
Family Reunion							
Dependant of refugee with indefinite leave	D	FAMILY REUNION		N	ILE	add initial and surname of sponsor	16
Dependant of refugee with limited leave	D	FAMILY REUNION	1a	N	Other	add initial and surname of sponsor	16
Dependant of humanitarian protectee (post 30/08/05)	D	FAMILY REUNION	1a	N	Other	add initial and surname of sponsor	16
Entry for employment: Work Permit							
Work Permit Holder	D	WORK PERMIT	2	Y	Other	add work permit no	17
Spouses/ CP/ Child of work permit holder	D	WORK PERMIT DEPENDANT	1	Y	Other	add initial and surname of work permit holder	17
Spouses/ CP/ partners of HSMP approval letter holder (non PBS)	D	HSMP PARTNER	1 + doc	Y	Other	add initial and surname of work permit holder	17
Child of HSMP approval letter holder (non PBS)	D	HSMP CHILD	doc	Y	Other	add initial and surname of work permit holder	17

Type of visa	Cat	Endorsement	Code	+POL	Duration	Add endorsement field	ECG Chapter
Entry for Non-Work Permit Employment							
Employment - work permit not required	D	FOR EMPLOYMENT WITH		Y	Other	add name of Firm/ visa category	18
Dependent spouse/ CP	D	TO ACC SPOUSE/CP		Y	Other	add initial and surname of spouse/ CP	18
Dependent spouse/ CP	D	TO JOIN SPOUSE/CP		Y	Other	add initial and surname of spouse/ CP	18
Dependent unmarried/ same-sex partner	D	TO ACC PARTNER		Y	Other	add initial and surname of partner	18
Dependent unmarried/ same-sex partner	D	TO JOIN PARTNER		Y	Other	add initial and surname of partner	18
Dependent child	D	TO ACC PARENT(S)		Y	Other	add initial and surname of working parent	18
Dependent child	D	TO JOIN PARENT(S)		Y	Other	add initial and surname of working parent	18
Other dependent relative (outside the Rules eg. Dependent parent)	D	TO ACC RELATIVE		Y	Other	add initial and surname of working relative	18
Other dependent relative (outside the Rules eg. Dependent parent)	D	TO JOIN RELATIVE		Y	Other	add initial and surname of working relative	18

Appendix 5: Leave to enter endorsements

Type of visa	Cat	Endorsement	Code	+POL	Duration	Add endorsement field	ECG Chapter
SAWS	D	AGRICULTURAL WORKER	4	N	max 6 months		18
Servants in Private Households accompanying employer with long-term visa	D	DOMESTIC WORKER (OTHER)	4	Y	max 1 year	(Do not state employer)	18
Servants in Private Households accomanying employer with visit visa	D	DOMESTIC WORKER(VISITOR)	4	N	6 months	(Do not state employer)	18
Spouses / CP / Child of Servant accompanying employer with long-term visa	D	DEPENDANT DOMESTIC WORKER OTHER	1	Y	max 1 year	add initial and surname of domestic worker	18
Spouses / CP / Child of Servant accompanying employer with visit visa	D	DEPENDANT DOMESTIC WORKER VISITOR	3	N	6 months	add initial and surname of domestic worker	18
ECAA	D	ECAA BUSINESS	2	Y	2 years		18
Off-shore worker	D	OFF-SHORE WORKER	2	N	1 year		18
Sole Representative	D	SOLE REPRESENTATIVE FOR EMPLOYMENT WITH	4	Y	2 years	add name of firm	18
UK Ancestry	D	UK ANCESTRY - EMPLOYMENT	1	Y	5 years		18

Type of visa	Cat	Endorsement	Code	+POL	Duration	Add endorsement field	ECG Chapter
Returning Residents							
Returning Residents who have ILE/ILR in the UK	D	RETURNING RESIDENT		N	ILE	(Issue for 2 years from last departure from UK)	20
The European Dimension							
EEA Family Permit	D	EEA FP: FAMILY MEMBER		N	6 months	add 'To Join' OR 'To Acc' (Name of EEA national)	21
EEA Family Permit - SWISS National	D	FAMILY MEMBER OF A SWISS NATIONAL		N	6 months	add 'To Join' OR 'To Acc' (Name of Swiss national)	21
Swiss Posted Workers	D	FOR EMPLOYMENT WITH	4	N	90 days	add company Name 'SWISS POSTED WORKER'	21
EU Employer 'Vander Elst'	D	VANDER ELST	4	Y	Other	add company Name	21
Primary carer/ parent of an EEA child	D	TO ACC EEA NATIONAL CHILD	3	Y	5 years		21
Primary carer/ parent of an EEA child	D	TO JOIN EEA NATIONAL CHILD	3	Y	5 years		21
Crew Members							
Crew members - seamen	D	JOINING SHIP	7	N	Other	add name of Ship	CRM 1
Crew members - airmen	D	JOINING AIRCRAFT	7	N	Other	add name of Aircraft	CRM 2

Type of visa	Cat	Endorsement	Code	+POL	Duration	Add endorsement field	ECG Chapter
Settlement Entry for Former Members of HM Forces and their Dependants							
Settlement after discharge from Gurkhas	D	SETTLEMENT - AF		N	ILE		29
Settlement after discharge from HM Forces	D	SETTLEMENT - AF		N	ILE		29
Spouse/CP of ex member of HM Forces	D	SETTLEMENT SPOUSE/CP		N	ILE	(where they've been married at least 2 years)	29
Spouse/CP of ex member of HM Forces	D	SPOUSE/CP	1	N	2 years	(where they've not been married 2 years)	29
Children - mother discharged member of HM Forces	D	SETTLEMENT ACC FATHER TO JOIN MOTHER		N	ILE	add name of mother	29
Children - father discharged member of HM Forces	D	SETTLEMENT ACC MOTHER TO JOIN FATHER		N	ILE	add name of father	29
Children - parent(s) present and settled in UK	D	SETTLEMENT TO JOIN PARENT(S)		N	ILE	add name of parent(s)	29
Children - parent admitted for settlement	D	SETTLEMENT ACCOMPANYING PARENT		N	ILE	add name of parent(s)	29

Type of visa	Cat	Endorsement	Code	+POL	Duration	Add endorsement field	ECG Chapter
Widow of member of armed forces	D	SETTLEMENT TO JOIN/ ACC		N	ILE	add name of relative in UK	29
Orphan of member of armed forces	D	SETTLEMENT TO JOIN/ ACC		N	ILE	add name of relative in UK	29
POINTS BASED SYSTEM							
Tier 1							
PBS Tier 1 General	D	TIER 1 (GENERAL) MIGRANT	1+doc	Y	3 years	(see Rule 245D)	PBS
PBS Tier 1 General	D	TIER 1 (GENERAL) MIGRANT	1	Y	3 years	(see Rule 245D)	PBS
PBS Tier 1 General dependent partner	D	TIER 1 (GENERAL) PARTNER	1+doc	Y	3 years	add initial and surname of migrant	PBS
PBS Tier 1 General dependent partner - no restriction on work (Rule 319D)	D	TIER 1 (GENERAL) PARTNER	1	Y	3 years	add initial and surname of migrant	PBS
PBS Tier 1 General dependent child	D	TIER 1 (GENERAL) CHILD	1	Y	3 years	add initial and surname of migrant	PBS

Type of visa	Cat	Endorsement	Code	+POL	Duration	Add endorsement field	ECG Chapter
PBS Tier 1 Entrepreneur	D	TIER 1 (ENTREPRENEUR) MIGRANT	1+ ownbus	Y	3 years		PBS
PBS Tier 1 Entrepreneur dependent partner	D	TIER 1 (ENTREPRENEUR) PARTNER	1+doc	Y	3 years	add initial and surname of migrant	PBS
PBS Tier 1 Entrepreneur dependent partner - no restriction on work (Rule 319D)	D	TIER 1 (ENTREPRENEUR) PARTNER	1+ unrestr	Y	3 years	add initial and surname of migrant	PBS
PBS Tier 1 Entrepreneur dependent child	D	TIER 1 (ENTREPRENEUR) CHILD	1	Y	3 years	add initial and surname of migrant	PBS
PBS Tier 1 Investor	D	TIER 1 (INVESTOR) MIGRANT	1+doc	Y	3 years		PBS
PBS Tier 1 Investor dependent partner	D	TIER 1 (INVESTOR) PARTNER	1+doc	Y	3 years	add initial and surname of migrant	PBS
PBS Tier 1 Investor dependent partner - no restriction on work (Rule 319D)	D	TIER 1 (INVESTOR) PARTNER	1+ unrestr	Y	3 years	add initial and surname of migrant	PBS

Type of visa	Cat	Endorsement	Code	+POL	Duration	Add endorsement field	ECG Chapter
PBS Tier 1 Investor dependent child	D	TIER 1 (INVESTOR) CHILD	1	Y	3 years	add initial and surname of migrant	PBS
PBS Tier 1 Post-Study Work	D	TIER 1 (POST STUDY) MIGRANT	1+doc	Y	2 years		PBS
PBS Tier 1 Post-Study dependent partner	D	TIER 1 (POST STUDY) PARTNER	1+doc	Y	2 years	add initial and surname of migrant	PBS
PBS Tier 1 Post-Study dependent partner - no restriction on work (Rule 319D)	D	TIER 1 (POST STUDY) PARTNER	1	Y	2 years	add initial and surname of migrant	PBS
PBS Tier 1 Post-Study dependent child	D	TIER 1 (POST STUDY) CHILD	1	Y	2 years	add initial and surname of migrant	PBS
Tier 2*							
PBS Tier 2 General (formerly Work Permit employment)	D	TIER 2 (GENERAL) MIGRANT	CoS	Y	max 3 years plus 1 month	add CoS no.	PBS
PBS Tier 2 Intra Company Transferree	D	TIER 2 (INT COM TRAN) MIGRANT	CoS	Y	max 3 years plus 1 month	add CoS no.	PBS
PBS Tier 2 Minister of Religion	D	TIER 2 (MIN OF REL) MIGRANT	CoS	Y	max 3 years plus 1 month	add CoS no.	PBS

Type of visa	Cat	Endorsement	Code	+POL	Duration	Add endorsement field	ECG Chapter
PBS Tier 2 Sportsperson	D	TIER 2 (SPORTSPEOPLE) MIGRANT	CoS	Y	max 3 years plus 1 month	add CoS no.	PBS
PBS Tier 2 dependent Partner	D	TIER 2 PARTNER	1+doc	Y	max 3 years plus 1 month	add initial and surname of migrant	PBS
PBS Tier 2 dependent Partner - no restriction on work (Rule 319D)	D	TIER 2 PARTNER	1	Y	max 3 years plus 1 month	add initial and surname of migrant	PBS
PBS Tier 2 dependent Child	D	TIER 2 CHILD	1	Y	max 3 years plus 1 month	add initial and surname of migrant	PBS
Tier 4**							
PBS Tier 4 (General) Student	D	TIER 4 (GENERAL) STUDENT	SPX	Y	length of course (245ZW)	add Tier 4 Sponsor Licence number	PBS
PBS Tier 4 (General) Student - officially or government sponsored	D	TIER 4 (GENERAL(S)) STUDENT	SPX	Y	length of course (245ZW)	add Tier 4 Sponsor Licence number	PBS
PBS Tier 4 (General) dependent Partner - Student leave at least 12 months	D	TIER 4 (GENERAL) DEP. PARTNER	1	Y	in line with student	add initial and surname of student	PBS

Type of visa	Cat	Endorsement	Code	+POL	Duration	Add endorsement field	ECG Chapter
PBS Tier 4 (General) dependent Partner - Student leave less than 12 months	D	TIER 4 (GENERAL) DEP. PARTNER	3	Y	in line with student	add initial and surname of student	PBS
PBS Tier 4 (General) dependent Child - Student leave at least 12 months	D	TIER 4 (GENERAL) DEP. CHILD	3	Y	in line with student	add initial and surname of student	PBS
PBS Tier 4 (General) dependent Child - Student leave less than 12 months	D	TIER 4 (GENERAL) DEP. CHILD	1	Y	in line with student	add initial and surname of student	PBS
PBS Tier 4 (Child) Student	D	TIER 4 (CHILD) STUDENT	SPX	Y	length of course (245ZW)	add Tier 4 Sponsor Licence number	PBS
PBS Tier 4 (Child) Student - officially or government sponsored	D	TIER 4 (CHILD(S)) STUDENT	SPX	Y	length of course (245ZW)	add Tier 4 Sponsor Licence number	PBS

Tier 5*

Type of visa	Cat	Endorsement	Code	+POL	Duration	Add endorsement field	ECG Chapter
PBS Tier 5 Youth Mobility	D	TIER 5 (YOUTH MOB) MIGRANT	Youth Mob	Y	2 years		PBS
PBS Tier 5 Charity/ Voluntary Worker	D	TIER 5 TW (CHARITY) MIGRANT	CoS	Y	max 12 months	add CoS no.	PBS
PBS Tier 5 Creative/ Sporting	D	TIER 5 TW (CRE-SPORT) MIGRANT	CoS	Y	max 12 months	add CoS no.	PBS
PBS Tier 5 Government Authorised Exchange	D	TIER 5 TW (EXCHANGE) MIGRANT	CoS	Y	max 2 years	add CoS no.	PBS
PBS Tier 5 International Agreement	D	TIER 5 TW (INT AGREE) MIGRANT	CoS	Y	max 2 years	add CoS no.	PBS
PBS Tier 5 Religious Worker	D	TIER 5 TW (RELIGIOUS) MIGRANT	CoS	Y	max 2 years	add CoS no.	PBS
PBS Tier 5 dependent Partner	D	TIER 5 TW PARTNER	1+ doc	Y	max 2 years	add initial and surname of migrant	PBS
PBS Tier 5 dependent Partner - no restriction on work (Rule 319D)	D	TIER 5 TW PARTNER	1	Y	max 2 years	add initial and surname of migrant	PBS
PBS Tier 5 dependent Child	D	TIER 5 TW CHILD	1	Y	max 2 years	add initial and surname of migrant	PBS

* Tier 2 and Tier 5 entry clearances to be issued in line with validity of sponsor licence (except Youth Mobility).

** Tier 4 entry clearances to be issued in line with Rules para 245ZW

Police registration is sometimes required for stays of more than 6 months for certain nationals aged 16 or over - see ECB16

Entry Clearance Codes and Conditions attached

Code 1 — No recourse to public funds

Code 1a — Leave to enter until *

Code 2 — No recourse to public funds. Work (and any changes must be authorised)

Code 3 — No work or recourse to public funds

Code 4 — No recourse to public funds. To work with * Changes must be authorised)

Code 7 — No recourse to public funds. Must leave the UK in *

ILE — Indefinite leave to enter the UK

CoS — CoS No* No recourse to public funds

SPX — SPX* No recourse to public funds. Work/Business as ILR in Tier 4 Rules

Youth Mob — Youth Mobility - No recourse to public funds. Work/business restricted as per YMS rules

+ Pol — Police Registration within 7 days of arrival in the UK

+ Doc — No employment as a doctor in training

+ Ownbus — Work limited to own business

+ Unrestr — No restriction on employment

+ Workhol — To work as a working holiday maker

Port and In-Country Endorsements

Code 5N — No work or recourse to public funds (arrival endorsement)

Indefinite leave to remain (in country endorsement)

Appendix 6

Reciprocal agreements

Benefits covered in conventions with European Union/European Economic Area member states

State	Retirement pension	Bereavement benefits	Guardian's allowance	Incapacity benefit (short-term)	Incapacity benefit (long-term)	Jobseeker's allowance	Maternity allowance	Disablement benefit	Industrial injuries benefits	Child benefit	Attendance allowance	Carer's allowance
Austria	✓	✓	✓	✓	✓	✓	✓	✓	✓	✓	-	-
Belgium	✓	✓	✓	✓	✓	✓	✓	✓	✓	✓	-	-
Cyprus	✓	✓	✓	✓	✓	✓	✓	✓	✓	-	-	-
Denmark	-	✓	✓	✓	✓	✓	✓	✓	✓	✓	✓	-
Finland	✓	✓	-	✓	✓	✓	✓	✓	✓	✓	-	-
France	✓	✓	-	✓	✓	✓	✓	✓	✓	✓	-	-
Germany	-	✓	✓	✓	✓	✓	✓	✓	✓	✓	✓	-
Iceland	✓	✓	✓	✓	✓	✓	-	✓	✓	-	-	-
Ireland	✓	✓	✓	✓	✓	✓	✓	✓	✓	-	-	-
Italy	✓	✓	✓	✓	✓	✓	✓	✓	✓	-	-	-
Luxembourg	✓	✓	✓	✓	✓	-	✓	✓	✓	-	-	-
Malta	✓	✓	✓	✓	✓	✓	-	✓	✓	-	-	-
Netherlands	✓	✓	✓	✓	✓	✓	✓	✓	✓	-	-	-
Norway	✓	✓	✓	✓	✓	✓	✓	✓	✓	✓	✓	-
Portugal	✓	✓	✓	✓	✓	✓	✓	✓	✓	✓	-	-
Spain	✓	✓	✓	✓	✓	✓	✓	✓	✓	✓	-	-
Slovenia	✓	✓	-	✓	✓	✓	✓	✓	✓	✓	-	-
Sweden	✓	✓	✓	✓	✓	✓	✓	✓	✓	✓	-	-

There is no agreement with Greece or Liechtenstein. The agreement with Gibraltar provides that, except for child benefit, the United Kingdom and Gibraltar are treated as separate European Economic Area countries. Although Northern Ireland is part of the United Kingdom, there is an agreement between Great Britain and Northern Ireland. This is because benefits in Northern Ireland and Great Britain are separate and administered under different social security legislation.

Benefits covered in conventions with non-European Union/ European Economic Area member states

State	Retirement pension	Bereavement benefits	Guardian's allowance	Incapacity benefit (short-term)	Incapacity benefit (long-term)	Jobseeker's allowance	Maternity allowance	Disablement benefit	Industrial injuries benefits	Child benefit	Attendance allowance	Disability living allowance	Carer's allowance
Barbados	✓	✓	✓	✓	✓	-	✓	✓	✓	✓	-	-	-
Bermuda	✓	✓	-	-	-	-	-	✓	✓	-	-	-	-
Bosnia-Herzegovina	✓	✓	-	✓	✓	✓	✓	✓	✓	✓	-	-	-
Canada	✓	-	-	-	-	✓	-	-	-	✓	-	-	-
Croatia	✓	✓	-	✓	✓	✓	✓	✓	✓	✓	-	-	-
Guernsey	✓	✓	✓	✓	✓	✓	✓	✓	✓	✓	✓	✓	-
Isle of Man	✓	✓	✓	✓	✓	✓	✓	✓	✓	✓	✓	✓	✓
Israel	✓	✓	✓	✓	✓	-	✓	✓	✓	✓	-	-	-
Jamaica	✓	✓	✓	-	✓	-	-	✓	✓	-	-	-	-
Jersey	✓	✓	✓	✓	✓	-	✓	✓	✓	✓	✓	✓	-
Kosovo	✓	✓	-	✓	✓	✓	✓	✓	✓	✓	-	-	-
Macedonia	✓	✓	-	✓	✓	✓	✓	✓	✓	✓	-	-	-
Mauritius	✓	✓	✓	-	-	-	-	✓	✓	-	-	-	-
Montenegro	✓	✓	-	✓	✓	✓	✓	✓	✓	✓	-	-	-
New Zealand	✓	✓	✓	✓	-	✓	-	-	-	✓	-	-	-
Philippines	✓	✓	-	-	-	-	-	✓	✓	-	-	-	-
Philippines	✓	✓	-	-	-	-	-	✓	✓	-	-	-	-
Serbia	✓	✓	-	✓	✓	✓	✓	✓	✓	✓	-	-	-
*Switzerland	✓	✓	✓	✓	✓	-	-	✓	✓	✓	-	-	-
Turkey	✓	✓	✓	✓	✓	-	✓	✓	✓	-	-	-	-
USA	✓	✓	✓	✓	✓	-	-	-	-	-	-	-	-

* From June 2002 an agreement with Switzerland allows Swiss nationals the right to rely on EU social security

Appendix 7

Passport stamps and other endorsements

Figure 1: Certificate of entitlement

Figure 2: Category D entry clearance

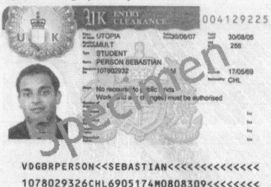

Figure 3: Category ABC visa

```
VCGBRPERSON<<SEBASTIAN<<<<<<<<<<<<<<
1078029326GE06905174M0802293<<<<<<<<
```

Figure 4: Green uniform format visa

```
VCGBR                    <<<<<<<<
7893287<<6HRV     0M0308234<<<<<<<<
```

Figure 5: Red residence permit

Figure 6: Indefinite leave to remain (both before and after December 2003)

Figure 7: Date stamp

Figure 8: Leave to remain with public funds restriction

Leave to remain in the United Kingdom on Condition that the holder maintains and Accommodates himself and any dependants Without recourse to public funds is hereby Given
 	
Until...
....
         on behalf of the Secretary of State
         Home Office
 	
Date	

CODE 1

Figure 9: Limited leave to enter (visitor or short-course student)

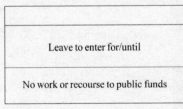

Leave to enter for/until

No work or recourse to public funds

CODE 3

Figure 10: Leave to remain with public funds restriction (before December 2003)

Figure 11: Leave to remain date stamp

Figure 12: Identity card

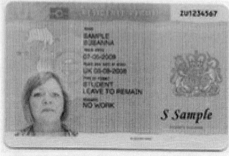

Figure 13: Residence permit confirming refugee status

Home Office
Immigration and Nationality Directorate

IMMIGRATION STATUS DOCUMENT

...gee Status

...ed on this document has been
...Secretary of State as a refugee
...e 1951 Geneva Convention
...Status of Refugees and its
...Protocol.

...ich leave to enter or remain in
...ngdom has been granted is
...d in the endorsement.

...d of leave indicated remains
...is able to work in the United
...t any immigration restrictions
...of work they can undertake.

This Immigration Status Document has been endorsed in place of a valid national passport or travel document and confers upon the person named leave to enter or remain in the United Kingdom for the period indicated. It does not certify the accuracy of the personal particulars, which are those supplied by the person who made the application. It remains the property of Her Majesty's Government and may be withdrawn at any time. It should not be tampered with or passed to an unauthorised person. Any case of loss or destruction should be immediately reported to the nearest police station and to the Immigration and Nationality Directorate at the address below: only after exhaustive enquiries can a replacement be issued in such circumstances. The Immigration Status Document of a deceased person should be returned to the Immigration and Nationality Directorate for cancellation.

Enquiries about the purpose, use, or validity of this document should be made to the Immigration and Nationality Directorate at.

Lunar House, 40 Wellesley Road, Croydon, CR9 2BY (Telephone 0870 606 7766)

ACD.2151

Figure 14: Letter explaining refugee status

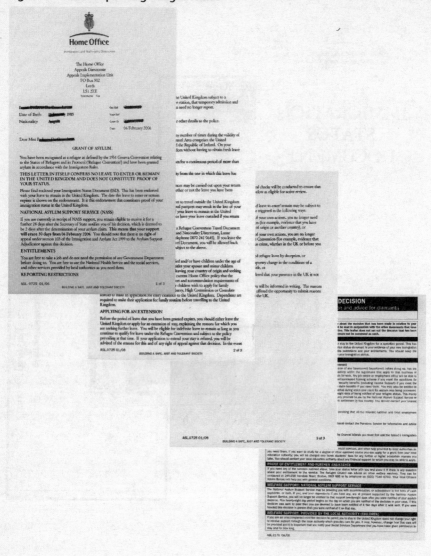

Figure 15: Residence permit confirming discretionary leave to remain

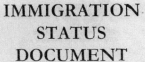

IMMIGRATION
STATUS
DOCUMENT

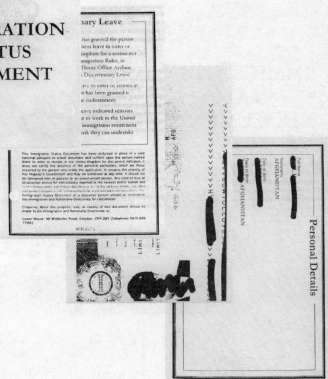

Figure 16: Letters explaining humanitarian protection or discretionary leave to remain

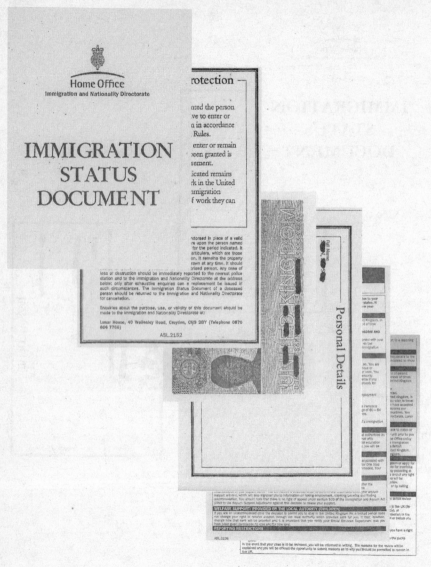

Figure 17: GV3

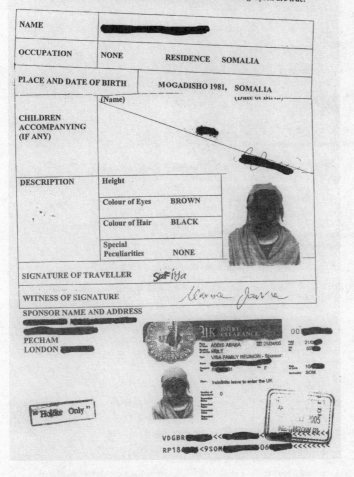

Figure 18: Refusal of leave to enter

Figure 19: Notice of illegal entry/administrative removal

Port Reference:
Home Office Reference: D██████   IS151A

Home Office

Lunar House
40 Wellesley Road
Croydon
CR9 2BY
Tel: 0870 606 7766 Fax:

NOTICE TO A PERSON LIABLE TO REMOVAL
(Illegal entrants and section 10 administrative removal cases)

COH ID: ██████

To: ██████████

I have considered all the information available to me and I am satisfied that you are **either**:

☐   A)   A person in respect of whom removal directions may be given in accordance with paragraphs 8 to 10A of Schedule 2 to the Immigration Act 1971 as:
      i.   an illegal entrant as defined in section 33(1) of the Immigration Act 1971
      ii.   a member of the family of such a person

OR

☒   B)   a person in respect of whom removal directions may be given in accordance with section 10 of the Immigration and Asylum Act 1999 (administrative removal) as:
      i)   a person who has failed to observe a condition of leave to enter or remain, or remains beyond the time limited by the leave;
      ii)   a person who used deception in seeking (whether successfully or not) leave to remain;
      iii)   a person whose indefinite leave to enter or remain has been revoked under section 76(3) of the Nationality, Immigration and Asylum Act 2002 (person ceasing to be a refugee).
      iv)   a member of the family of such a person

LIABILITY TO DETENTION   You are therefore a person who is liable to be detained under paragraph 16(2) of Schedule 2 to the Immigration Act 1971 pending a decision whether or not to give removal directions and, where relevant, your removal in pursuance of such directions.

Date: ██December 2006   On behalf of the Secretary of State

Important notice for persons detained under the Immigration Act 1971.

You may on request have one person known to you or who is likely to take an interest in your welfare informed at public expense as soon as practicable of your whereabouts.

IS151A 04/06

Figure 20: Decision to remove for illegal entrants/those subject to administrative removal

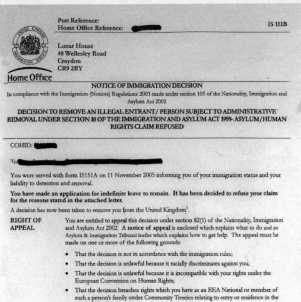

Port Reference:
Home Office Reference: ████████   IS 151B

Home Office

Lunar House
40 Wellesley Road
Croydon
CR9 2BY

NOTICE OF IMMIGRATION DECISION

In compliance with the Immigration (Notices) Regulations 2003 made under section 105 of the Nationality, Immigration and Asylum Act 2002

DECISION TO REMOVE AN ILLEGAL ENTRANT/ PERSON SUBJECT TO ADMINISTRATIVE REMOVAL UNDER SECTION 10 OF THE IMMIGRATION AND ASYLUM ACT 1999- ASYLUM/HUMAN RIGHTS CLAIM REFUSED

COHID: ████████

To ████████████████████

You were served with form IS151A on 11 November 2005 informing you of your immigration status and your liability to detention and removal.

You have made an application for indefinite leave to remain. It has been decided to refuse your claim for the reasons stated in the attached letter.

A decision has now been taken to remove you from the United Kingdom[1].

RIGHT OF APPEAL   You are entitled to appeal this decision under section 82(1) of the Nationality, Immigration and Asylum Act 2002. A notice of appeal is enclosed which explains what to do and an Asylum & Immigration Tribunal leaflet which explains how to get help. The appeal must be made on one or more of the following grounds:

- That the decision is not in accordance with the immigration rules;
- That the decision is unlawful because it racially discriminates against you;
- That the decision is unlawful because it is incompatible with your rights under the European Convention on Human Rights;
- That the decision breaches rights which you have as an EEA National or member of such a person's family under Community Treaties relating to entry or residence in the United Kingdom;
- That the decision is otherwise not in accordance with the law;
- That a discretion under the immigration rules should have been exercised differently;
- That your removal from the United Kingdom as a result of the decision would:
  - breach the United Kingdom's obligations under the 1951 Refugee Convention;
  - be incompatible with your rights under the European Convention on Human Rights.

You should not appeal on grounds which do not apply to you. You must also give arguments and any supporting evidence which justifies your grounds.

el
[1] Sections 82(2)(g), 82(2)(h), 82(2)(i) of the 2002 Act.
Where a decision to remove has been made under section 10 of the Immigration and Asylum Act 1999, any leave previously granted is invalidated by the service of this notice (section 10(8) of that Act (as amended)).

[IS 151B] 06/06

Figure 21: Removal directions

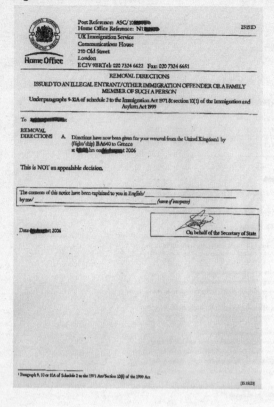

Figure 22: Notice of temporary admission

Port Reference: {MAINREF}
Home Office Reference: {HOREF}

IS 96NW

UK IMMIGRATION SERVICE
Enforcement Policy unit
Floor, Green Park House
29 Wellesley Road, CROYDON CR0 2AJ

Tel: Fax:

Home Office

IMMIGRATION ACT 1971 - NOTIFICATION OF TEMPORARY ADMISSION TO A PERSON WHO IS LIABLE TO BE DETAINED

To: {Name}

Date of Birth: {Bd1}   Nationality: {Nat1}

LIABILITY TO DETENTION

A.   You are a person who is liable to be detained*.

TEMPORARY ADMISSION RESTRICTIONS

B.   I hereby authorise your (further) temporary admission to the United Kingdom subject to the following restrictions**:

■   You **must** reside at:

{Address1}

■   You **must** report to: {Report_To}

at   {Reporting_Location}

on   {Report_On} at {Report_At}hrs.

and then on: {Report_on_2}   at   {Report_at_2}hrs.

■   You **may not** enter employment, paid or unpaid, or engage in any business or profession.

ANY CHANGE OF RESTRICTION

■   If these restrictions are to be changed, an Immigration Officer will write to you.

■   Although you have been temporarily admitted, you remain liable to be detained
■   You have NOT been given leave to enter the United Kingdom within the meaning of the Immigration Act 1971

Date **31 January 2002**

Immigration Officer

* Paragraph 16 of Schedule 2 to the Act
** Paragraph 21 of Schedule 2 to the Act

[IS 96NW Temporary Admission —— VC2]

Figure 23: Application registration card

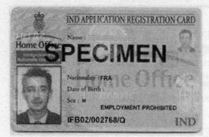

Figure 24: Embarkation stamp

Figure 25: Worker Registration Scheme

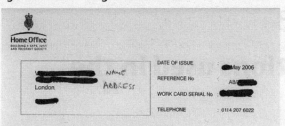

Accession State Worker Registration Scheme

Thank you for your application to register on the Accession State Worker Registration scheme. I am pleased to inform you that we have approved your application and that you are now registered.

Your worker registration card is attached below. If you have any queries about this document, then please contact Work Permits (UK) on the telephone number above.

Managed Migration
Home Office
PO Box 3468
Sheffield S3 8WA

www.workingintheuk.gov.uk

Accession State Worker Registration Scheme
Registration Card

SURNAME :
FORENAME(S) :
DATE OF BIRTH :
NATIONALITY :
REFERENCE No : A8/
DATE OF ISSUE : May 2006

This worker registration card should be retained as evidence of your registration with the Accession State Worker Registration Scheme.

PLEASE DO NOT LOSE · REPLACEMENTS MAY NOT BE ISSUED

WORK CARD SERIAL No

Date of Issue: May 2006

ER REGISTRATION SCHEME
CERTIFICATE

CEMENTS MAY NOT BE ISSUED

n the Accession State Worker Registration
e have approved your application.

It authorises you to work for the employer

no longer working for the employer
hich it is issued.

This certificate expires on the date you cease working for the specified employer.

This certificate should be retained with your worker registration card.

Name :
Date of Birth : 1955
Nationality :
Unique Reference Number: A8/
Job start date :
Employer's Name : C
Employer's Address :

Appendix 8

Abbreviations used in the notes

AC	Appeal Cases
All ER	All England Reports
Art(s)	Article(s)
CA	Court of Appeal
CMLR	Common Market Law Reports
COD	Crown Office Digest
Crim App R	Criminal Appeal Reports
ECJ	European Court of Justice
ECR	European Court Reports
EEA	European Economic Area
ECHR	European Convention on Human Rights
ECtHR	European Court of Human Rights
EU	European Union
EULR	European Union Law Reports
EWCR	England and Wales Court of Appeal
EWHC	England and Wales High Court
FLR	Family Law Reports
HC	High Court
HL	House of Lords
HLR	Housing Law Reports
Imm AR	Immigration Appeal Reports
INLR	Immigration and Nationality Law Reports
IRLR	Industrial Relations Law Reports
KB	King's Bench Reports
LGR	Local Government Reports
para(s)	paragraphs(s)
PC	Privy Council
QB	Queen's Bench Reports
QBD	Queen's Bench Division
r(r)	rule(s)

Reg(s)	regulation(s)
s(s)	section(s)
Sch(s)	Schedule(s)
SLT	Scots Law Times
UKAIT	United Kingdom Asylum and Immigration Tribunal
UKHL	United Kingdom House of Lords
UKIAT	United Kingdom Immigration Appeal Tribunal
UKSC	United Kingdom Supreme Court
UKUT	United Kingdom Upper Tribunal
WLR	Weekly Law Reports

Acts of Parliament

AI(TC)A 2004	Asylum and Immigration (Treatment of Claimants etc) Act 2004
BNA 1981	British Nationality Act 1981
CSPSSA 2000	Child Support, Pensions and Social Security Act 2000
FLRA 1969	Family Law Reform Act 1969
IA 1971	Immigration Act 1971
IA 1988	Immigration Act 1988
IAA 1999	Immigration and Asylum Act 1999
JSA 1995	Jobseekers Act 1995
NAA 1948	National Assistance Act 1948
NIAA 2002	Nationality, Immigration and Asylum Act 2002
SSA	Social Security Act 1998
SSAA 1992	Social Security Administration Act 1992
SSCBA 1992	Social Security Contributions and Benefits Act 1992
TCA 2002	Tax Credits Act 2002
WRA 2007	Welfare Reform Act 2007
WRPA 1999	Welfare Reform and Pensions Act 1999

Regulations and other statutory instruments

Each set of regulations has a statutory instrument (SI) number and date. You ask for them by giving their date and number.

A(IWR) Regs	The Accession (Immigration and Worker Registration) Regulations 2004 No.1219
AS Regs	The Asylum Support Regulations 2000 No.704
ASA(P) Rules	The Asylum Support Appeals (Procedure) Rules 2000 No.541
CB Regs	The Child Benefit (General) Regulations 2006 No.223
CB &GA(AA) Regs	The Child Benefit and Guardian's Allowance (Administrative Arrangements Regulations 2003 No.494
CTB Regs	The Council Tax Benefit Regulations 2006 No.215

CTB(SPC) Regs	The Council Tax Benefit (Persons who have attained the qualifying age for state pension credit) Regulations 2006 No.216
CTC Regs	The Child Tax Credit Regulations 2002 No.2007
ESA Regs	The Employment and Support Allowance Regulations 2008 No.794
ESA(TP)(EA) Regs	The Employment and Support Allowance (Transitional Provisions, Housing Benefit and Council Tax Benefit) (Existing Awards) (No.2) Regulations 2010 No.1907
GA (Gen) Regs	The Guardian's Allowance (General) Regulations 2003 No.495
HB Regs	The Housing Benefit Regulations 2006 No.213
HB(SPC) Regs	The Housing Benefit (Persons who have attained the qualifying age for state pension credit) Regulations 2006 No.214
HPG(A) Regs	The Health in Pregnancy Grant (Administration) Regulations 2008 No.3109
HPG(EA) Regs	The Health in Pregnancy Grant (Entitlement and Amount) Regulations 2008 No.3108
I(CERI)O	The Immigration (Control of Entry through the Republic of Ireland) Order 1972 No.1616
I(EEA) Regs	The Immigration (European Economic Area) Regulations 2006 No.1003
I(LER)O	The Immigration (Leave to Enter and Remain) Order 2000 No.1161
IA(POAFAS) Regs	The Immigration and Asylum (Provision of Accommodation to Failed Asylum Seekers) Regulations 2005 No.930
IS Regs	The Income Support (General) Regulations 1987 No.1967
JSA Regs	The Jobseeker's Allowance Regulations 1996 No.207
SFCWP Regs	The Social Fund Cold Weather Payments (General) Regulations 1988 No.1724
SFM&FE Regs	The Social Fund Maternity and Funeral Expenses (General) Regulations 2005 No.3061
SMP Regs	The Statutory Maternity Pay (General) Regulations 1986 No.1960
SMP(PAM) Regs	The Statutory Maternity Pay (Persons Abroad and Mariners) Regulations 1987 No.418
SPC Regs	The State Pension Credit Regulations 2002 No.1792
SPPSAP(G) Regs	The Statutory Paternity Pay and Statutory Adoption Pay (General) Regulations 2002 No.2822

SPPSAP(PAM) Regs	The Statutory Paternity Pay and Statutory Adoption Pay (Persons Abroad and Mariners) Regulations 2002 No.2821
SS(AA) Regs	The Social Security (Attendance Allowance) Regulations 1991 No.2740
SS(Con) Regs	The Social Security (Contributions) Regulations 2001 No.1004
SS(C&P) Regs	The Social Security (Claims and Payments) Regulations 1987 No.1968
SS(CTCNIN) Regs	The Social Security (Crediting and Treatment of Contributions, and National Insurance Numbers) Regulations 2001 No.769
SS(DLA) Regs	The Social Security (Disability Living Allowance) Regulations 1991 No.2890
SS(EEEIIP) Regs	The Social Security (Employed Earners' Employment for Industrial Injuries Purposes) Regulations 1975 No.467
SS(GA) Regs	The Social Security (Guardian's Allowance) Regulations 1975 No.515
SS(HR)A Regs	The Social Security (Habitual Residence) Amendment Regulations 2004 No.1219
SS(IA)CA Regs	The Social Security (Immigration and Asylum) Consequential Amendments Regualtions 2000 No.636
SS(ICA) Regs	The Social Security (Invalid Care Allowance) Regulations 1976 No.409
SS(IB) Regs	The Social Security (Incapacity Benefit) Regulations 1994 No.2946
SFWFP Regs	The Social Fund Winter Fuel Payment Regulations 2000 No.729
SS(IB-ID) Regs	The Social Security (Incapacity Benefit – Increases for Dependants) Regulations 1994 No.2945
SS(IIAB) Regs	The Social Security (Industrial Injuries) (Airmen's Benefits) Regulations 1975 No.469
SS(IIMB) Regs	The Social Security (Industrial Injuries) (Mariners' Benefits) Regulations 1975 No.470
SS(IIPD) Regs	The Social Security (Industrial Injuries) (Prescribed Diseases) Regulations 1985 No.967
SS(NIRA) Regs	The Social Security (Northern Ireland Reciprocal Arrangements) Regulations 1976 No.1003
SS(OB) Regs	The Social Security (Overlapping Benefits) Regulations 1979 No.597
SS(PA)A Regs	The Social Security (Persons from Abroad) Amendment Regulations 2006 No.3317

SS(WB&RP) Regs	The Social Security (Widow's Benefit and Retirement Pensions) Regulations 1979 No.642
SS&CS (DA) Regs	The Social Security and Child Support (Decisions and Appeals) Regulations 1999 No.991
SSB(Dep) Regs	The Social Security Benefit (Dependency) Regulations 1977 No.343
SSB(PA) Regs	The Social Security Benefit (Persons Abroad) Regulations 1975 No.563
SSB(PRT) Regs	The Social Security Benefit (Persons Residing Together) Regulations 1977 No.956
SSP Regs	The Statutory Sick Pay (General) Regulation 1982 No.894
SSP(MAPA) Regs	The Statutory Sick Pay (Mariners, Airmen and Persons Abroad) Regulations 1982 No.1349
TC(CN) Regs	The Tax Credits (Claims and Notifications) Regulations 2002 No.2014
TC(Imm) Regs	The Tax Credits (Immigration) Regulations 2003 No.653
TC(R) Regs	The Tax Credits (Residence) Regulations 2003 No.654
TP(FT) Rules	The Tribunal Procedure (First-tier Tribunal)(Social Entitlement Chamber) Rules 2008 No.2685
TP(SEC) Rules	The Tribunal Procedure (Social Entitlement Chamber) Rules 2008 No.2685
WTC(EMR) Regs	The Working Tax Credit (Entitlement and Maximum Rate) Regulations 2002 No.2005

Other information

API	Asylum Policy Instructions
ASGN	Asylum Support Guidance Notes
DMG	Decision Makers Guide
GM	Housing Benefit and Council Tax Benefit Guidance Manual
IDI	Immigration Directorate Instructions
IR	Immigration Rules
SF Dir	Social Fund Directions

References like CIS/142/1990 aand R(IS) 1/07 are to commissioners' decisions. References like CH/426/2008[2009] UKUT 34(AAC) are references to decisions of the Upper Tribunal.

Index

How to use this Index

Entries against the bold headings direct you to the general information on the subject, or where the subject is covered most fully. Sub-entries are listed alphabetically and direct you to specific aspects of the subject.

AA	Attendance allowance	IS	Income support
CA	Carer's allowance	I-ESA	Income-related employment and support allowance
C-ESA	Contributory employment and support allowance	I-JSA	Income-based jobseeker's allowance
C-JSA	Contribution-based jobseeker's allowance	JSA	Jobseeker's allowance
CTB	Council tax benefit	MA	Maternity allowance
CTC	Child tax credit	NI	National insurance
DLA	Disability living allowance	PC	Pension credit
EEA	European Economic Area	SAP	Statutory adoption pay
ESA	Employment and support allowance	SDA	Severe disablement allowance
EU	European Union	SF	Social fund
HB	Housing benefit	SMP	Statutory maternity pay
IB	Incapacity benefit	SPP	Statutory paternity pay
IIDB	Industrial injuries disablement benefit	SSP	Statutory sick pay
		WTC	Working tax credit

A
A2 nationals 33
   accession worker card 34
   aggregation 178
   child in education 244
   EU right of residence 239
A2 states 147
A8 nationals 33
   aggregation 177
   child in education 244
   EU right of residence 239
   Worker Registration Scheme 33
A8 states 147
abroad
   child abroad 108
      child benefit 109
      CTB 108
      CTC 109
      ESA 108
      GA 109
      HB 108
      I-JSA 108
      IS 108
      PC 108
   entitlement to benefit abroad
      AA 97, 138
      bereavement benefits 92, 138
      C-ESA 89, 137
      C-JSA 88, 137
      CA 97, 139
      child benefit 87
      CTB 86, 137
      CTC 86
      DLA 97, 138
      GA 88
      HB 84, 137
      I-ESA 83, 137
      I-JSA 80, 137
      IB 89, 137
      industrial injuries benefits 95
      IS 79, 137
      MA 99, 137
      PC 84
      retirement pensions 90, 138
      statutory employment benefits 99
      WTC 86
   ordinary residence 74
   partner abroad 103
      CTB 106
      CTC 107
      dependent adult increases 107
      HB 106

I-ESA 105
I-JSA 105
IS 105
PC 106
WTC 107
travel with indefinite leave 43
see also: temporary absence abroad
absence
child abroad 108
ordinary residence 74
partner abroad 103
temporary absence abroad 75
accession worker card 34, 228
accommodation
asylum seekers 294, 306
security of tenure 299
failed asylum seekers 312
overcrowding 13
recourse to public funds 13
administrative removal 45
advisers 3
Advocate General's opinion 155
age
evidence 134
aggregation
A2/A8 nationals 178
EU co-ordination rules 177
family benefits 201
industrial injuries benefits 195
invalidity benefits 187
special non-contributory benefits 204
unemployment benefits 197
aircrew 9
Algeria
CTC 62
EU agreements 257
non-contributory benefits 61
social fund payments 61
anti-test-case rule 155
appeals
asylum support 316
failed asylum seekers 267, 280
refusal of NI number 130
application registration card 44
apportionment
EU co-ordination rules 178
armed services
leave to enter and remain 9
single state principle 174
association agreements 257
Turkish nationals 15
asylum seekers 17, 263
16/17-year-olds leaving care 287
accommodation 306, 312
adequate accommodation 294
application refused 21
application registration card 44
applying for asylum 17

expenses 307
bail 18
benefits 288
care and attention needs 285
caseowners 264
children 20
Children Act support 287
claiming as soon as reasonably
practicable 269
community care 284
dependants 268, 269
definition of asylum seeker 17, 266
destitute 268, 272, 273, 293
destitution plus test 285
detention 18
dispersal 298, 306
employment 19
essential living needs 304
eviction from accommodation 299
exceptional leave 21
failed asylum seekers 21, 272
future changes 18
health benefits 298
humanitarian protection 20
in-country applications 18
leave outside the rules 21
means-tested benefits 60
proof of status 44
recording a claim 267
standard acknowledgement letter 44
support 263
tax credits 288
temporary admission 18
temporary protection 17
travel expenses 308
see also: failed asylum seekers
asylum support 263, 264
accommodation 299, 306
adequate accommodation 294
amount of support 304
appeals 316
application form 292
applying for support 292, 297
assets 310
backdating 308, 327
challenging a decision 300
change of circumstances 298
children 266
Children Act support 287
claiming as soon as reasonably
practicable 269
clothing 296
community care 284
community care support 265
conditions 297
contributing to support 309
dependants 268, 269
destitute 268, 273, 293

dispersal 298, 306
education costs 308
emergency support 272
entitlement 266
essential living needs 296
exclusions 269
expenses of applying for asylum 307
hard cases support 272
health benefits 298
legal framework 303
maternity payment 306
misrepresentation 310
one-stop agencies 264
overpayments 309, 310
recovery from a sponsor 311
repaying support 309
Section 4 support 265, 272
suspension 270, 282
temporary support 272, 297
travel expenses 308
types of support 263, 303
waiting for a support decision 297
asylum support appeals 316
decision to remit 329
decisions 325
hearing procedure 324
judicial review 329
notice of appeal 319
oral hearings 323
paper hearings 322
procedures 317
representation 319
right to appeal 317
setting aside a decision 328
striking out an appeal 321
time limits 317, 321
UKBA response 322
withdrawing the appeal 329
attendance allowance
entitlement abroad 97
EU co-ordination rules 186, 207
exporting benefit 210
immigration conditions 51
ordinarily resident 72
payment abroad 138, 187
residence conditions 51, 96
terminal illness 96
azure card 311

B
backdating
asylum support 308, 327
bail
asylum seekers 18
illegal entrants 43
bereavement allowance
EU co-ordination rules 194
residence conditions 93

bereavement benefits
EU co-ordination rules 170
immigration conditions 51
payment abroad 138
reciprocal agreements 255
residence conditions 51, 92
bereavement payment
residence conditions 93
British citizens
proof of status 38
reciprocal agreements 252
right of abode 6, 38
right to reside 119
British citizenship 6
acquiring citizenship at birth 7
British dependent territories citizens
reciprocal agreements 252
British nationals 6
right of abode 6
British overseas citizens
reciprocal agreements 252
British subjects
reciprocal agreements 252
budgeting loan
residence conditions 102

C
carer's allowance
dependent adult increases 107
entitlement abroad 97
EU co-ordination rules 186, 207
exporting benefit 210
immigration conditions 51
ordinarily resident 72
payment abroad 139, 187
residence conditions 51, 97
Case Resolution Directorate 264
certificate of patriality 39
challenging a decision
asylum support appeals 328
Channel Islands
reciprocal agreements 251
charities 141
child benefit
child abroad 109
entitlement when abroad 87
EU co-ordination rules 170, 201
exporting benefit 203
immigration status 51
ordinarily resident 72
payment abroad 202
reciprocal agreements 255
residence conditions 51, 87
right to reside test 117, 118
child tax credit
child abroad 109
entitlement when abroad 86
EU co-ordination rules 170, 201

exporting benefit 203
immigration status 51
ordinarily resident 72
partner abroad 107
payment abroad 202
person subject to immigration control 62
refugees 67
residence conditions 51, 86
right to reside test 117, 118
children
asylum support 266
child abroad 108
child benefit 109
CTB 108
CTC 109
ESA 108
GA 109
HB 108
I-JSA 108
IS 108
PC 108
Children Act support 287
discretionary leave 20
in education 243
ordinary residence 74
proof of parentage 136
Christmas bonus
EU co-ordination rules 189
civil partners
ending a partnership 242
person subject to immigration control
means-tested benefits 65
proof of relationship 136
civil servants
single state principle 174
claims
benefit claims 126
EU co-ordination rules
family benefits 202
industrial injuries benefits 196
invalidity benefits 187
MA 208
retirement pensions 193
SMP 208
special non-contributory benefits 206
SPP 208
SSP 208
clothing grants 140
co-habitation
presumption of marriage 136
co-operation and association agreements
257
cold weather payments
residence conditions 101
Commission, the 147
common travel area 110

Commonwealth citizens
freely landed 41
right of abode 6
right to reside 119
community care
applying for support 285
asylum seekers 265, 284
care and attention needs 285
community care grant
residence conditions 102
competent state 171
how long does UK remain competent
state 175
constant attendance allowance
residence conditions 94
Council of the European Union 148
conventions and agreements 256
Social Charter 256
council tax benefit
child abroad 108
couples 66
entitlement when abroad 86
habitual residence test 110
immigration conditions 51
partner abroad 106
payment abroad 137
person from abroad 110
residence conditions 51, 85
right to reside test 117
couples
CTB 66
CTC 66
different immigration statuses 64
means-tested benefits 65
NI numbers 131
tax credits 66
HB 66
IS/I-JSA/I-ESA 65
partner abroad 103
CTB 106
CTC 107
dependent adult increases 107
HB 106
I-ESA 105
I-JSA 105
IS 105
PC 106
WTC 107
PC 66
proof of relationship 136
treated as a couple 105
WTC 66
criminal offence
suspension of asylum support 270
crisis loan
residence conditions 102

Croatia
means-tested benefits 60
WTC 62

D
date of birth
providing evidence of age 134
death grants
EU co-ordination rules 206
decisions
EU law 151
delays
awarding benefits 129
dental treatment
asylum seekers 298
dependants' increases
reciprocal agreements 255
deportation 45
destitute
asylum seekers 268, 293
expenses of applying for asylum 307
detainees
applying for Section 4 support 301
detention
asylum seekers 18
diplomatic staff
leave to enter and remain 9
single state principle 174
direct effect
EU law part of UK legal system 149
Directives
EU law 151
disability
failed asylum seekers unable to leave UK
275
disability living allowance
children 67
entitlement abroad 97
EU co-ordination rules 170, 186, 204, 207
exporting benefit 210
immigration status 51
ordinarily resident 72
payment abroad 138
residence conditions 51, 96
terminal illness 96
disablement benefit
EU co-ordination rules 170, 195
residence conditions 94
discretionary leave 20
children 20
right to reside 119
discrimination
EU co-ordination rules 176
dispersal
asylum seekers 298, 306
divorce
right of residence 242
DNA testing 137

E
economically inactive people
EU right of residence 244
education
receiving services 237
education maintenance allowance 140
EEA
see: European Economic Area
employed person
EU co-ordination rules 163
family benefits 203
sickness, maternity and paternity
benefits 208
employment
asylum seekers 19
employing migrant workers 11
leave to enter and remain 11
points-based system 15
sponsorship 15
employment and support allowance,
contributory
entitlement abroad 89
EU co-ordination rules 185
immigration conditions 52
payment abroad 137, 187
residence conditions 52, 88
employment and support allowance, income
related
child abroad 108
couple 65
entitlement when abroad 83
EU co-ordination rules 170, 204
habitual residence test 110
housing costs 82
immigration conditions 52
ordinarily resident 72
partner abroad 105
payment abroad 137
person from abroad 110
reciprocal agreements 254
residence conditions 52, 82
right to reside test 117
English language lessons
asylum seekers 308
entry clearance 39
obtaining a visa 9
entry clearance officers 4
equal treatment 176
agreements
CTC 62
non-contributory benefits 61
EU co-ordination rules 176
EU
see: European Union
European Convention on Social and Medical
Assistance 256, 337

European Court of Justice 148, 153
Advocate General's opinion 155
judgments 155
procedure 155
referrals 153
European Economic Area
member states 23
reciprocal agreements 251
benefits covered 253
people covered 252
European Economic Area nationals 23, 146
A2 nationals 33, 239
A8 nationals 33, 239
employed in two or more EEA states 174
EU right of residence 223
exclusion from UK 35
family members 27
means-tested benefits 60
non-contributory benefits 61
habitual residence test 115
interim benefit payments 156
legal basis
benefits/tax credits 151
means-tested benefits 60
permanent right of residence 25
family members 31
proof of status 44
public funds 32
qualified person 24
registration certificate 26, 44
removal from UK 35
residence cards 31
right of admission 24
right to reside 24, 116
WTC 62
European Free Trade Area 146
European Parliament 147
European Union 145
co-ordination of social security 159
decisions 151
Directives 151
EU treaties 149
institutions 147
interpretation of EU law 150
legal basis
benefits/tax credits 151
member states 146
principles of EU law 219
reciprocal agreements
benefits covered 253
people covered 252
recommendations 151
Regulations 150
right of residence 223
rights under EU law 218
supremacy of EU law over domestic law
149

treaties 150
using EU law 152, 218, 223
European Union co-ordination of benefits
159, 184
aggregation 177
family benefits 201
industrial injuries benefits 195
invalidity benefits 187
unemployment benefits 197
apportionment 178
benefits covered 165
competent state 171
death grants 206
declarations of benefits 168
discrimination 176
employed in two or more EEA states 174
employed person 163
exporting benefits 178
industrial injuries benefits 196
invalidity benefits 189
retirement pensions 194
survivors' benefits 194
unemployment benefits 198
family benefits 170, 201
family members 164
habitual residence 204
industrial injuries benefits 170, 195
international transport workers 174
invalidity benefits 169, 185
legal basis 159
maternity benefits 169, 207
non-contributory benefits 166
old age benefits 170, 189
overlapping benefits from more than one
state 180
paternity benefits 169, 207
personal scope of the rule 161
refugees 164
self-employed person 163
sickness benefits 169, 207
single state principle 171
special arrangements 174
social advantage rule 165
social and medical assistance 168, 171
social security benefits 166, 169
special non-contributory benefits 166,
170, 204
stateless people 164
students 163
subject to legislation of member state 162
survivors' benefits 170, 194
temporary employment in another EEA
state 173
third-country nationals 164
transitional arrangements 162
unemployment benefits 170, 196
who is covered 161
widowers 164

widows 164
winter fuel payments 191
European Union nationals
co-ordination of social security 161
employed in two or more EU states 174
subject to the legislation of a member
state 162
European Union Treaty 149
benefits and tax credits 151
exercising Treaty rights 222
provisions 219
evidence
age 134
immigration status 134
exceptional leave to enter or remain
asylum seekers 21
exceptionally severe disablement allowance
EU co-ordination rules 170, 195
residence conditions 94
expenses
asylum support 307
exporting benefits
anti-test case rules 156
EU co-ordination rules 178
family benefits 203
industrial injuries benefits 196
invalidity benefits 189
retirement pensions 194
sickness, maternity and paternity benefits
210
survivors' benefits 194
unemployment benefits 198
extension of stay 42

F
failed asylum seekers
accommodation 312
additional Section 4 support 313
appeals 280
applying for Section 4 support 301
criteria for support 273
fresh representations to Home Office 276
human rights 276, 281
judicial review 276
no safe route of return 276, 281
pregnancy 275
reasonable steps to leave UK 274
Section 4 support 311
sick or disabled 275
see also: Section 4 support
family benefits 201
EU co-ordination rules 170, 201
aggregation 201
children of pensioners 203
claims 202
employed person 203
overlapping benefits 202
unemployed person 203

exporting benefits 203
payment abroad 202
reciprocal agreements 255
family members
A2 nationals 34
A8 nationals 33
British citizens 29
child abroad 108
definition 103, 241
EEA nationals 27
EU co-ordination rules 161, 164
extended family 28, 242
non-EEA nationals 241
partner abroad 103
partners with different immigration
statuses 64
right of admission 30
right of residence 28, 241
family permit 30
fiancé(e)s
entitlement to claim benefits
means-tested benefits 65
First-tier Tribunal (Asylum Support) 316
appeal procedures 317
decision to remit 329
decisions 325
hearing procedure 324
oral hearings 323
paper hearings 322
setting aside a decision 328
withdrawing the appeal 329
former workers
child in education 243
EU right of residence 231, 238
right to reside 119
free school lunches 139
freedom of movement
EEA nationals 222
funeral payments
residence conditions 100

G
guardian's allowance
child abroad 109
entitlement when abroad 88
EU co-ordination rules 201
exporting benefit 203
immigration status 52
payment abroad 202
reciprocal agreements 255
residence conditions 52, 88

H
habitual residence
EU co-ordination rules 115, 204
habitual residence test 110
benefits affected 110
complaints 114

deemed to be habitually resident 111
definition 111
EEA nationals 115
establishing habitual residence 111
evidence 113
reclaiming 114
returning UK residents 114
health benefits
asylum seekers 298
health in pregnancy grant
immigration conditions 52
ordinarily resident 72
person subject to immigration control 66
residence conditions 52
right to reside test 117, 118
Home Office
links with benefit authorities 49
household
child abroad 108
definition 104
partner abroad 103
housing benefit
child abroad 108
couples 66
entitlement when abroad 84
habitual residence test 110
immigration conditions 52
partner abroad 106
payment abroad 137
person from abroad 110
residence conditions 52, 84
right to reside test 117
housing costs
ESA 83
IS 80
JSA 82
human rights
asylum seekers 284
EU law 220
failed asylum seekers 276, 281
humanitarian protection 20
right to reside 119

I
Iceland
co-ordination of social security 161, 163
rights as EEA nationals 24
Identity and Passport Service 4
identity cards 41
illegal entry 43
administrative removal 45
immigration control
*see: person subject to immigration
control*
immigration law 3
immigration officers 4

immigration status 5
benefit entitlement 55
determining status 38
evidence 134
families with different statuses 64
means-tested benefits 60
subject to immigration control 5
tax credits 62
in-country applications 18
incapable of work
EU right of residence 238
family members 242
retaining worker status 231
incapacity benefit
dependent adult increases 107
entitlement abroad 89
EU co-ordination rules 186
immigration conditions 52
ordinarily resident 72
payment abroad 137
reciprocal agreements 254
residence conditions 52, 88
income support
child abroad 108
children 65
couples 65
entitlement when abroad 79
EU co-ordination rules 170, 204
habitual residence test 110
housing costs 80
immigration conditions 52
partner abroad 105
payment abroad 137
person from abroad 110
residence conditions 52, 79
right to reside test 116
indefinite leave to enter or remain 10
entry clearance 40
EU co-ordination rules 164
means-tested benefits 60
returning to the UK 10
right to reside 119
travel abroad 43
industrial injuries benefits
entitlement abroad 95
EU co-ordination rules 170, 195
aggregation 195
claims 196
exporting benefits 196
immigration conditions 52
payment abroad 196
reciprocal agreements 254
residence conditions 52, 94
interim relief 156
international transport workers
EU co-ordination rules 174

invalidity benefits
aggregation 187
EU co-ordination rules 169, 185
exporting benefits 189
reciprocal agreements 254
Isle of Man
reciprocal agreements 251
Israel
CTC 62
EU agreements 257
social fund payments 61

J
jobseeker's allowance, contribution-based
entitlement abroad 88
EU co-ordination rules 170, 196
exporting benefit 198
immigration conditions 52
payment abroad 137, 197
reciprocal agreements 253
residence conditions 52, 88
jobseeker's allowance, income-based
child abroad 108
couples 65
entitlement when abroad 80
available for and actively seeking work 81
holidays from jobseeking 82
housing costs 82
receiving training allowance 82
EU co-ordination rules 170, 204
habitual residence test 110
immigration conditions 53
partner abroad 105
payment abroad 137
person from abroad 110
residence conditions 53, 80
right to reside test 117
judicial review
asylum support appeals 329
failed asylum seekers 276

L
leave outside the rules 21
habitual residence 111
leave to enter or remain 8
applying for leave 9
asylum seekers 17
conditions of leave 9
EEA nationals 24
employment 11
entry clearance 39
exemptions from usual conditions 9
extending leave 10
Immigration Rules 8
indefinite leave 10
leave to remain 41
limited leave 10, 41

non-contributory benefits 61
port of entry applications 40
proof of status 39
recourse to public funds 11, 57
refugees 19
sponsorship 14
travel documents 42
Turkish nationals 15
leaving the UK
passport endorsements 45
legal aid
asylum support appeals 319
lex laboris rule 171
liability to maintain rules 59
Liechtenstein
co-ordination of social security 161, 163
rights as EEA nationals 24
limited leave to enter or remain 10
entry clearance 41
extension of stay 42
means-tested benefits 60
overstayers 43
right to reside 119

M
Macedonia
means-tested benefits 60
WTC 62
maternity allowance
dependent adult increases 107
entitlement when abroad 99
EU co-ordination rules 207
exporting benefit 210
immigration conditions 53
payment abroad 137
reciprocal agreements 254
residence conditions 53, 99
maternity benefits
EU co-ordination rules 169, 207
employed/self-employed people 208
unemployed claimants 209
exporting benefits 210
payment abroad 208
reciprocal agreements 254
see also: statutory maternity pay
maternity payment
asylum seekers 306
means-tested benefits
person subject to immigration control 60
residence conditions 78
medical treatment
EU co-ordination rules 207
receiving services 237
migrant workers 11
points-based system 15
sponsorship 15

Morocco
CTC 62
EU agreements 257
non-contributory benefits 61
social fund payments 61
multiple nationalities 6

N

National Asylum Support Service 263
national insurance contributions 131
Class 1 contributions 132
Class 2 contributions 132
Class 3 contributions 133
Class 4 contributions 133
contribution record 133
credits 133
national insurance numbers 126
applications 127
delays 129
refusal 130
requirement 126
nationality
British nationality 6
multiple nationalities 6
non-contributory benefits
EU co-ordination rules 166, 170, 204
aggregation 204
claims 206
habitual residence 204
person subject to immigration control 61
Northern Ireland
reciprocal agreements 251
Norway
co-ordination of social security 161, 163
rights as EEA nationals 24

O

occupational diseases
EU co-ordination rules 170, 195
old age benefits
EU co-ordination rules 170, 189
sickness, maternity and paternity
benefits 209
one-stop agencies 264
ordinary residence
absence from the UK 74
benefits affected 72
children 74
definition 72
involuntary residence 74
on arrival 73
temporary purpose 73
young people 74
overlapping benefits
EU co-ordination rules 180, 202
overpayments
asylum seekers 309
asylum support 310

overstayers 43

P

parents
proof of parentage 136
part-time workers
EU co-ordination rules 163
passports
illegible stamps 45
transferring endorsements 45
past presence test 72
AA 96
DLA 96
payment
payment of benefit abroad
AA 138
bereavement benefits 138
C-ESA 137
C-JSA 137, 197
CA 139
CTB 137
DLA 138
HB 137
I-ESA 137
I-JSA 137
IB 137
industrial injuries benefits 196
IS 137
MA 137
retirement pensions 138
pension credit
child abroad 108
couples 66
entitlement when abroad 84
EU co-ordination rules 170, 204
habitual residence test 110
immigration conditions 53
partner abroad 106
person from abroad 110
presence test 110
residence conditions 53, 83
right to reside test 117
permanent right of residence
caring for a child 244
EEA nationals 25
family members 31
residence cards 228
EEA nationals 26
family members 31
person subject to immigration control 55
children
means-tested benefits 65
claiming benefits 49, 59
couples 66
CTC 62
definition
benefit rules 56
immigration rules 5

foreign partner 65
means-tested benefits 60
non-contributory benefits 61
recourse to public funds 62
who can claim benefits 60
WTC 62
police
powers 5
pregnancy
asylum seekers 285, 306
retaining worker status 232
Section 4 support 275
premiums
residence conditions 78
presence conditions 70
definition 71
past presence 72
presumption of legitimacy 137
proportionality 219
public funds
see: recourse to public funds

R
reciprocal agreements 71, 250
benefits covered 253
benefits not covered 250
people covered by the agreements 252
with countries outside EEA 251
with EEA member states 251
recommendations
EU law 151
recourse to public funds 11, 62
accommodation 13
adequate maintenance 12
definition
EEA nationals 32
person subject to immigration control
12, 62
EEA nationals 32
person subject to immigration control 12
reduced earnings allowance
residence conditions 94
refugees 19
application refused 21
definition 17
discretionary leave 20
entitlement to claim benefits 67
EU co-ordination rules 161, 164
habitual residence 111
students 68
tax credits 67
travel documents 43
regulations
EU law 150
removal
EEA nationals 35
residence cards 228

residence certificates
EEA nationals 228
residence conditions 70
AA 96
bereavement benefits 92
C-ESA 88
C-JSA 88
CA 97
child benefit 87
CTB 85
CTC 86
DLA 96
GA 88
habitual residence 77
HB 84
I-ESA 82
I-JSA 80
IB 88
industrial injuries benefits 94
IS 79
MA 99
ordinary residence 72
past presence 72
PC 83
presence 71
retirement pensions 90
right to reside 77
SAP 98
SMP 98
social fund 100
SPP 98
SSP 98
WTC 86
residence permits
EEA nationals 227
residence tests 71
habitual residence 77
ordinary residence 72
past presence 72
presence 71
right to reside 77
retired people
EU right of residence 238
family members 242
retirement allowance
residence conditions 94
retirement pensions
calculating pension in the EEA 192
dependent adult increases 107
entitlement abroad 90
EU co-ordination rules 189
Category D pension 190
exporting benefits 194
immigration conditions 53
ordinarily resident 72
payment abroad 138, 194
reciprocal agreements 255
residence conditions 53, 90

revisions
EU law 153
right of abode
British citizens 6
British nationals 6
Commonwealth citizens 6
definition 7
evidence of right of abode 38
right of admission
family members
EEA nationals 30
right of residence 223
A2 and A8 nationals 239
economically inactive people 244
extended right of residence 225
family members 241
initial right of residence 224
permanent right of residence 225
retired people 238
self-employed people 234
self-sufficient people 235
service providers and users 236
students 235
workers 229
workseekers 233
right to reside 118
EEA nationals 24
extended right to reside
EEA nationals 24
family members 30
family members 30
initial right to reside
EEA nationals 24
family members 30
permanent right of residence
EEA nationals 25
family members 31
registration certificate
EEA nationals 26
family members 31
transitional protection 117
UK nationals
family members 29
right to reside test 116
child benefit 118
CTB 118
CTC 118
HB 118
health in pregnancy grant 118
I-ESA 118
I-JSA 118
IS 118
PC 118
workseekers 118

S
San Marino
CTC 62
EU agreements 257
non-contributory benefits 61
social fund payments 61
savings
asylum support 310
school transport 140
seamen 9
single state principle 174
Seasonal Agricultural Workers Scheme 34
Section 21 services 286
Section 4 support 272, 311
accommodation 312
additional Section 4 support 313
amount of payments 312
applications 300
asylum seekers 265
breach of conditions 283
criteria for support 273
decisions 300
destitution 273
disability 275
discontinued 282
exclusions 282
fresh representations to Home Office 276
human rights 276
judicial review 276
no viable route of return 276
payment methods 311
pregnancy 275
reasonable steps to leave the UK 274
repaying support 314
review enquiry letter 282
sickness 275
suspension 282
self-employed person
child in education 244
EU co-ordination rules 163
sickness, maternity and paternity
benefits 208
EU right of residence 234
self-supporting people 235
comprehensive sickness insurance 236
EU right of residence 235
not self-supporting 244
separation
right of residence 242
service providers and users
EU right of residence 236
severe disablement allowance
EU co-ordination rules 186
immigration conditions 53
residence conditions 53

sickness
failed asylum seekers unable to leave UK 275
retaining worker status 231
sickness benefits
EU co-ordination rules 169, 207
employed/self-employed people 208
unemployed claimants 209
exporting benefits 210
payment abroad 208
reciprocal agreements 254
see also: statutory sick pay
sight tests
asylum seekers 298
single state principle
EU co-ordination rules 171
exceptions 173
special arrangements 174
social advantage rule
family members 165
social and medical assistance
EU co-ordination rule 168, 171
Social Charter 256, 341
social fund
immigration conditions 53
residence conditions 53, 100
social services 141
applying for support 285
sponsorship 14
asylum seekers 311
employment 15
liabilities of sponsors 58
tax credits 62
undertakings 14
spouses
ending a marriage 242
entitlement to claim benefits
means-tested benefits 65
proof of relationship 136
standard acknowledgement letter 44
stateless people 164
co-ordination of social security 161
travel documents 43
statutory adoption pay
entitlement abroad 99
immigration conditions 53
residence conditions 53, 98
statutory maternity pay
entitlement abroad 99
EU co-ordination rules 207
exporting benefit 210
immigration conditions 53
payment abroad 208
residence conditions 53, 98
statutory paternity pay
entitlement abroad 99
EU co-ordination rules 169, 207
exporting benefit 210

immigration conditions 53
payment abroad 208
residence conditions 53, 98
statutory sick pay
entitlement abroad 99
EU co-ordination rules 207
exporting benefit 210
immigration conditions 53
payment abroad 208
residence conditions 53, 98
students
comprehensive sickness insurance 236
EU co-ordination rules 163
EU right of residence 235
refugees 68
right to reside 119
supersessions
EU law 153
Sure Start maternity grant
residence conditions 100
survivors' benefits
benefits 194
EU co-ordination rules 161, 164, 194
exporting benefits 194
Switzerland
co-ordination of social security 161, 163
registration certificate 44
rights as EEA nationals 24

T
tax credits
immigration conditions 51
residence conditions 51
temporary absence abroad 75
AA 97
bereavement benefits 92
C-ESA 89
C-JSA 88
CA 97
child abroad 108
child benefit 87
CTB 86
CTC 86
DLA 97
GA 88
habitual residence test 115
HB 84
I-ESA 83
I-JSA 80
IB 89
industrial injuries benefits 95
IS 79
MA 99
partner abroad 103
PC 84
retirement pensions 90
statutory employment benefits 99
WTC 86

temporary admission
asylum seekers 44
illegal entrants 43
temporary protection 17
terminal illness 96
time limits
asylum support appeals 317, 321
travel expenses
asylum seekers 308, 324
Treaty of Rome 149
Tunisia
CTC 62
EU agreements 257
non-contributory benefits 61
social fund payments 61
Turkey 15
CTC 62
EU agreements 257
means-tested benefits 60
non-contributory benefits 61
social fund payments 61
WTC 62

U
UK Border Agency 4, 263
UK nationals
reciprocal agreements 252
right of residence
family members 29
using EU law 219
UK residence permit 41
unemployment
EU co-ordination rules
family benefits 203
sickness, maternity and paternity
benefits 209
retaining worker status 231
unemployment benefits
EU co-ordination rules 170, 196
aggregation 197
exporting benefits 198
payment abroad 197
reciprocal agreements 253

V
vignettes 39
visas
entry clearance 9

W
widowed parent's allowance
EU co-ordination rules 194
residence conditions 93
widowers' benefits
EU co-ordination rules 164
widows' benefits
EU co-ordination rules 164

winter fuel payments
EU co-ordination rules 191
residence conditions 101
work permits 11
Worker Registration Scheme 33
certificates 228
workers
child in education 243
CTC 62
definition 229
EEA nationals 25
EU right of residence 229
habitual residence 111
non-contributory benefits 61
retaining worker status 231
right to reside 119
tax and social advantages 229
working tax credit
couples 66
entitlement when abroad 86
immigration conditions 53
ordinarily resident 72
person subject to immigration control 62
refugees 67
residence conditions 53, 86
workseekers
EU right of residence 233
right to reside test 118

Y
young people
ordinary residence 74

Training at CPAG

CPAG courses provide comprehensive rights training for advisers and detailed coverage of up-to-the minute legislative changes. Our tutors are expert in their areas of work and draw on the extensive training experience of CPAG's own welfare rights specialists. Courses include:

- An introduction to welfare rights
- Rights of EU/EEA nationals
- Immigration law and social security
- Right to reside and habitual residence
- ESA transfers and appeals
- Welfare reform.

For full course information and online booking please see our website (details below). Our courses can also be tailored to meet the needs of specific groups, including those not normally concerned with welfare rights. To assess your training needs, we are happy to discuss your requirements for 'in-house' training to meet the internal needs of your organisation.

CPAG's London-based courses are Law Society and Bar Council accredited and carry continuing education points. They are also approved by The Institute of Legal Executives and the UK College of Family Mediators. Courses in Scotland have Law Society Scotland accreditation.

Contacts for further information:

London   Judy Allen, Training Co-ordinator,
tel: 020 7812 5228   email: jallen@cpag.org.uk
website: www.cpag.org.uk/training

Scotland   Pauline Chalmers, Training Administrator
Tel: 0141 552 3420   email: pchalmers@cpagscotland.org.uk
website: www.cpag.org.uk/scotland/training

CPAG Handbooks order form

Use this form to get more copies of this or other CPAG handbooks
– or visit our online shop at www.onlineservices.cpag.org.uk/shop

Title	Price £	Total £
Benefits for Migrants Handbook 5th edition	23.00	
Welfare Benefits and Tax Credits Handbook 2011/12 (due April 2011)	39.00	
Fuel Rights Handbook 15th edition (January 2011)	19.00	
Council tax Handbook 9th edition (due summer 2011)	17.00	
Child Support Handbook 2011/12 (due summer 2011)	27.00	
Student Support & Benefits Handbook: England, Wales and N. Ireland 2011/12 (due autumn 2011)	13.50	
Benefits for Students in Scotland Handbook 2011/12 (due autumn 2011)	13.50	
Debt Advice Handbook 9th edition (September 2010)	22.00	
Personal Finance Handbook 3rd ed. (November 09)	16.50	
Paying for Care Handbook 6th edition (March 2009)	19.50	
	Subtotal £	
Add P&P: order value £10.01—£100, add £3.00; £100.01—£400, add £5.99; order value £400+, add £9.99	P&P £	
Optional donation towards CPAG's work against child poverty	£	
	Grand total £	

I enclose a cheque/PO for £_____ payable to Child Poverty Action Group

Title _____ First name _____ Second name _____

Organisation _____ Dept _____

Address _____

_____ Postcode _____

Email _____

Return form with payment to:

Child Poverty Action Group, 94 White Lion St, London N1 9PF

Tel: 020 7837 7979   Email: bookorders@cpag.org.uk